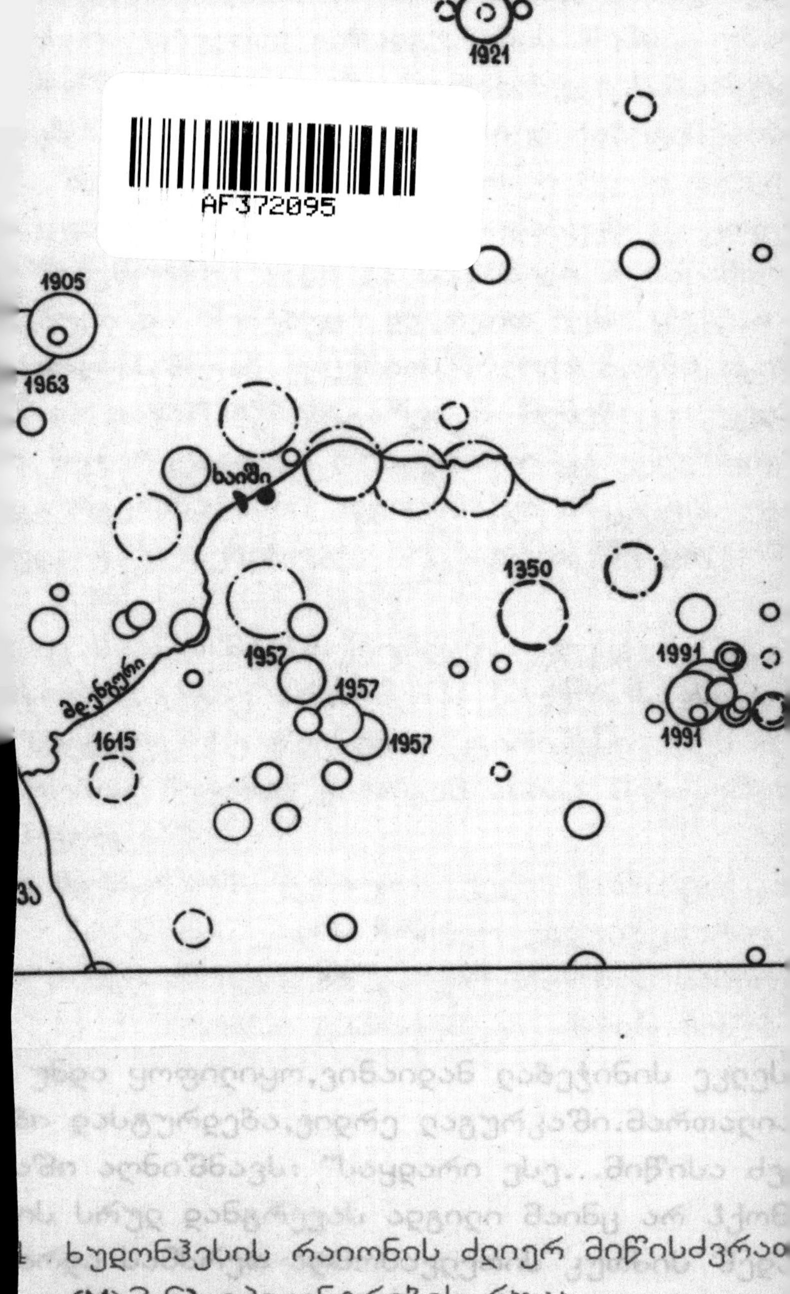

ხუდონჰესის რაიონის ძლიერ მიწისძვრაი (M≥3.6) ეპიცენტრების რუკა.

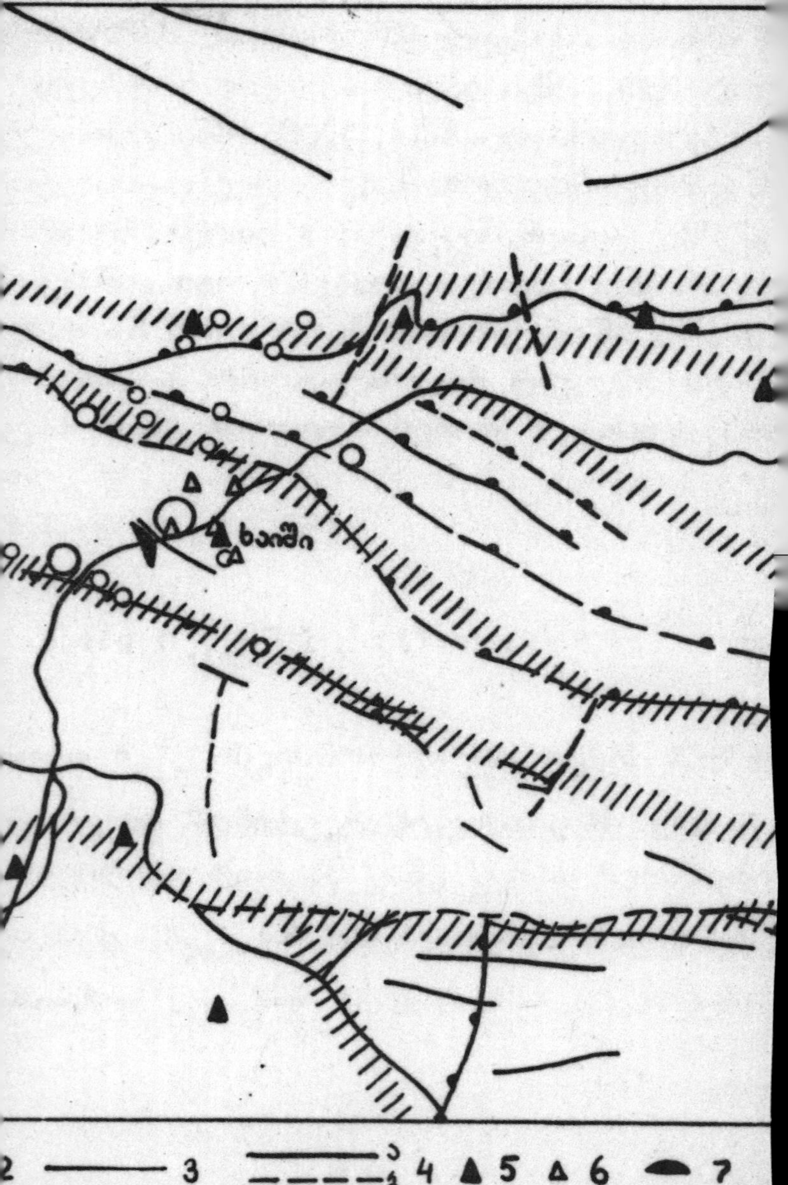

2 — 3 — 4 ▲ 5 △ 6 ➖ 7

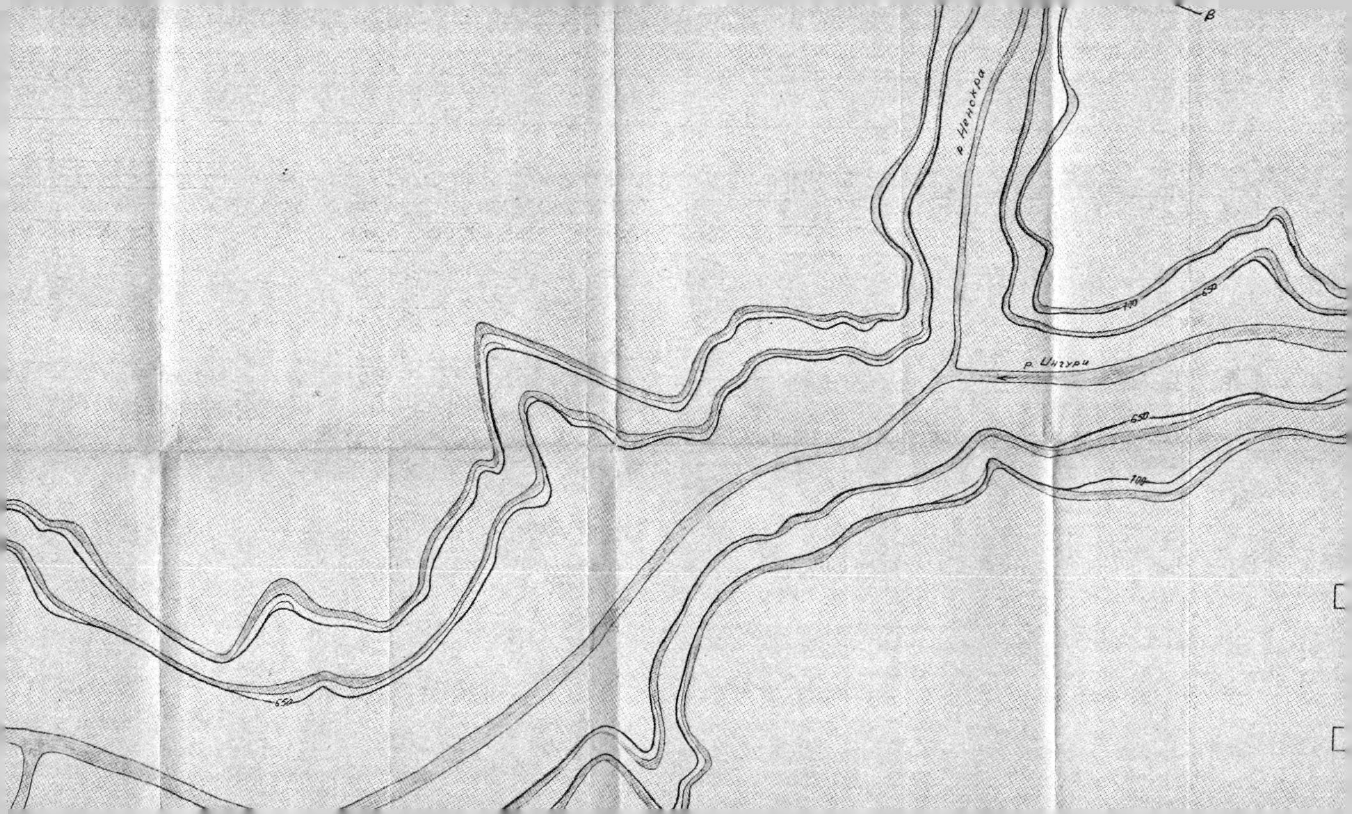

р. Ненскра
р. Ингури
650
700
650
700
650

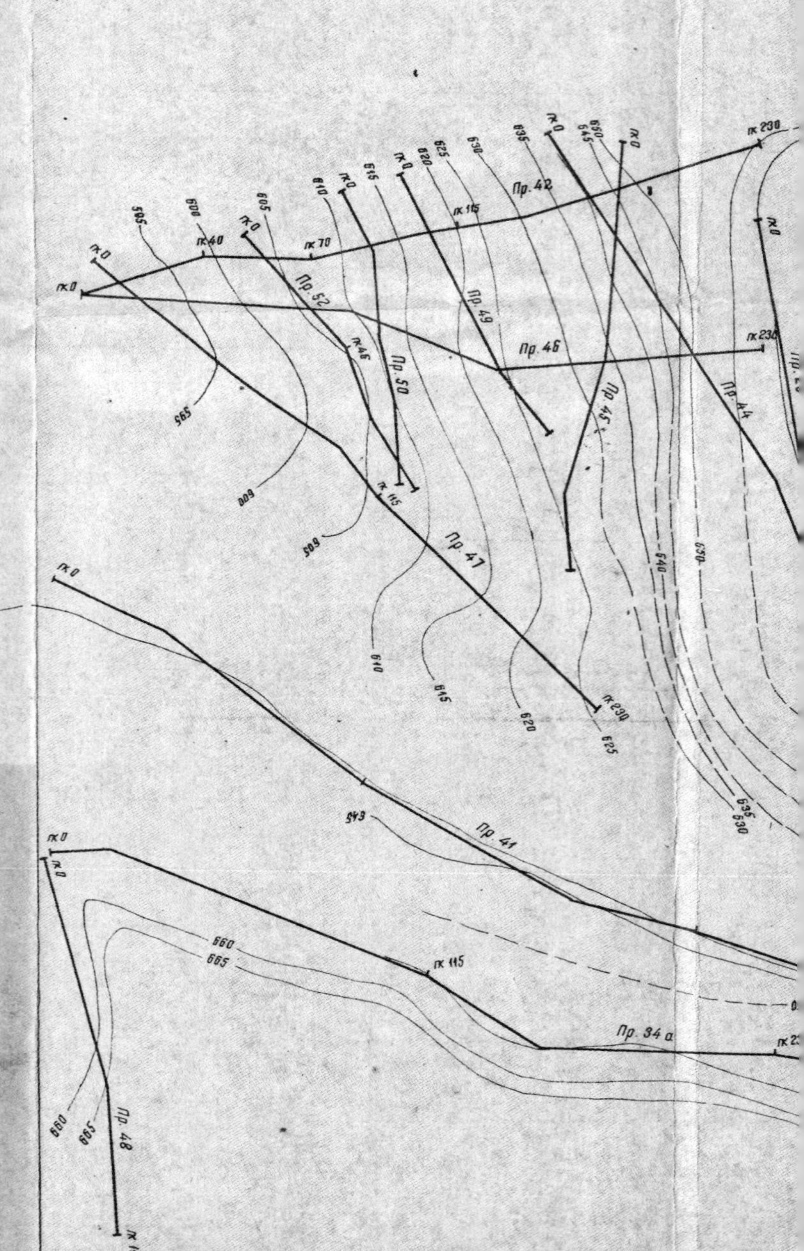

пк 230
пк 0
Пр. 42
пк 115
Пр. 49
Пр. 46
Пр. 52
Пр. 50
Пр. 47
Пр. 45
Пр. 44
пк 230
пк 46
пк 40
пк 70
пк 0
595
600
605
610
615
620
625
630
635
640
645
650
595
600
605
610
615
620
625
630
635
640
650
пк 115
пк 230
Пр. 41
645
пк 115
Пр. 34 а
пк 2
660
665
Пр. 48
660
665

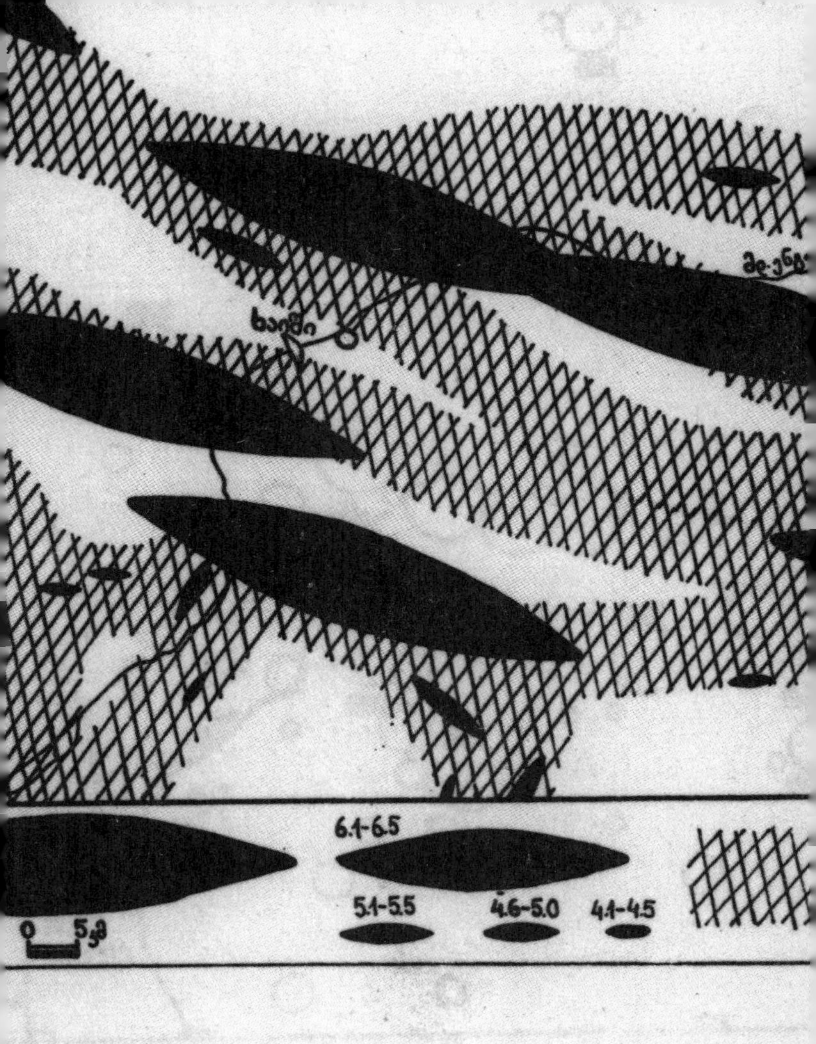

ა.3 ხუდონჰესის ახლომბელ ზონაში ძლიერი

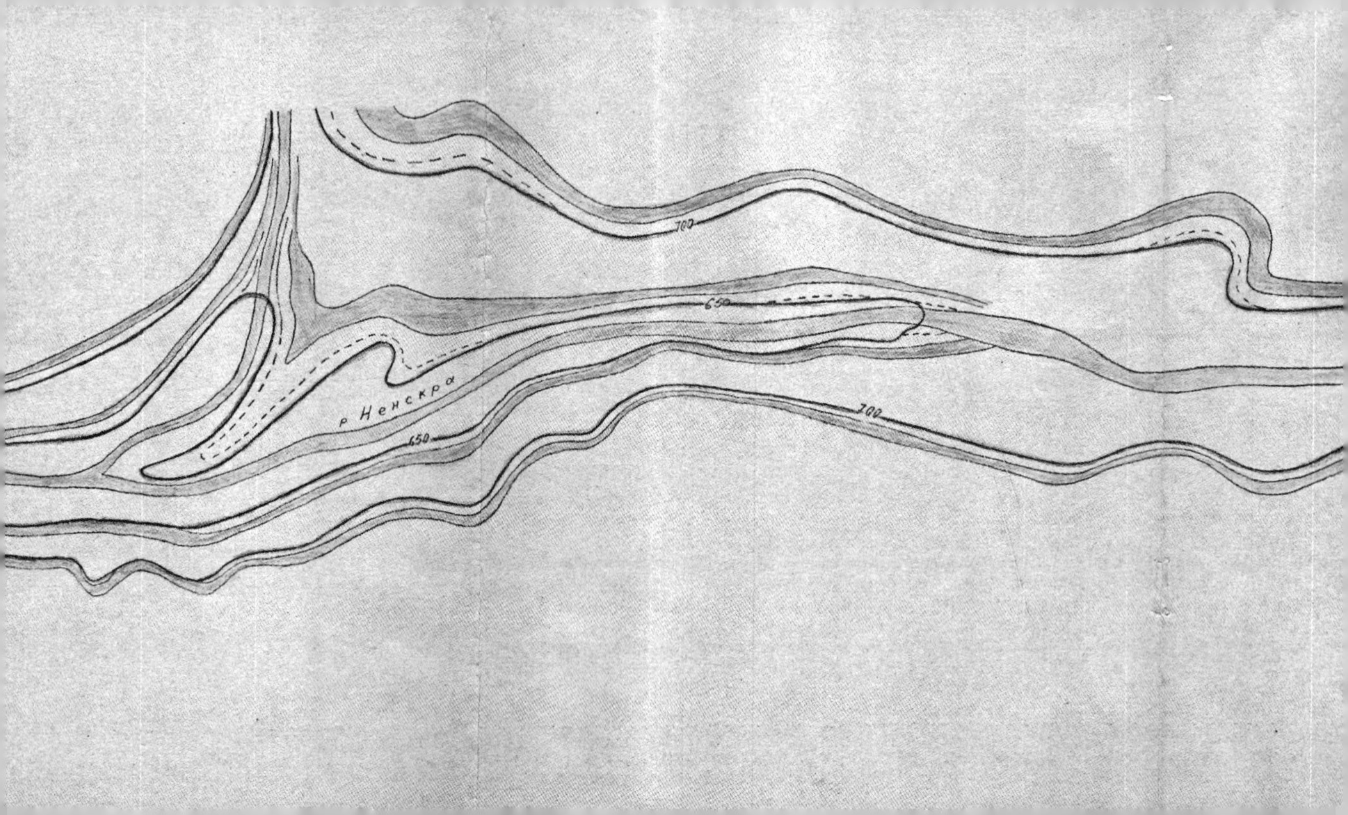
700
650
700
р. Ненскра

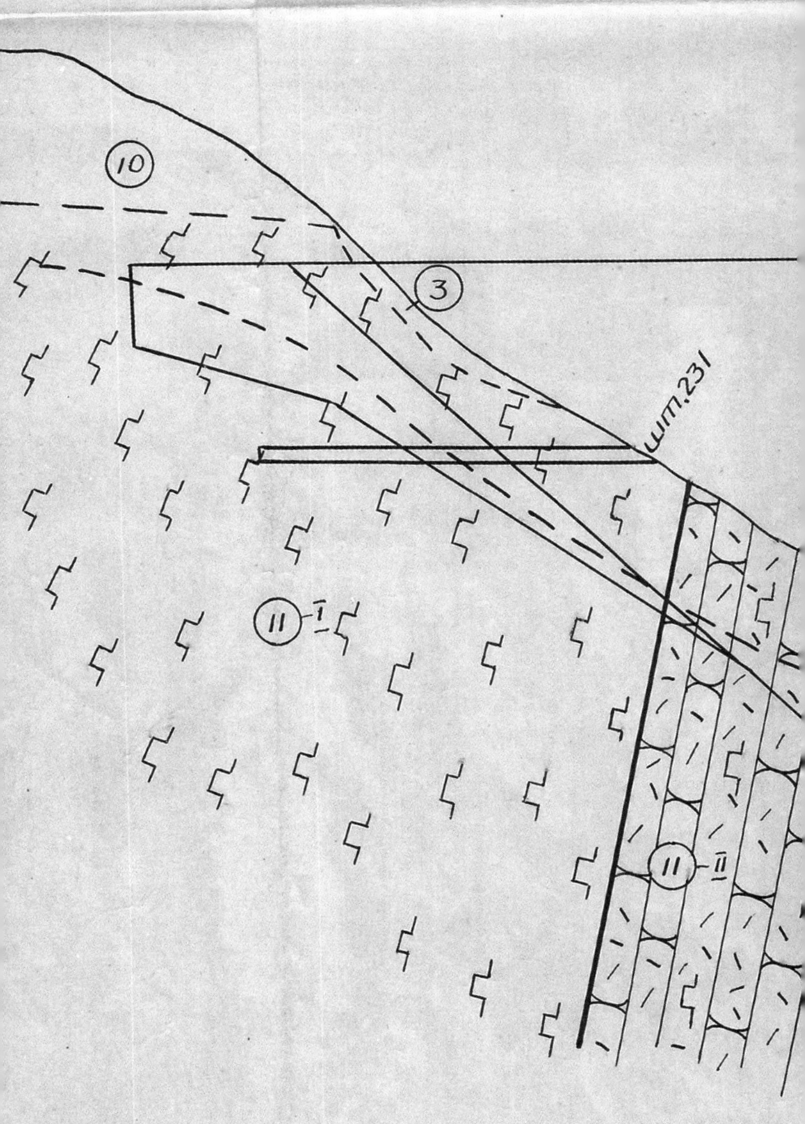
10
3
Шт.231
II
II
I
II
конп

Разрез
Верхне-Худонскому створу на р.Ингу...
зональностью по степени трещи-
новатости и деформируемости
М 1:2000
НПУ
Скв.304
Скв.236
Скв.299
Скв.259
Шт.221
2.9
Шт.205
Шт.232
Шт.212
0.20
0.20
0.10
0.51
0.28
1.87
1.45
0.76
0.76
0.1
0.20
0.33
0.40
0.48
0.27
0.23
0.35
1.0
302
300
11 - III
11 - III
11 - IV
Зоны с различными значениями КТП (%)
и модуля деформации Едф·10³ кг/см²
КТП/Едф
>5
<10
1-2
25-50
<0.5
>100
>2
<25
0.5-1
50-100
-3.0
.0

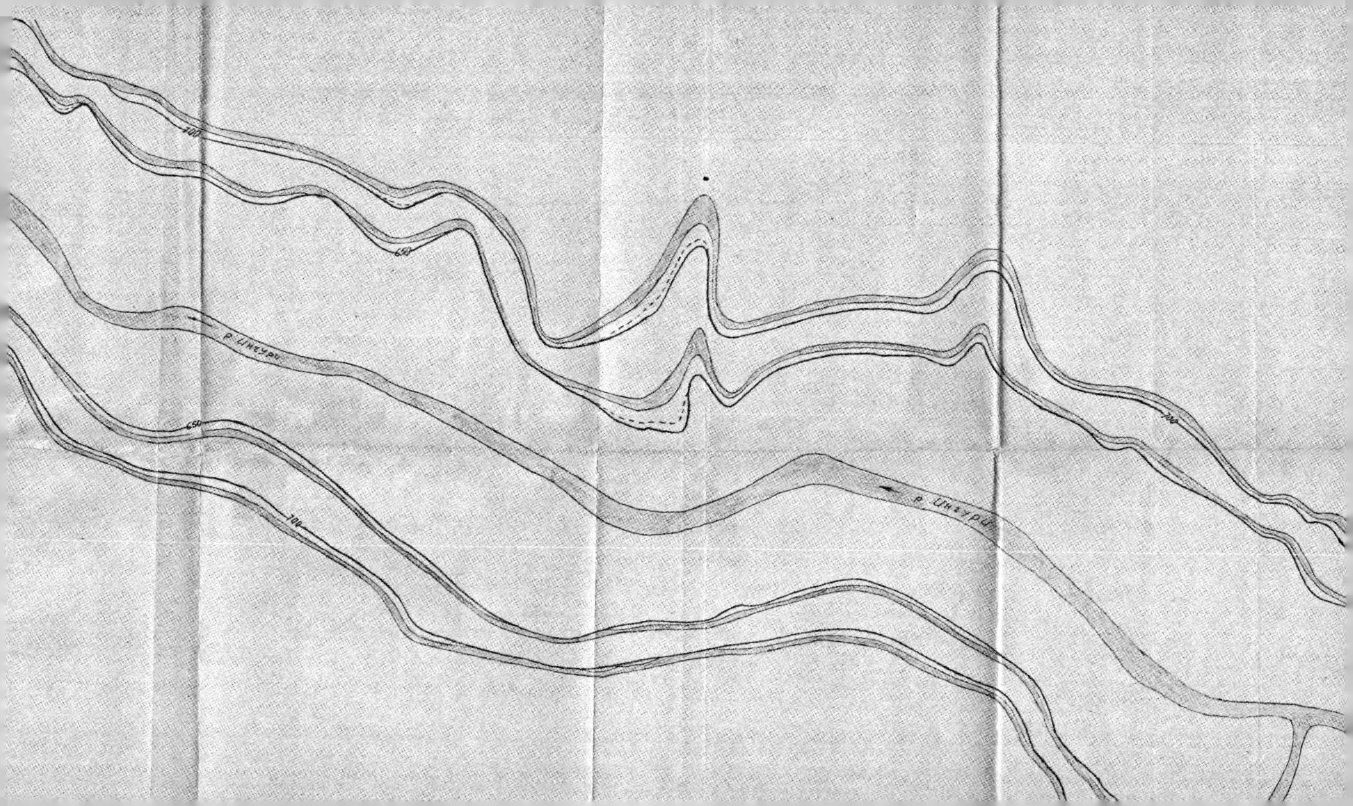

700
650
р. Ингури
650
700
700
р. Ингури

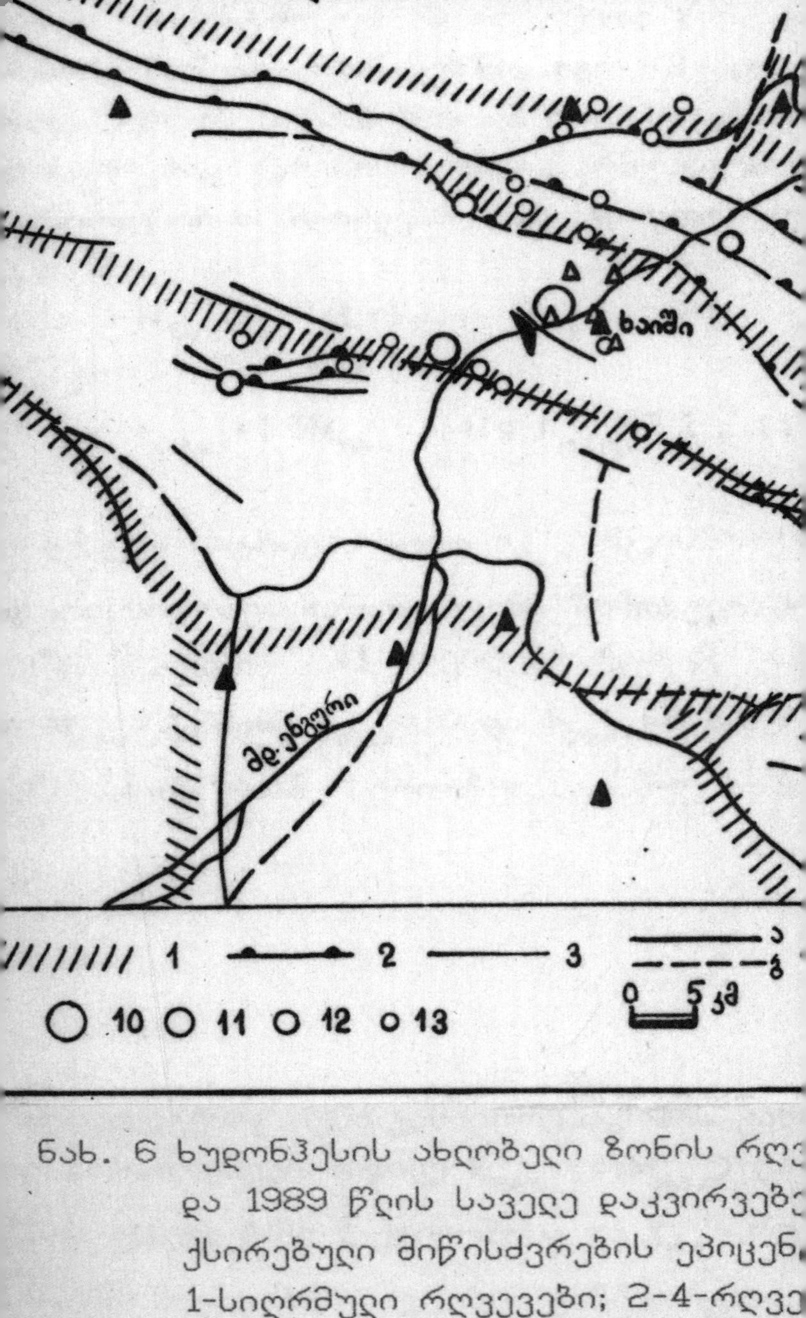

ნახ. 6 ხუდონჰესის ახლობელი ზონის რდე
და 1989 წლის სავეელე დაკვირვებ
ქსირებული მიწისქვრების ეპიცენ
1-სიღრმული რღვევები; 2-4-რღვე

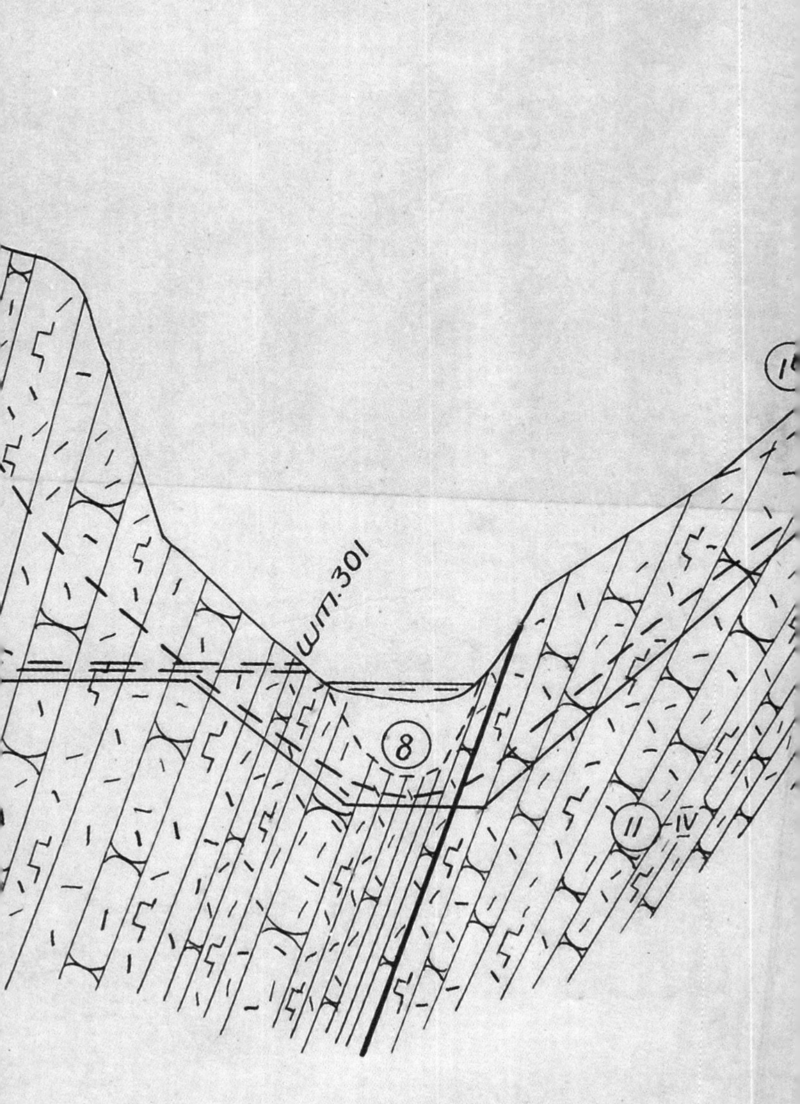
шт.301
8
II
IV
651,5

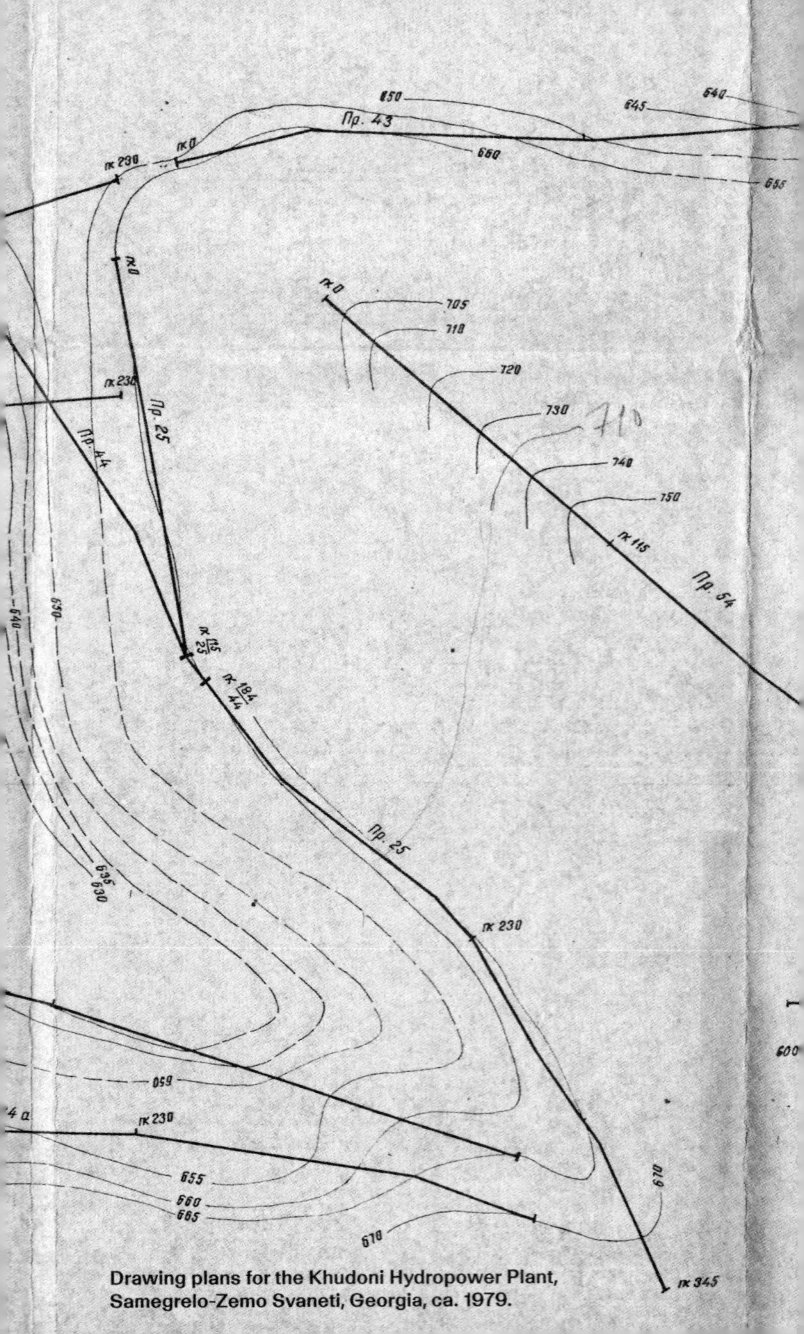

Drawing plans for the Khudoni Hydropower Plant, Samegrelo-Zemo Svaneti, Georgia, ca. 1979.

The Mountain Speaks to the Sea

Tekla Aslanishvili

S

y

s

t

e

m

s

&

T

e

r

r

i

t

o

r

i

e

s

Edited by Silvia Franceschini
Onomatopee #261

Contents

Foreword

The Mountain Speaks to the Sea delves into artist, filmmaker, and essayist Tekla Aslanishvili's experimental film trilogy produced between 2020 and 2024. Positioned between an artist's book and a reader, it provides a broader perspective on the role of moving image and artistic research in the making and unmaking of infrastructures and unravelling the social, ecological, and geopolitical complexities of the contemporary world. Featuring essays and conversations with scholars in visual culture, political science, and critical geography, the book brings the research and references behind Aslanishvili's cinematic works to the forefront. The texts are interspersed with a series of stills from each film, with their sequence reflecting on how film can be translated into printed matter.

The publication follows a reverse chronology, beginning with the most recent film, *The Mountain Speaks to the Sea* (2024), moving backwards through the creation of *A State in a State* (2022), and concluding with the first film of the trilogy, *Scenes from Trial and Error* (2020). Though not initially intended as a trilogy, the films have organically developed from one another. Collectively, they seek to make sense of Georgia's recent transformation in relation to global, political, and economic changes, focusing on how large-scale infrastructure projects have reshaped the dynamics between governments, people, and their lands. The introductory text by curator Silvia Franceschini, *Thinking with Conditions: Tekla Aslanishvili's Topographic Tales*, recounts this evolution, highlighting the connections between the films and the way Aslanishvili uses history to interpret the contemporary "fetish for logistics".[1]

Aslanishvili's cinematic project *The Mountain Speaks to the Sea* (2024) reassembles fragmented (hi)stories of restructuring labour and life around global energy politics. By intertwining personal and distant histories with myths and future orientations, the film examines how energy infrastructures are reforming not only social and geological landscapes but also the making and unmaking of state borders and practices of statecraft. In his essay, *Rivers Shape Mountains: Mountains Become Rivers*, artist and interdisciplinary researcher Ifor Duncan reads Aslanishvili's film within a broader reflection on the impact of hydropower projects on river and watery ecosystems. Drawing on diverse references, from environmental humanities to literature, he explores the agency of rivers in the context of large geopolitical and infrastructural processes.

In her essay *Water Movement, Hybrid Ecosystems, and Infrastructural War—The Image as a Method*, scholar and research collaborator of the artist, Alexandra Aroshvili, unfolds the making of *The Mountain Speaks to the Sea* by going deep into the context in which it emerged, connecting the Soviet Hydro-industrial past, with the extractive operations behind Georgia's contemporary energy politics. She reflects on the relationship between cinema, politics, and infrastructure, drawing examples from Harun Farocki's essay documentary film *Images of the World and the Inscription of War* (1989), and building connections to the production of *The Mountain Speaks to the Sea*. She considers how both filmmakers "speak to the power of images to reveal the presence of things or phenomena that aren't immediately apparent".[2]

Aslanishvili's experimental documentary films *A State in a State* (2022) and *Scenes from Trial and Error* (2020) blend intimate stories and geopolitical narratives in the Caucasus and Caspian regions which undergo macro-infrastructural transformations. Both films go against the grain in their reading of the grand promises of connectivity, challenging the dominant vision of the New Silk Road. While disclosing the intricate geopolitical networks and the extractive operation behind the making of infrastructure, they observe the social fabric woven along transit routes, excavating their potential for building lasting, transnational kinship among the people who live and work around them.

In her essay *Infrastructures of Friendship*, researcher and collaborator of the artist, Evelina Gambino, unfolds the collaborative methods involved in making the films and focuses on the acts of solidarity enacted by railway workers to resist the political violence performed by the state. Through a feminist lens grounded in a gendered analysis of capitalism, Gambino notes that infrastructures are made of and make relations, allowing distant subjects, sites, and events to belong to an ecosystem. Timothy Mitchell, a distinguished political scientist and professor at Columbia University, adds a layer of insight into these processes by proposing the concept of infrastructural consciousness. This features in the conversation *Economies of Delay* between Mitchell, Aslanishvili, and Gambino—originally conducted for *A State in a State*'s voiceover—where they unpack Mitchell's research on how "infrastructures work on time".[3]

This publication accompanies the 2024 exhibition *The Mountain Speaks to the Sea* at Onomatopee, which is the first exhibition of Tekla Aslanishvili in the Netherlands.[4] Following the transformation of matter from solid to liquid, travelling across rivers and railways in the South East Caucasus and the Caspian Sea region, readers are invited to immerse themselves in the gradual unfolding of complex geopolitical histories filtered through
the lens of infrastructure and moving image.

The Mountain Speaks to the Sea is the first publication in the series *Systems & Territories*, a five-year research program exploring how regimes of governance shape territories. The program centres on monographic and thematic exhibitions and publications that emerge from long-term investigations and collaborations between artists, researchers, and communities. It critically examines the categories, structures, and ideologies that uphold global modernity, as well as the ways in which geopolitics intersects with themes such as decolonisation, gender, infrastructure, and labour.

Thinking with Conditions

Tekla
Aslanishvili's

Topographic
Tales

Silvia
Franceschini

Since the second post-Soviet decade, massive infrastructural interventions have dominated Georgia's national imagination. Located on the dividing line between Europe and Asia, between Russia, Turkey, Iran, Afghanistan, and the Black Sea, the country is envisioned to be turned into a transit corridor of natural resources into Europe, and a pivotal point within the Eurasian development strategy Belt and Road Initiative.[1] But the promise of these transformations, which is reshaping the country's internal geography as well as the arrangements of global powers, lands in a territory impacted by decades of uncertainty, wars and economic crisis, interrupted by harsh privatisation of spaces and services. Additionally, Georgia is assuming a new geopolitical role in light of the current Russian-Ukrainian war.

It is precisely within these cracks that the work of Tekla Aslanishvili moves, offering a layered picture of geopolitical transformations by connecting past narratives with future orientations to show how deeper, complex histories feed a contemporary "fetish for logistics".[2] Her cinematic work foregrounds the inherent multiplicity—of narratives and practices, but also of temporalities and spatial formations—at play in development projects of planetary scale.

Aslanishvili's practice is characterized by its critical engagement with themes of progress and the extending fault lines between people, governments, and the land they inhabit. Using a situated and collaborative approach to filmmaking, she constructs experimental documentaries addressing the connection between exploitation and the spatial forms produced by the expansion of transnational logistics. Another recurring motif of Aslanishvili's works is the complex dynamic of urban planning and development, as expressed in the project of building new cities. Her works explore how these projects are artificially imposed on the social, ecological, and cultural fabric of existing territories and communities.

All these trajectories intertwine in a trilogy of films created by the artist between 2020 and 2024. Although not initially conceived as a trilogy, the films naturally evolved from one another, developing across multiple geographies into a cohesive cinematic experience that portrays the landscapes impacted by infrastructural projects.

In 2018, the artist accidentally discovered an abandoned area on the shores of the Black Sea—a city embryo, consisting of three main elements: a sculpture, a municipal building, and a small stretch of road connecting them. This territory, fabricated by a series of speculative designs, was the trace of what was supposed to develop as a smart city and a deep sea port out of the existing wetlands of Anaklia, a seaside region located near Abkhazia, a contested territory that has been at the centre of conflicts since the collapse of the Soviet Union. Discovering remnants of the potential city marked the beginning of a long-term research culminating in the film *Scenes from Trial and Error* (2020), where Aslanishvili closely observes the project of transforming a little fishing village into a 'smart city' and major port called Lazika, reclaiming Georgia's place as a critical geopolitical node in the logistical landscapes of the Great Silk Road.

As evidenced through Aslanishvili's body of inter-disciplinary work, the idea for the project dates back to Soviet times and gained even greater importance in the post-Soviet period. As former president Eduard Shevardnadze states in a TV interview featured in the film, Georgia needed to "find its place in the modern world",[3] and the government sought to shape a new national identity by drawing on the semi-mythical history of the country, which once played a central role along the ancient Silk Road. His successor, President Mikheil Saakashvili, even revived and inserted himself into the legend of the Argonauts from Greek mythology, drawing a parallel between Jason discovering the rich land of Colchis, now modern-day Georgia, and his own arrival in the same territory during a maritime crisis, which awakened him to the region's beauty and immense potential for development. As Aslanishvili notes in her essay, *Scenes from a Reclamation*, co-authored with Orit Halpern: "In Anaklia, reclamation of the distant past has become the grounds for a speculative future, one that escapes all resource, material, and monetary limits."[4] The futuristic city of Lazika, however, was never built.

Halpern, a professor of digital cultures and smart city expert, is one of four invited narrators featured in *Scenes from Trial and Error*, who comment on the processes involved in smart city development from different temporal, geographic, and professional perspectives. As the film unfolds, their insights flow alongside and against the visual backdrop of a failed urban project.

Other protagonists are the executive director of Anaklia's city project and the architect Niko Japaridze, designer of the municipality building, now in ruins, who narrates over long shots of the empty glass volume and a cow slowly crossing the road. The montage is built on a mismatch between multiple speeches and scenes from the swampland of Anaklia, emphasizing how this form of worldmaking functions against the logic of habitation.

Scenes from Trial and Error reveals how the mere anticipation of the project reshaped the way that people interacted with their land, starting with the relocation of part of the population under the promise of a new life in the future city. By exploring the derelict infrastructural landscapes and relating architectural frictions that have emerged in Anaklia, the film observes how planning strategies and operational logics of large-scale infrastructural investments inevitably result in the failed fantasy of a technologically managed smooth urban life.

The camera zooms on architecture built to compose the future smart city, among which is a pier sculpture designed by German architect Jürgen Hermann Mayer. Mayer's parametric design, devised of a series of steel fins hanging from an interior skeleton, was meant to be a landmark for Georgia's second-largest city—a city which is nowhere in evidence. When the camera stretches northward up the beach from the sculpture and pier there is nothing but a vast port construction site. Aslanishvili refers to China

Miéville's novel *The City & the City*, where a performative border between two fictional cities is created through the act of seeing and unseeing the architecture of the respective sites.[5] Similarly, in Anaklia the idea was that the people from Abkhazia—a conflict zone with Georgia since the collapse of the USSR, located on the northern part of the sea—would observe a "performance of modernity",[6] staged through the architecture along the shoreline with no function but high symbolic value.

Mayer, the favourite architect of President Saakashvili, had designed many other key sites for logistics operations in Georgia, including the station building for the Baku-Tbilisi-Kars railway line in Akhalkalaki. Through her research, the artist gradually realized that this railway was more than just a way of transporting goods and people, it acted as a means for negotiating political relations between Azerbaijan, Georgia, Armenia, and Turkey. This marked the beginning of Aslanishvili's journey towards her next film, *A State in a State* (2022), which similarly explores the intersection of war, political upheaval, and economic factors.

The film begins its narration with the artist's voice looking out of the window of her apartment, observing the changing seasons over the railway. *A State in a State* follows the railway's transit route which is part of the New Silk Road, running from Baku in Azerbaijan via the Georgian capital Tbilisi to Kars in Türkiye, touching the fragile political boundaries that have emerged in the South Caucasus and Caspian regions since the collapse of the Soviet Union. The railroad was built in the aftermath of the war between Armenia and Azerbaijan, during which Azerbaijan and Turkey closed their borders and cut transit links with Armenia, isolating the country. Despite this, both nations still needed alternative transit routes, and since Georgia lies between them they began investing in new railway lines, such as the Baku-Tbilisi-Kars (BTK) railway. This project is also part of the Middle Corridor, or Trans-Caspian International Transport Route, which connects Europe and China via Georgia, Azerbaijan, and the Caspian Sea. While the corridor has been in development for years, the ongoing war between Ukraine and Russia has heightened its importance as an alternative transit route. The film critically examines the construction of this vast infra-structure, revealing the realities that exist on the periphery of these anticipated opportunities for connectivity.

In a range of interviews with journalists, railway workers, and researchers, Aslanishvili captures the complex political and social entanglements of these post-Soviet states and explores how railways are used as instruments of exclusion and geopolitical sabotage.

At the same time, she flags strategies adopted by workers to counter state coercion and the transnational bonds formed between people who live and work around these infra-structures. Evelina Gambino notes: "As a socio-technical system of almost unfathomable proportions, the railways that crossed the Soviet

Union allowed the emergence and circulation of a set of techno-political relations and subjectivities that have largely been severed in the wake of the Soviet collapse."[7]

Alongside narration from Gambino and political scientist Timothy Mitchell, the film voice-over is structured as a compilation of stories from individuals living and working within these infra-structures, sharing their own experiences and histories. For Aslanishvili, the film thus became a medium for conducting research with others, assembling diverse voices and perspectives to explore the intersection of local histories, geographies, and temporalities where these infra-structures emerge. This approach to filmmaking, which collages various voices and narratives into a single storyline crafted by the author, renegotiates the boundaries of essay film—a genre that seeks to rethink the critical potential of montage.

Another fundamental element of *A State in a State* is landscape. The film provides an impressive insight into the region between the Caspian and Black Seas through a landscape interrupted by infrastructure. Through both documentary-style and carefully long-staged cinematic shots, the film captures roads and railways across the four seasons, highlighting the resilience of these infrastructures as they withstand extreme temperatures and adapt to the changing environment around—an environment both powerful in its impressive natural beauty and fragile due to the extractive operations driven by the development projects.

Thinking with Conditions

In all of Aslanishvili's films, there is a profound investment in shaping the landscapes cinematically. However, the way her images are composed and infrastructures are depicted is never glorious or apologetic of their large scale. On the contrary, the scale of such projects is reshaped in relation to the rest of the elements of the story. The power of landscape in contrast to the technological frontiers is enhanced even more by a sophisticated sound design by composers Nika Pasuri and Ani Zakareishvili. As if it were an opera, the music interweaves with the narrative to build the rhythm of the film together.

The last film of the trilogy, *The Mountain Speaks to the Sea* (2024), is based on the energy infrastructure of the South Caucasus. The experimental two-channel documentary, developed in collaboration with Alexandra Aroshvili, co-founder of the Fair Energy Politics Collective,[8] follows the rivers of the South Caucasus, tracing their paths from the mountains to the Black Sea, mapping the material and social infrastructures surrounding them through the shifting seasons. This work is a continuation of the previous two films, engaging with the promises of big infrastructural transformation and connectivity while excavating layers of myths, historical and current border formation, and practices of statecraft. The main trigger for the film was the Black Sea submarine cable project, a new energy bridge taking renewable energy to Europe, built to strengthen its energy security in the aftermath of the Russian invasion of Ukraine. The project's ambitious scale is prompting Georgia to reposition its role as a new energy hub. This includes the reactivation of planned dams, the construction of which was halted during and after Soviet rule, as well as the use of energy produced by mega-dams built in the Soviet Union such as the majestic Enguri HPP—the world's highest arched dam at the time of its construction—now divided by the administrative boundary line between Georgia and Abkhazia.

The Mountains Speaks to the Sea pays specific attention to the region of Svaneti in northwest Georgia, where the unregulated pro-liferation of crypto-mining is disrupting existing energy infrastructures, and intended dam projects endanger local ecological and social landscapes. While mapping the shifting fracture zones between local and national governments and practices of touristification and exploitation, it also investigates Indigenous practices of self-organization and control deployed by the local population to protect their infrastructures and environment.

Various maps move the viewer around a geography which becomes the film's central subject. Soviet cartography of rivers shows their path from the Caucasian Mountains to the Black Sea and allows us to envision them as a commu-nicating vessel between two geographical points. Maps therefore become a linguistic and narrative element offering a mobile topography through shifting territories.

Delving further, the film examines the layers of infrastructure developed throughout Soviet times, particularly the creation of new modes of knowledge production around hydropower projects. This process also fostered the rise of a new scientific intelligentsia, tasked with living and working within these infrastructures. As the narrative unfolds, the focus shifts to the tensions between the tacit knowledge of coexisting with nature and the scientific expertise required for these ambitious projects.

The Mountain Speaks to the Sea incorporates archival footage from Soviet national scientific films, as well as one of the earliest ethnographic films by Georgian director Mikheil Kalatozov, *Salt for Svanetia* (1930). Depicting the construction of an important road in the region of Svaneti, it is used in Aslanishvili's film as a backdrop against which the post-Soviet reality emerges. Through meticulous shots that reframe architectures and landscapes in the same way as Kalatozov's montage, Aslanishvili's moving image work responds to how the Soviet film shaped the captivating aura around these infrastructures. Historical footage intertwines with contemporary material and existing videos such as journalistic clips, and the interplay between past and present narratives creates a polyphonic dialogue that brings together multiple temporalities.

For Aslanishvili, the medium of film allows the viewer to comprehend the complexity of infrastructure — how infrastructure is all about control, sovereignty, and other kinds of power dynamics and human relations. At the same time, because the trilogy puts historical documentaries into conversation with contemporary footage, it's possible to reflect on the role of moving images in the making and unmaking of the infrastructures themselves. During Soviet times, cinema was a key tool for promoting large-scale state projects. Cinematographers like Dziga Vertov and Oleksandr Dovzhenko filmed the development of Soviet industrialization, portraying hydropower stations, factories, and railways, whose images have become emblems of the Soviet Union's leap into modernity. In this sense, we can say that cinema, modernity, and infrastructure are inextricably entangled. To be modern is to be synchronized with infrastructure: "To live within and by means of infrastructure."[9] Cinema is emblematic of modernity: it compresses and captures time and space. Positioned between infrastructure and modernity, the cinematic experience dictates who is included or excluded, shaping how we see and experience the world. As Anu Thapa states: "Cinema goes therefore from being an emblem of modernity to containing and constructing modernity … To consider cinema as an infrastructure is to blur the distinctions between infrastructure and apparatus, aesthetics and politics, ontology and epistemology."[10]

Aslanishvili's films reinstate the materiality and physicality of infrastructures to highlight the processes and the contingencies of their formation. Deeply engaged in the relationship between bodily acts of labour and the abstraction of science, her work weaves together intimate histories with the macro-infrastructural transformations that mark Georgia's recent past.

By deconstructing the capability of infrastructures to 'enchant',[11] Aslanishvili's films inform what she calls 'infrastructural imaginaries'—a way of thinking about what infrastructures are, where they are located, who controls them, and what they do as "ubiquitous and seemingly innocuous features of our world".[12]

By showing often disastrous outcomes of infrastructural projects—abandonment, depopulation, unrealized expectations, and broken promises—Aslanishvili's films urge us to consider: What if the failure of infrastructural imagination is inherently embedded in the promise of a better future?

By bridging the gaps between geographic and topographic thought and historical layering, Aslanishvili's research and films critically explore how infrastructures establish their significance in relation to socio-economic, geopolitical, and environmental conditions. In this way, filming became a way for her to 'think with conditions'[13] —considering how the promise of infrastructure can contribute to the "mobilization of affect and the senses of desire, pride, and frustration, feelings which can be deeply political."[14]

Aslanishvili's film trilogy reveals the deep interconnections between space and time, geography and history, within the realm of infrastructural imagination. The films offer glimpses of a world where lands and cultures, their mythical and real pasts—whether the legend of the Argonauts or Soviet industrialization—as well as the present day and possible futures, derive meaning from a territory's ability to channel transcontinental flows of resources. Infrastructures become a lens through which governments, shaped by the pressures of advancing transglobal capitalism, view history. This geopolitical worldview interprets human history and predicts its future through the lens of space.

1	The so-called 'New Silk Road'.

2	Tekla Aslanishvili and Orit Halpern, *Scenes from a Reclamation*, e-flux Architecture, February 2020, https://www.e-flux.com/architecture/new-silk-roads/313102/scenes-from-a-reclamation/.

3	*Scenes from Trial and Error*, directed by Tekla Aslanishvili (2020).

4	Tekla Aslanishvili and Orit Halpern, *Scenes from a Reclamation*, e-flux Architecture, February 2020, https://www.e-flux.com/architecture/new-silk-roads/313102/scenes-from-a-reclamation/.

5	From the lecture delivered by Tekla Aslanishvili and Evelina Gambino, "(Re)making Anaklia, the architecture of ruin," at the Tbilisi Architecture Biennial, 2020.

6	Ibid.

7	Evelina Gambino, "Infrastructures of Friendship," in *The Mountain Speaks to the Sea*, ed. Silvia Franceschini (Eindhoven: Onomatopee Projects, 2024).

8	The Fair Energy Politics collective is an activist group founded in Georgia in 2021 operating mainly against Namakhvani dam construction.

9	Paul N. Edwards, "Infrastructure and Modernity: Force, Time, and Social Organization in the History of Sociotechnical Systems," in *Modernity and Technology*, ed. Thomas J. Misa, Philip Brey, Andrew Freenberg (Cambridge: The MIT Press, 2003): 185–225.

10	Anu Thapa, "Cinema and/as infrastructure in interwar avant-gardes and empire aviation documentaries," Necsus, June 7, 2023. https://necsus-ejms.org/cinema-and-as-infrastructure-in-interwar-avant-gardes-and-empire-aviation-documentaries/.

11	Penny Harvey & Hannah Knox, "The Enchantments of Infrastructure," *Mobilities* 7, no. 4 (2012). https://doi.org/10.1080/17450101.2012.718935.

12	Keller Esterling, *Extrastatecraft: The Power of Infrastructure Space* (London: Verso Books, 2016).

13	For Denise Ferreira da Silva, to 'think with conditions' means to think through a transformative approach that acknowledges and engages with the lived experiences and histories of diverse communities. See: Denise Ferreira da Silva in conversation with Stefanie Hessler, https://www.novembermag.com/content/denise-ferreira-da-silva.

14	Brian Larkin, "The Politics and Poetics of Infrastructure," *Annual Review of Anthropology* 42 (2013). https://doi.org/10.1146/annurev-anthro-092412-155522.

Water Movement, Hybrid Ecosystems

and

Infrastructural War

The Image as a Method

Alexandra Aroshvili

"When the sea surges against the land, irregularly, not haphazardly, this motion binds the look without fettering it and sets free the thoughts.

The surge that sets the thoughts in motion is here being investigated scientifically in its own motion—in the large wave channel at Hannover.

The motions of water are still less researched than those of light."

— Harun Farocki, *Images of the World and the Inscription of War*, 1989

Harun Farocki's 1989 essay documentary film, *Images of the World and the Inscription of War*, begins with a depiction of a wave-measuring laboratory in Hannover, where water waves crash against a concrete channel. This footage of water movement in a scientific laboratory, which presents a picture familiar to the human eye of the intersection of nature and technology, is accompanied by the calm, unruffled voice of a female narrator reading the introduction to this essay.

This film tells the story of the first aerial photographs of Auschwitz, accidentally taken in 1944 by American pilots while photographing the nearby IG Farben factory before bombing it. IG Farben was a chemical and pharmaceutical industrial complex that produced products for various military and genocidal purposes, including Zyklon B, used in the gas chambers. However, until 1977, these photographs were not deciphered as depicting a concentration camp; they were perceived as pictures of an economic

Water Movement, Hybrid Ecosystems

Farocki tells the story of one the most horrific events in history: by showing unfamiliar images of mathematical and technological instruments of measurement, alongside a critical analysis of capitalism, consumerism, media, technology, war, reconnaissance, and the military industry.

However, the footage of the Hannover laboratory, shown in the prologue and epilogue and flashing several more times throughout the film, is the sole fragment among many events linked by the narrator's commentary which transcends the film's primary narrative, functioning as an overarching perspective or a detached symbol of hope. Many researchers suggest that in this film—the release of which coincides with the end of the Cold War and the period of global concern about nuclear arms—Farocki expresses a certain hope through the depiction of the Hannover laboratory, speculating that a thorough study of water could potentially lead to the replacement of nuclear energy.

In light of today's energy crises, which are once again intertwined with wars, and set against the backdrop of cataclysms related to the climate crisis and a global strategy for Green Transition—a strategy that involves both developed and developing countries in a new industry of renewable energy production, prioritizing hydro and green energy—complex, multi-layered, and critical methods are needed to reveal the conflicts, contradictions, and particularities associated with this transition. These needs render Farocki's essay documentary filmmaking, or other critical and experimental anthropological

target prepared for bombing. It wasn't until the political situation changed that they were allowed to be seen as evidence of a death camp.

By exploring image-making and its historical significance, Farocki's film delves into the military-industrial complexities of capitalism — tracing the evolution from the earliest methods of photographic measurement to the creation of simulated realities, examining the relationship between the concepts of 'enlightenment' and 'reconnaissance', and revealing connections between countless seemingly unrelated events — ultimately offering an impressive method of research. This method, rather than confronting familiar, contradictory narratives, seeks out connections, echoes, and unknown combinations, thus caring for the multi-layered diversity of the world. This is how

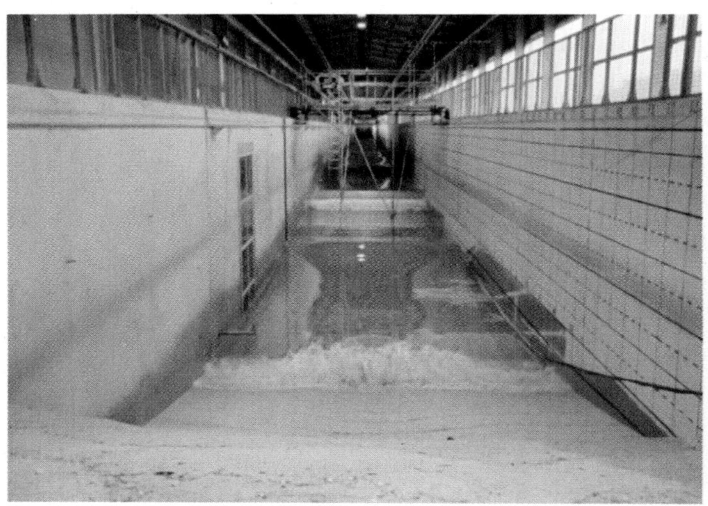

Film still. Harun Farocki, *Images of the World and the Inscription of War*, 1989.

methods, more relevant than ever; methods that were, in turn, born precisely when the crises of planetary and modern political projects first collided.[1] These methods that strive to bridge disciplines fragmented by modernity, divergent histories, geographies, and socio-political or economic complexities are especially instrumental in documenting the large-scale infrastructures involved in the production and transit of energy. This is why, when Tekla Aslanishvili and I began working on her film, *The Mountain Speaks to the Sea*, which traces the past and present of developing hydro infrastructures in the South Caucasus, our goal was not to artificially link non-connectables but to uncover hidden connections—connecting processes that are distant in space and time, which render rivers as extractable resources. From the beginning, it was clear that we needed a multifaceted and somewhat experimental research method in the face of this complexity, which is further complicated by its im/materiality, symbolic meanings, the inscrutability of natural forces, and the promises and waste of infrastructure. This complexity also intersects with intricate global economic, neocolonial, multi-scalar imperial, and social interests.

Over the last decades, Georgia has attempted to overcome the severe economic, social, public, and moral crisis that arose during the collapse of the Soviet Union. Through aggressive economic privatisation, deregulation, and intensive use of natural resources, it now finds itself entangled in a confused mix of historical, geographical, political, economic, cultural, and social factors. This complexity physically manifests in foreign direct investments and their results, in infrastructure-led development, and the emergence of speculative sectors of the economy, such as the crypto mining industry with its in/formal farms, free industrial zones, and illegal infrastructure in mountainous regions. An example of this is Svaneti, which, due to its severe geography and status as a high-mountainous region, is supplied with free electricity. In addition to being characterized by natural climatic conditions favourable for the crypto industry (ideal for cooling miners), it is also a region associated with significant hydroelectric resources. It is home to the Enguri HPP, Georgia's largest hydropower plant, which had the tallest arch dam in the world at the time of its construction. Also, Svaneti is the region where the construction of the 704 MW Khudoni Hydropower Plant (HPP) and the 280 MW Nenskra Dam is planned. Although the Khudoni HPP was initially conceived during the Soviet era, and the Nenskra Dam has been under consideration since 2015, neither project has been constructed to date. Here are also located other medium and small hydropower plants such as the 20 MW Mestiachala HPP, which was rebuilt after being damaged by a river flood upon its commissioning in 2019. These examples represent only a fraction of the numerous hydropower plants either temporarily halted due to protests or currently under construction, scattered not just across Svaneti but throughout Georgia.

Georgia's hydroelectric potential has been historically significant since before the Soviet Union. This was particularly evident in the early Soviet era when the first hydropower plants were built, contributing to industrialization through the development of hydropower in a country abundant in water resources. However, the aggressive policy of maximizing water resource exploitation began more recently in Georgian history, following the global financial crisis of 2008 and the intensification of the climate crisis, when international financial institutions started funding 'greenfield' projects in developing countries. The planning of new hydro projects or the renewal of Soviet-era projects is particularly dangerous and unjustifiable in a small country filled with seismically active, populated valleys—especially when unfolding against a backdrop of significant scientific setbacks such as hydroelectric projects that are being developed without essential geological, seismic, engineering, or technical studies, or merely on a formal basis. Moreover, the agreements concluded between the state and private companies building hydroelectric power plants are often critiqued as exploitative.[2] In addition to civic protests and political, corrupt, or private interests, there are conflicts and contradictions around issues of preserving ancient natural monuments and cultural heritage that are important to indigenous populations and historical mountain regions. This includes layers of sacred and religious significance, such as the practice of swearing on icons. In the case of Svaneti,

Alexandra Aroshvili

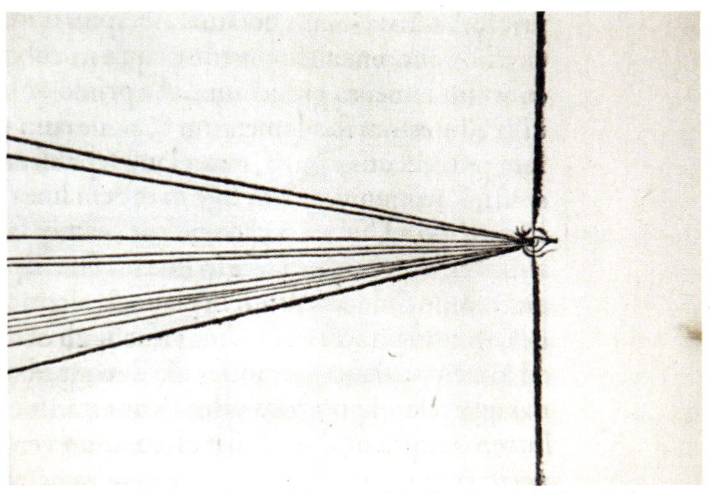

Film still. Harun Farocki, *Images of the World and the Inscription of War*, 1989.

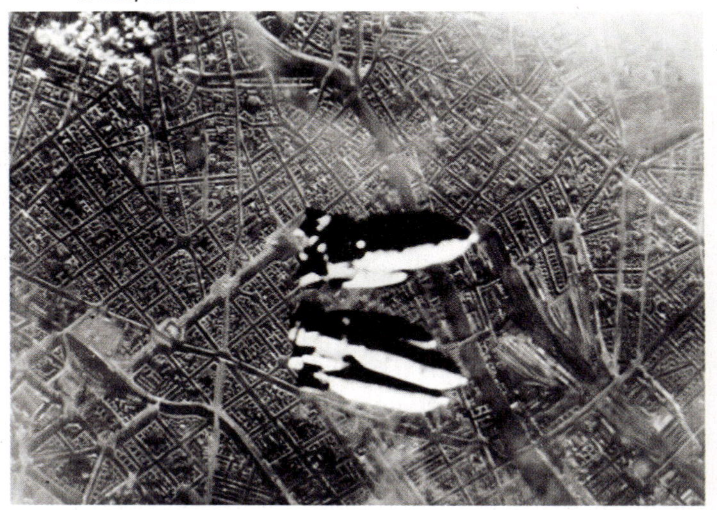

Film still. Harun Farocki, *Images of the World and the Inscription of War*, 1989.

this has been revived in contemporary opposition to infrastructure projects and speculative economic practices, particularly against the construction of hydroelectric power plants and crypto mining.

These stories are endless, much like the multi-layered nature of the processes they describe, which besides involving historical, geographical, architectural, ecological, cultural-ethnographic, socio-economic, and geopolitical layers, also encompass many as-yet-unnamed and thus emotional, impressive, hidden, and invisible worlds. Additionally, numerous hybrid ecosystems are affected; suspicious electric cables that invade forests and infrastructural waste from the construction of hydropower facilities—that began and later were stopped—are now scattered in nature, embedded in biodiversity, covered with moss, and half-buried. These infrastructural ecosystems create mixed biotechnological diversities that for the eye (and therefore the mind) stimulate and release different thoughts, much like the Hannover wave. For Farocki, this universal measuring organ does not need to get close to its object to 'taste' it.[3]

It is to the eye that the image best shows the homogeneity between the seemingly unrelated sectors of mineral extraction and hydropower. In recent years, as I have researched extractivism in Georgia—ranging from traditional mineral extraction to its extension into the human body through the flow of migrant women into the global care market and the extraction of their psycho-emotional resources—I have constantly thought about the seemingly invisible, yet evident materiality of these processes. However, since 2020, when I got involved in one of the largest public movements against the construction of the hydroelectric power station 433MW Namakhvani HPP cascade, it became increasingly clear to me that the term 'resource curse'—widely spread in literature about extractivism—best matches the historical rhetoric about Georgia's abundance in water resources and hydropower potential. Most visibly, it materially manifests in the construction of hydropower facilities and resistance to them. The 'resource curse' refers to a state where, by engaging in unequal trade conditions, one or more resource-rich countries are irreversibly impoverished and made miserable by extracting their resources and exporting them to the world market. The term specifically implies that, apart from severe socio-ecological catastrophes, extractivism also fosters economic disasters.

Until 2022, Georgia's hydroelectric boom was primarily justified by arguments for energy independence and expected consumption growth. However, the government was unable to articulate the sources of this expected growth in energy use and failed to substantiate the necessity for new hydroelectric facilities—neither in direct confrontations, nor in work meetings, nor in their unilateral rhetoric. They had no argument on the topic of cryptocurrency mining either, although they spoke of economic growth and the volume of investments that would be generated from the construction of

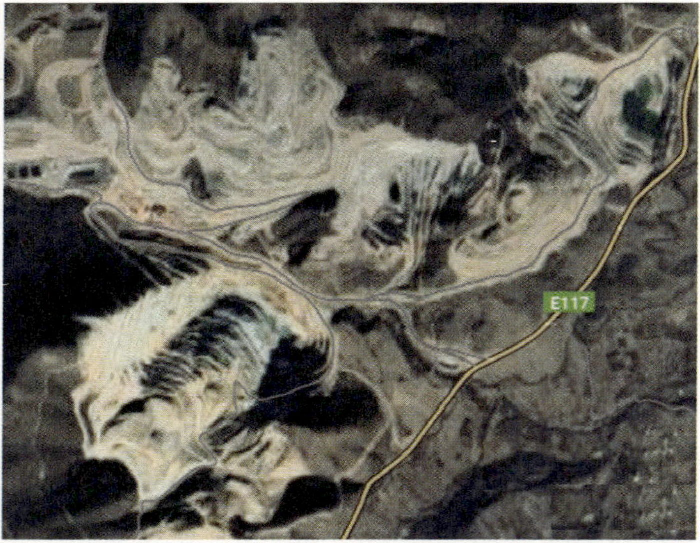

Water Movement, Hybrid Ecosystems

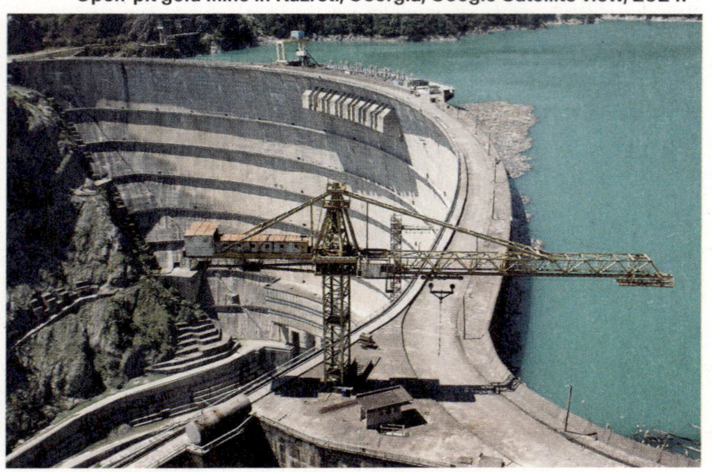

Open-pit gold mine in Kazreti, Georgia, Google Satellite view, 2024.

Enguri Hydro Power Plant, photo by the author, 2019.

hydroelectric facilities. The Russia-Ukraine war in 2022 changed the geopolitical landscape and global resource politics, creating new demands for energy independence from Russia and new trade routes, thereby revitalizing the dormant, and constantly up-in-the-air regional and logistical significance of the South Caucasus. This was followed by the memorandum of the Black Sea electric cable project under the EU initiative, which will supply 'green' energy to the EU via a large underwater cable from Azerbaijan through Georgia. This will be the largest underwater electric cable in the world, crossing not only the sea but also the entire territorial length of Georgia.

The issue of the cable shifted the rhetoric from energy independence to energy export, intensifying the idea of restarting the construction of all hydropower facilities that had been suspended due to protests during and after Soviet rule, and highlighted Georgia's main comparative advantage in the world market — hydro resources. Against this backdrop, we began working on the film.

Just like the waves crashing against a concrete surface in the Hannover laboratory, these processes also release and stimulate thoughts: they crash directly against complex socio-cultural and ethnographic beliefs and effects, internal geopolitical agitations of the country, and political — seemingly unrelated — events. They directly crash against religious and community narratives, social and environmental science crises, and the global or local boundaries of political power.

Water Movement, Hybrid Ecosystems

Still, like the movement of water in Farocki's film, this complex, multi-layered world appears to exist as the overhead view of the content of all this, reflecting an archaic cycle of natural reproduction and the constant transformation of energy. From ice to snow, snow to water, and water to energy, this cycle interweaves rivers, soils, forests, rocks, and minerals with economic transformations and concentrated capital, leading to social and environmental disasters. This takes us back to glaciers and headwaters, to mountaineers and skiers in the Upper-Svaneti mountains, and to the electricity powering the multiple snow economies and infrastructures that violently crash against each other. It also leads us to the energy abduction and its results—ski lift stoppages, damaged infrastructure, power cables running through forests to feed the hidden bitcoin farms, and so on.

What is invisible at first glance becomes visible to the eye in the images, in the montage, and in the technical potential of cinema. A woman's voice in Farocki's film states: "Perhaps some would find it incredible, but it is a fact proved by experience: in a scale picture one does not see everything, but one sees many things better than on the spot." This speaks of the power of images to reveal the presence of things or phenomena that aren't immediately apparent. In Farocki's film, we primarily observe images taken from an overhead view—photography allows us to look at something, as the narrator says, through the eyes of God. Google Maps satellites allow us to view any point on Earth. For a long time, through this satellite, I have observed the vast quarries left by extractive practices all over the world. The scale and shapes of these quarries are best perceived from above, and the layers left by open-pit mining and the horizontal terraces simultaneously remind me of ancient Roman amphitheatres, at the heart of which someone or something else must have been sacrificed, meticulously repeating these forms.

In the case of mineral extraction, you can see an open wound in the land directly on the surface of the earth. Due to the solid material structure of the earth, the picture of its gutting is clearly visible; however, water, with its hydrological liquid structure existing in the form of waves, tides, or river currents, with its pressure and dispersion capabilities, with all its fluid materiality, is difficult to be perceived as a material object of extractivism. It is difficult to imagine cutting into water, as we do into the land. But if we look at dams, they are man-made cutting quarries in the surface of the water, the horizontal concrete layers of which meticulously repeat these forms of various historical manifestations of violent infrastructure—from Roman amphitheaters to open quarries. Cutting on the surface of the water is possible by damming it up.

The feeling I had while we were filming—passing along the narrow tunnel through the concrete body of the Enguri HPP Dam, which took us to the other side of the dam to view the touristic sight of water jets dispersing from the hydropower station—was identical to the feeling

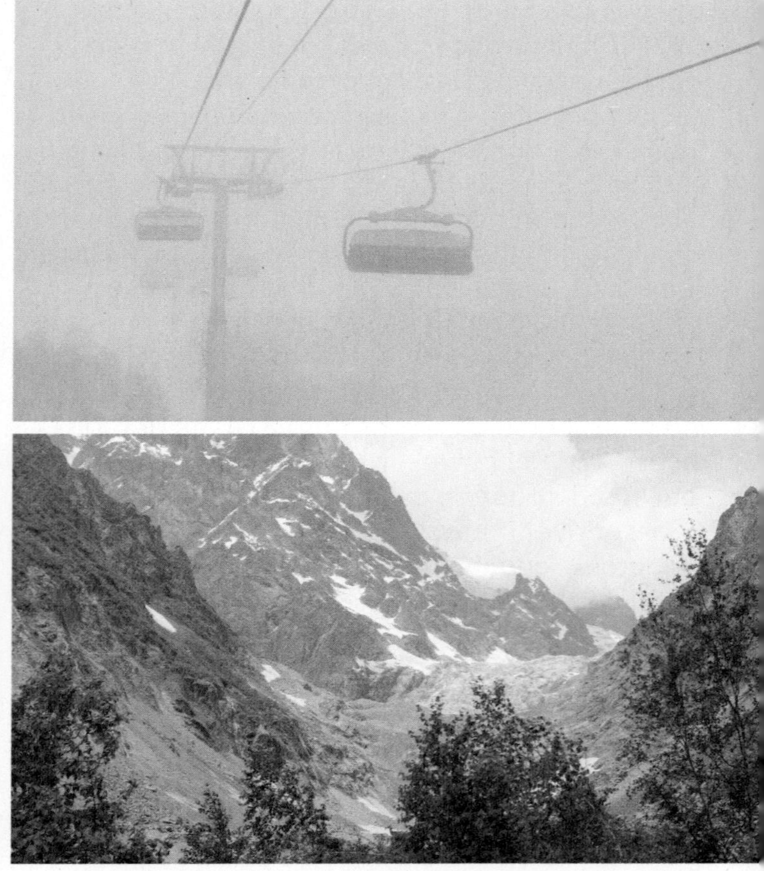

Film stills. Tekla Aslanishvili, *The Mountain Speaks to the Sea*, 2024.

I had when I saw the open quarries for mineral extraction. A looming 271-metre-high wall behind you, a damp, narrow path ahead, with millions of cubic metres of water retained. The sense of disaster that emerges as a possible scenario —what could happen if the dam breaks—is a

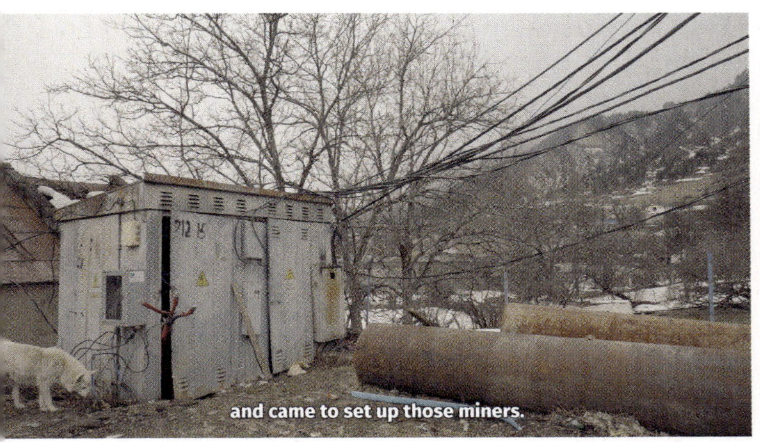

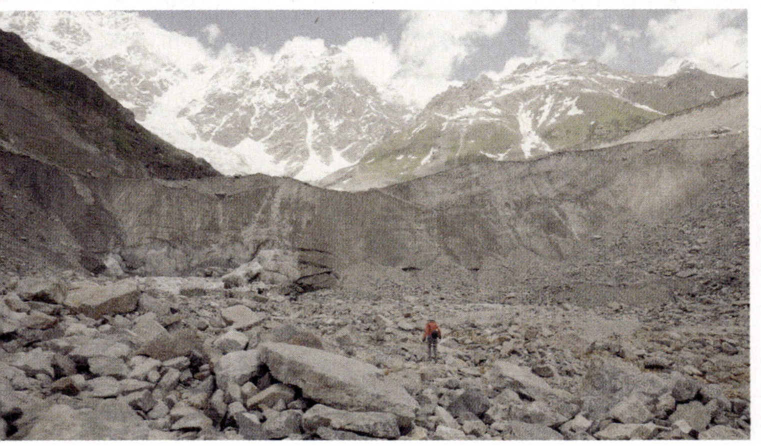

seemingly irrational, bodily experience. The enduring, gigantic infrastructure of the Soviet legacy evokes admiration as a result of the hydro-industrial past, yet it significantly differs from the post-Soviet infrastructural war—a hydro-technocratic future full of catastrophes, just as the method of mineral extraction differs in these two historical periods. Georgia has been mining manganese for a century and a half, but it was precisely due to the extractivist method of mining—gutting at all costs—that it became a place of catastrophe. These lands can collapse at any moment; houses stand on them, there are gardens, animals and people walk about, there are cemeteries and churches, yet they crumble and fall into the ground, huge cracks appear, and the surface of the earth separates from each other. In one of the villages, I met a woman who showed me two trees standing in her yard. These two walnut trees, two metres apart and facing each other on the downhill, were once a single tree, which, as a result of these processes, split in half one day and separated. Grass had already grown between them, obliterating the material traces of their separation. It was an incredible sight that transcends the physical and provokes thoughts about "what is possible at all".[4] It was equally unbelievable to see the remains of the construction of one of the abovementioned dams, Khudoni HPP in Svaneti, which began in the 1980s, scattered in the wilderness as concrete elements covered with moss. They looked like mausoleums or pyramids from ancient times, which had already integrated into the existing environment and formed a hybrid ecosystem. Near these mausoleum-like structures, I had a strong feeling that I was standing in a place that would have been underwater if protests at the time had not stopped the construction of this facility. The undulating concrete surface covered with moss creates a sense of mixed and hybrid nature, similar to the feeling one might experience from perceiving the scale of a dam or from standing on mudflats. The structures and surfaces themselves tell us much more than the knowledge about them.

But the parallels between cutting the surfaces of land and water are not merely metaphorical, poetic, or visual similarities. Primarily, they are methodological, which is reflected in the similarity of material forms — 'methodological' meaning they share the same logic. The rampant extraction of minerals for export to the global market mirrors the resource curse seen in the aggressive policy of maximizing water resource utilization for exporting electricity to the global market. Both practices are done at the expense of destroying local environments and populations, and have been shaped by war and global power shifts, such as the emergence of new extractivist geographies in the process of Green Transition.

Water movements have been sufficiently studied; yet this knowledge is often used to maintain the existing power status quo and hierarchies, where small, resource-rich countries are sacrificed to meet the demands of the capitalist centre, akin to humans in the very heart of ancient Roman amphitheatres. It is clear that individuals living in specific locations and the environments there are still easily classified and deemed insignificant.

Analysing photos of the camp that were later deciphered, the narrator of Farocki's film states: "When there was reclassification—either work or death—Inherent is the notion that along with contempt for humanity is the false idolization of work."[5] To compare anything to the brutality and sheer, terrifying evil that characterizes this event in history would be inappropriate, and is not

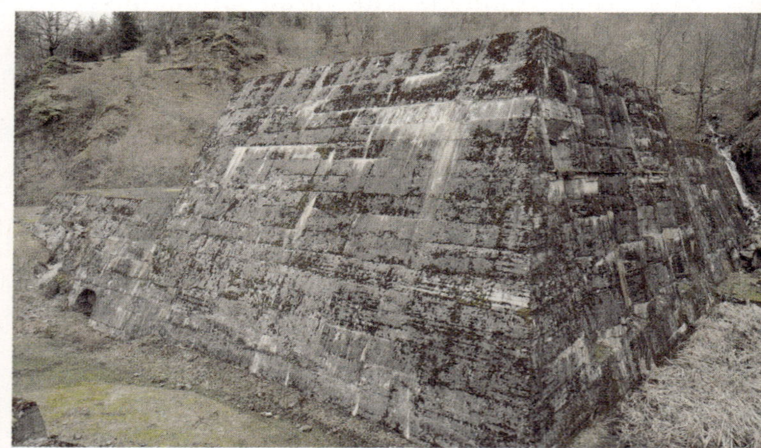

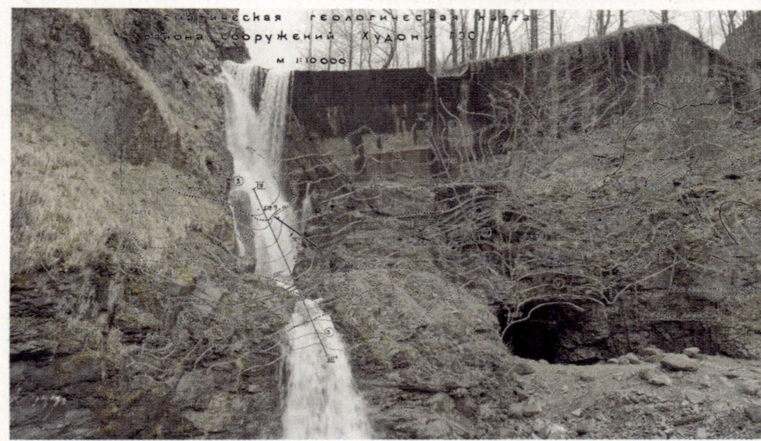

Film stills. Tekla Aslanishvili, *The Mountain Speaks to the Sea*, 2024.

the purpose of this essay. But what is interesting is the method Farocki uses, and why he chooses to tell the story of the concentration camp in a way that prompts us to think about the potential of water resources. By discovering "how close the one is to the other: the industry to the camp"

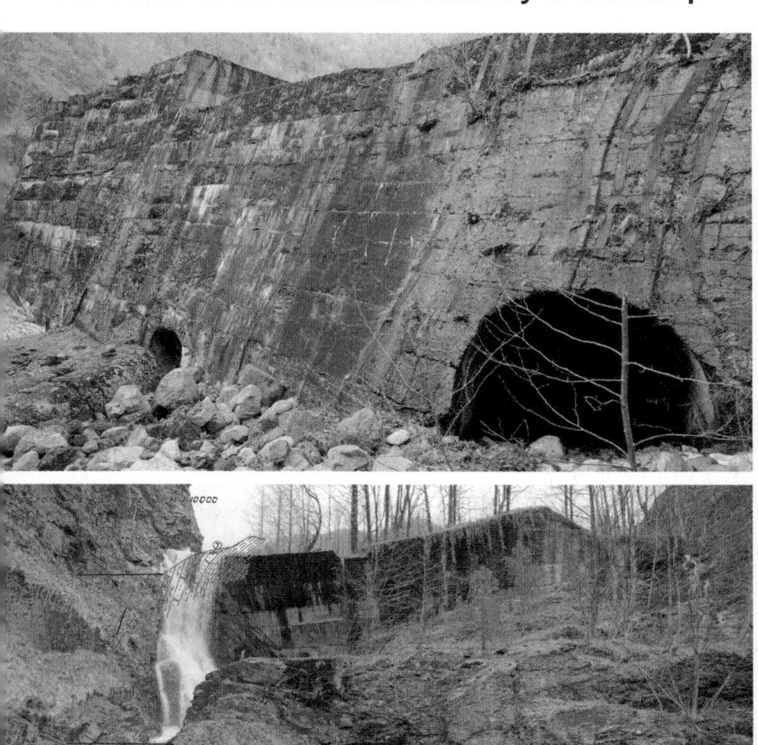

(IG Farben factory that was photographed alongside Auschwitz), he highlights the structural, material factors upon which totalitarianism is built, and revisits the question that Arendt raised about the fundamental claims such systems make of absolute domination over humans: "What is possible at all?"[6]

Deploying these methods in research on extractivism and the sacrifice zones derived from it may reveal that specific places and the people who inhabit them are graded according to the value that can be extracted from them. This, along with the devaluation of people and the environment, represents the false idolization of value production that has always been characteristic of capitalism.

In another part of Farocki's film, besides overhead views captured accidentally, we see other photos taken by the Nazis themselves in these camps. The narrator tells us that these photographs reveal what the eye of their photographer could not perceive: that "Apart from death and work, there was a black market, there were love stories and resistance groups," which culminates with the story of the Auschwitz uprising in 1944 and the escape of two prisoners. This is what the system always misses, what is beyond the reach of surveillance: including all natural and human phenomena not subject to market exchange that cannot be fully commoditised, like the flow of rivers, forms of care and reproduction, the renewability of life, and the already well-studied yet sometimes spontaneous movements which constantly create hybrid ecosystems that give rise to new worlds. The growing resistance of local populations against traditional extractivism or new energy policies are the conflicts that crash as agitated waves against the new extractivist horizons, the new military-industrial complexes of capitalism, with their new wars, manufactured images, and new waves of repression.

Wherever it is suspended, in natural rocks or in wide concrete channels of the laboratory, the wave crashes against the earth. Instead of capturing the thoughts or an eye, it stirs them up and sets them free. As we try to show in our film; floodings that are often social contain a whole system of movements that are still less studied compared to water and light.

Water Movement, Hybrid Ecosystems

1   Here I am referring to the historical coincidence of the initial reports about the climate crisis and the failure of socialism (the collapse of the Soviet Union), which both occurred in the year 1989. Bruno Latour talks about this in his seminal book, *We Have Never Been Modern*, trans. Catherine Porter (Cambridge, MA: Harvard University Press, 1993). Farocki's film, *Images of the World and the Inscription of War*, was released in the same year. On the one hand it is directly connected to these events, with its unique methodology and hope for the advancement of hydrological sciences. On the other hand, it preemptively employs a method that Latour proposes later.

2   In 2021, a secret agreement between the state and a Turkish company concerning one of the largest hydroelectric station projects, the Namakhvani HPP, was revealed. This contract was so clandestine that it was assessed by various organizations as well as the Ministry of Justice of the country as compromising state interests. Despite these assessments, the construction continued until it was halted by widespread public opposition across Georgia.

3   In the film *Images of the World and the Inscription of War*, Farocki presents photographs of Algerian women, originally taken by a French photographer. No one had ever seen them without a veil, which left only their eyes uncovered. As the mouths of the Algerian women are being shown, the female narrator comments in the background: "A mouth, to be able to taste something, must come close to its object. The eye, to be able to see, can remain at a distance from its object."

4   *Images of the World and the Inscription of War*, directed by Harun Farocki (Harun Farocki Filmproduktion, 1989).

5   Ibid.

6   The question refers to a citation of Arendt regarding concentration camps by a narrator in *Images of the World and the Inscription of War*, directed by Harun Farocki: "Laboratories in which experiments were carried out to see whether the fundamental claim of totalitarian systems—that human beings are capable of being totally dominated—is correct. Here, the question was to establish what was possible and to obtain proof that absolutely everything is possible." Hannah Arendt, *The Origins of Totalitarianism* (New York: Schocken Books, 1951).

The Mountain Speaks to the Sea

72:00'
Georgia, Germany
2024

Director and Editor	Tekla Aslanishvili
Research and Script	Tekla Aslanishvili, Alexandra Aroshvili
Cinematography	Nikoloz Tabukashvili
Music	Nika Pasuri, Ani Zakareishvili
Graphic Design	Viktor Bone
Typography	Dato Simonia
Sound Mastering	Luka Telia
Color	Niko Tarielashvili

Supported by the Graduate School / The Berlin Centre for Advanced Studies in Arts and Sciences (BAS), Kommission für künstlerische und wissenschaftliche Vorhaben (KKWV) at the UdK Berlin, and Critical Media Lab Basel.

The Mountain Speaks to the Sea reassembles fragmented (hi)stories of labour and life restructured around the realm of energy politics. This two-channel experimental documentary follows the rivers of the Central South Caucasus across different seasons, tracing their paths from mountains and glaciers to the Black Sea, mapping the material and social infrastructures woven around them. The film's narrative culminates in the EU-Georgia joint initiative to construct the world's longest high-voltage power grid beneath the Black Sea, designed to transmit renewable energy from the Caucasus and Caspian regions to Europe and reduce dependence on Russian fossil fuels. The cable acts as a potential catalyst for reshaping energy geographies, reactivating sites of energy extraction that were halted due to protests during and after Soviet rule. Binding together personal, scientific, and political histories with myths and future projections, the documentary explores how hydro-energy infrastructures function as organizational tools across three interlinked spheres: the production of knowledge, the making and unmaking of political and physical borders, and the practices of statecraft.

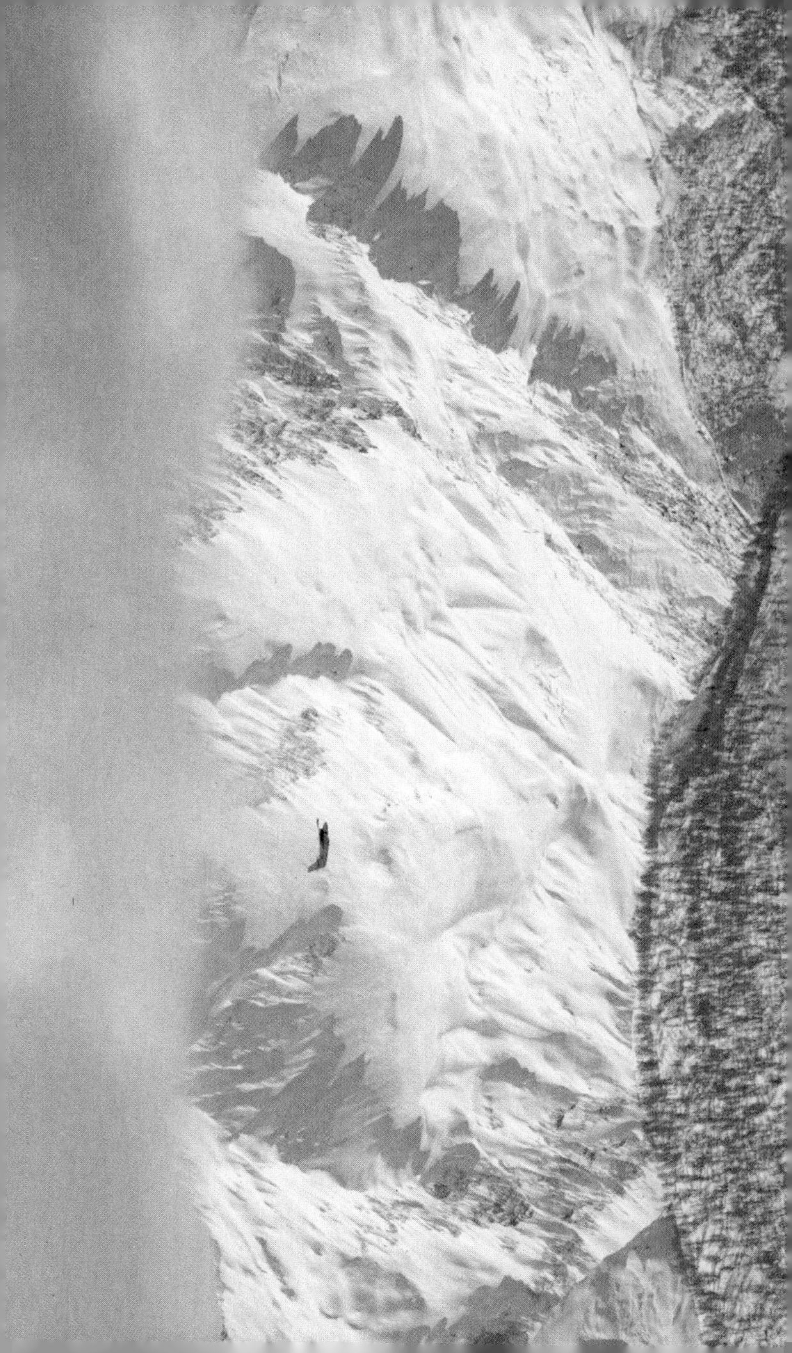

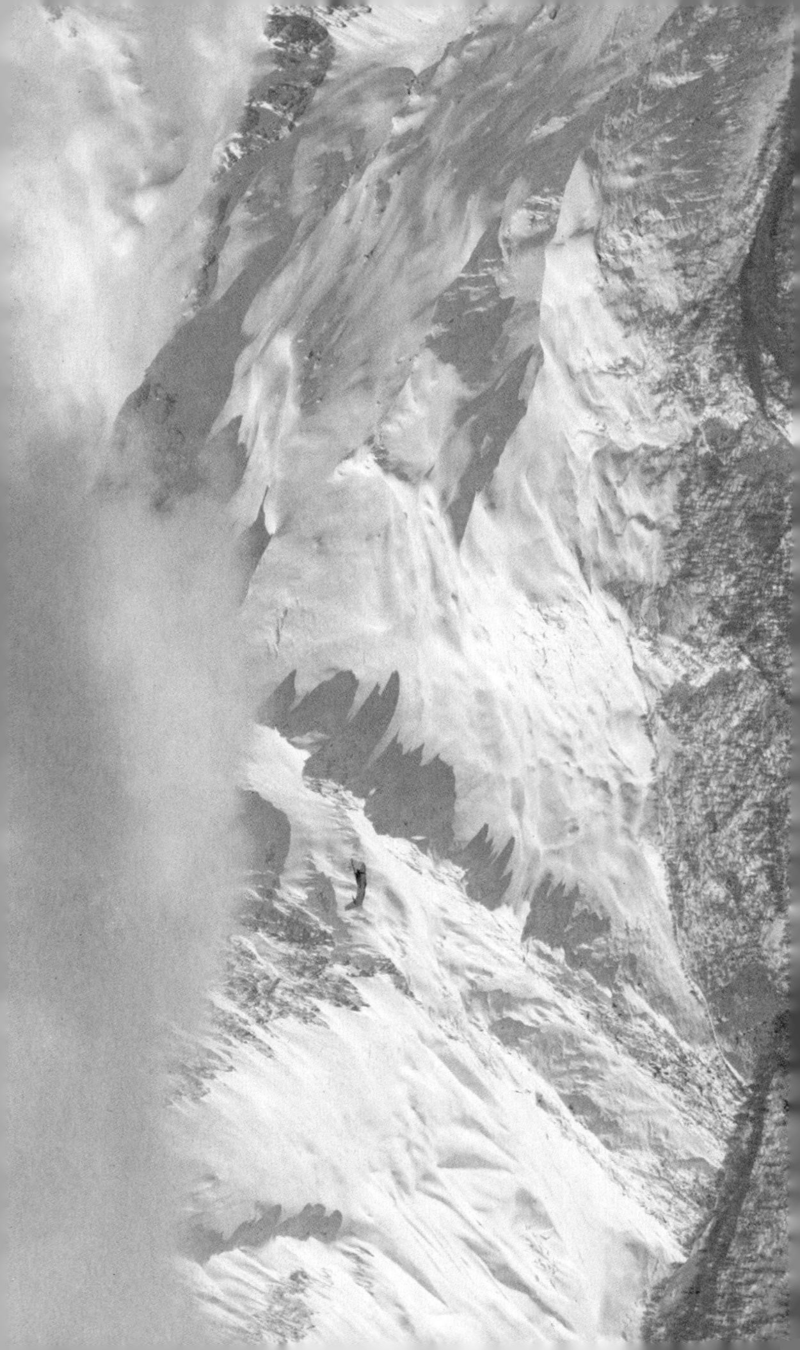

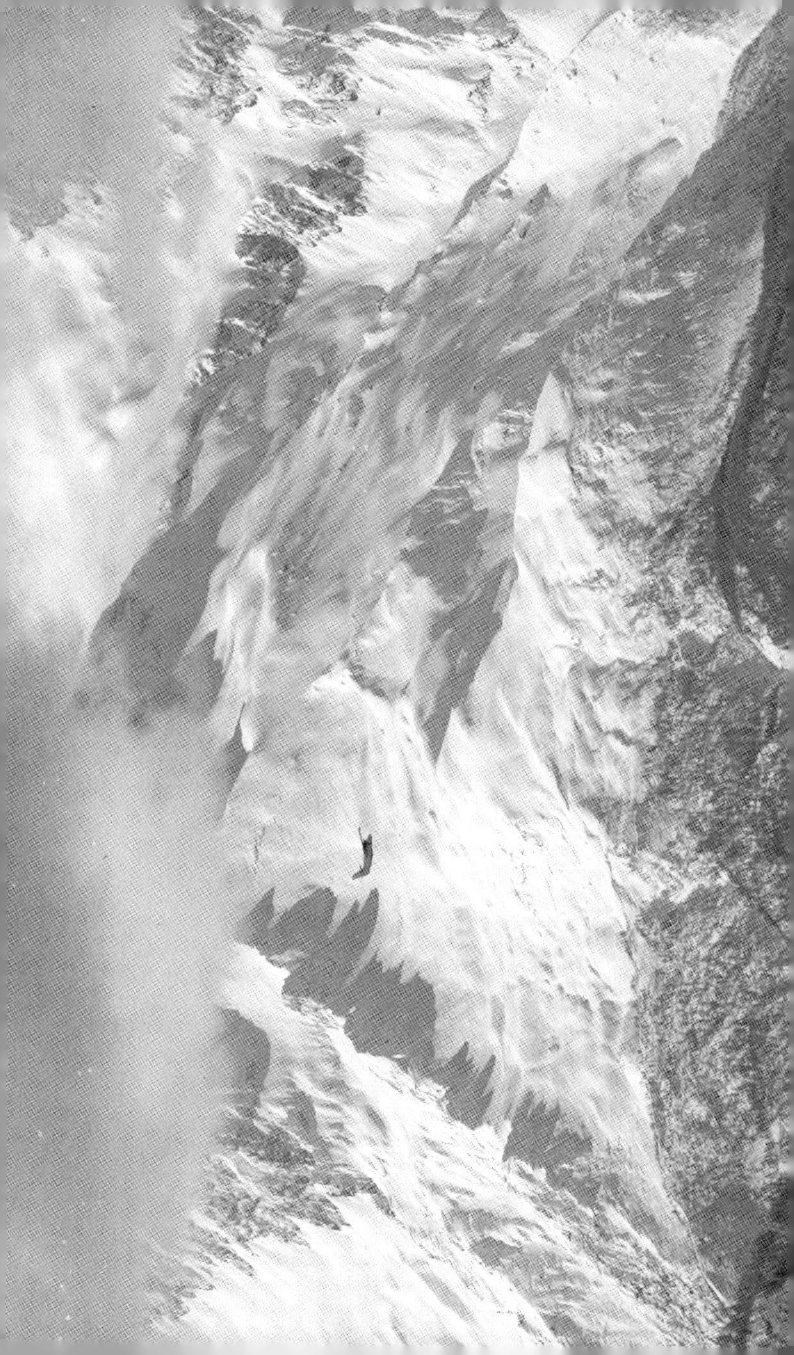

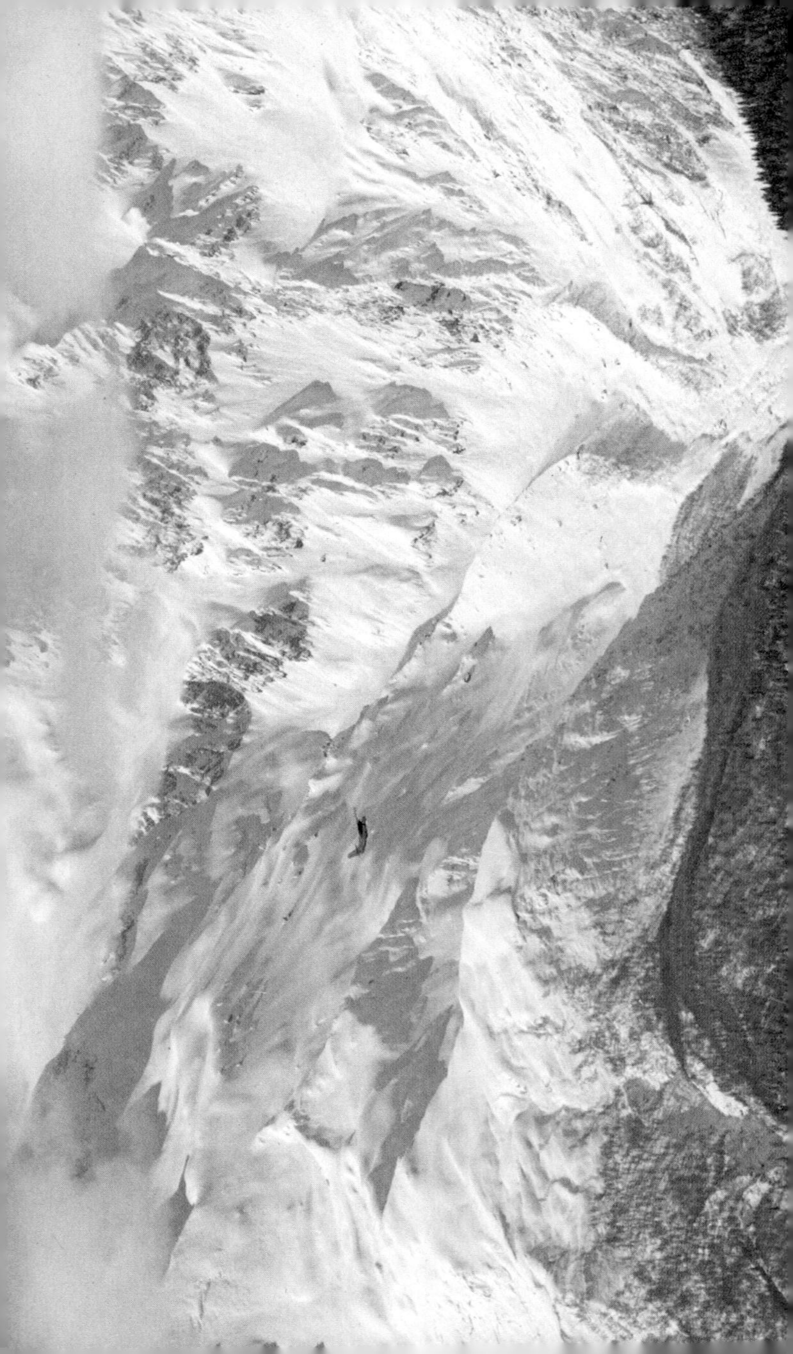

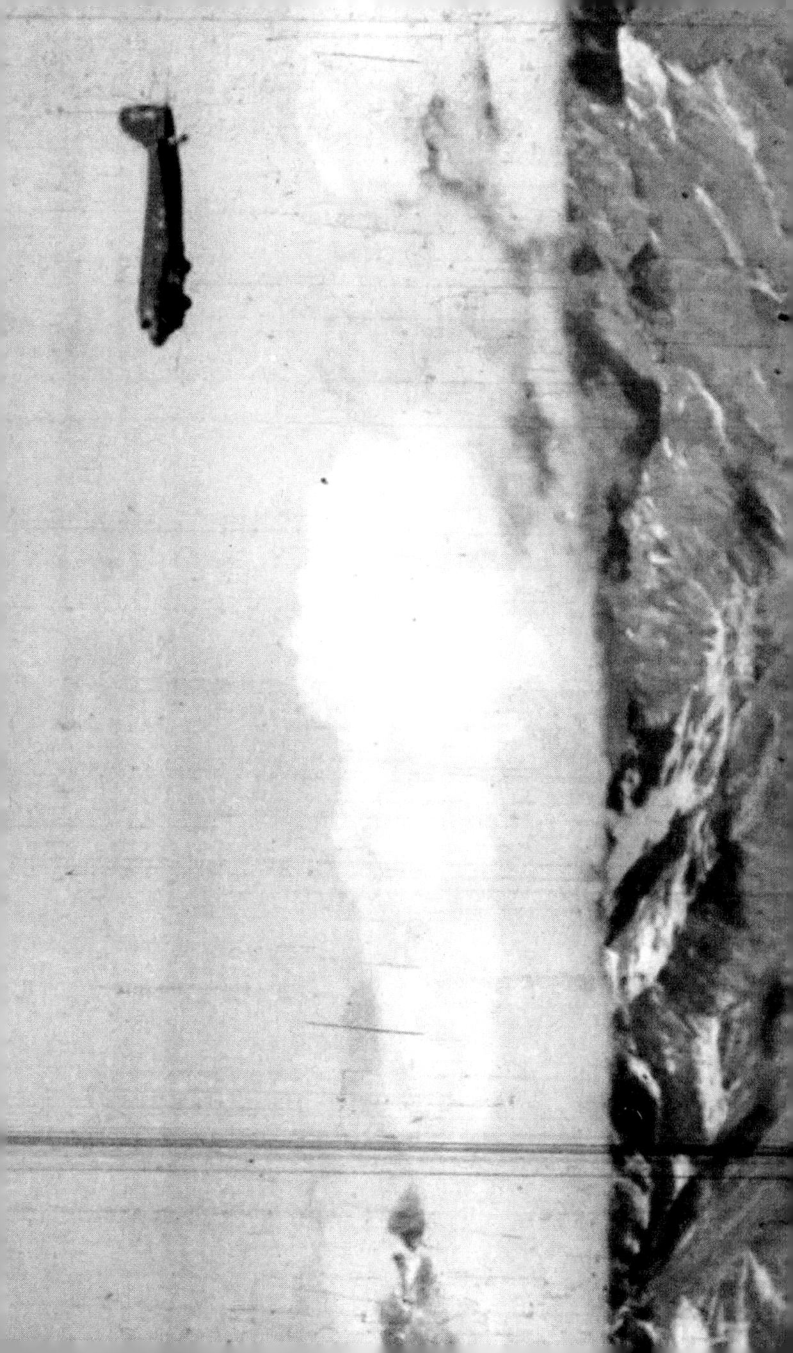

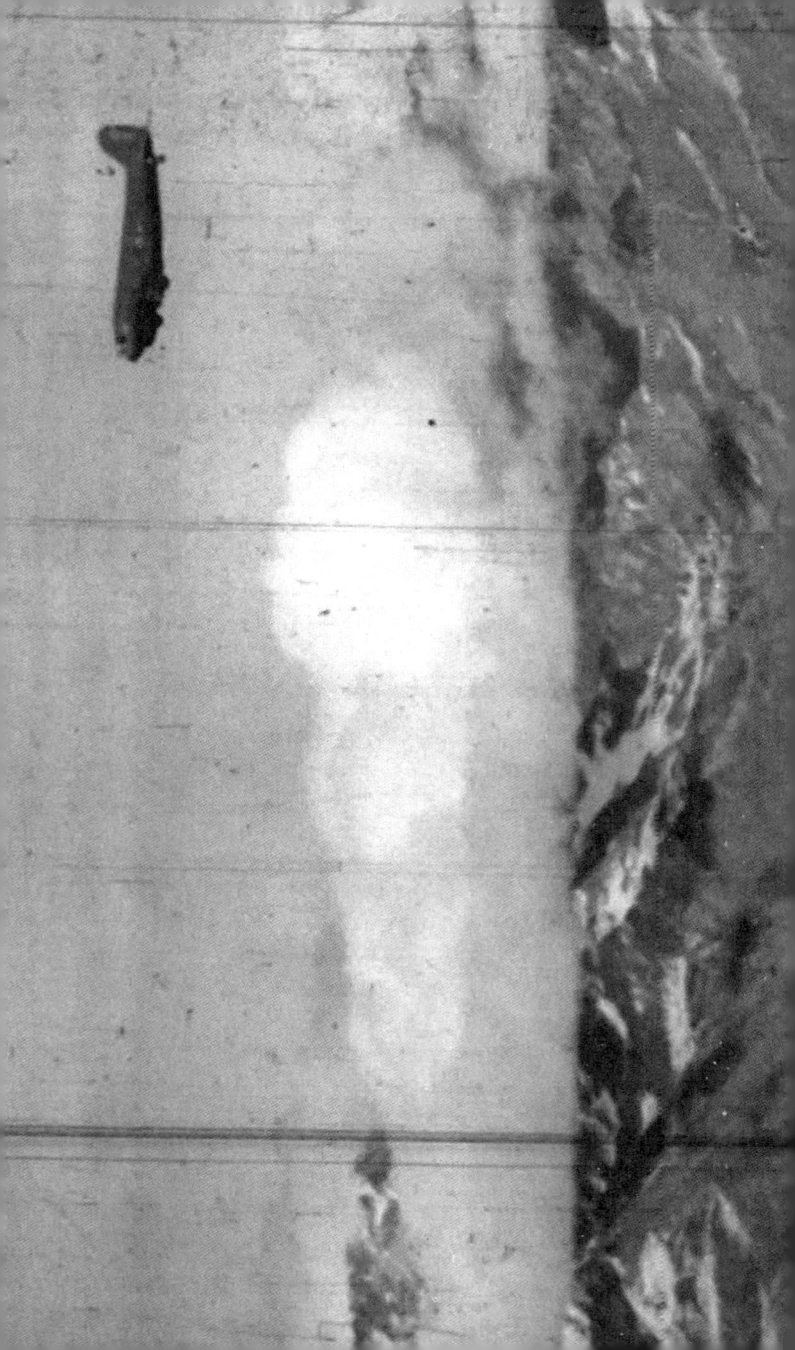

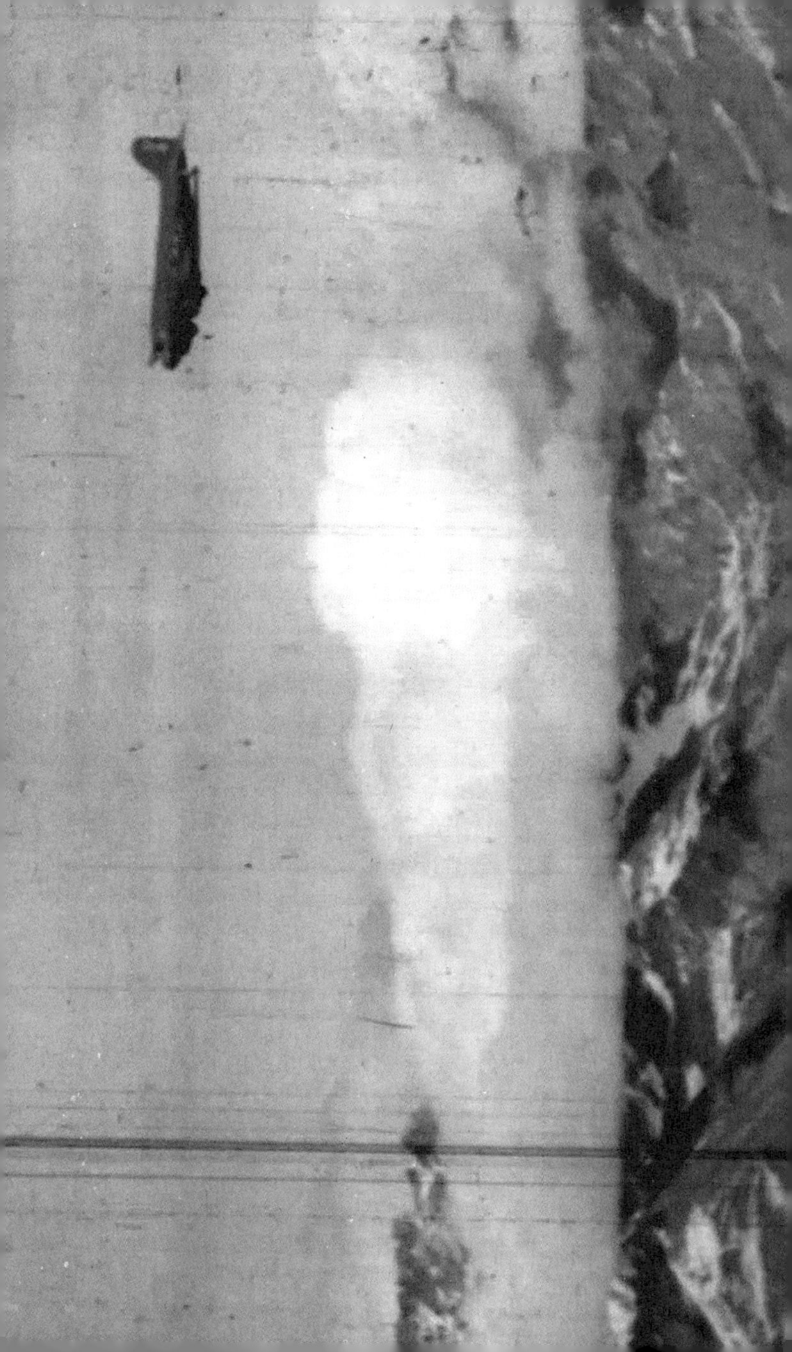

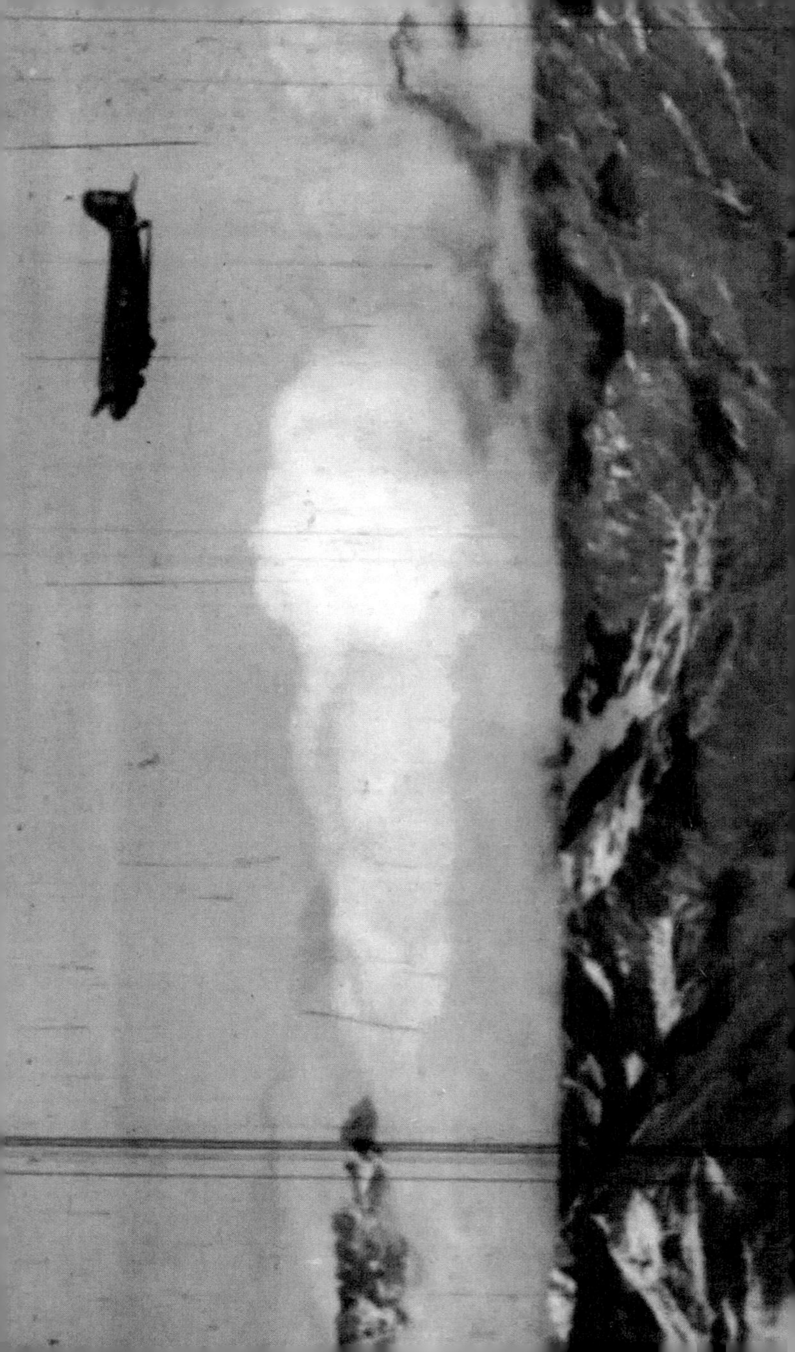

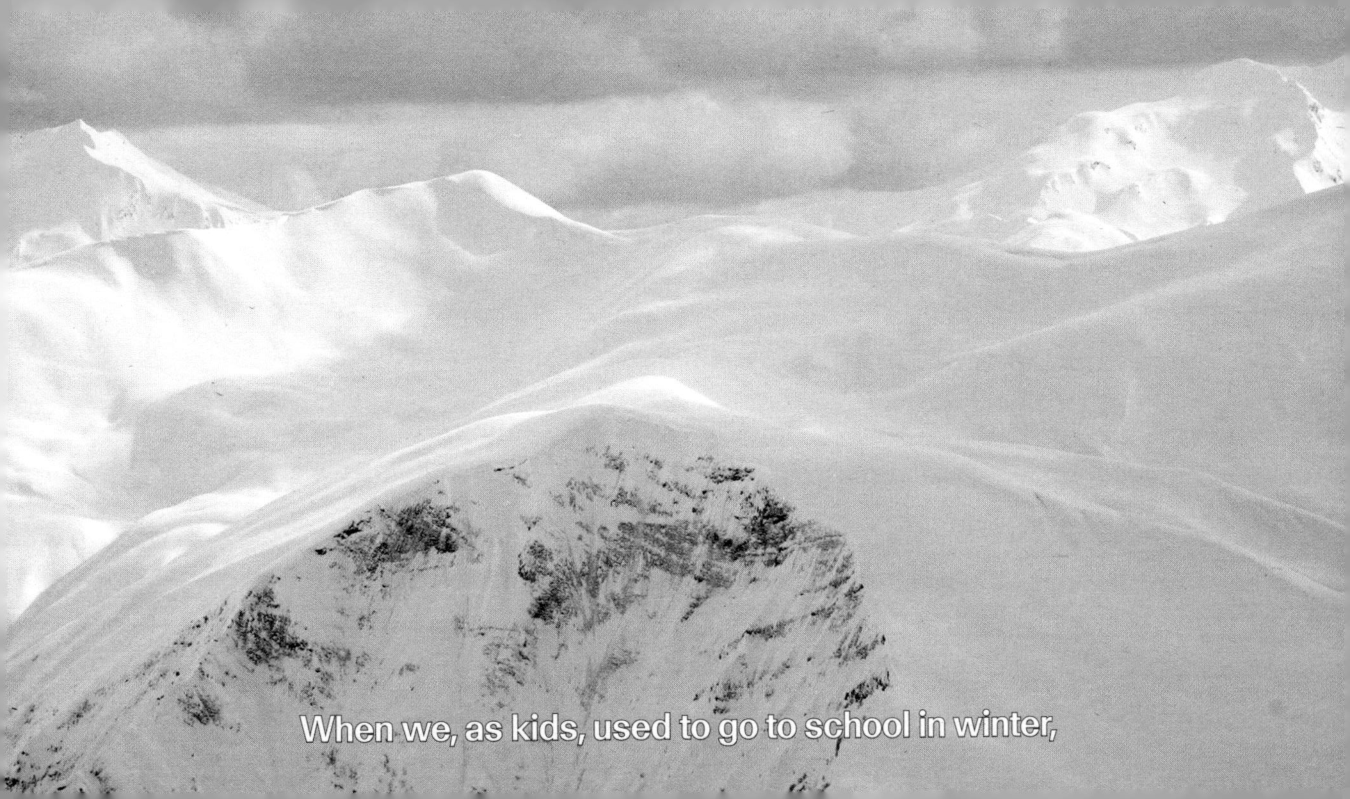
When we, as kids, used to go to school in winter,

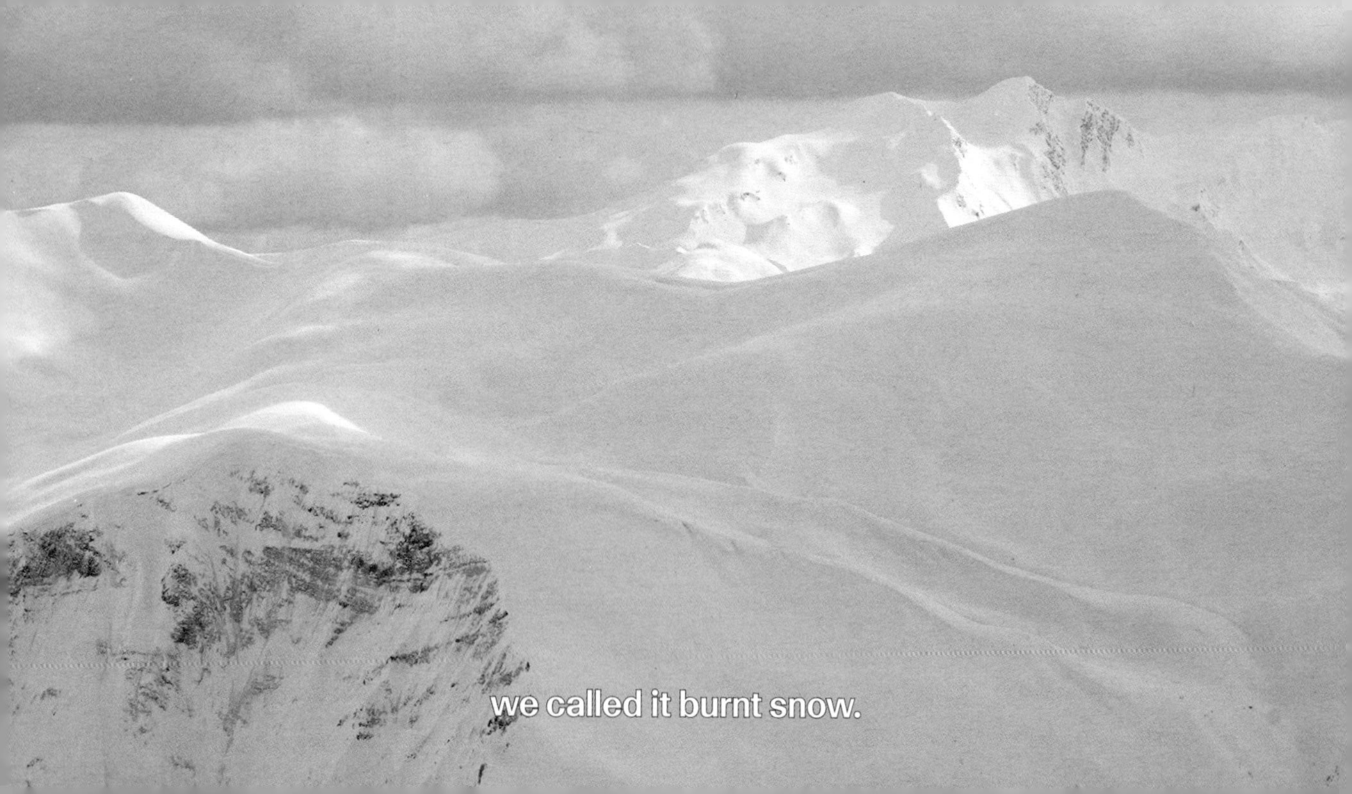
we called it burnt snow.

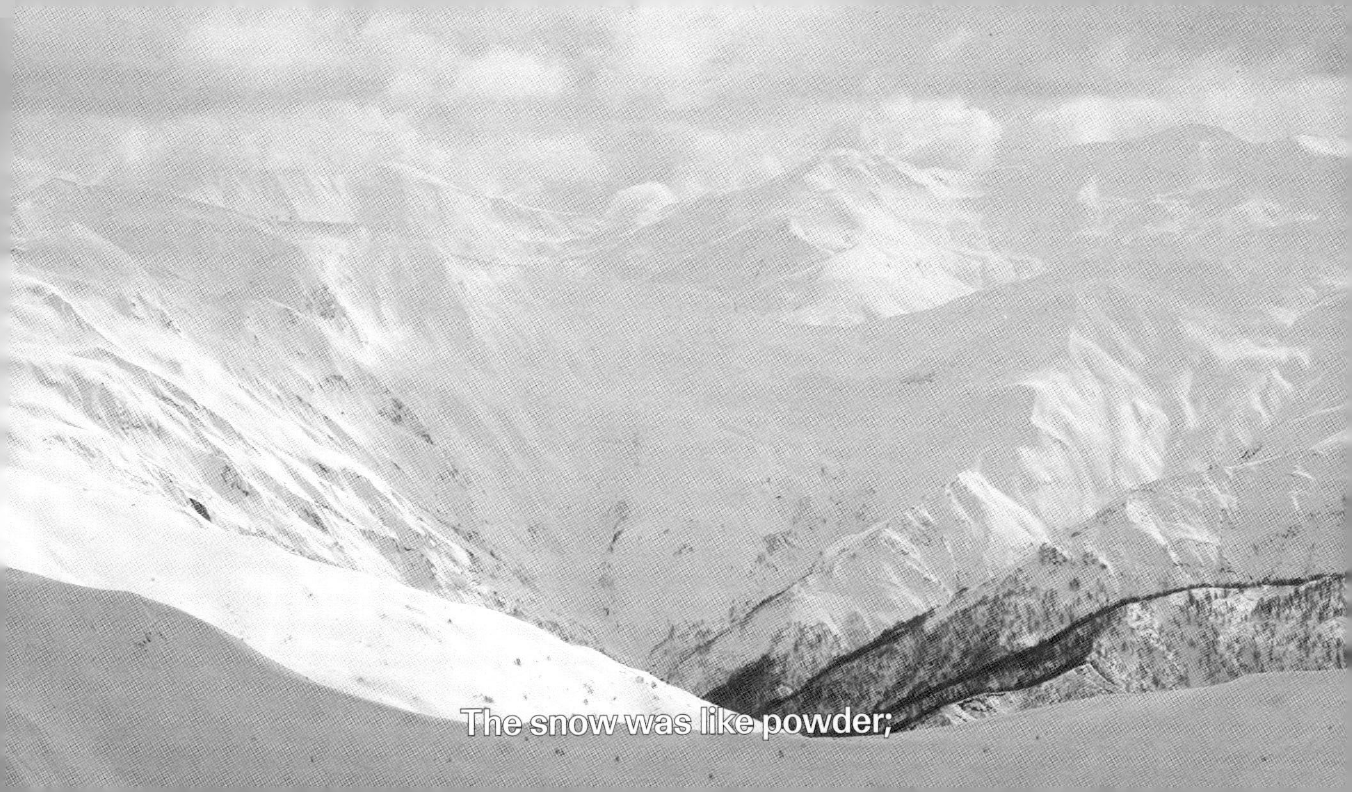
The snow was like powder;

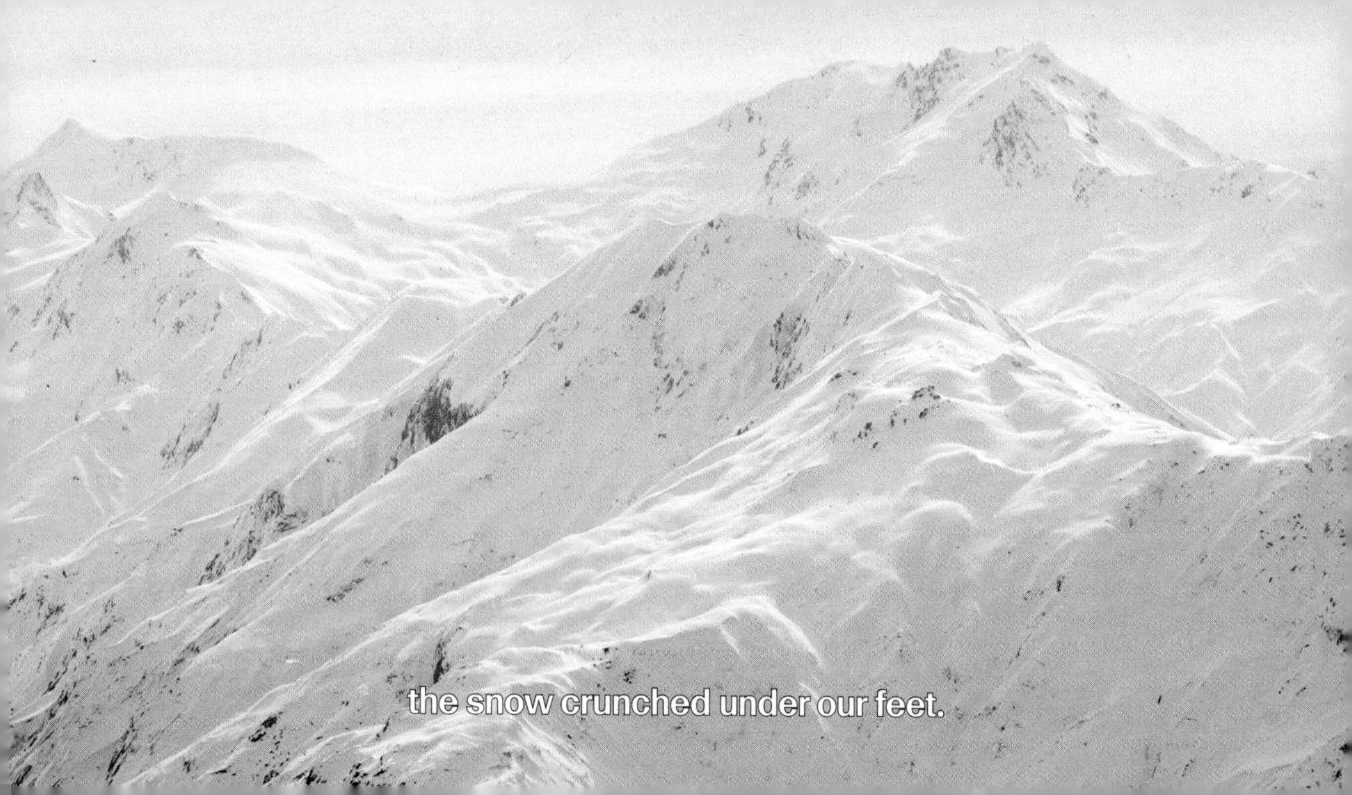
the snow crunched under our feet.

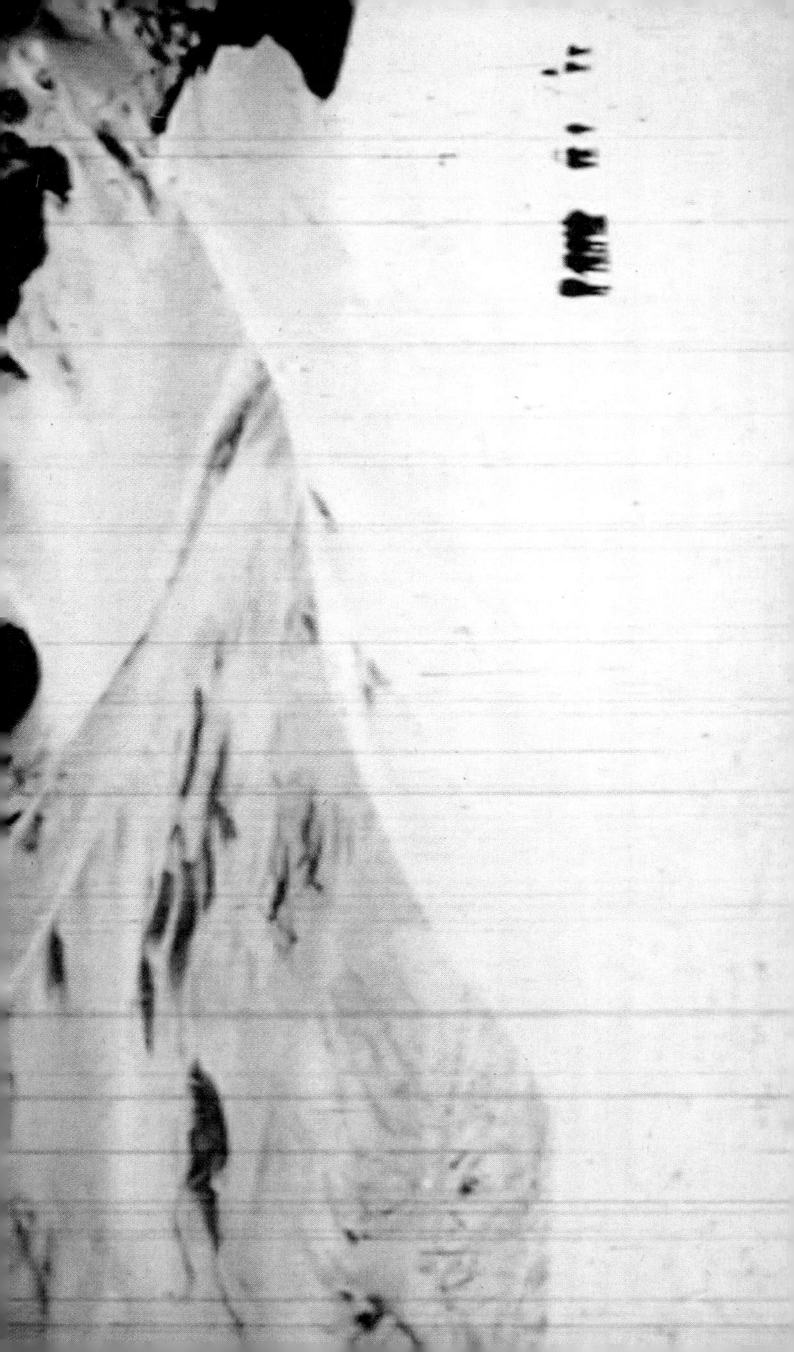

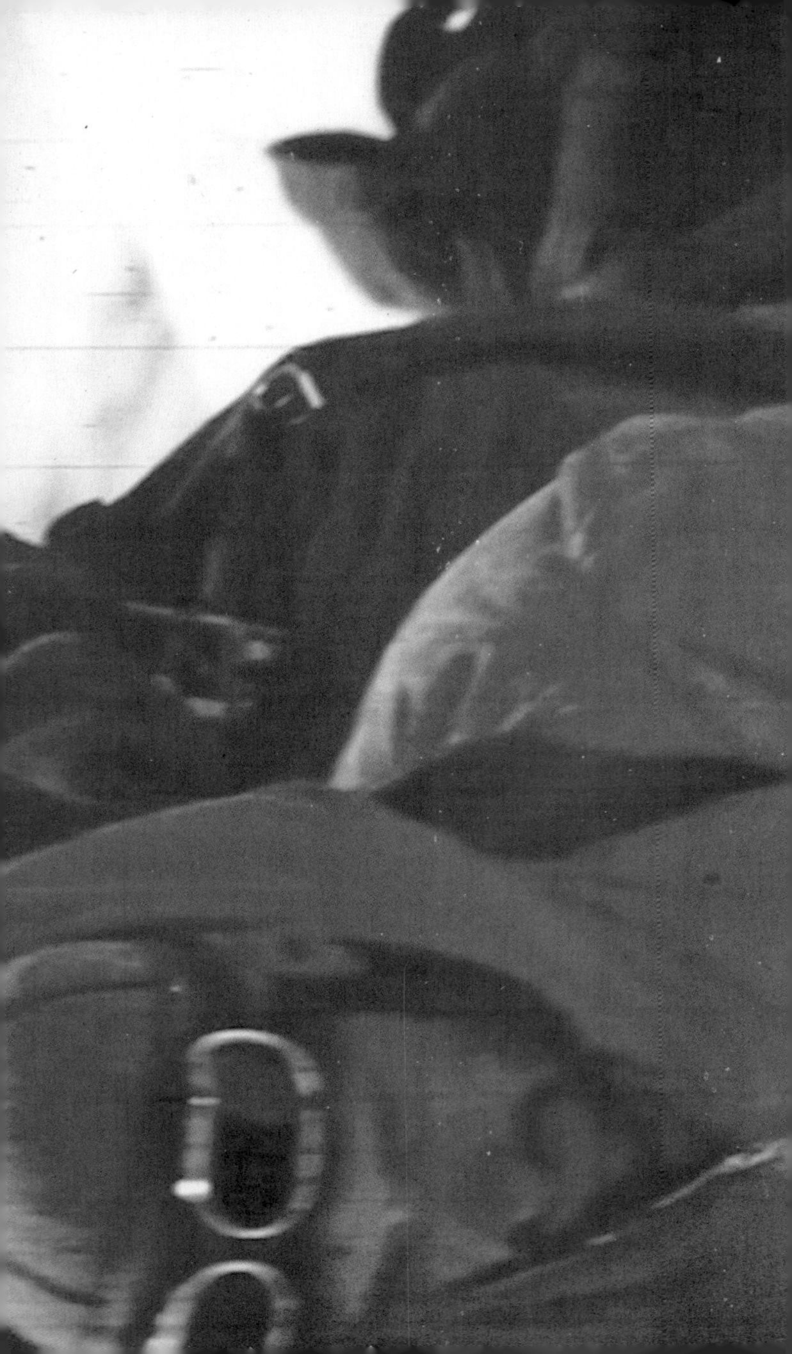

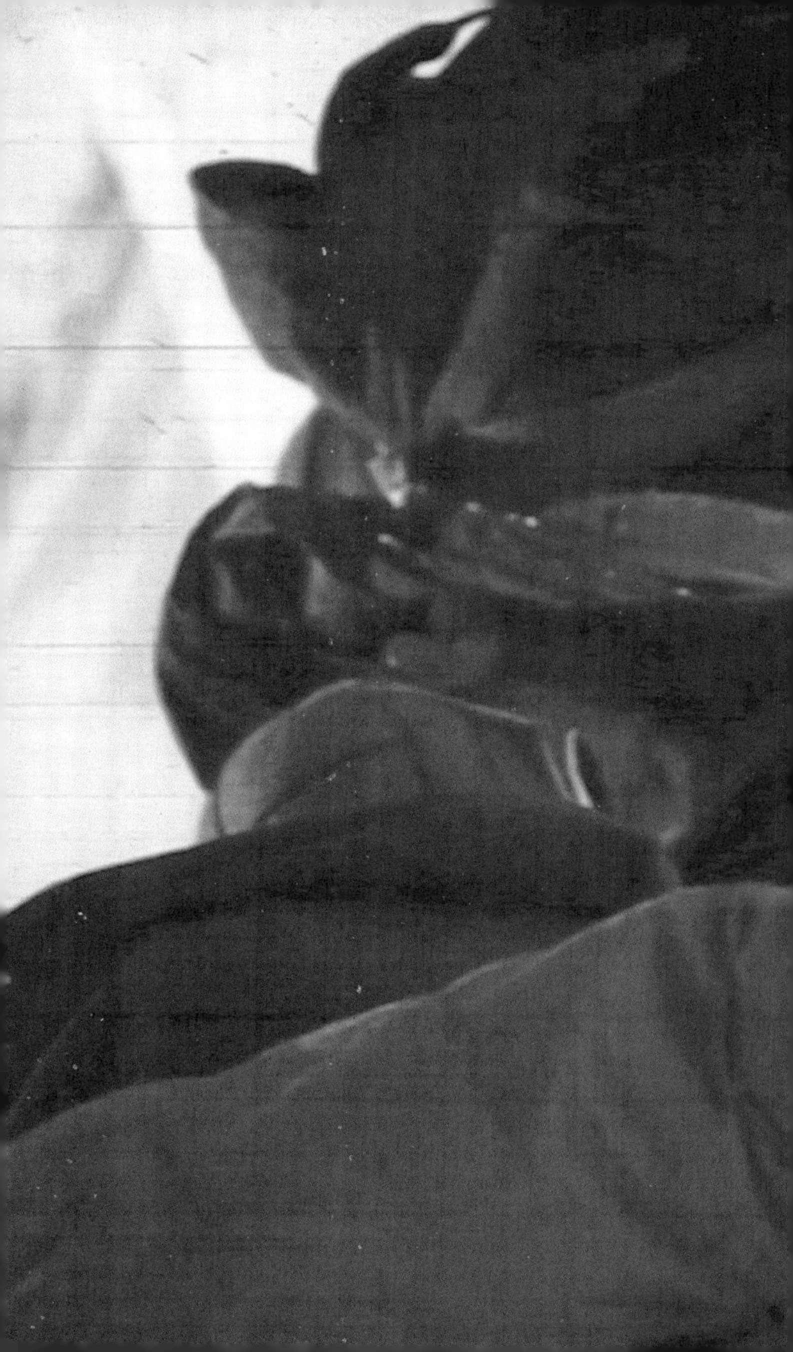

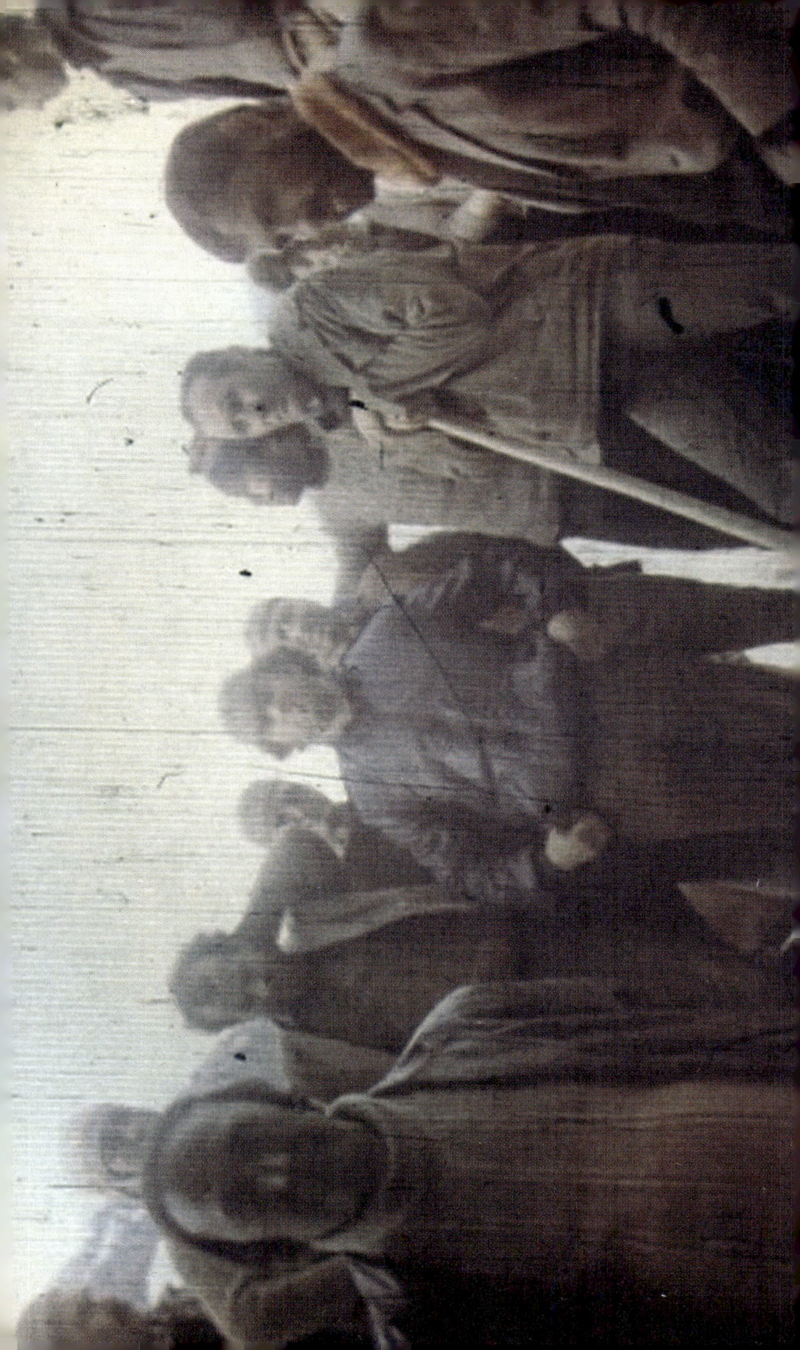

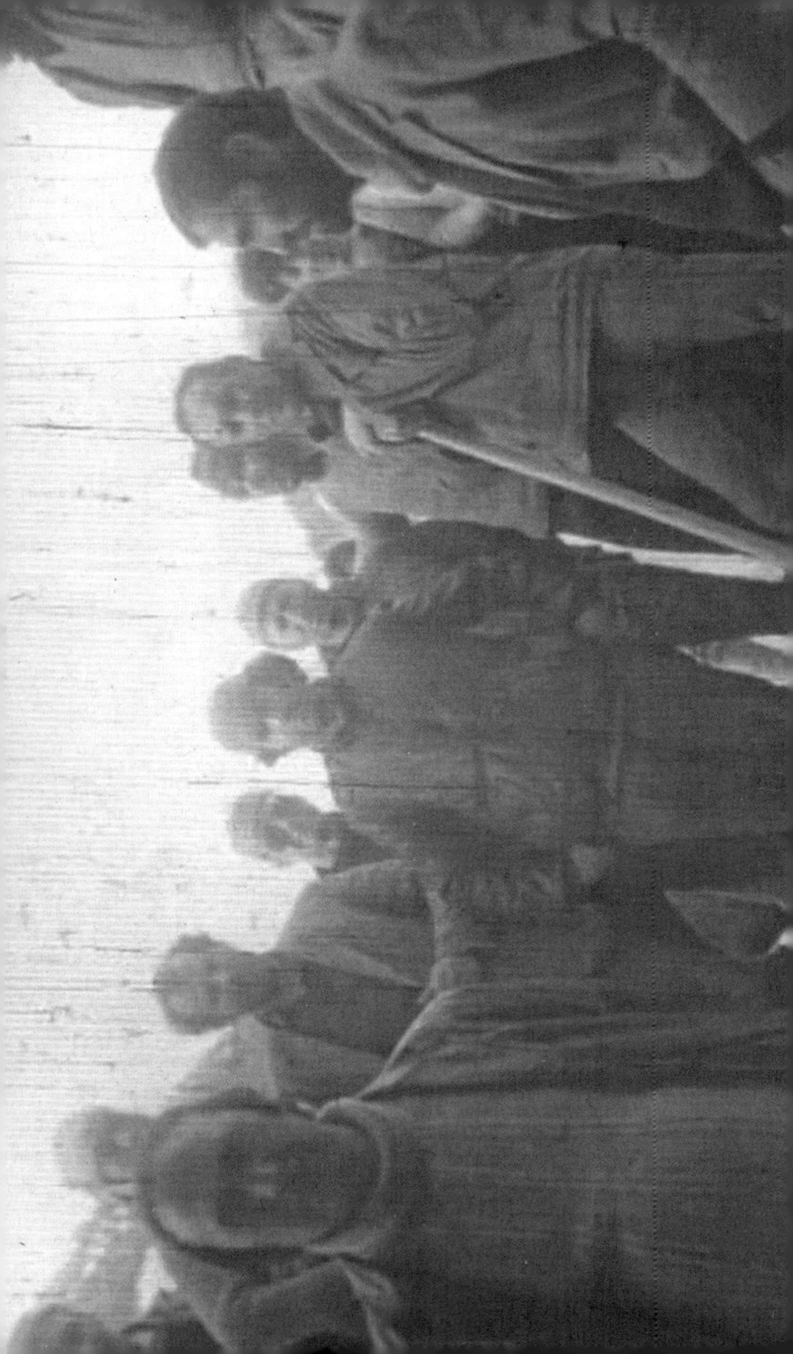

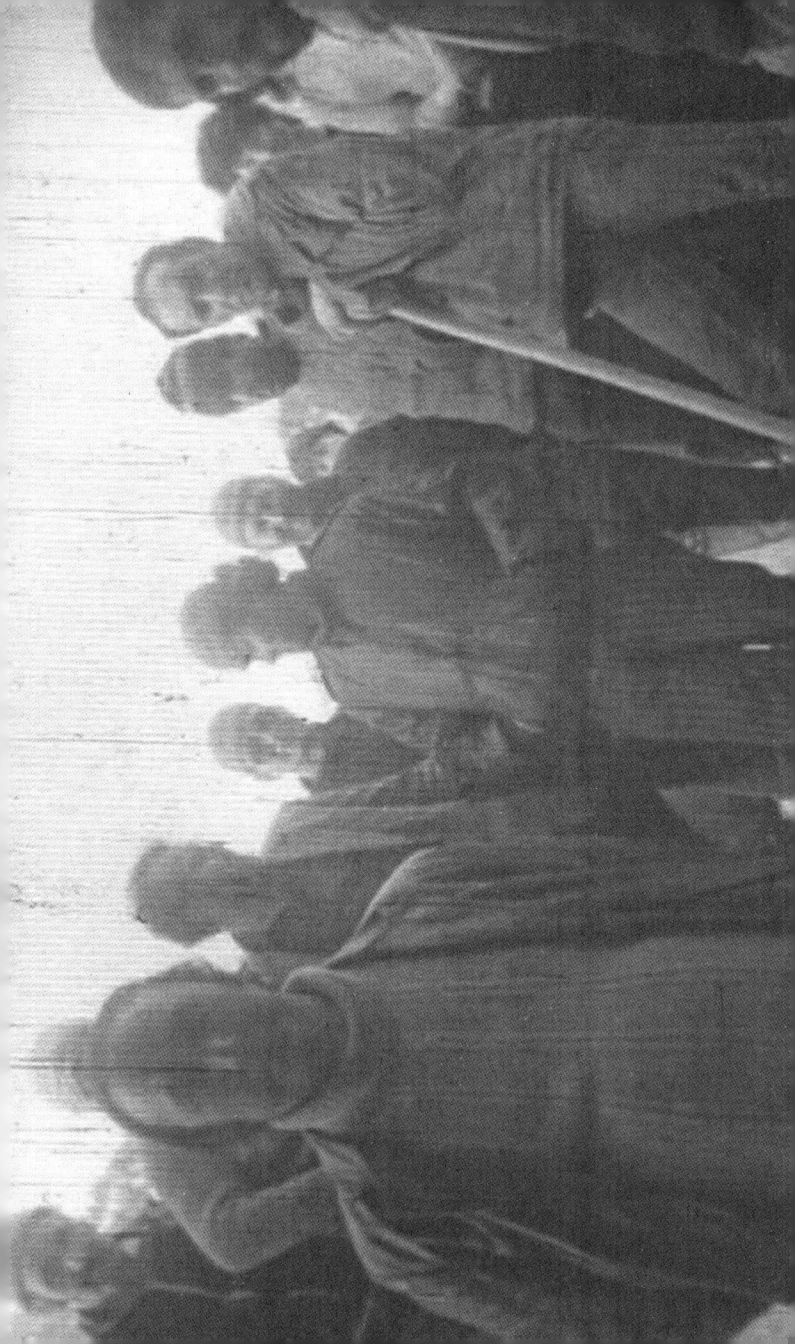

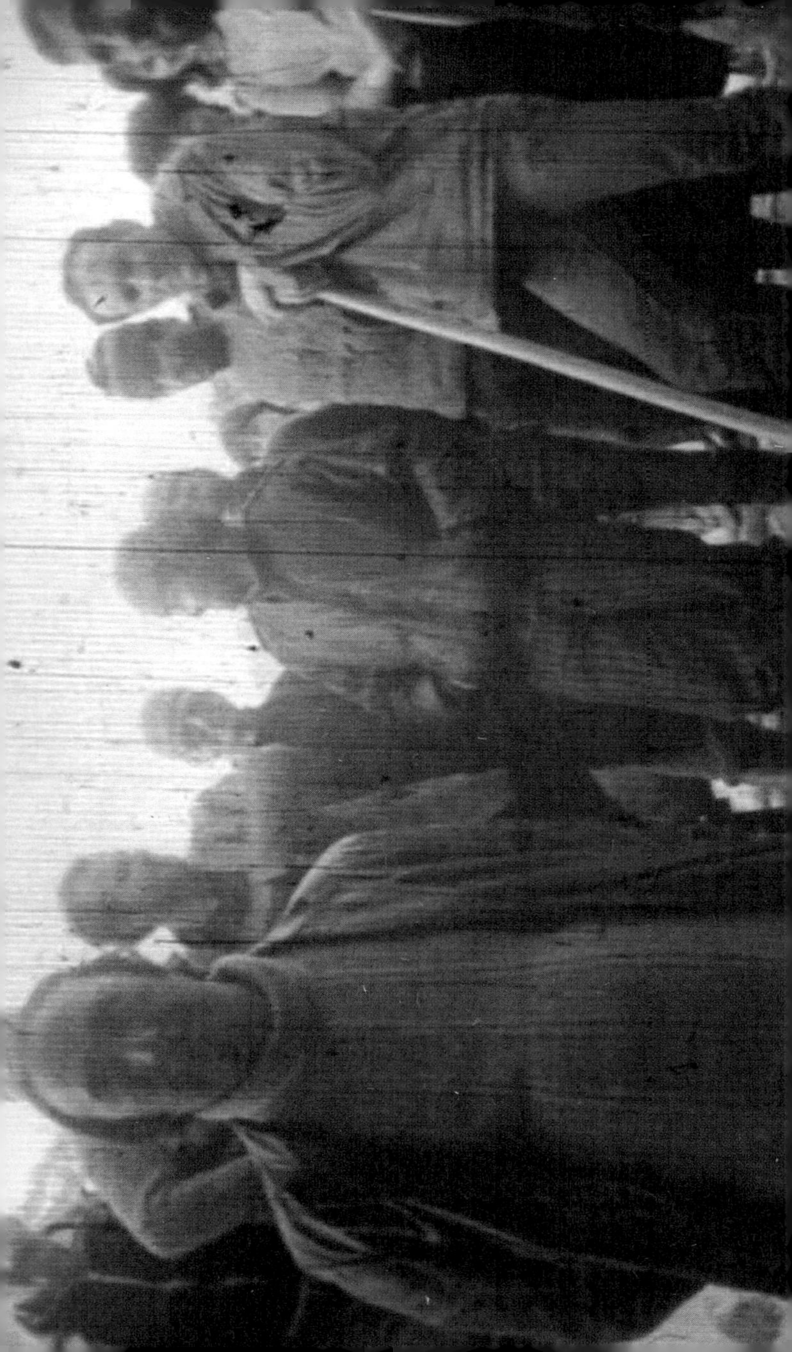

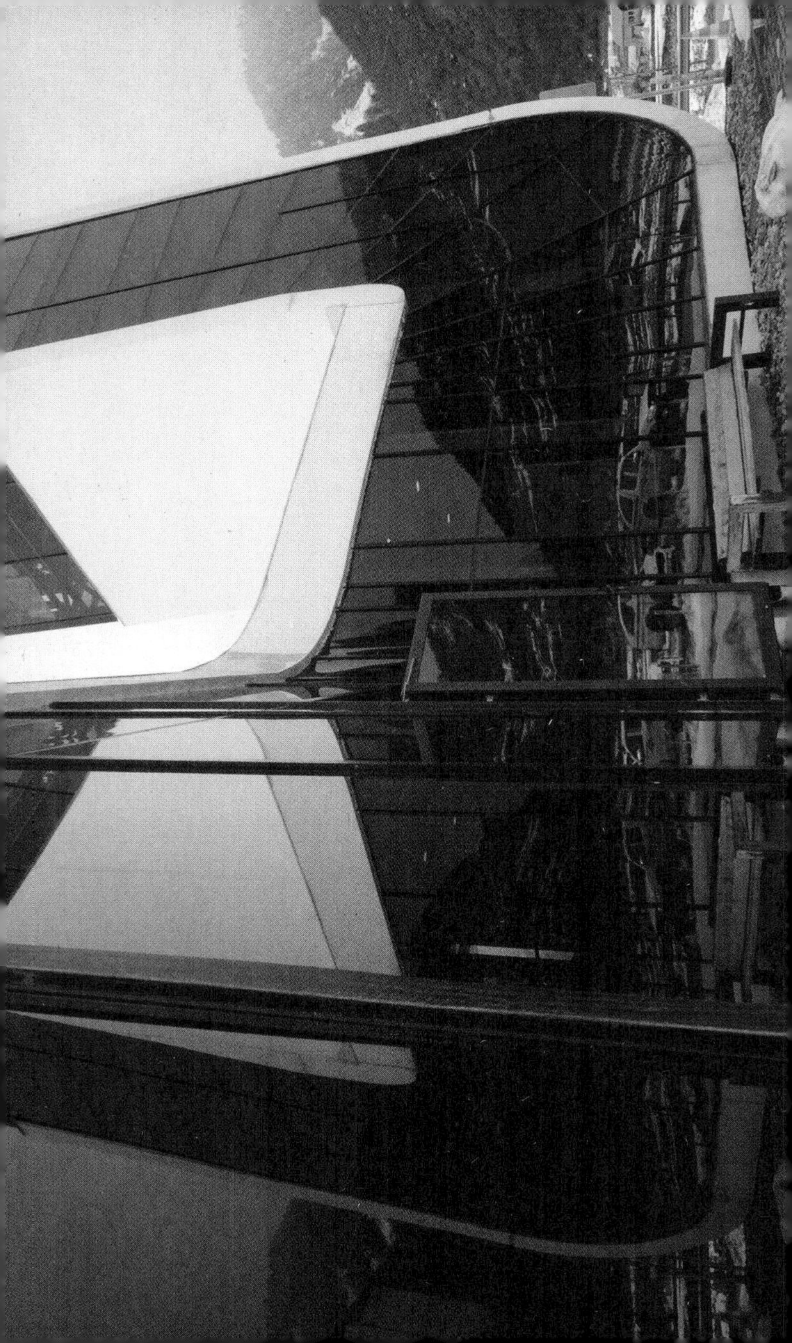

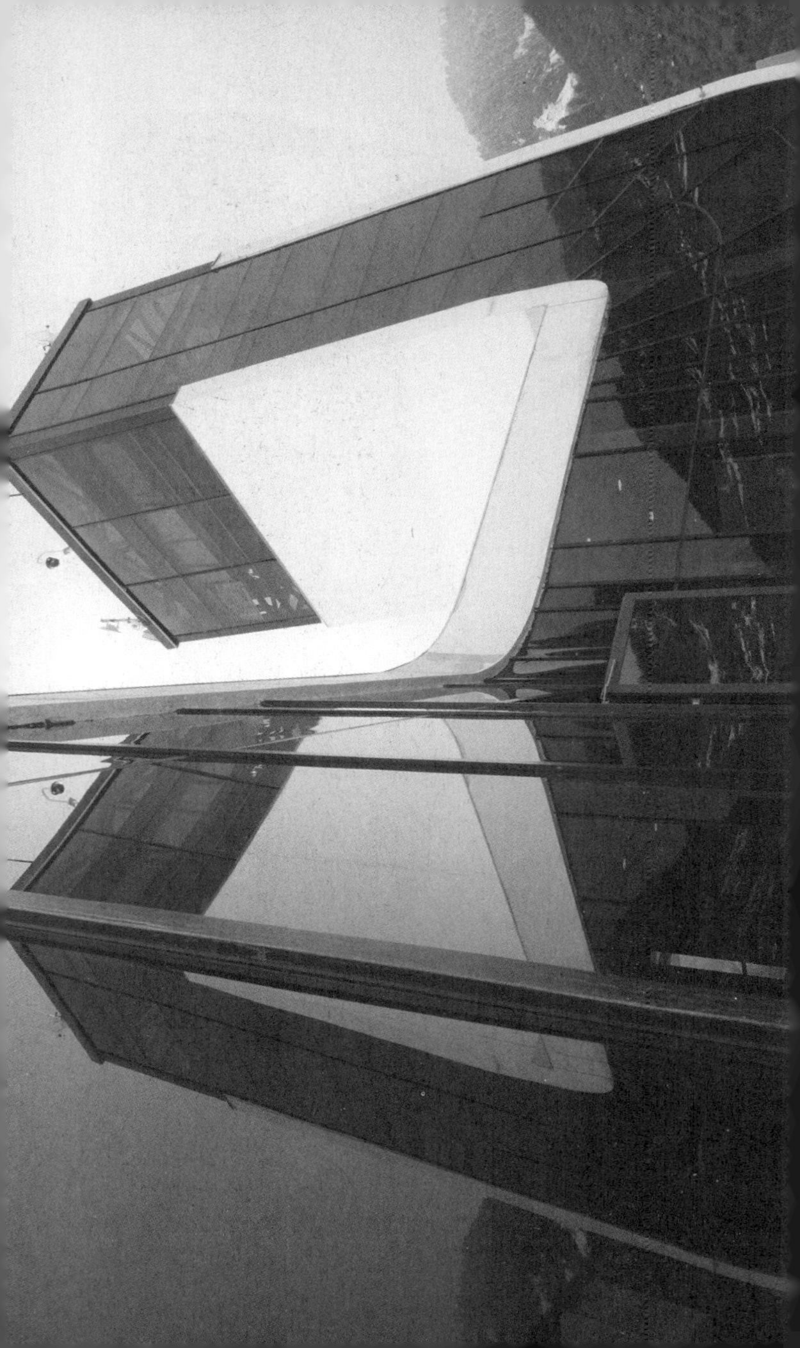

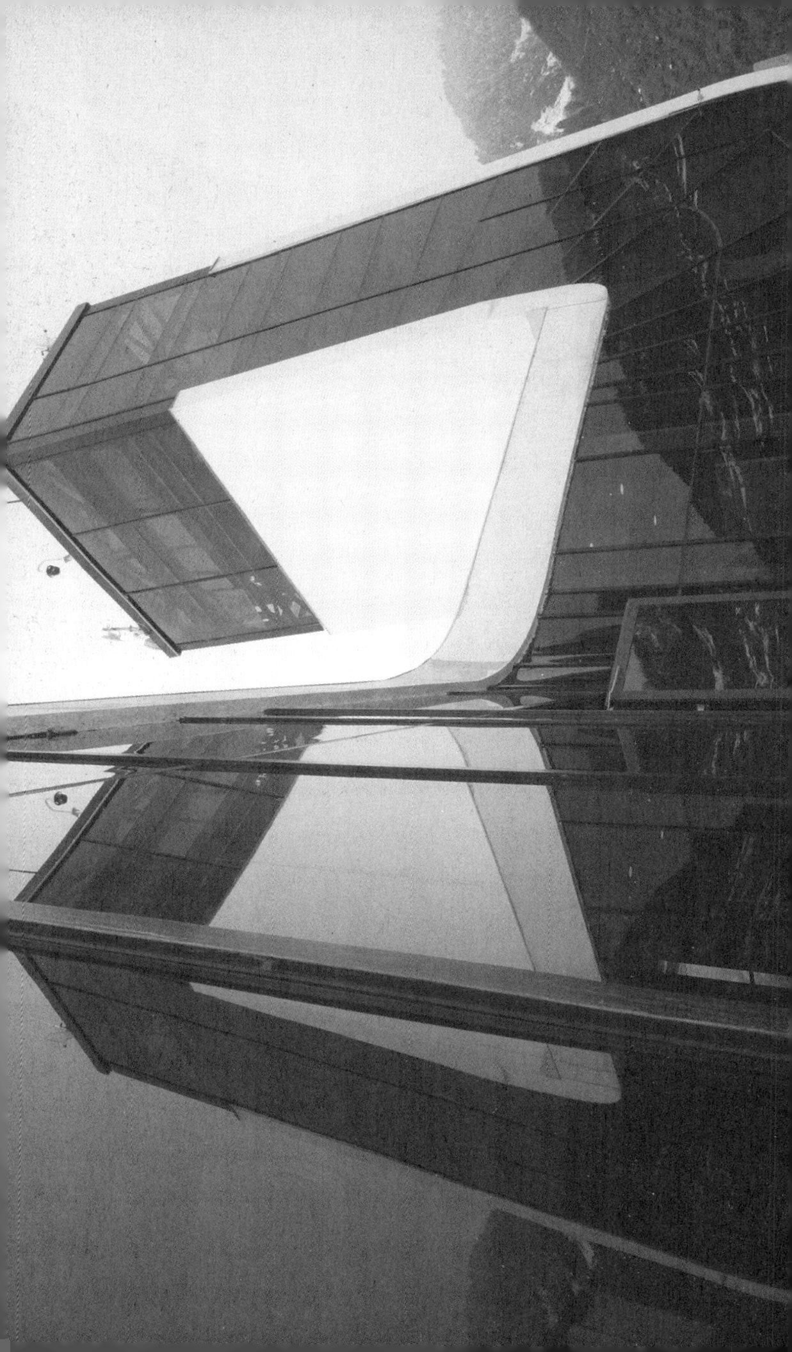

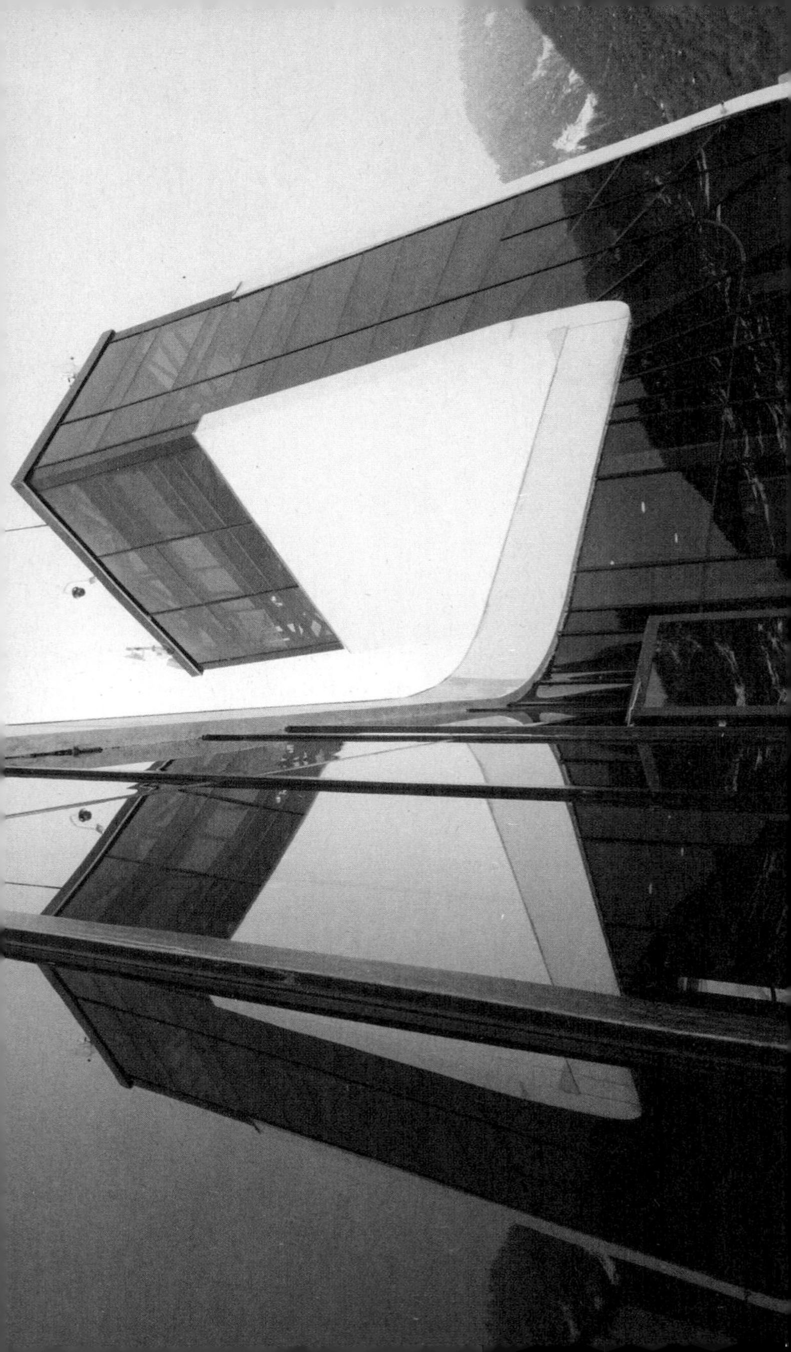

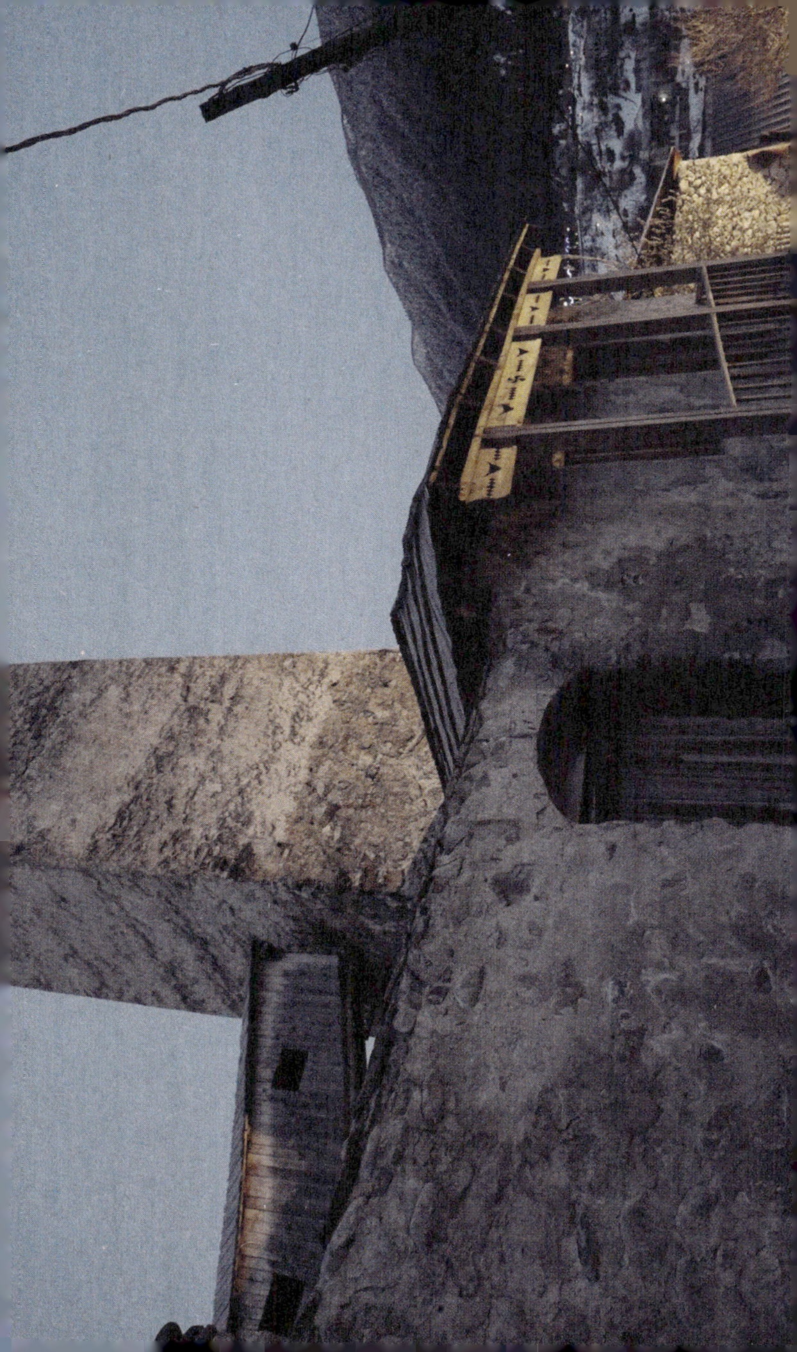

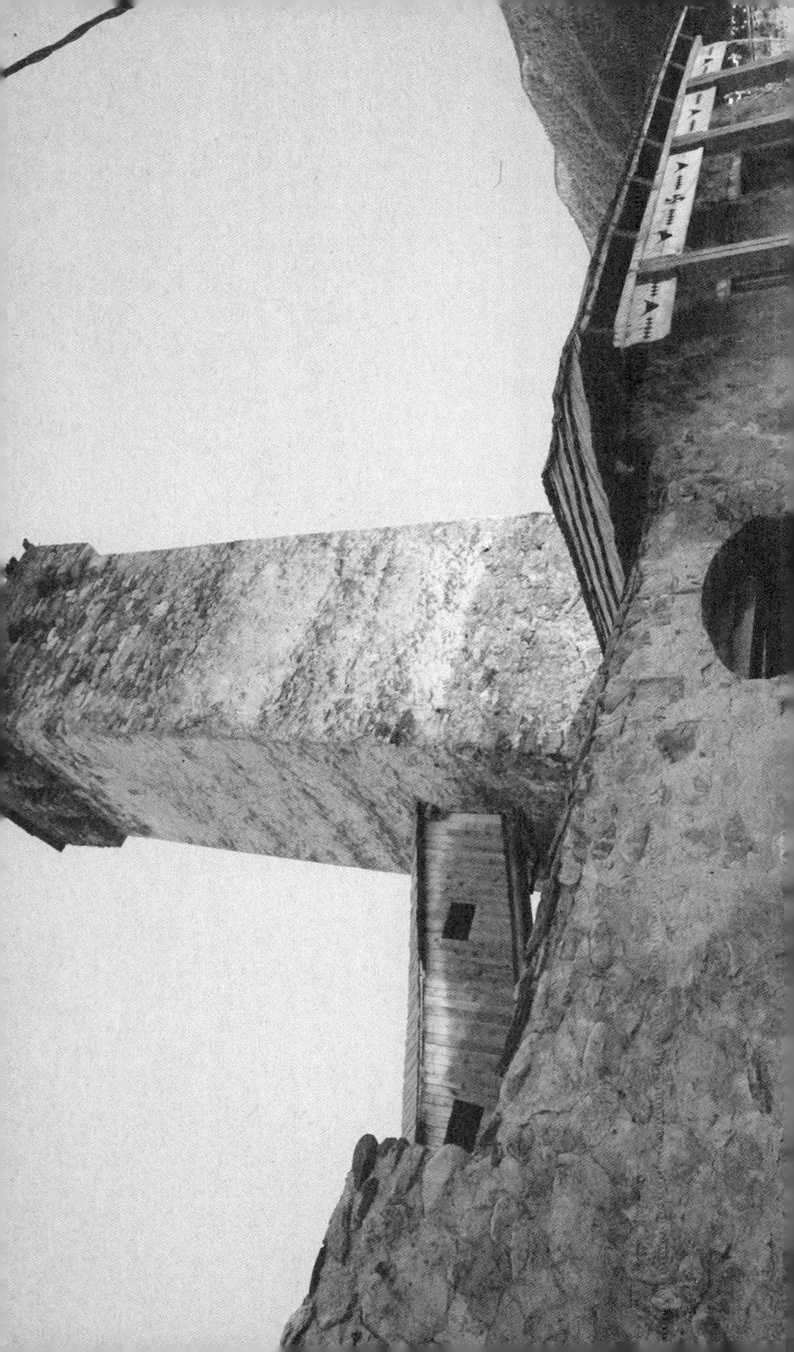

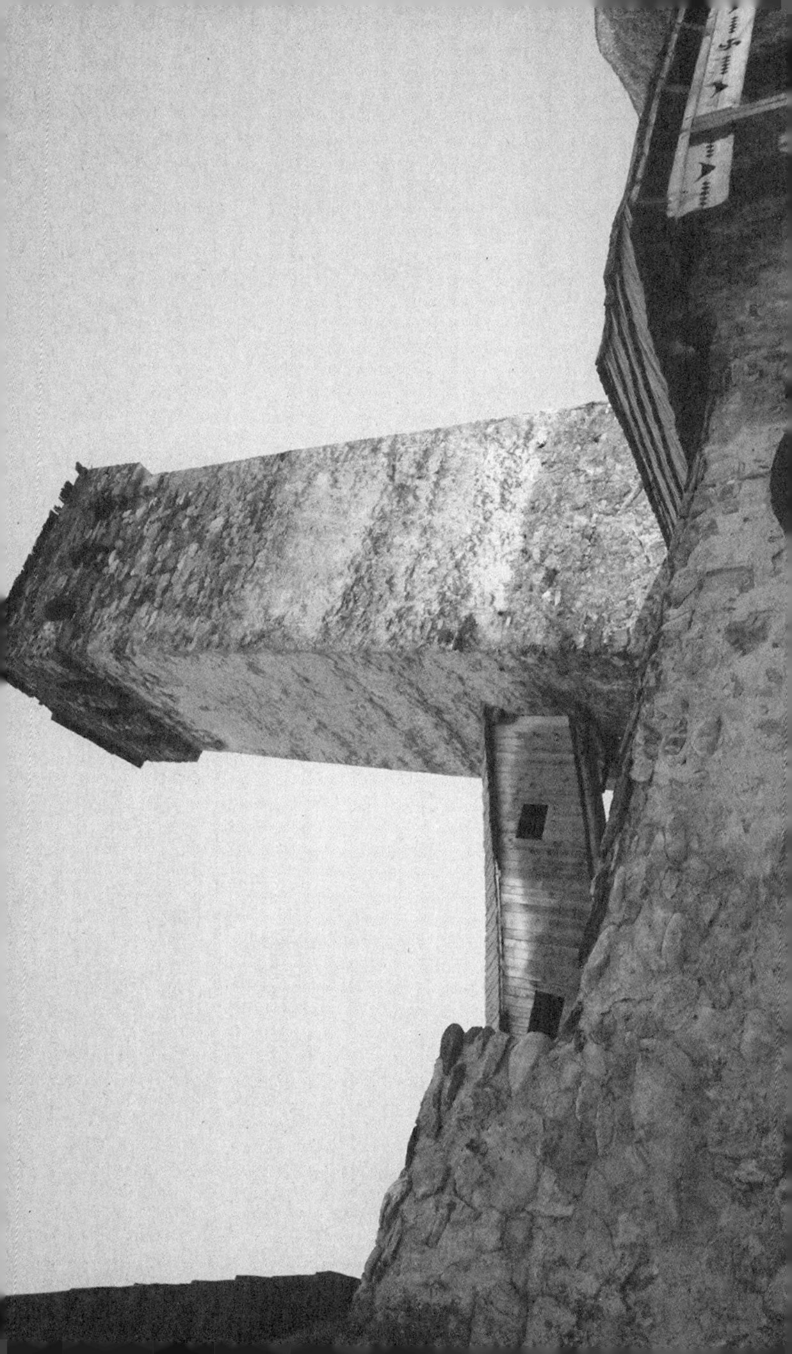

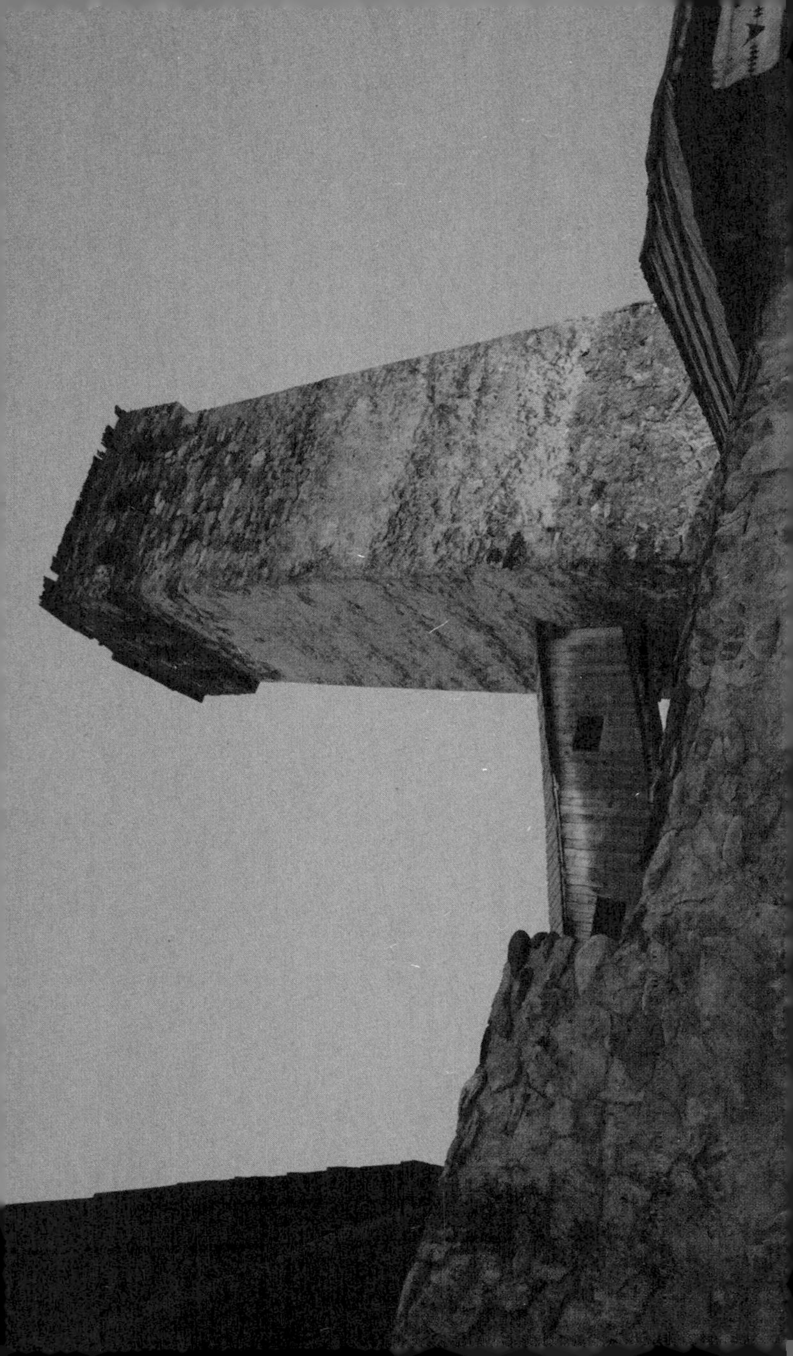

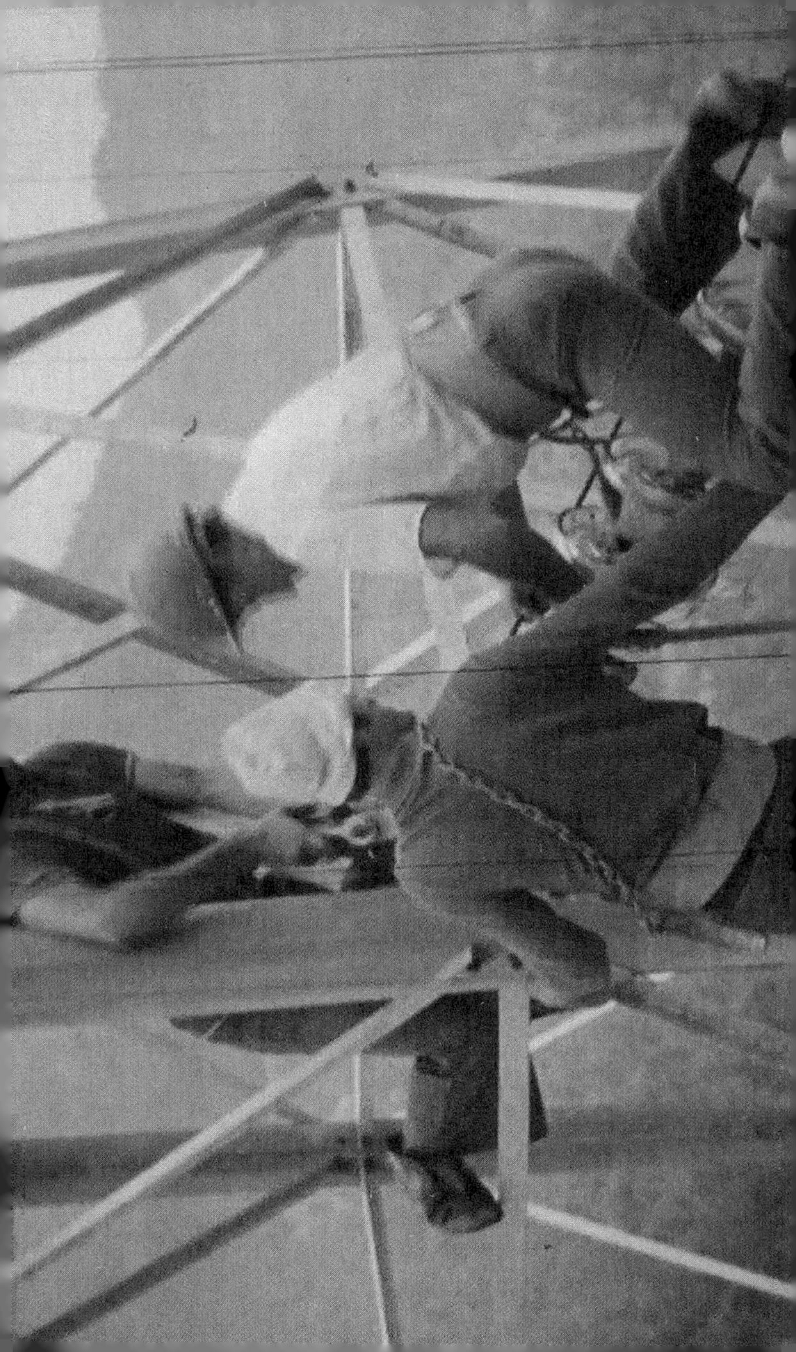

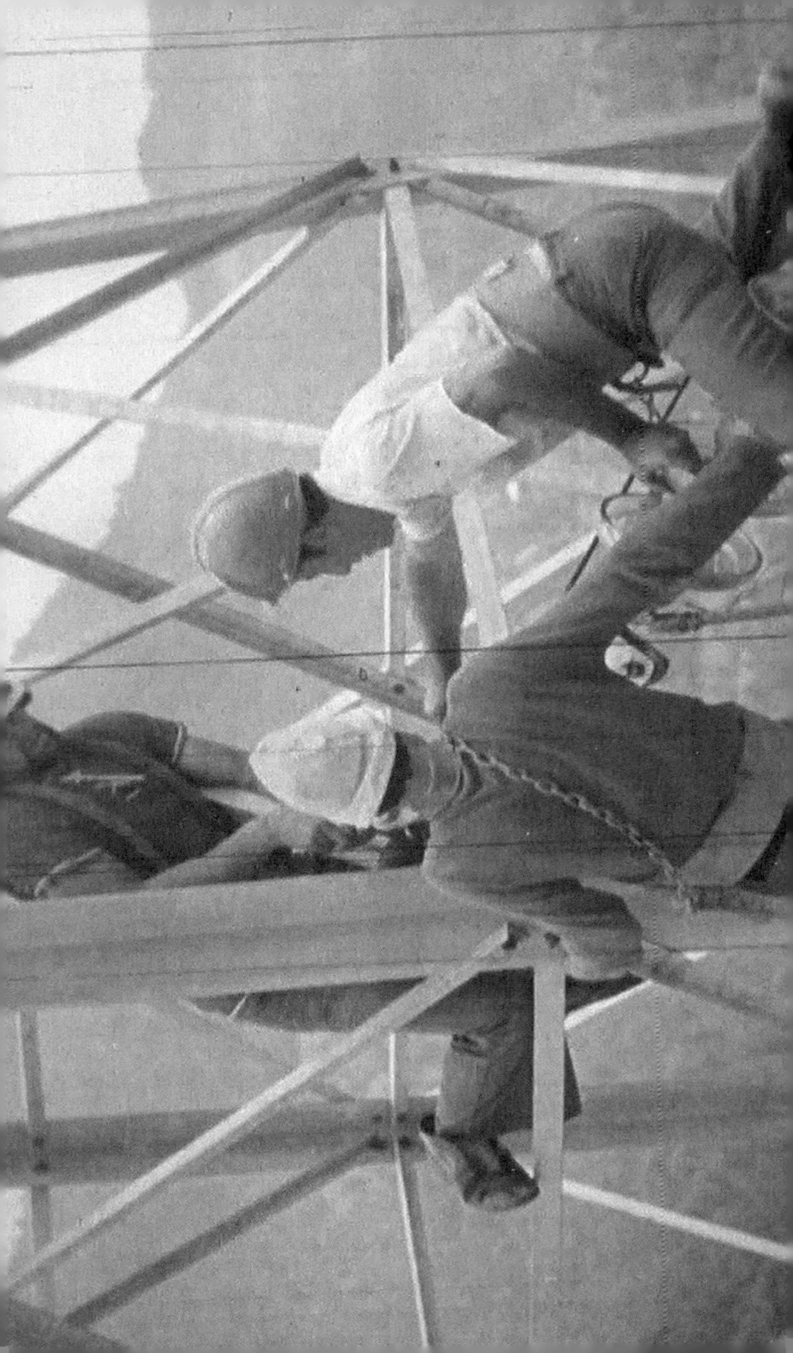

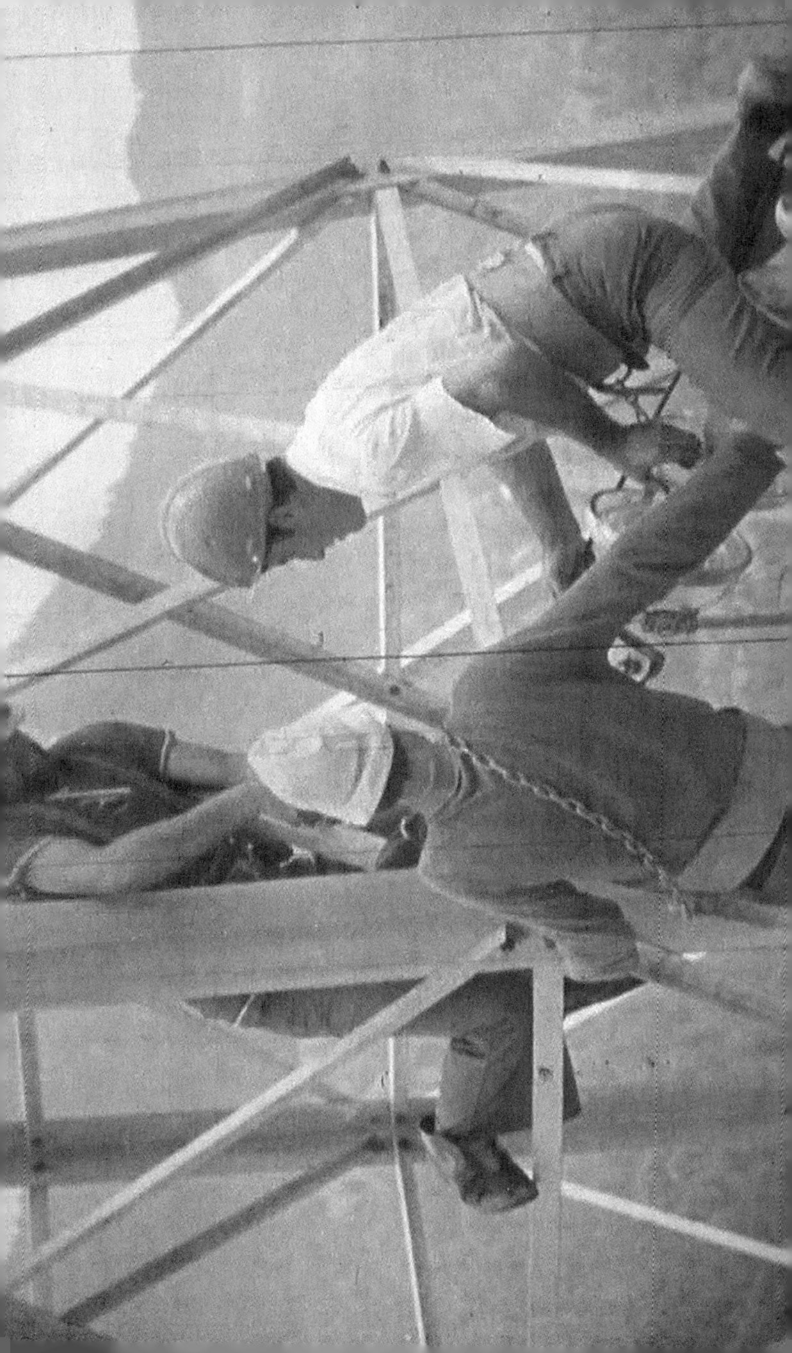

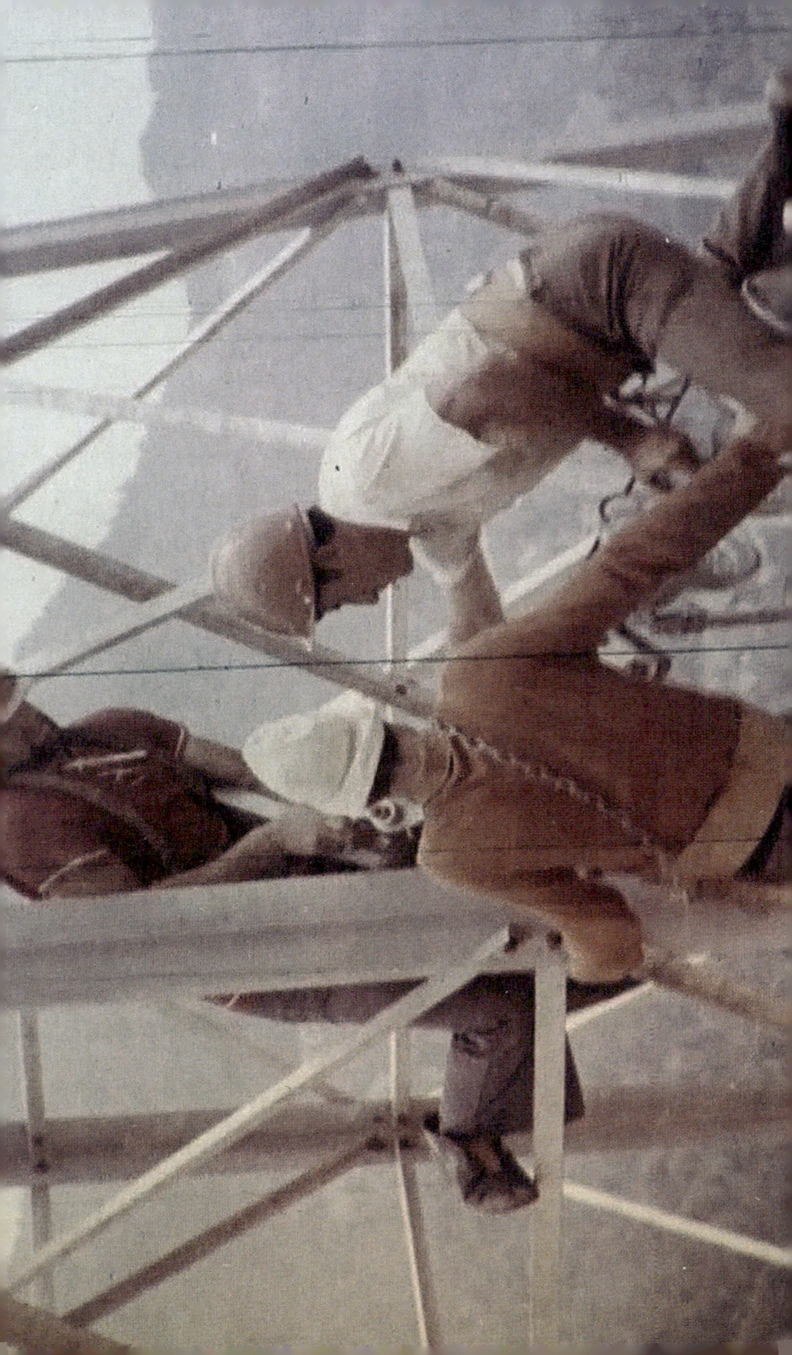

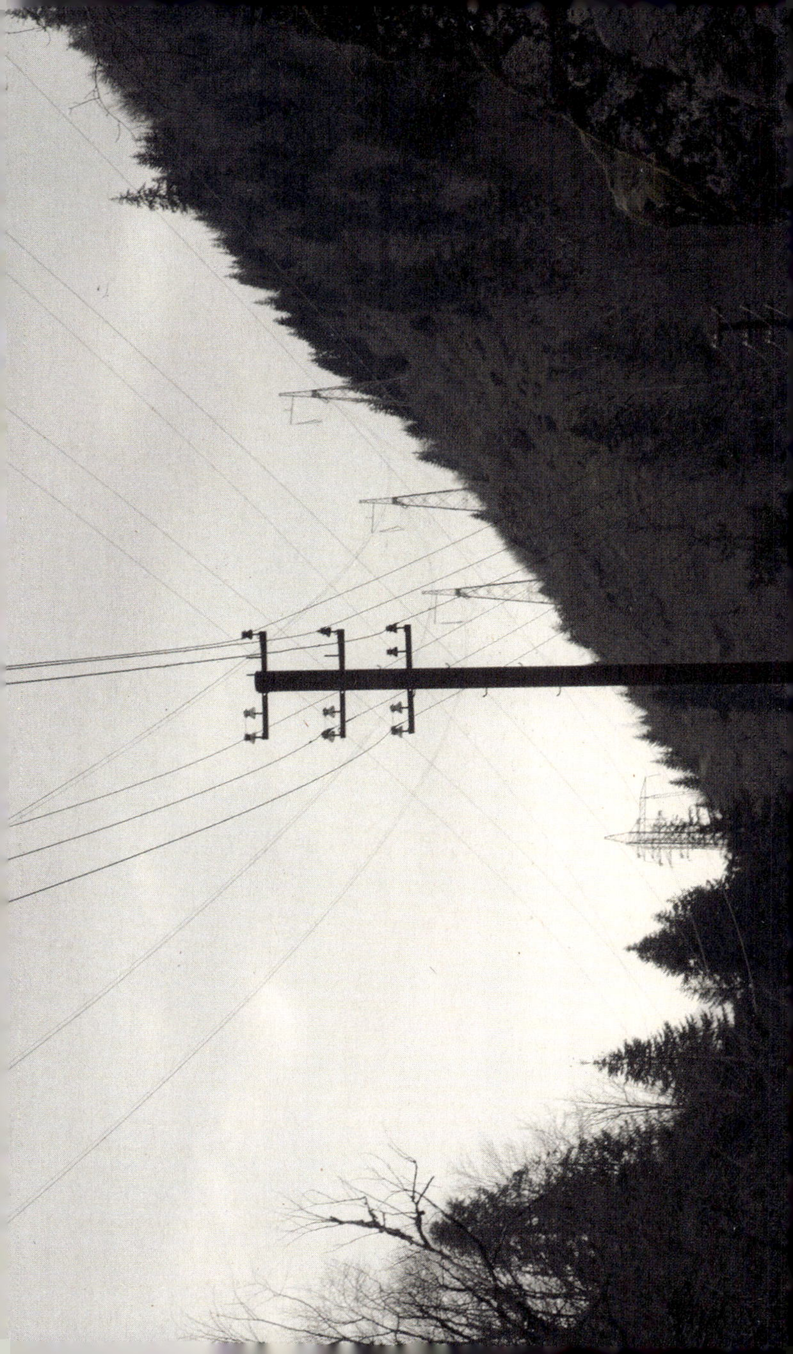

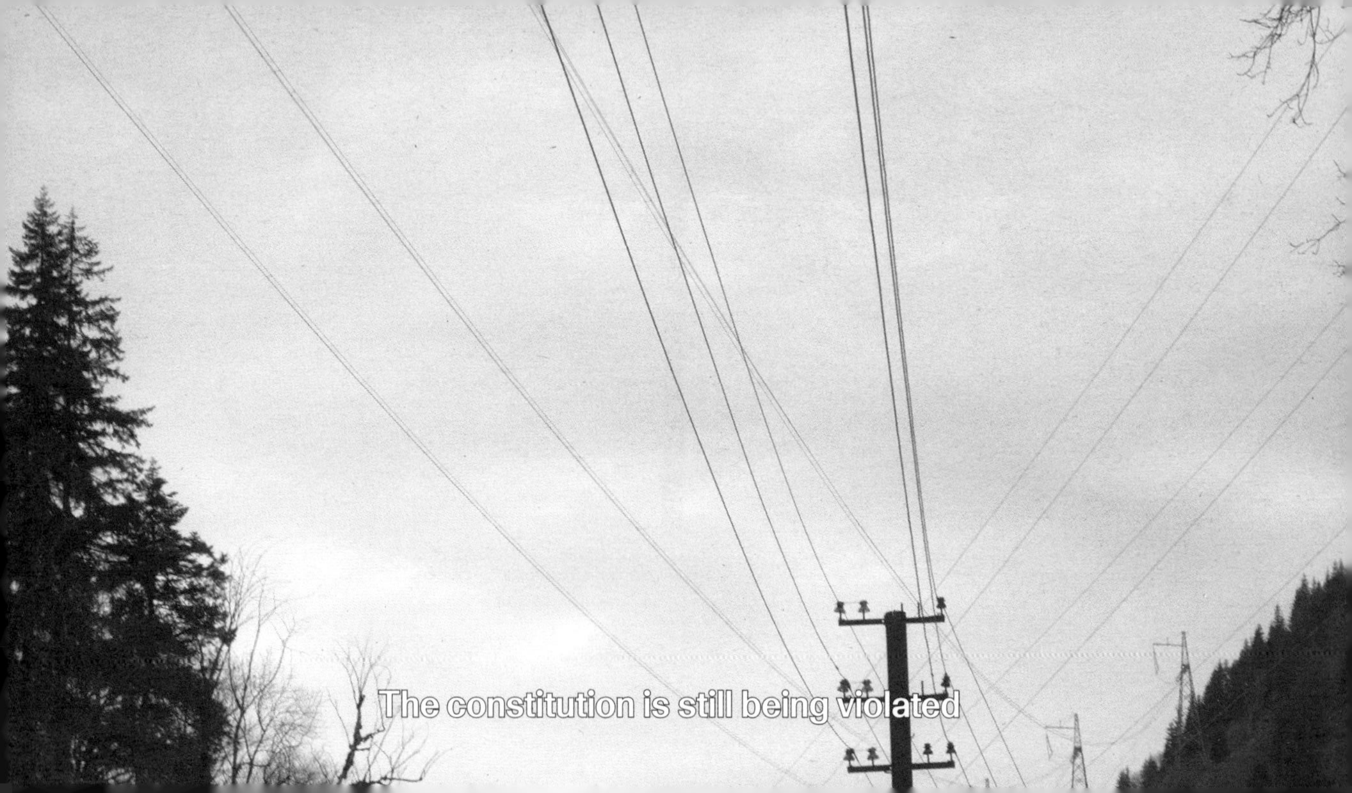
The constitution is still being violated

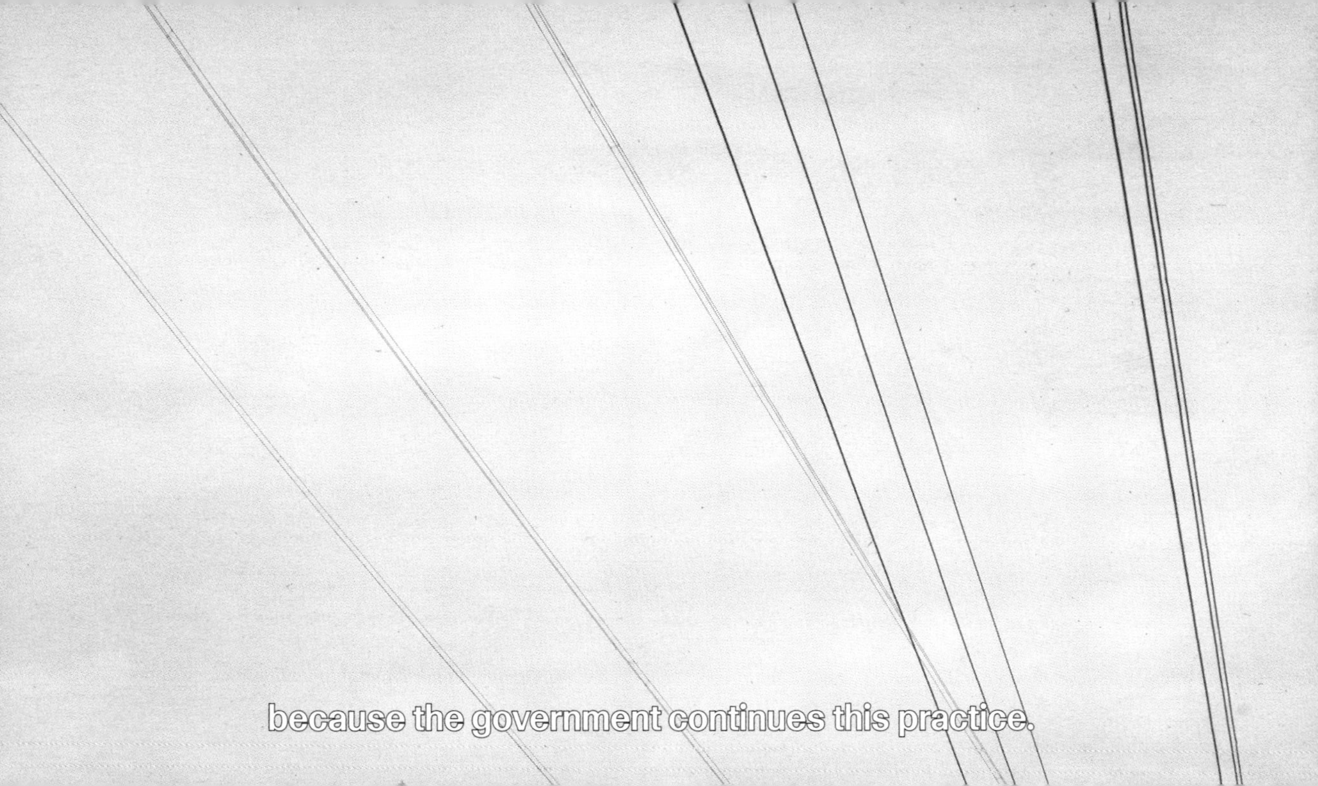
because the government continues this practice.

1TV.GE

The second issue is

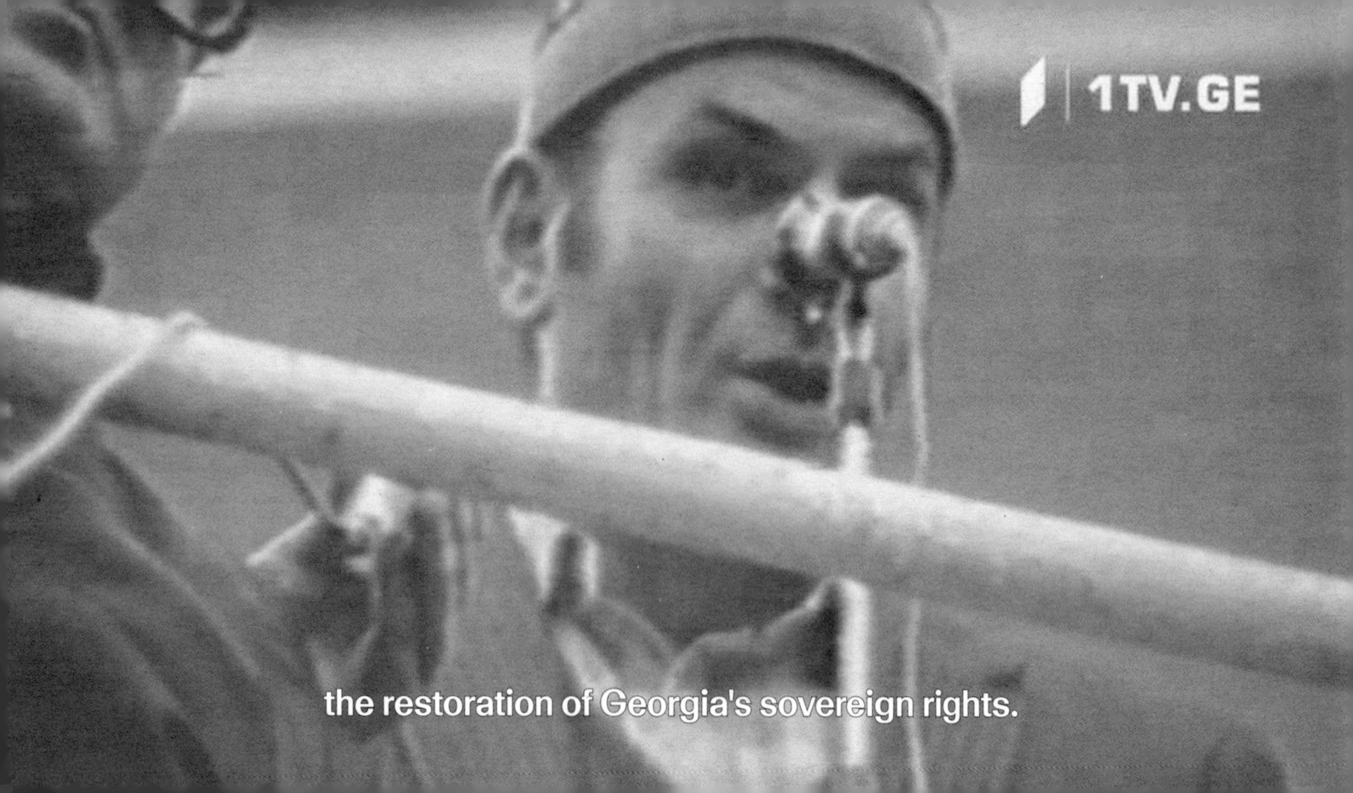

1TV.GE

the restoration of Georgia's sovereign rights.

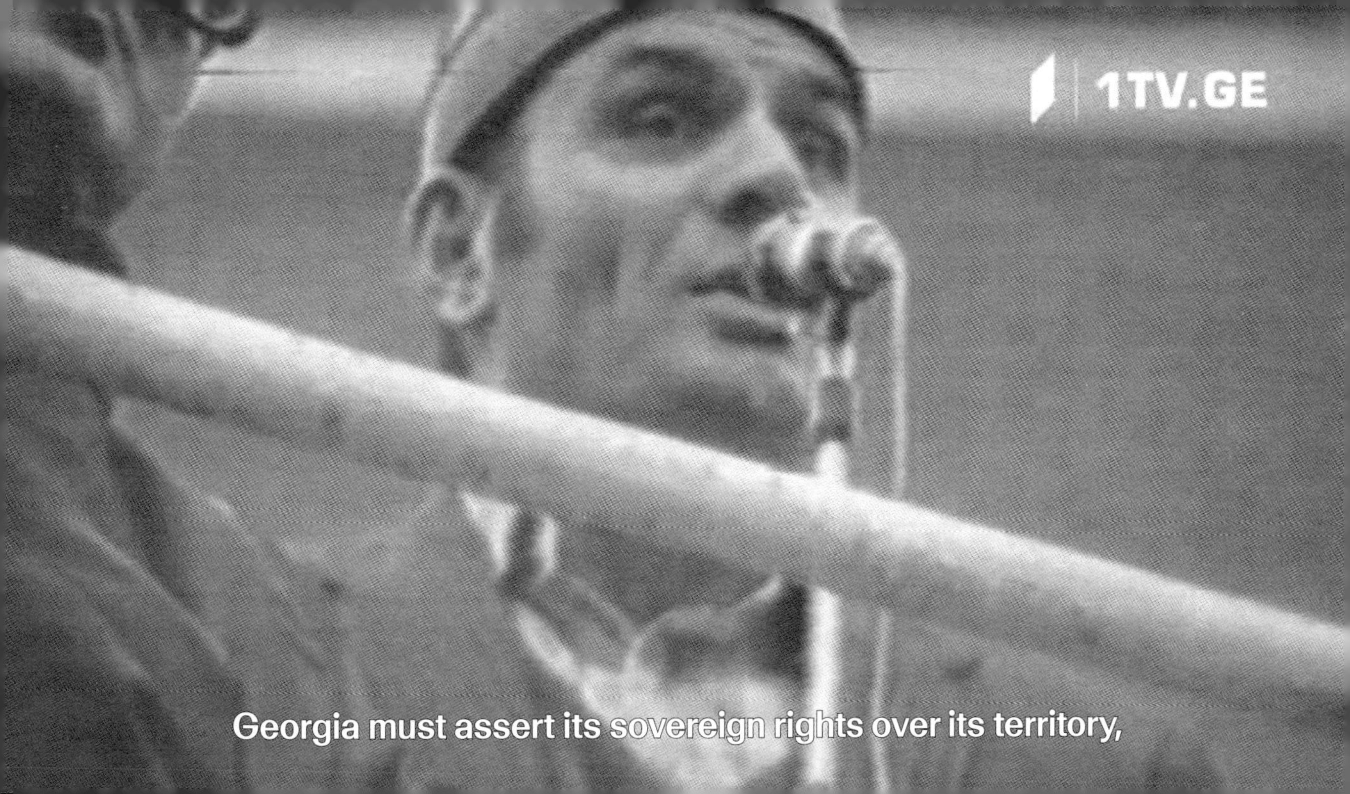

1TV.GE
Georgia must assert its sovereign rights over its territory,

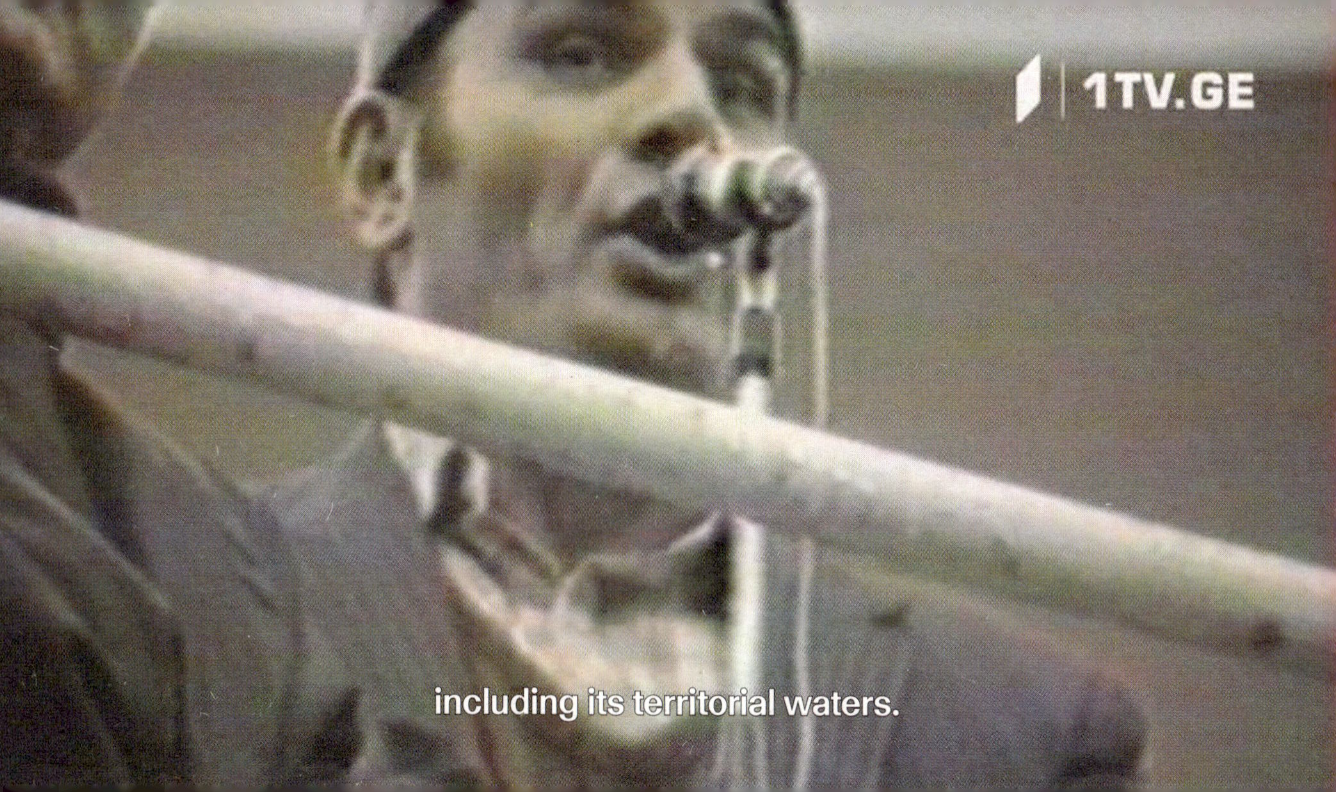
1TV.GE
including its territorial waters.

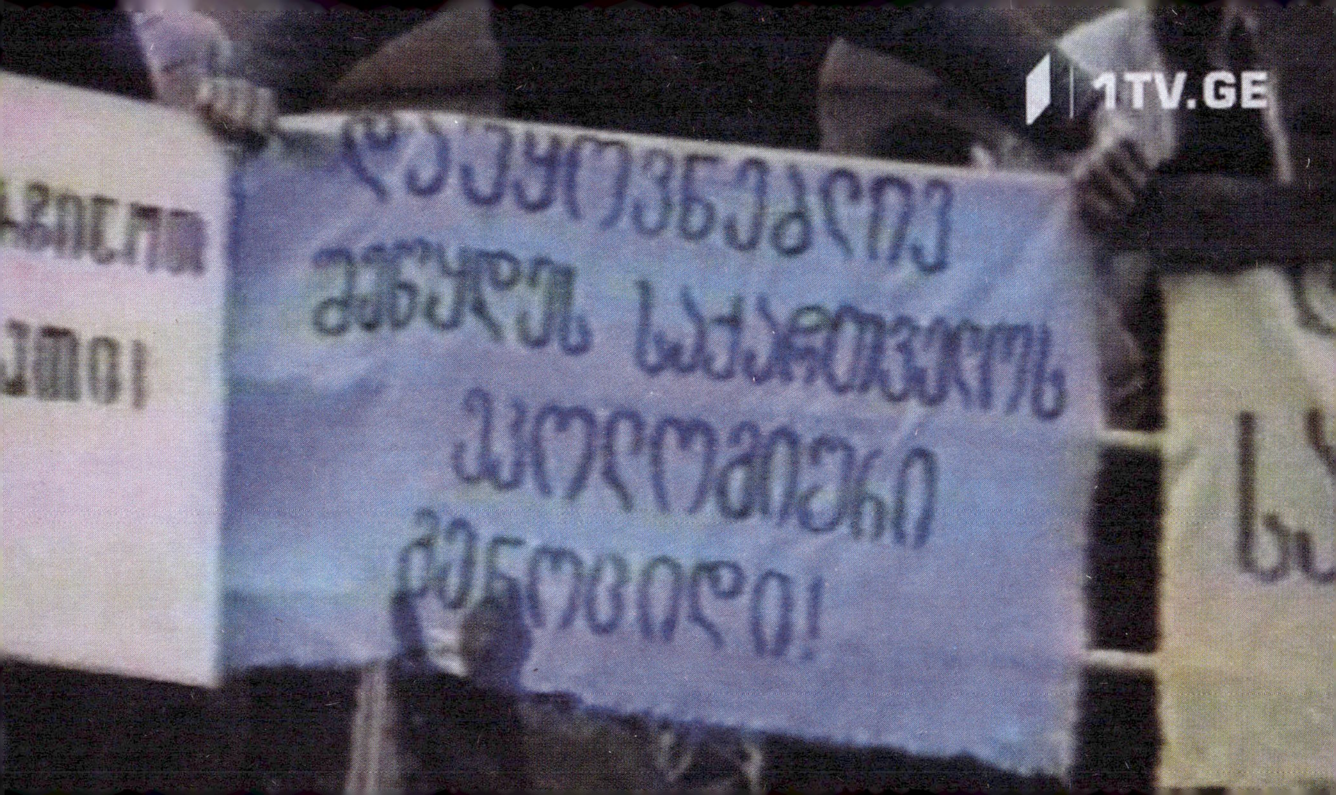

დაუყოვნებლივ
გვინდა სამართლის
პოლიტიკური
გამოძიება!

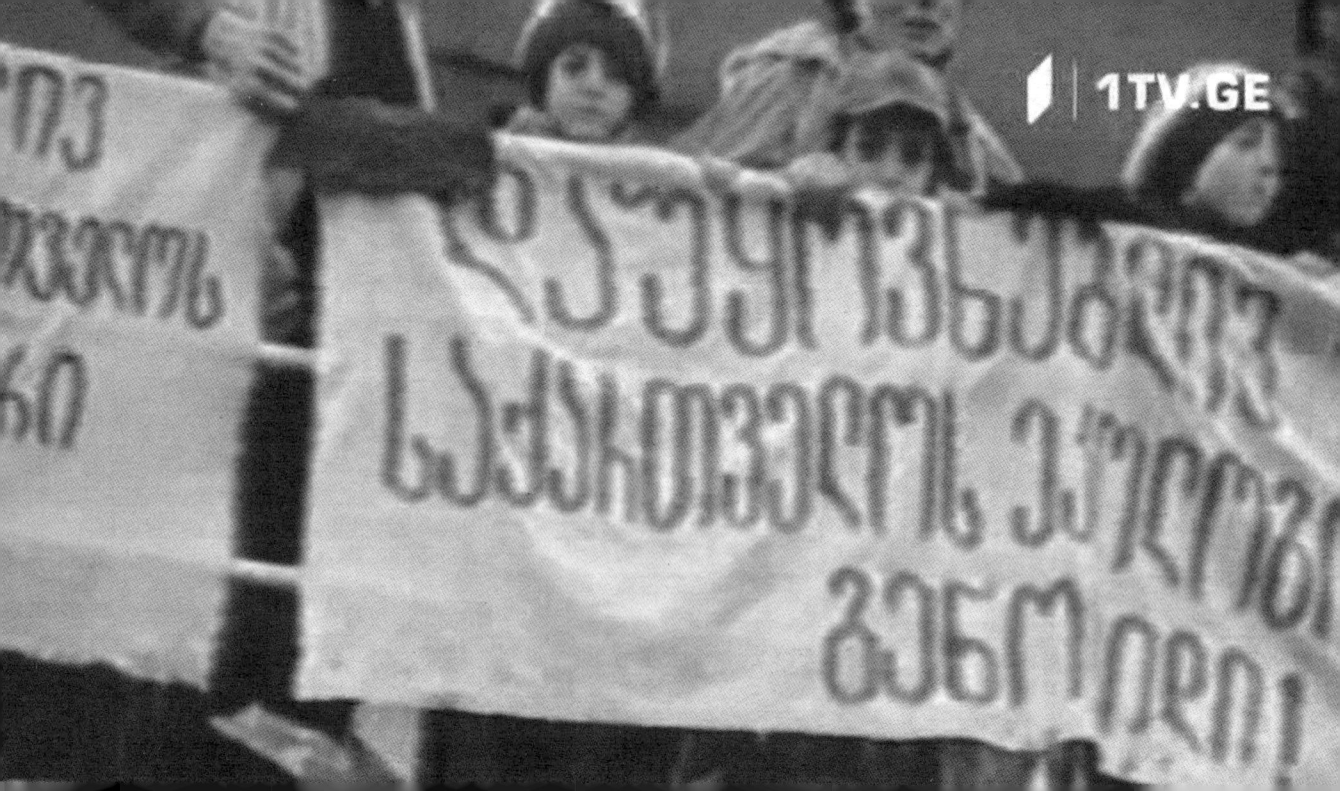
დაუყოვნებ...
საქართველოს პოლიტი...
ვანო თ...
1TV.GE

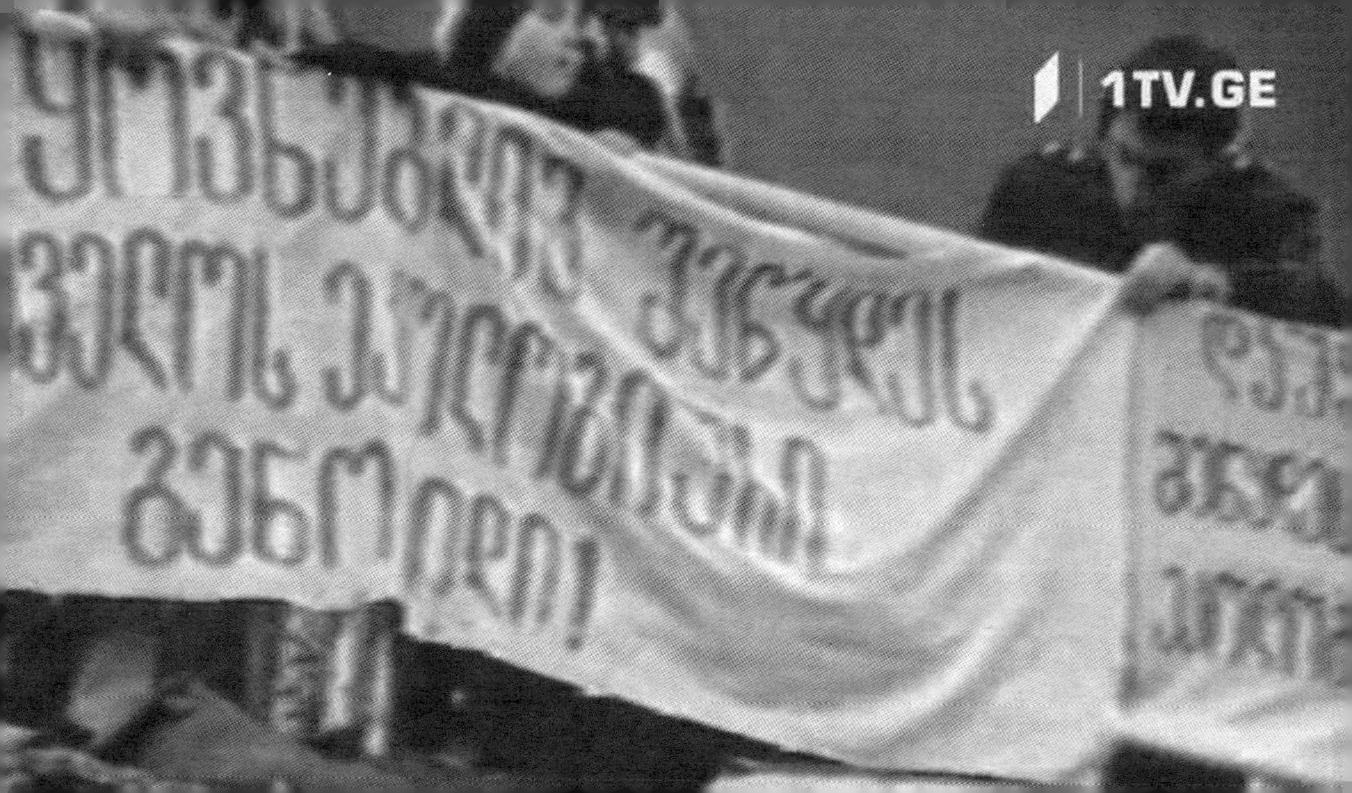
ყოვნების
ვადის ქველი
გენოცა
ხსოვნა 1990 წელი
1TV.GE

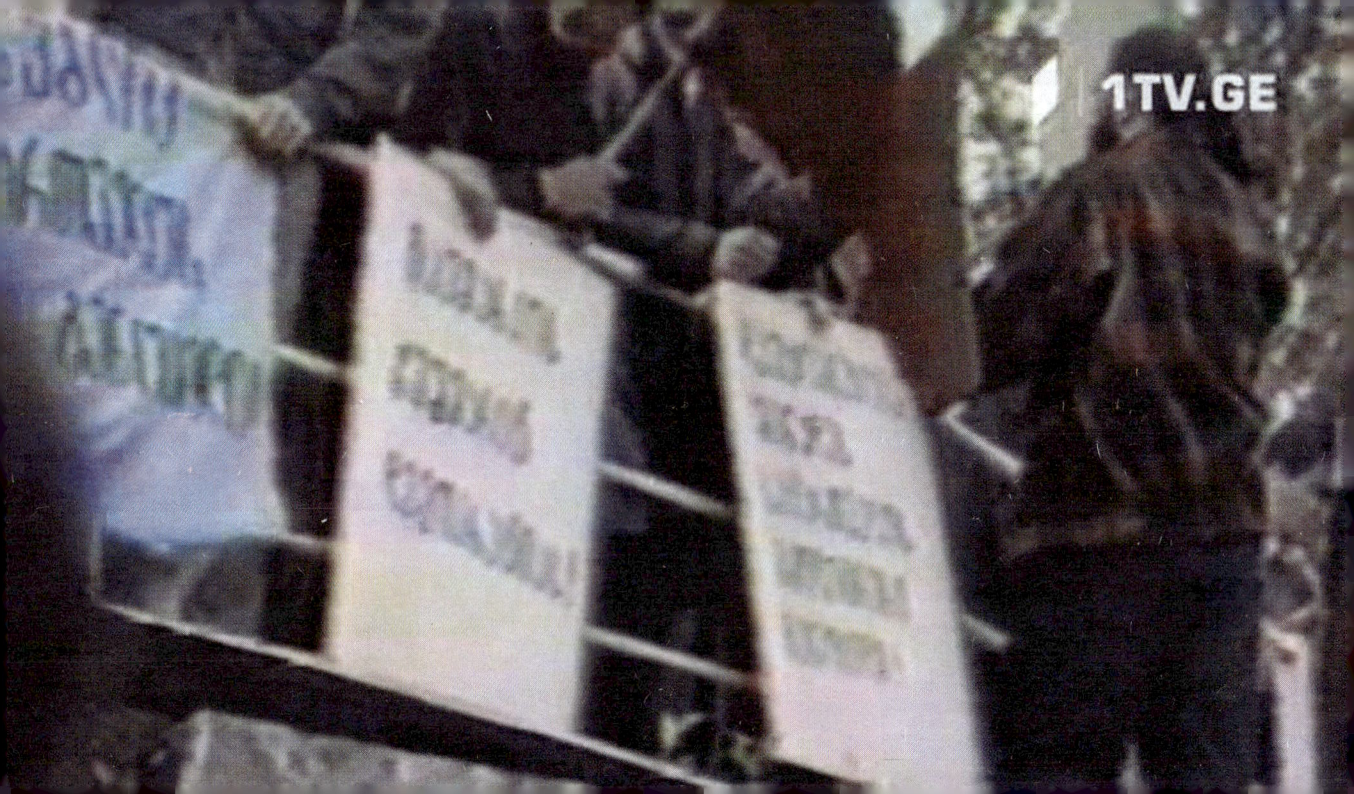
1TV.GE

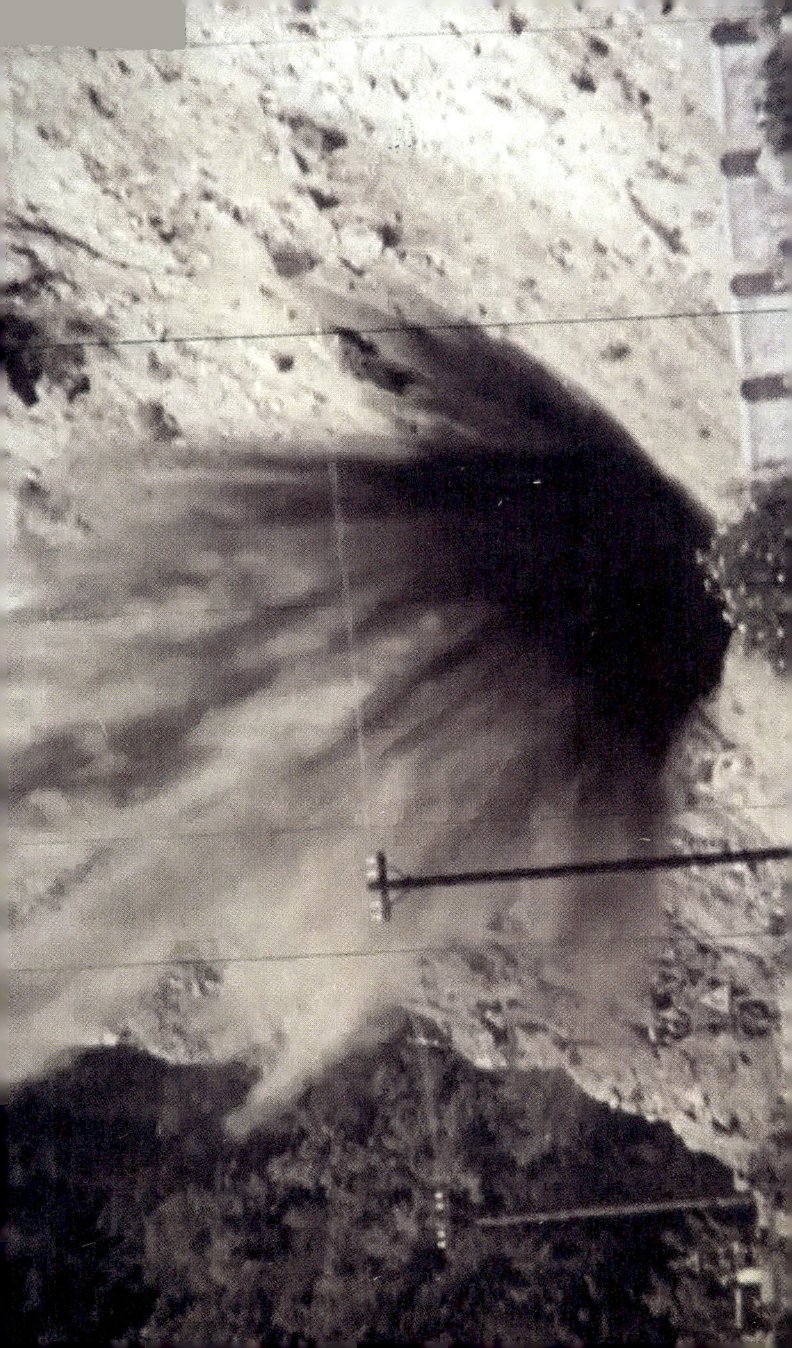

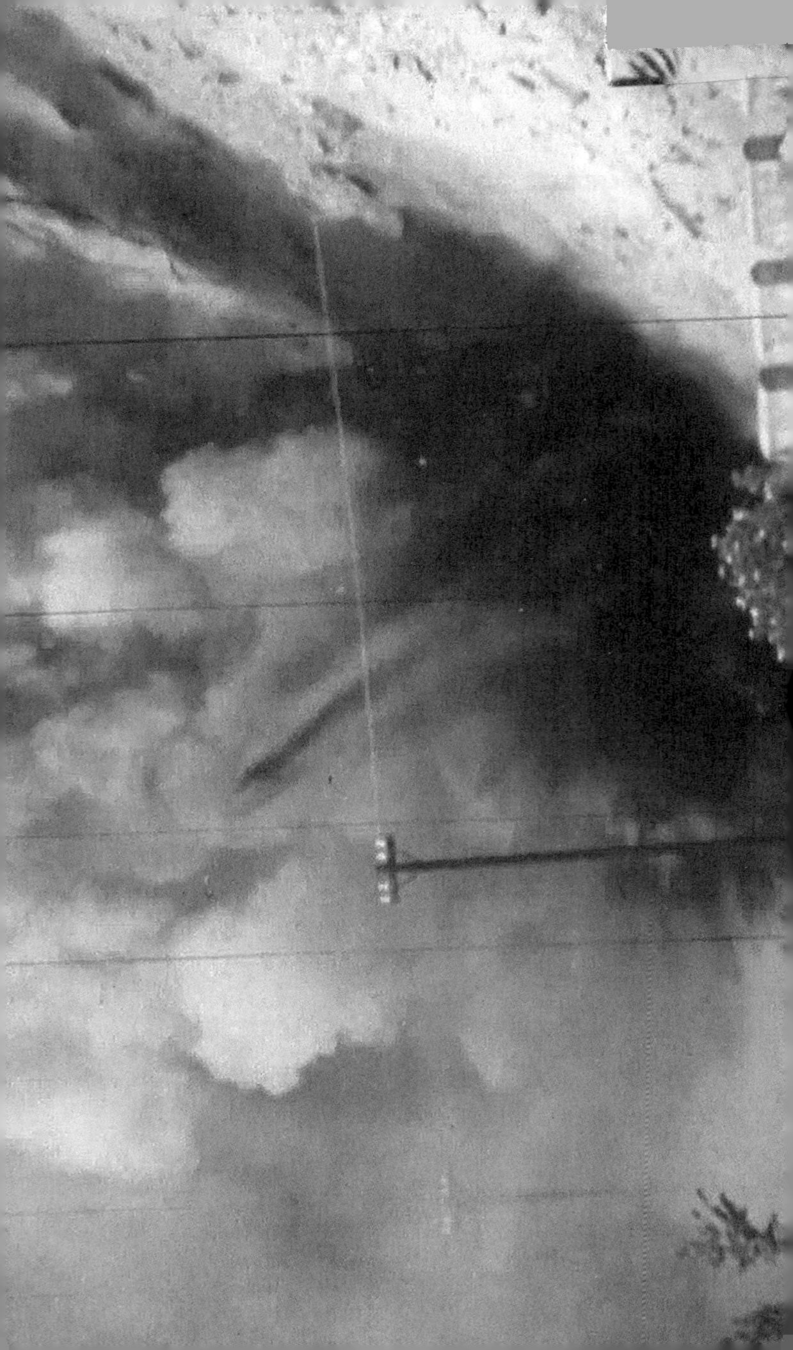

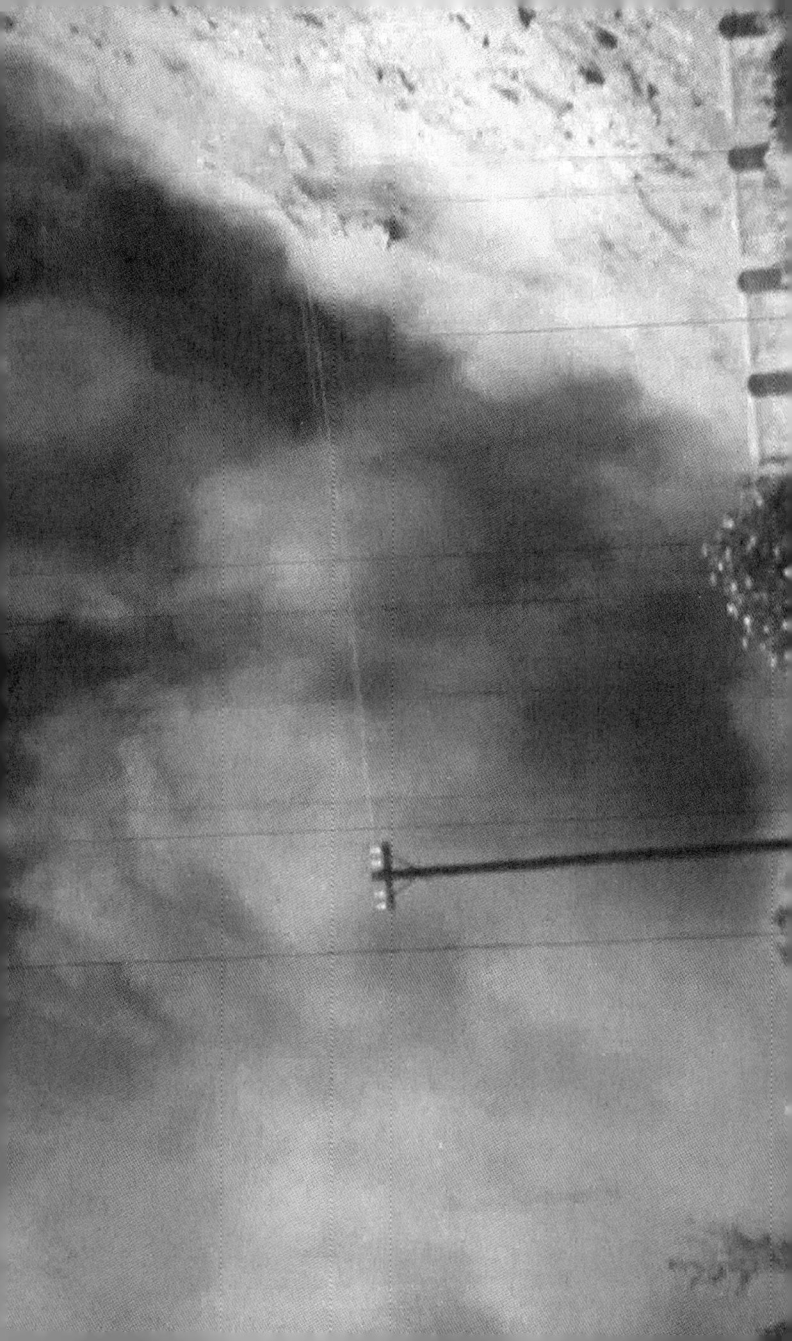

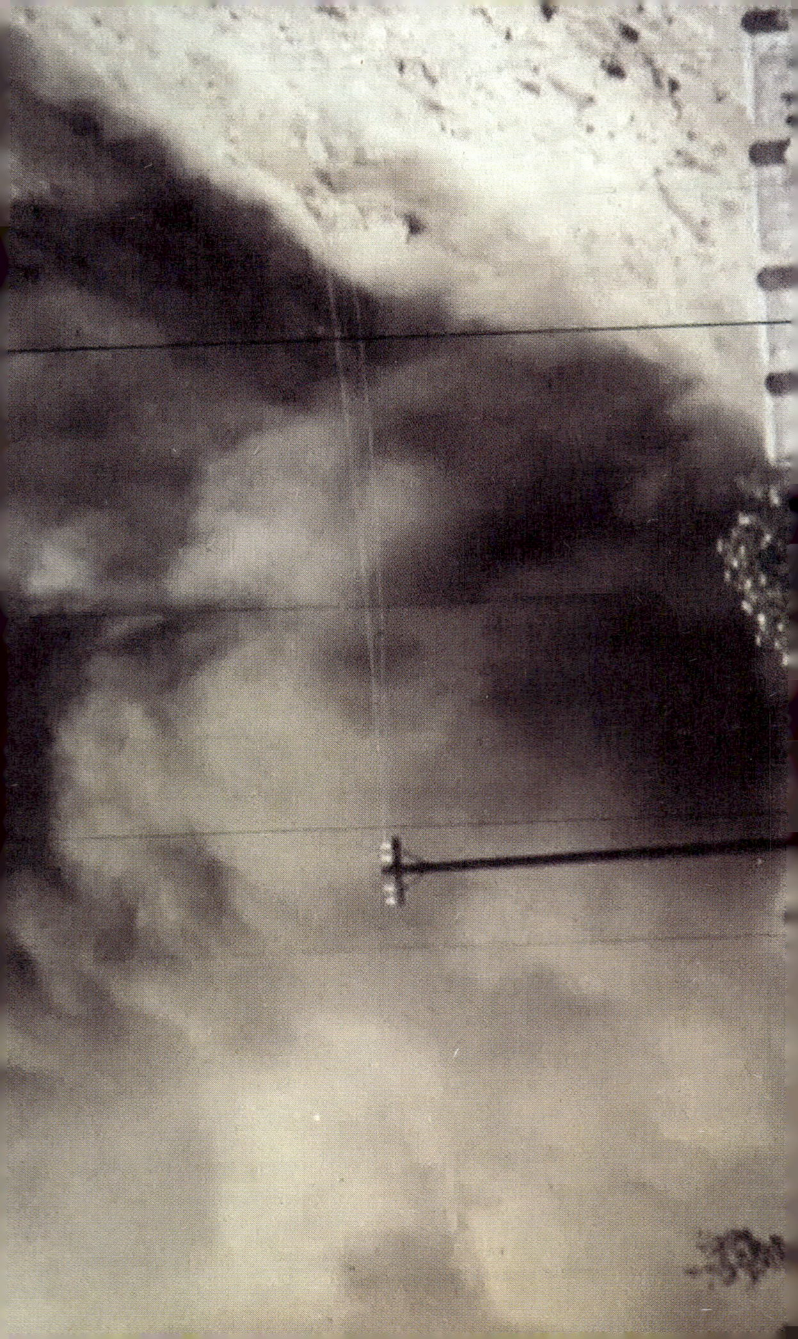

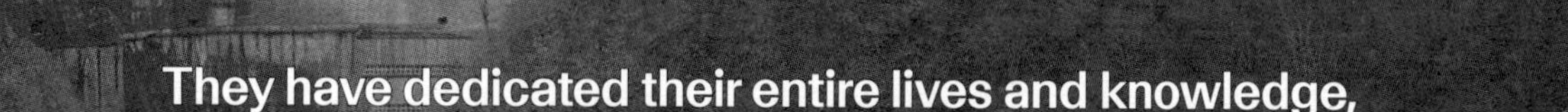

They have dedicated their entire lives and knowledge,

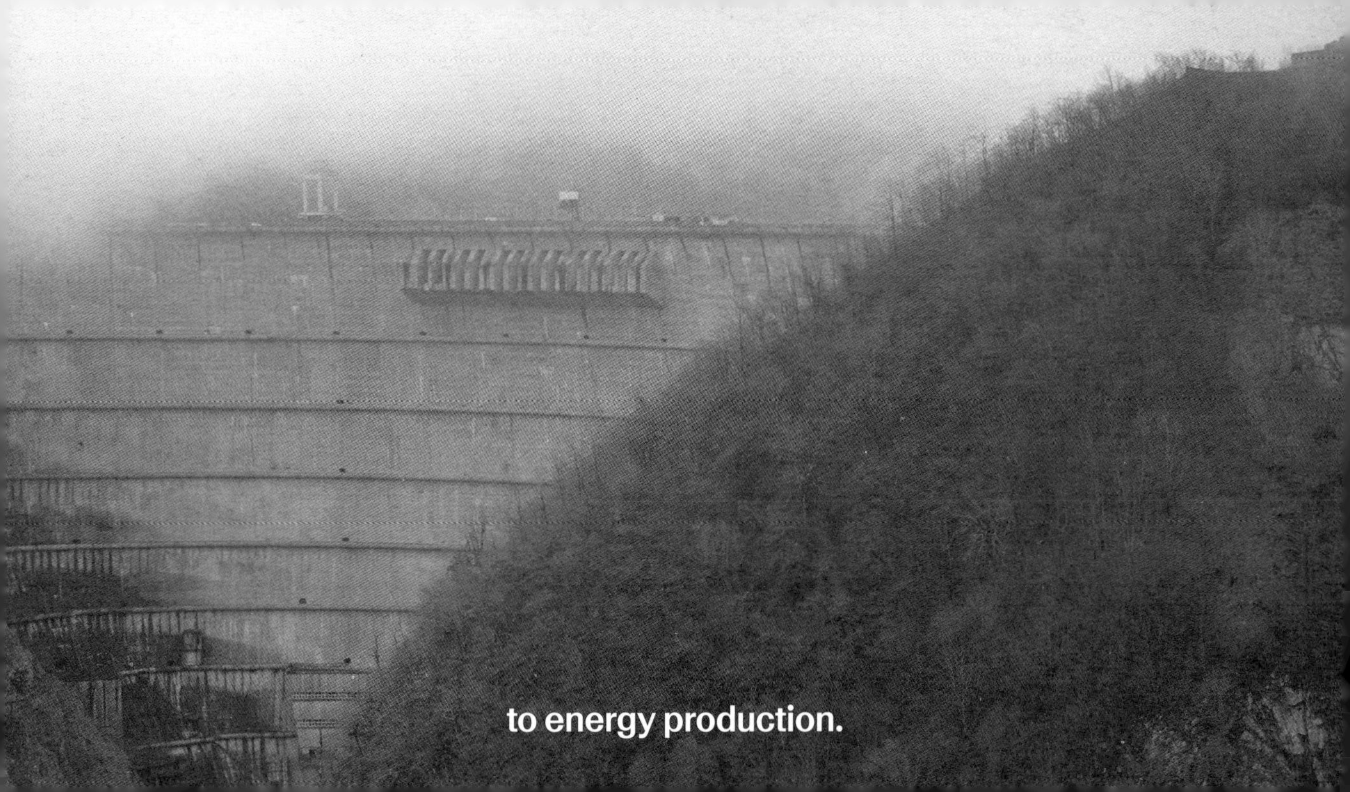
to energy production.

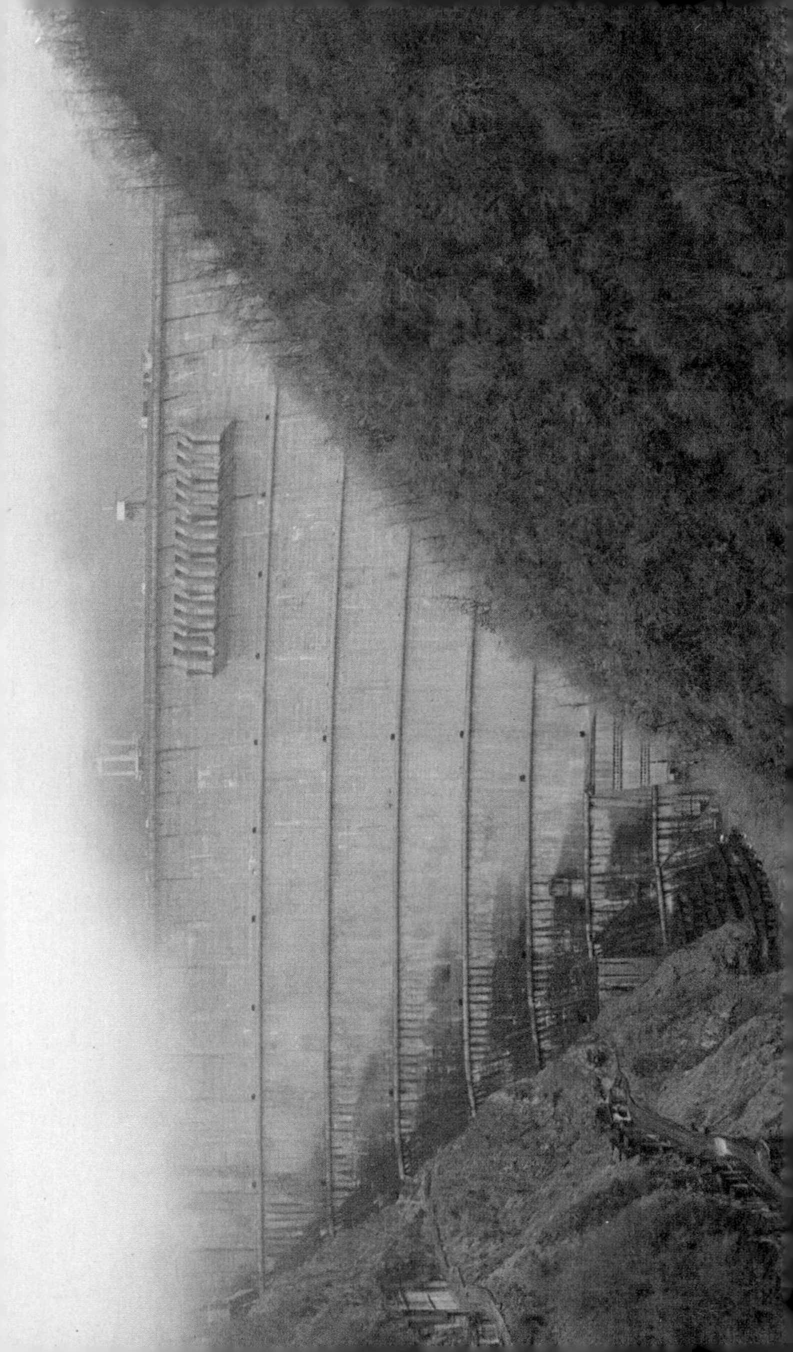

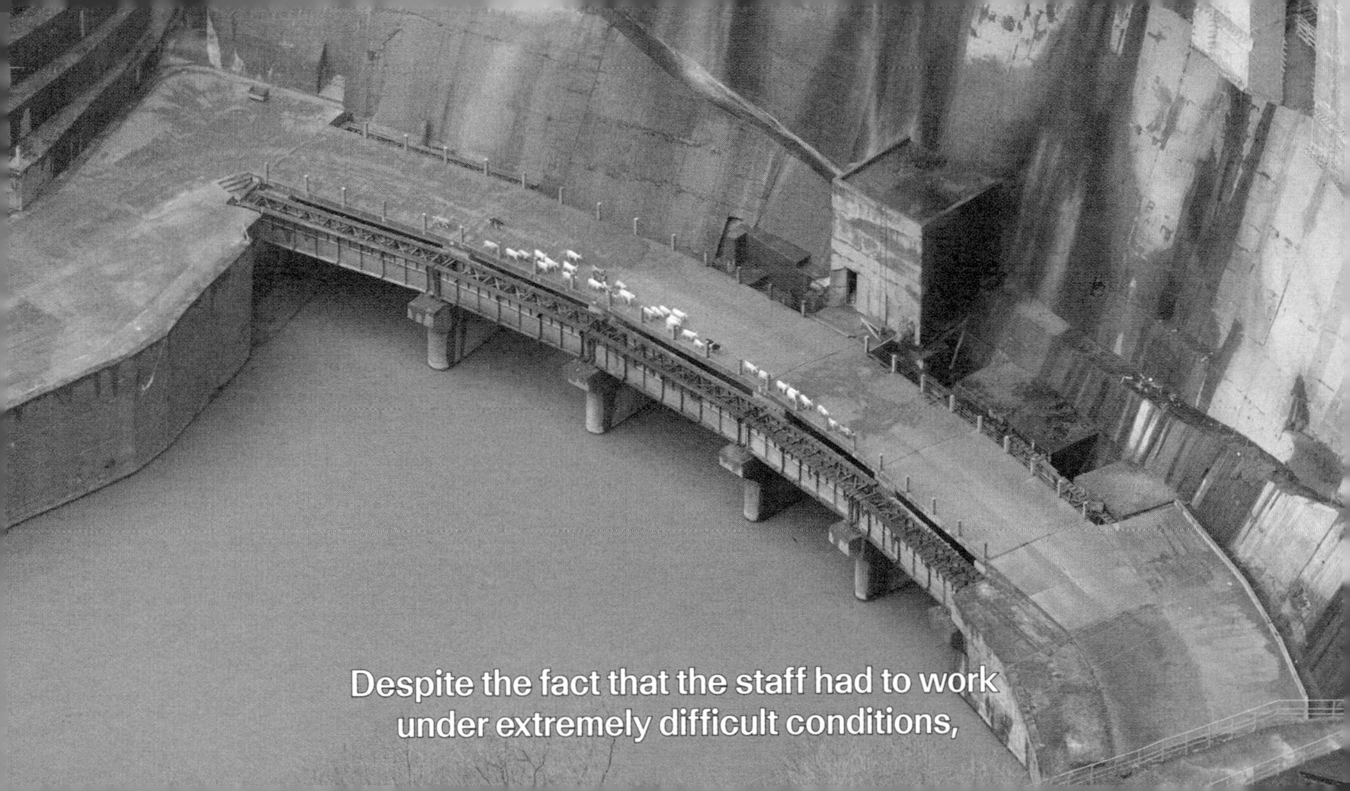

Despite the fact that the staff had to work
under extremely difficult conditions,

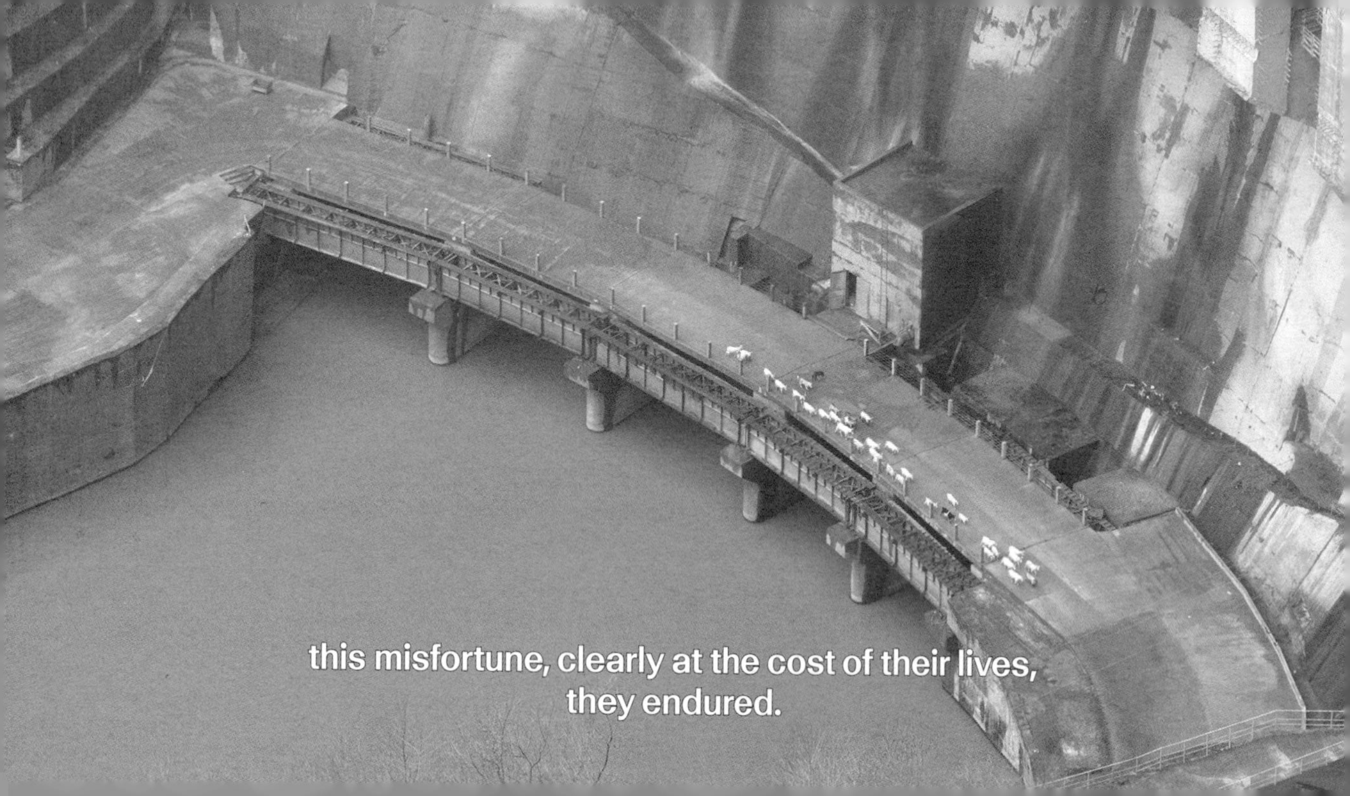

this misfortune, clearly at the cost of their lives,
they endured.

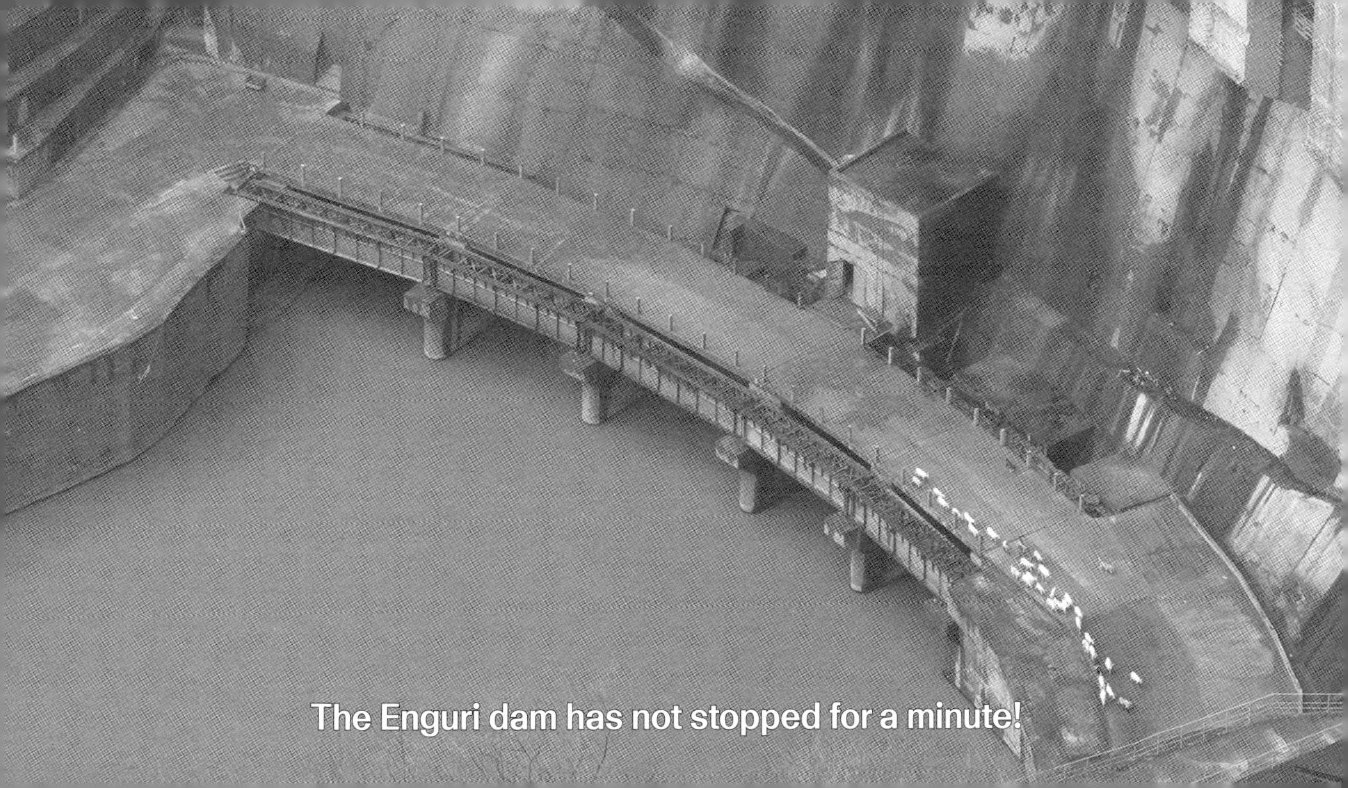

The Enguri dam has not stopped for a minute!

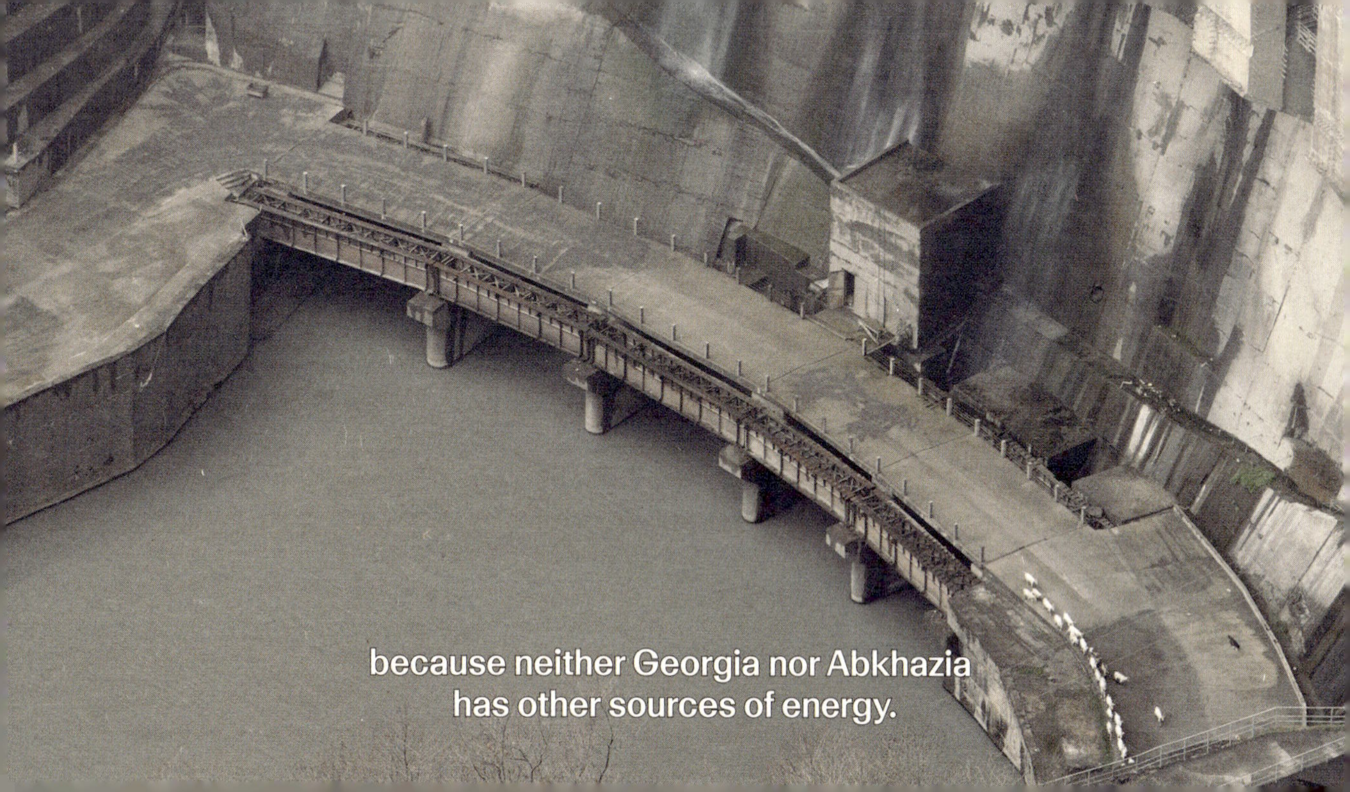
because neither Georgia nor Abkhazia
has other sources of energy.

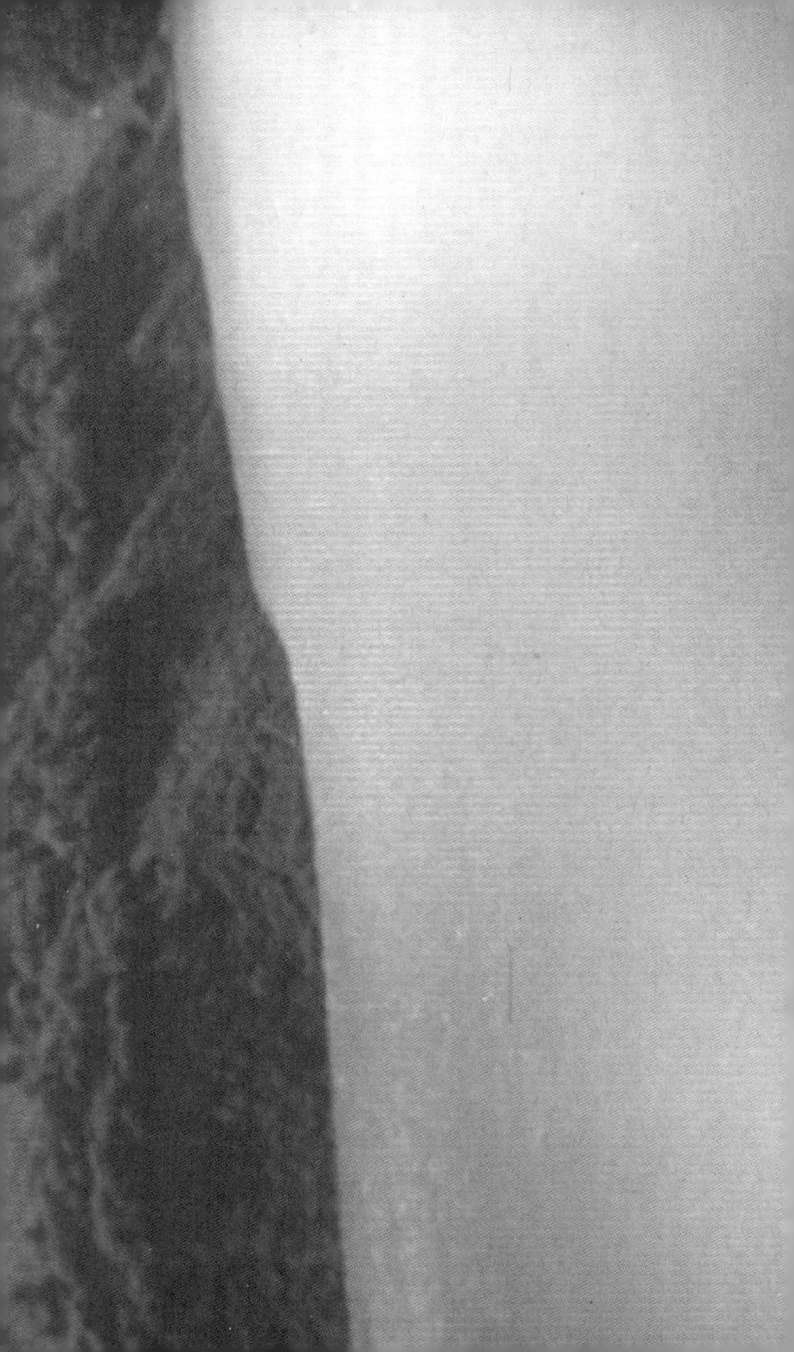

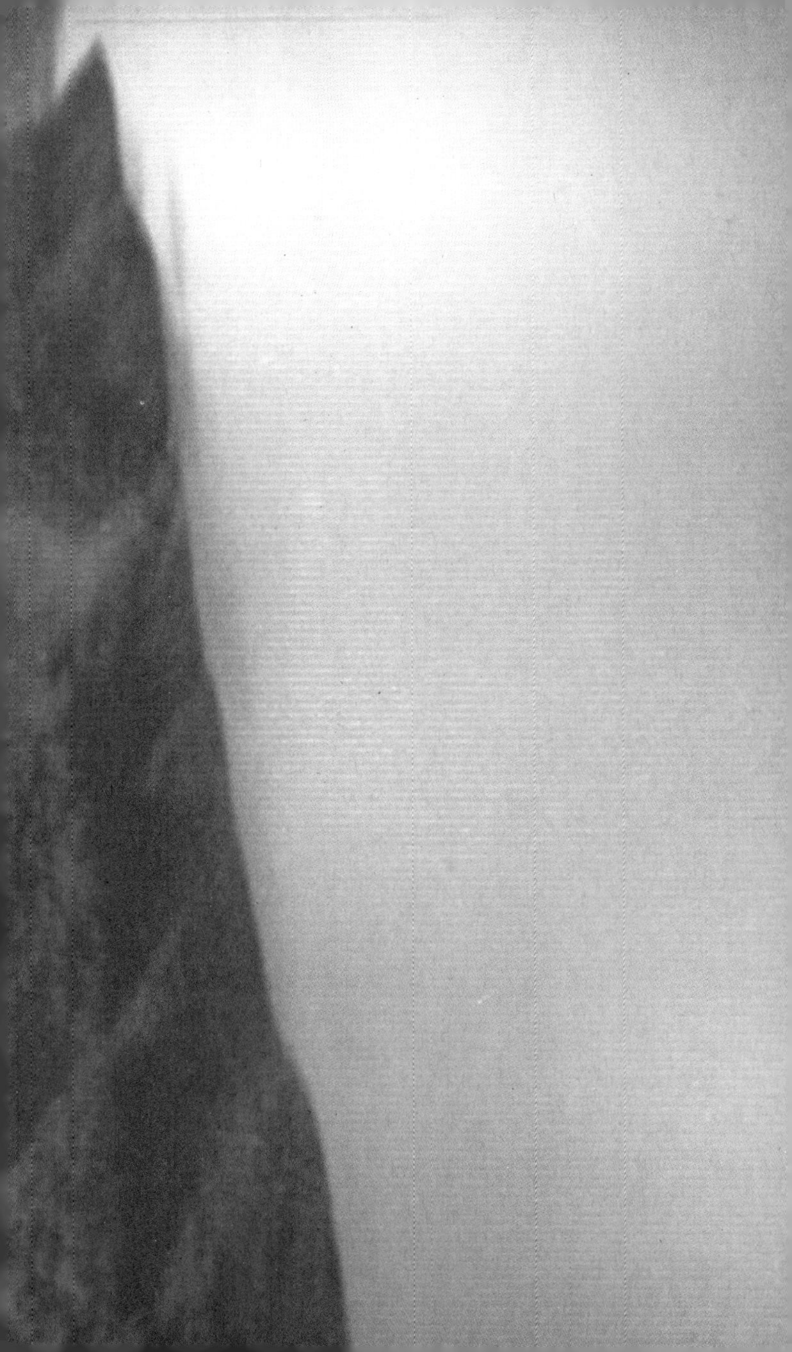

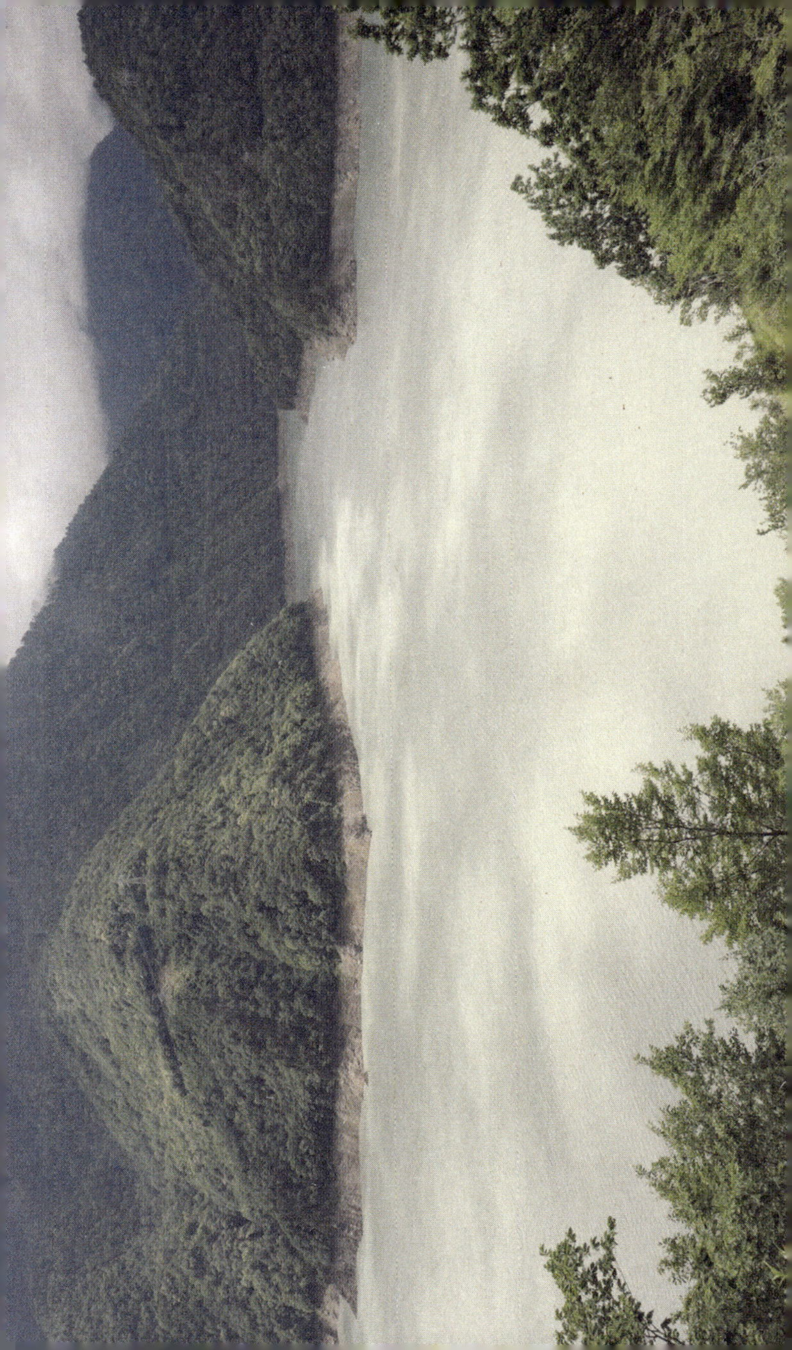

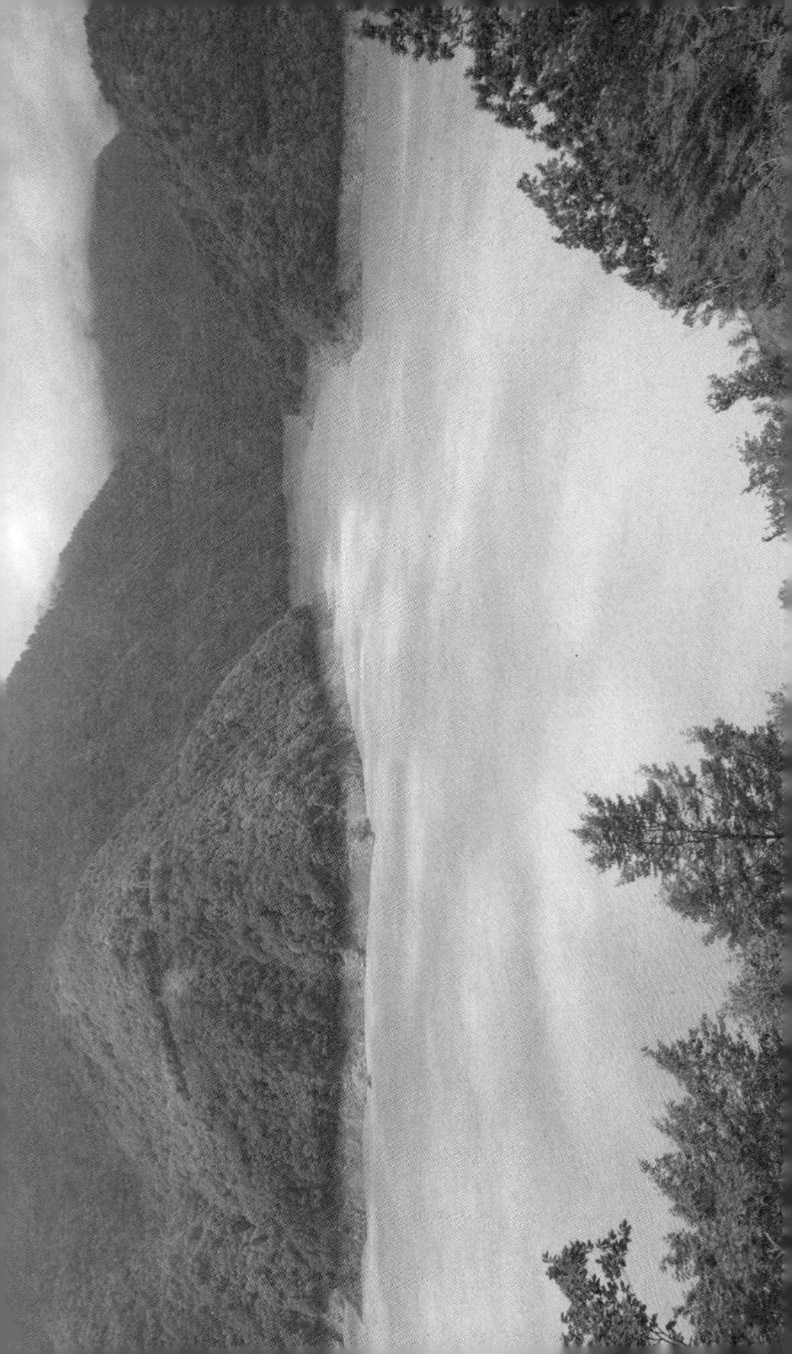

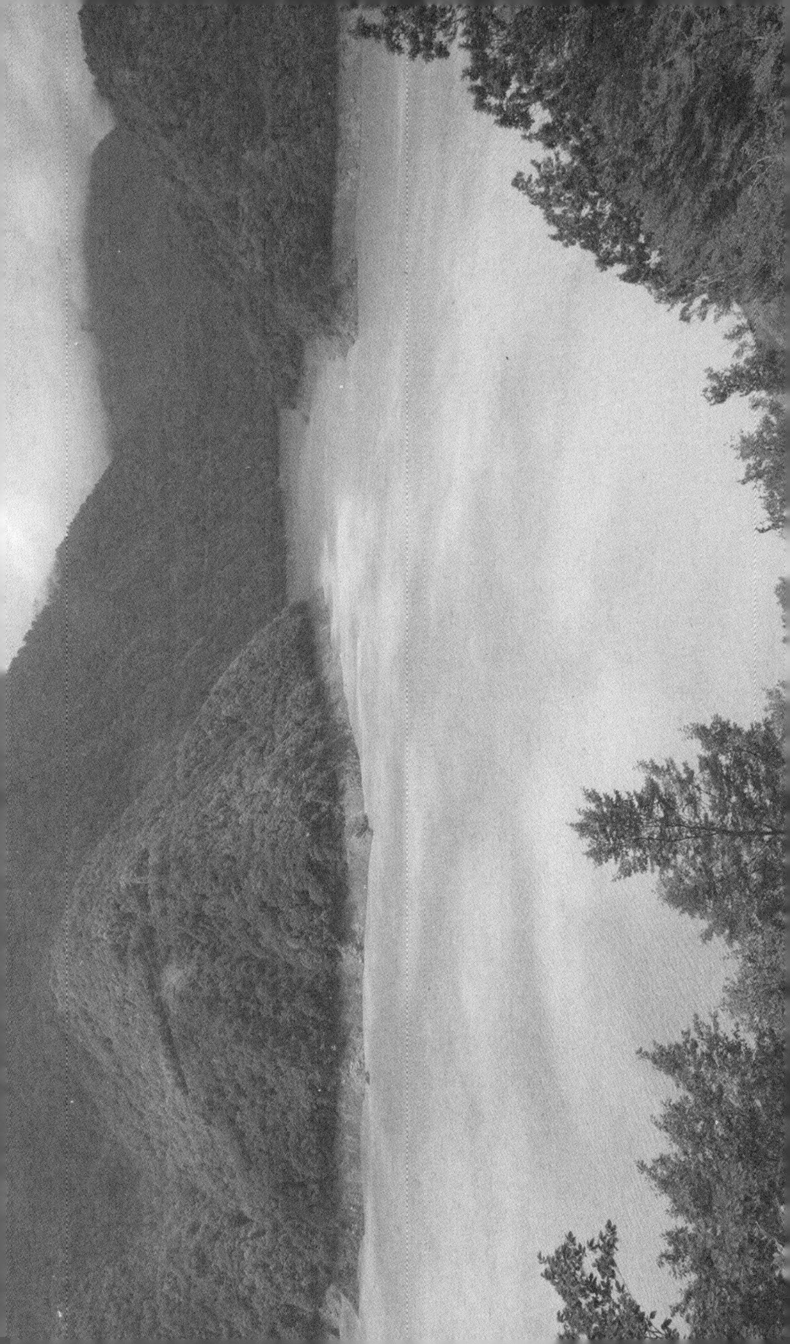

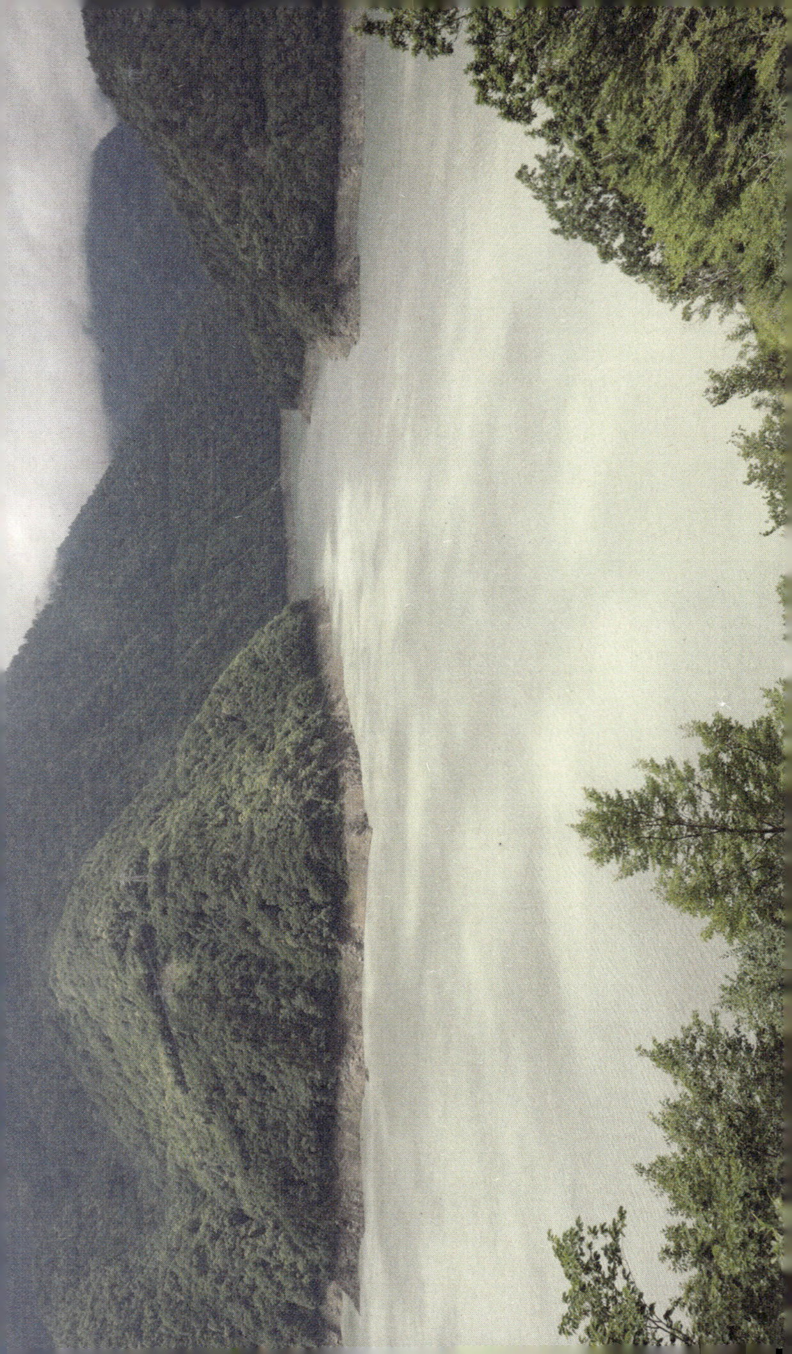

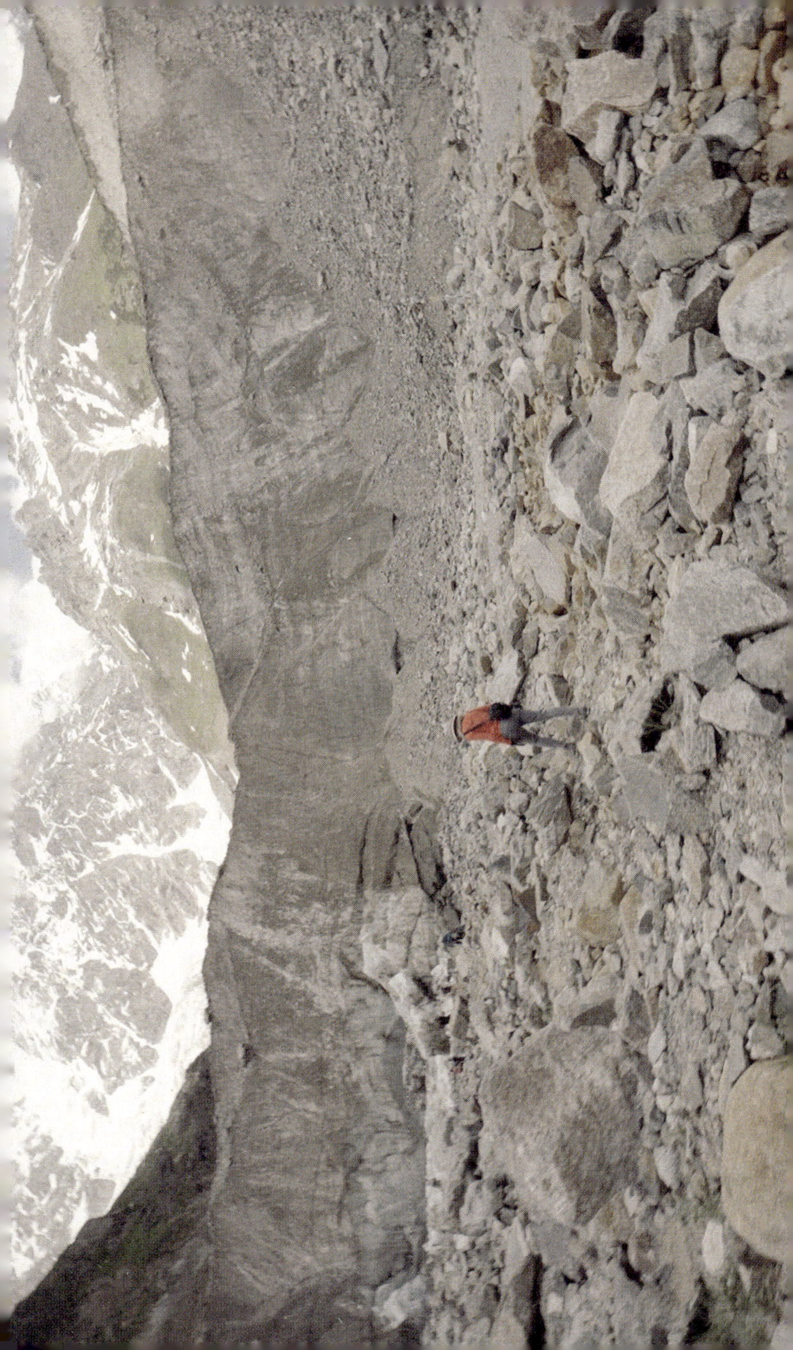

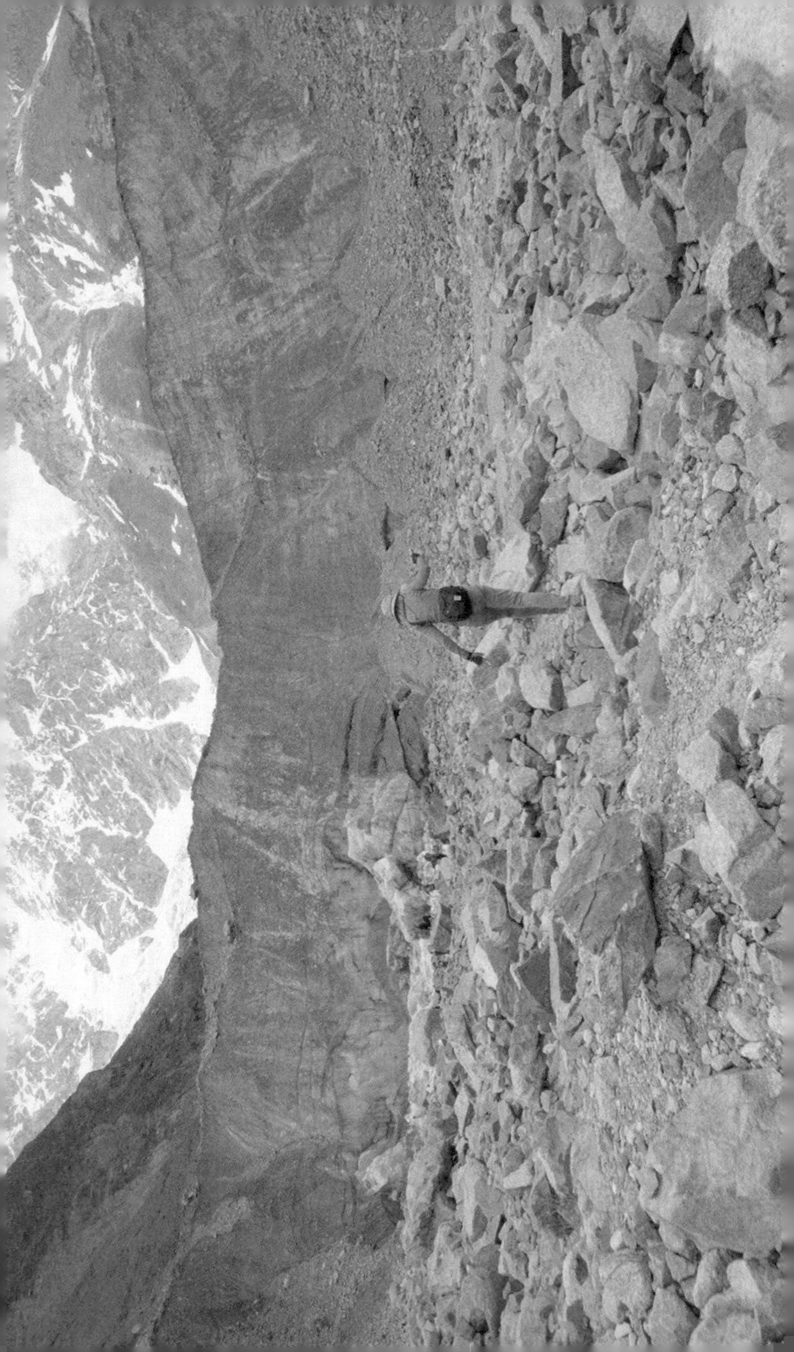

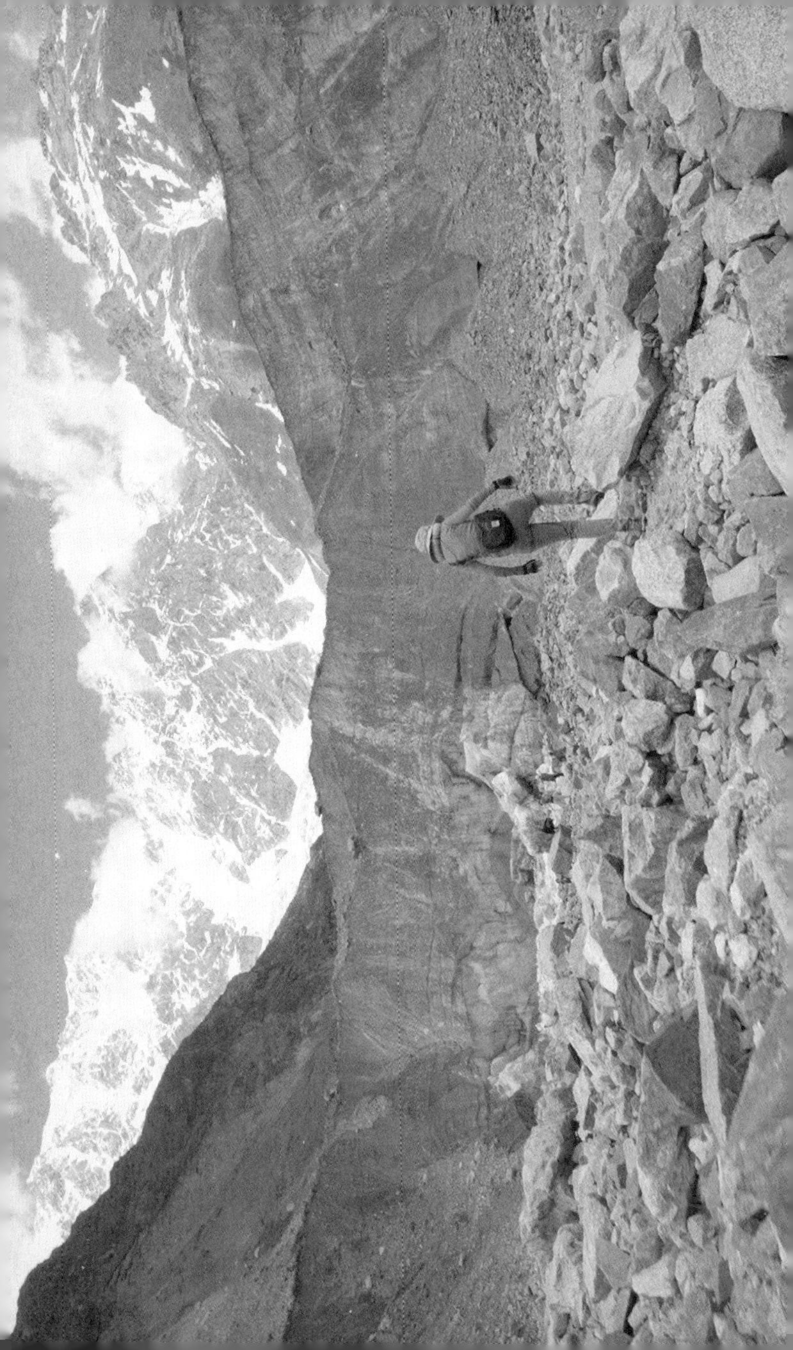

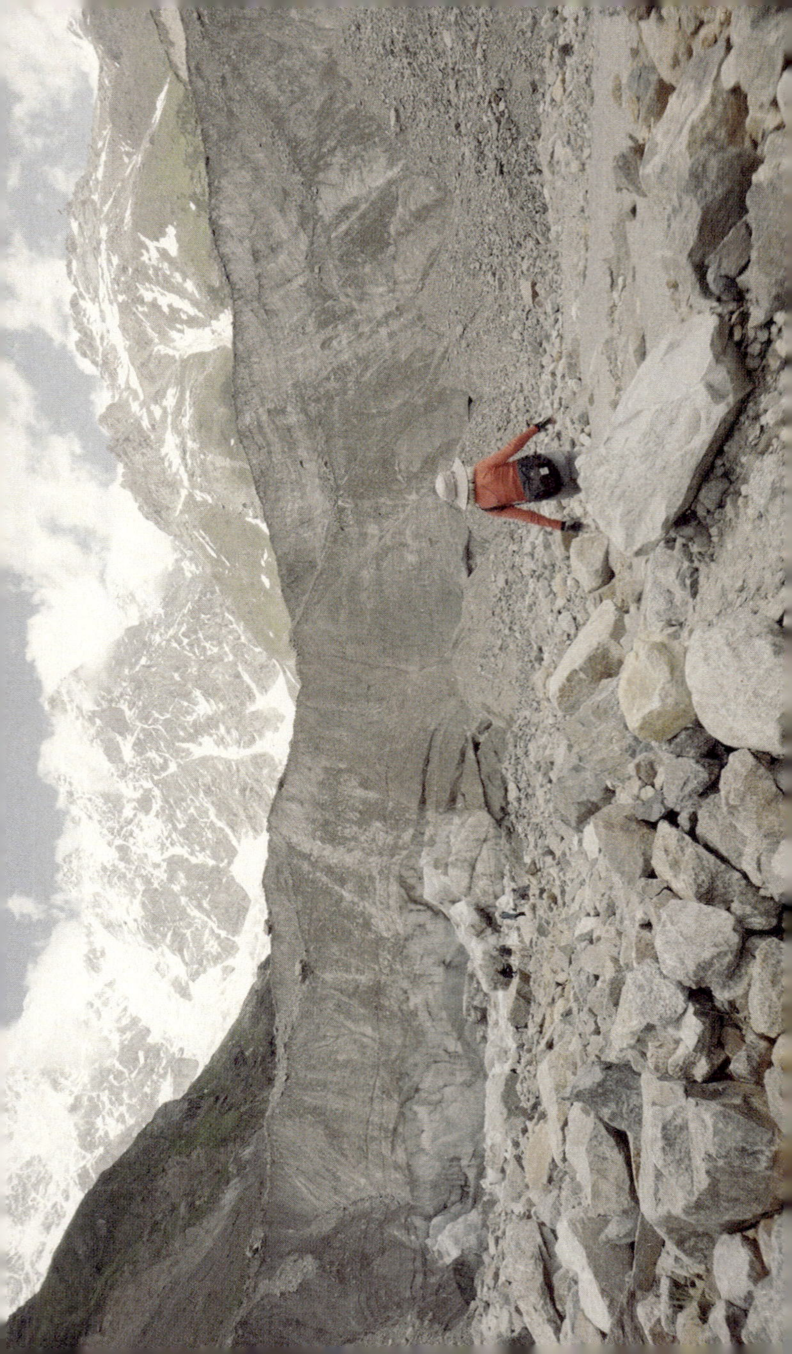

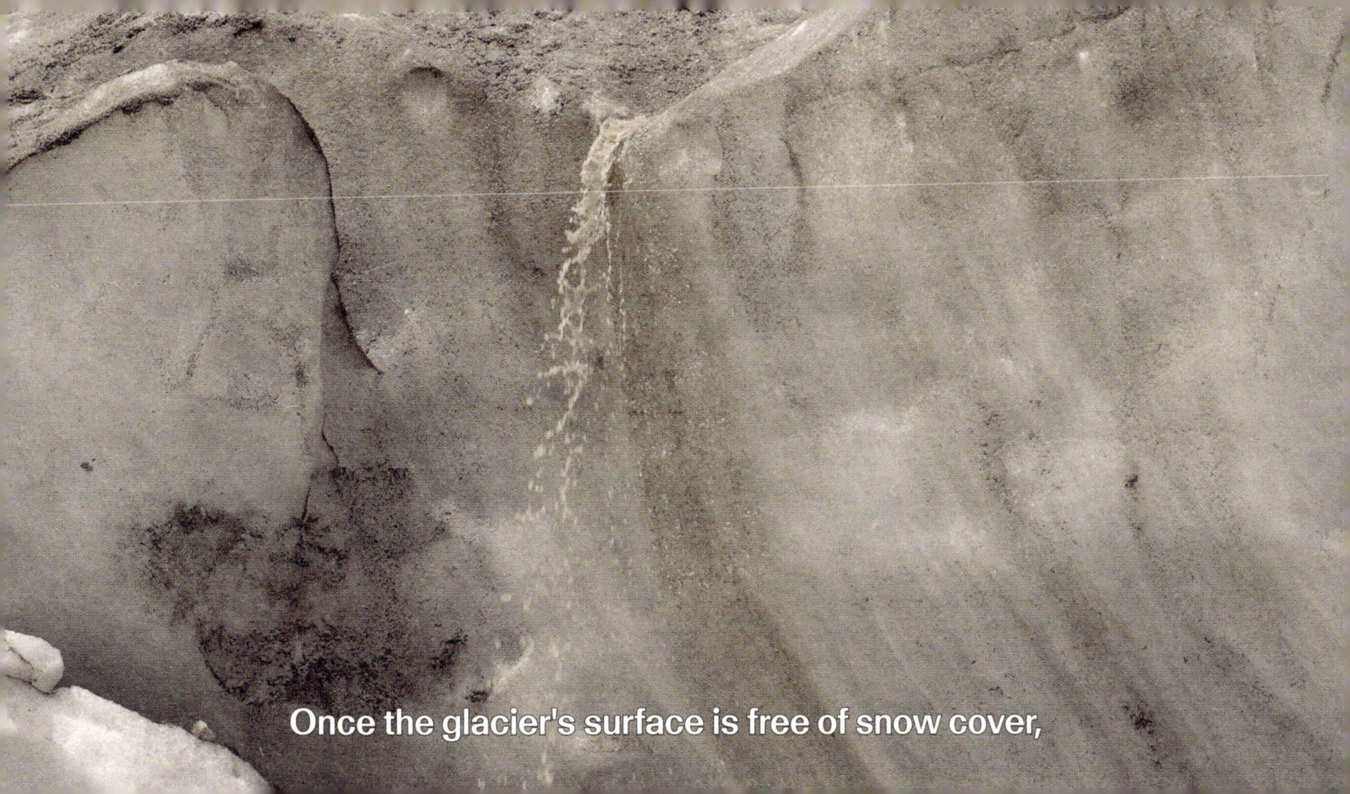

Once the glacier's surface is free of snow cover,

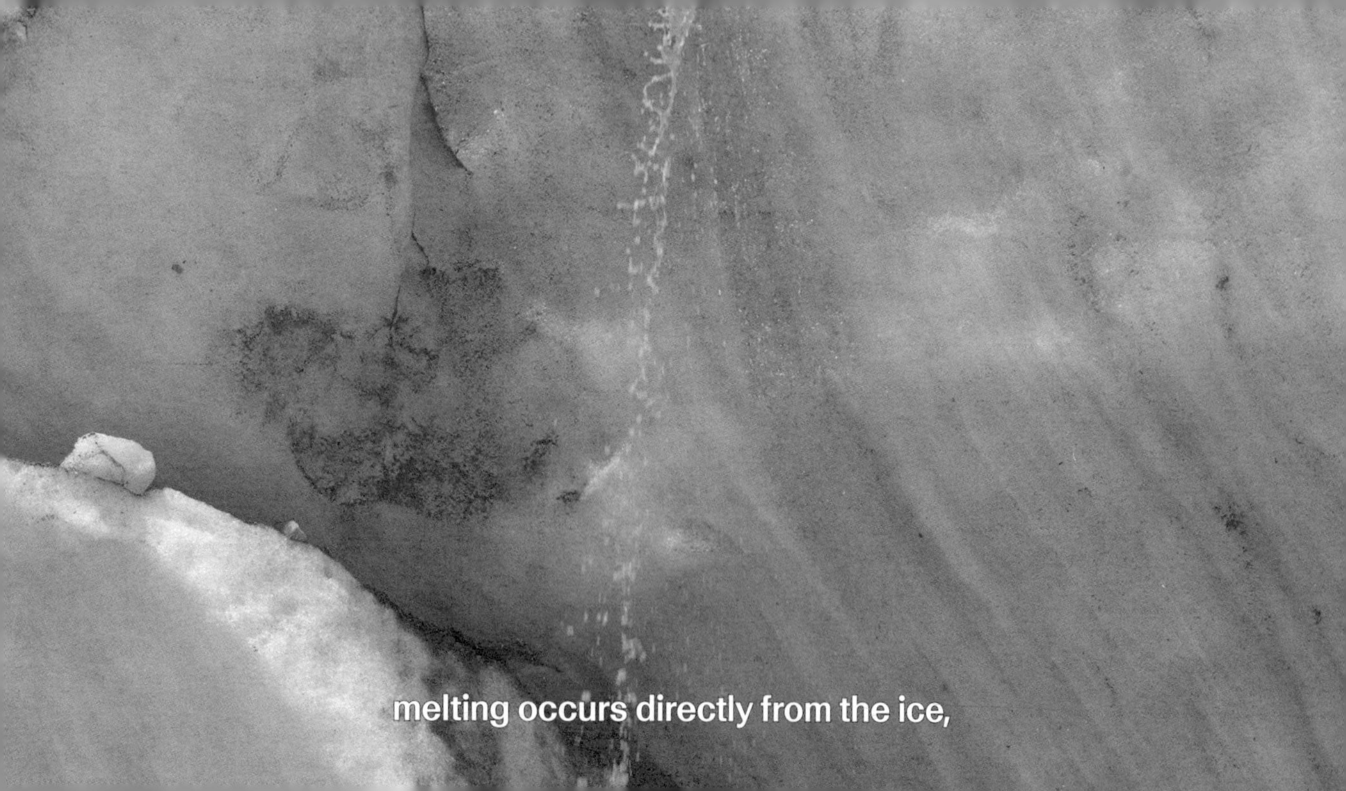
melting occurs directly from the ice,

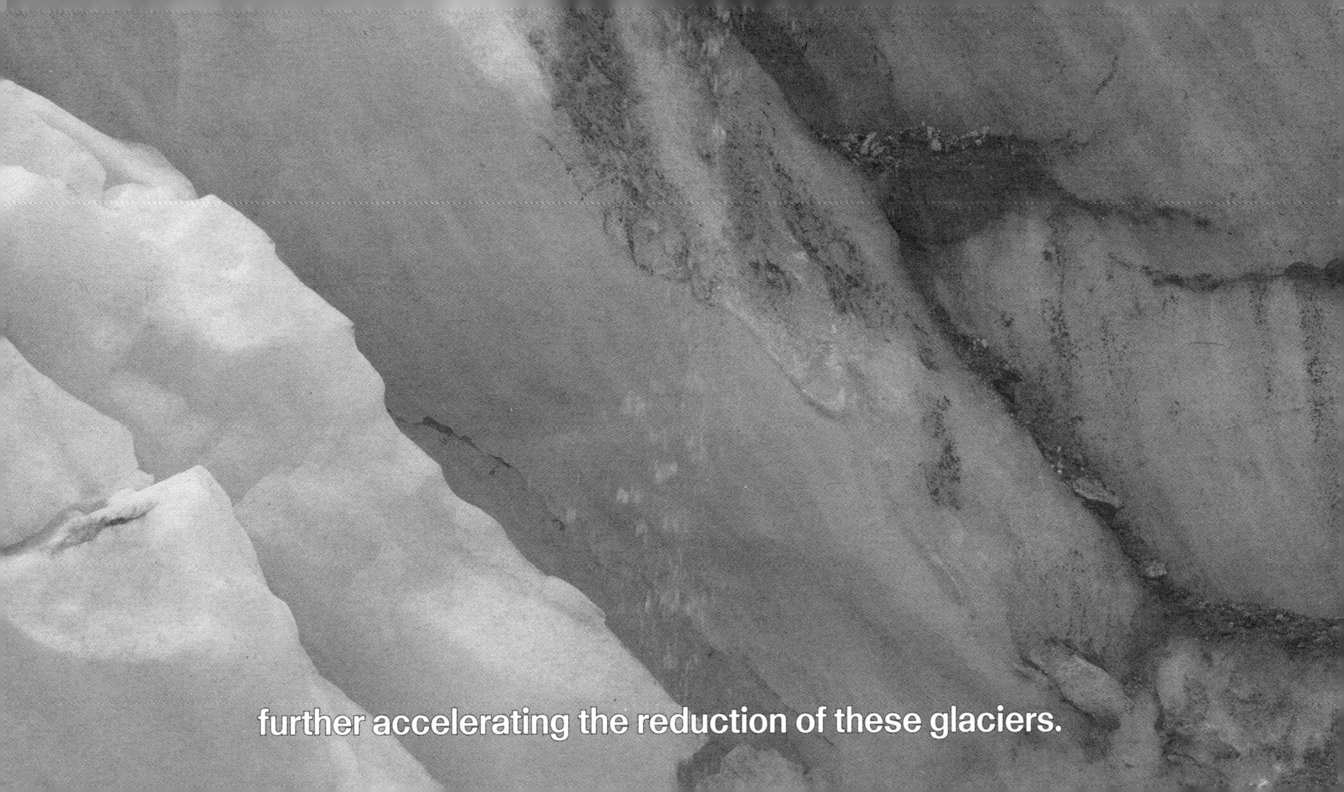

further accelerating the reduction of these glaciers.

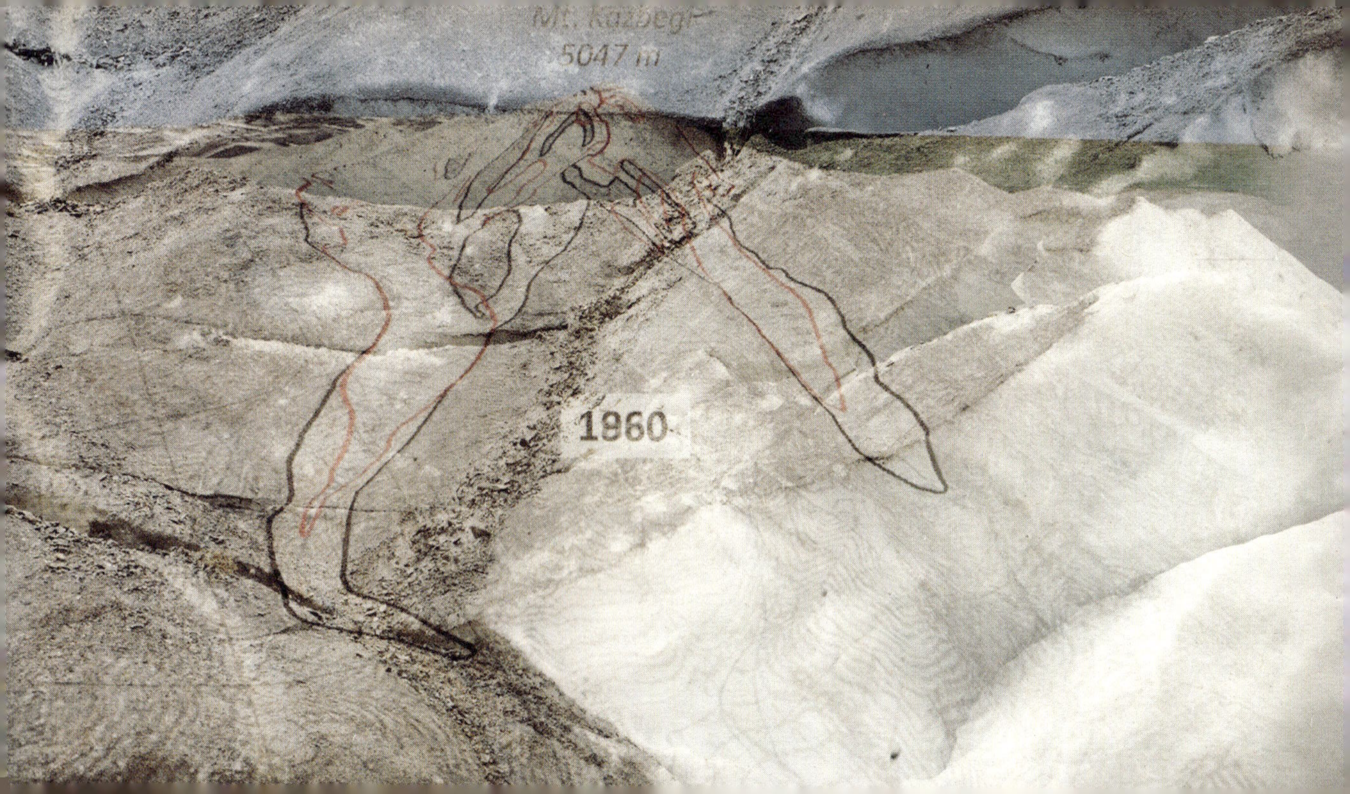

Mt. Kazbeg-
5047 m
1960

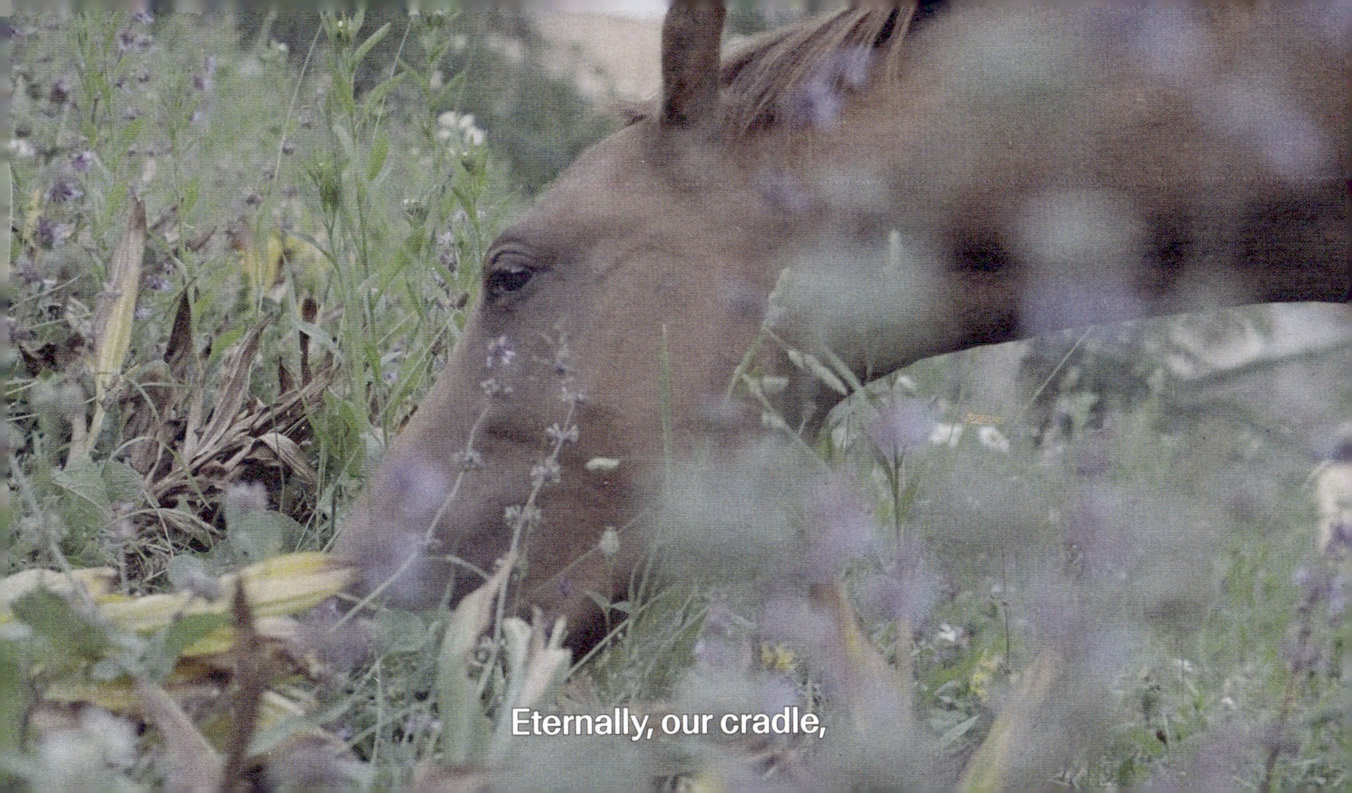
Eternally, our cradle,

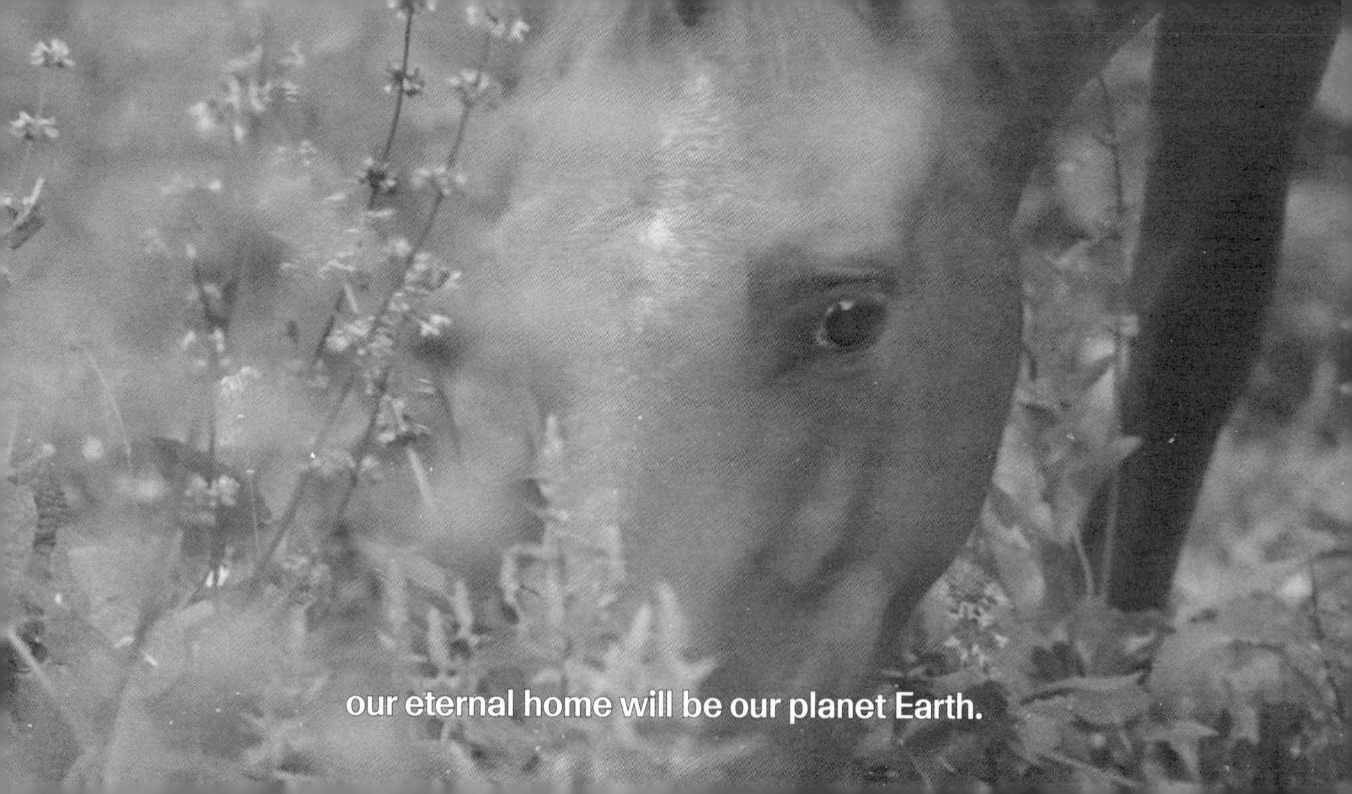
our eternal home will be our planet Earth.

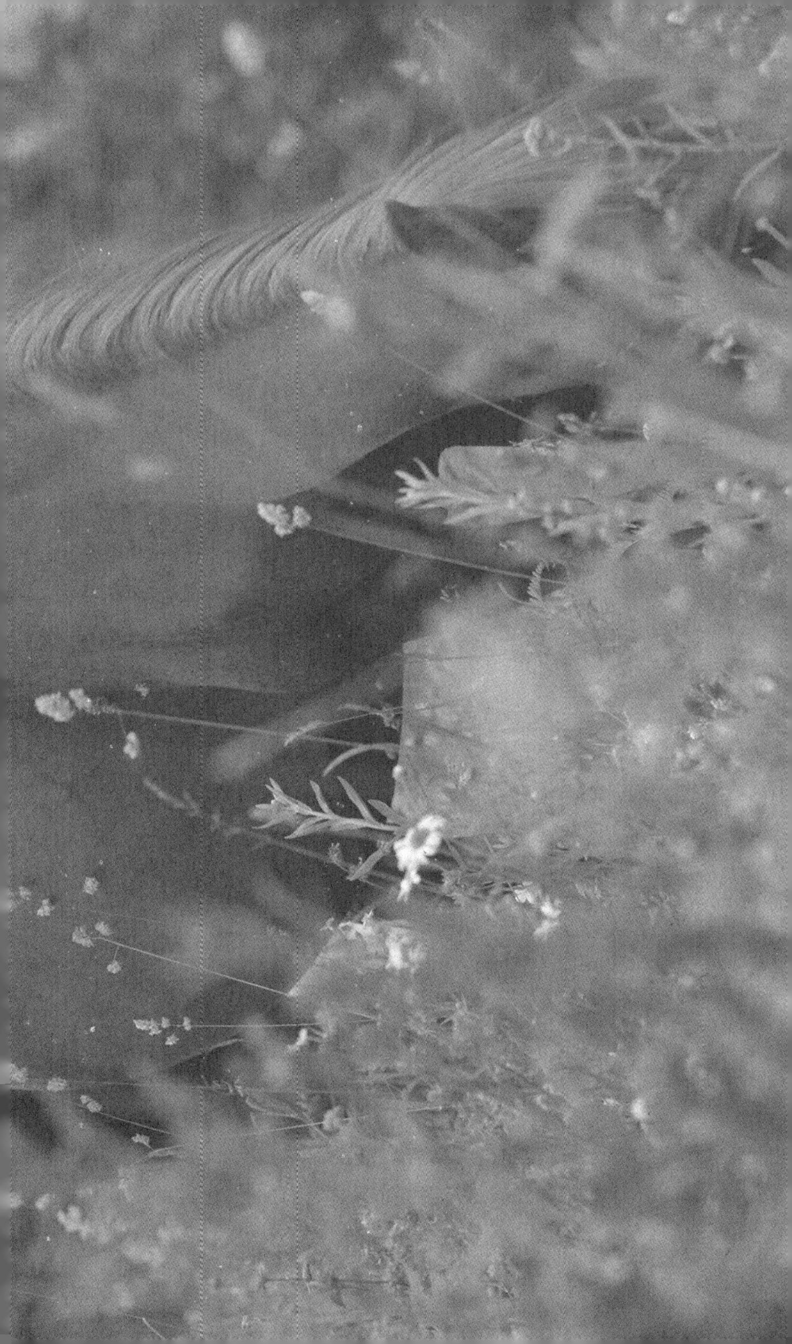

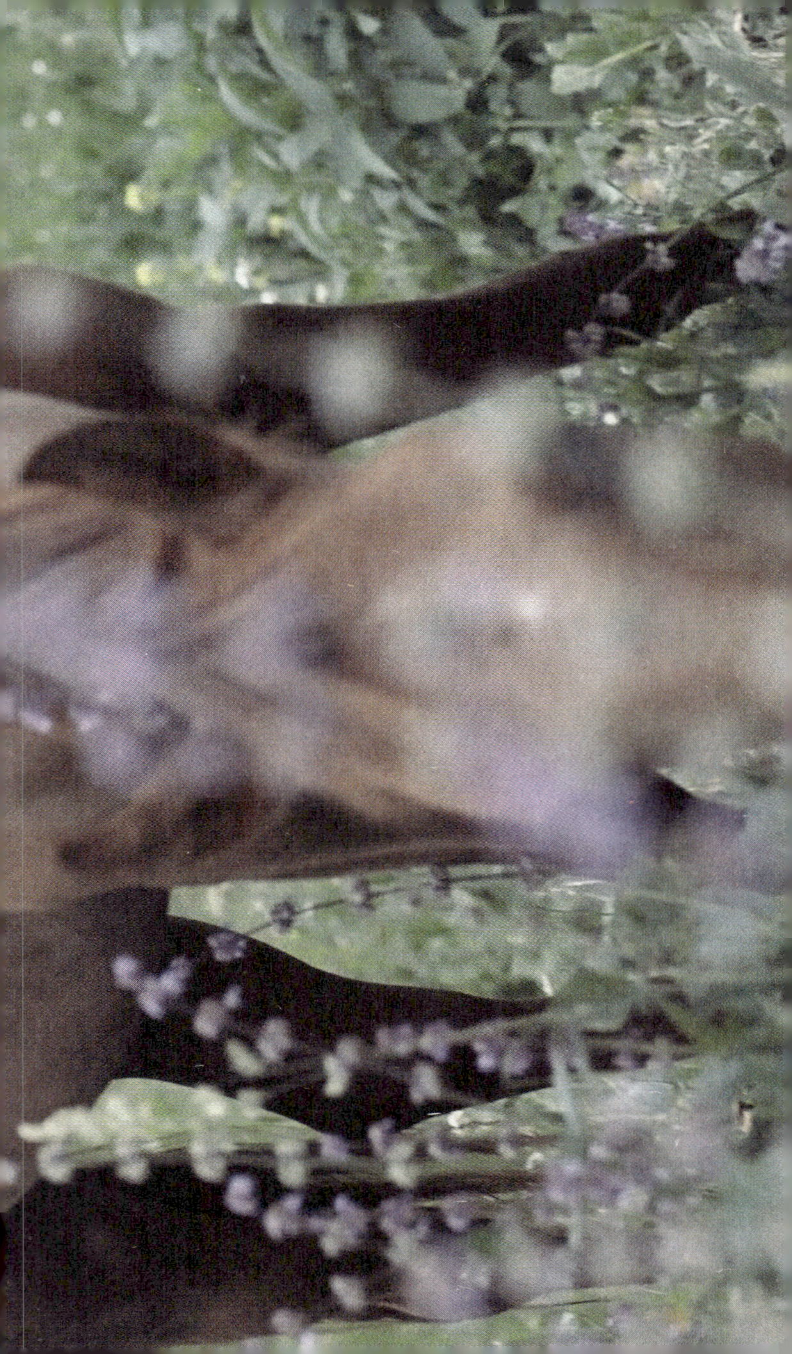

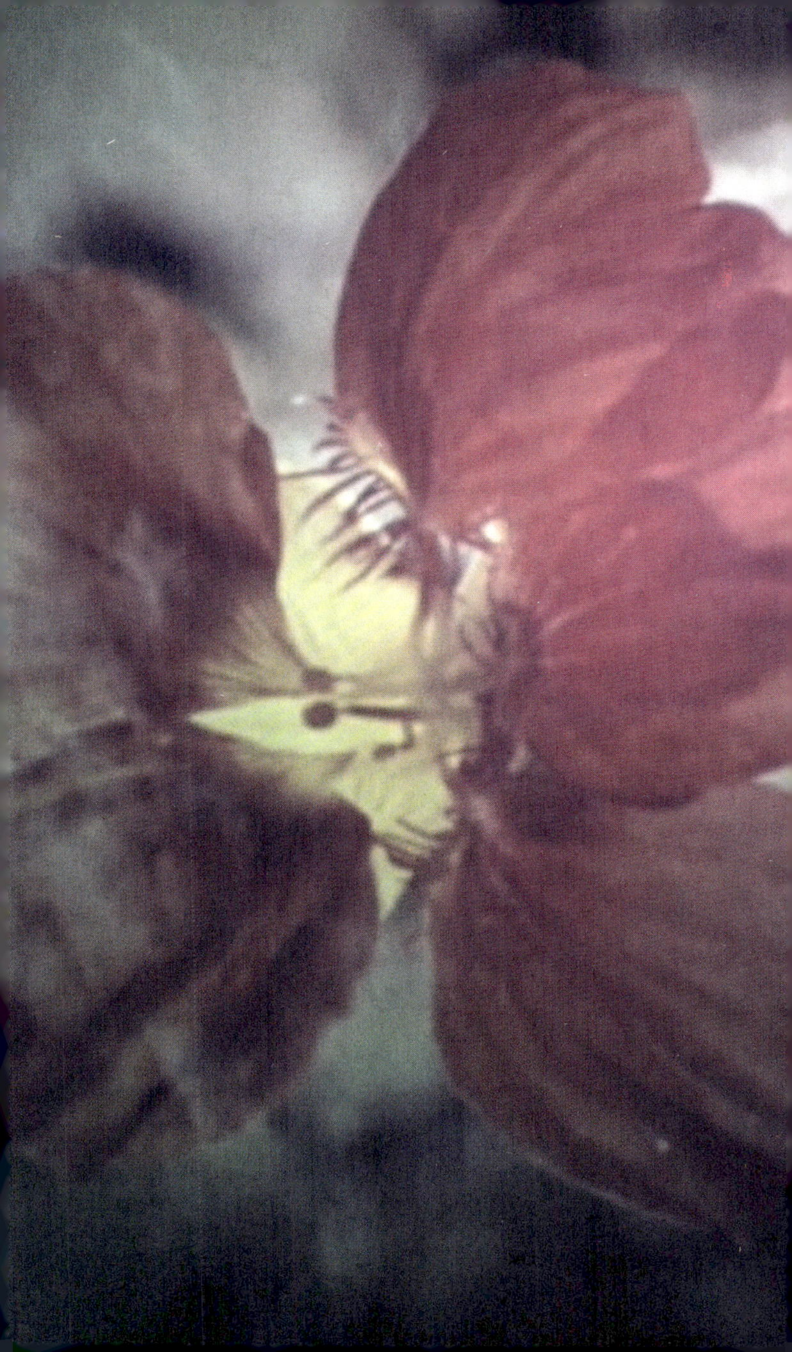

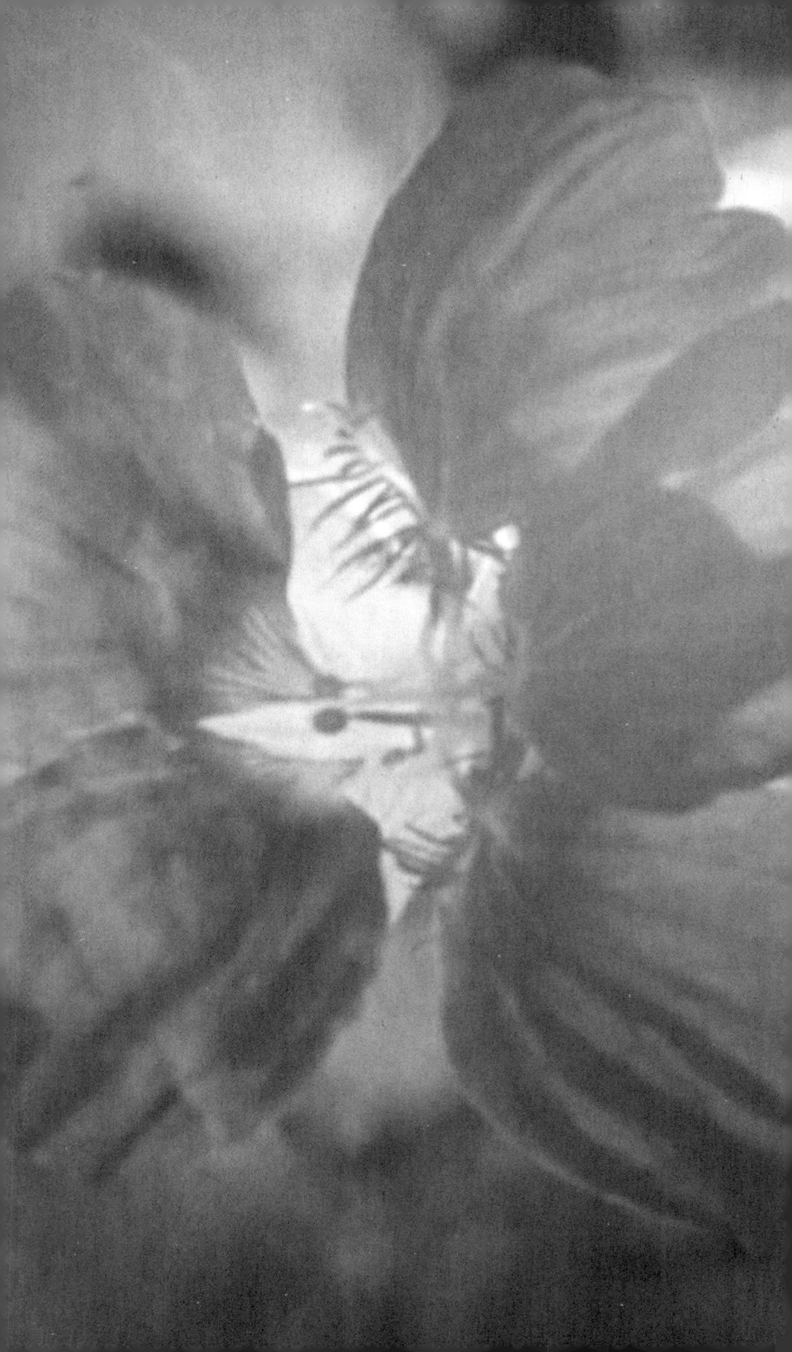

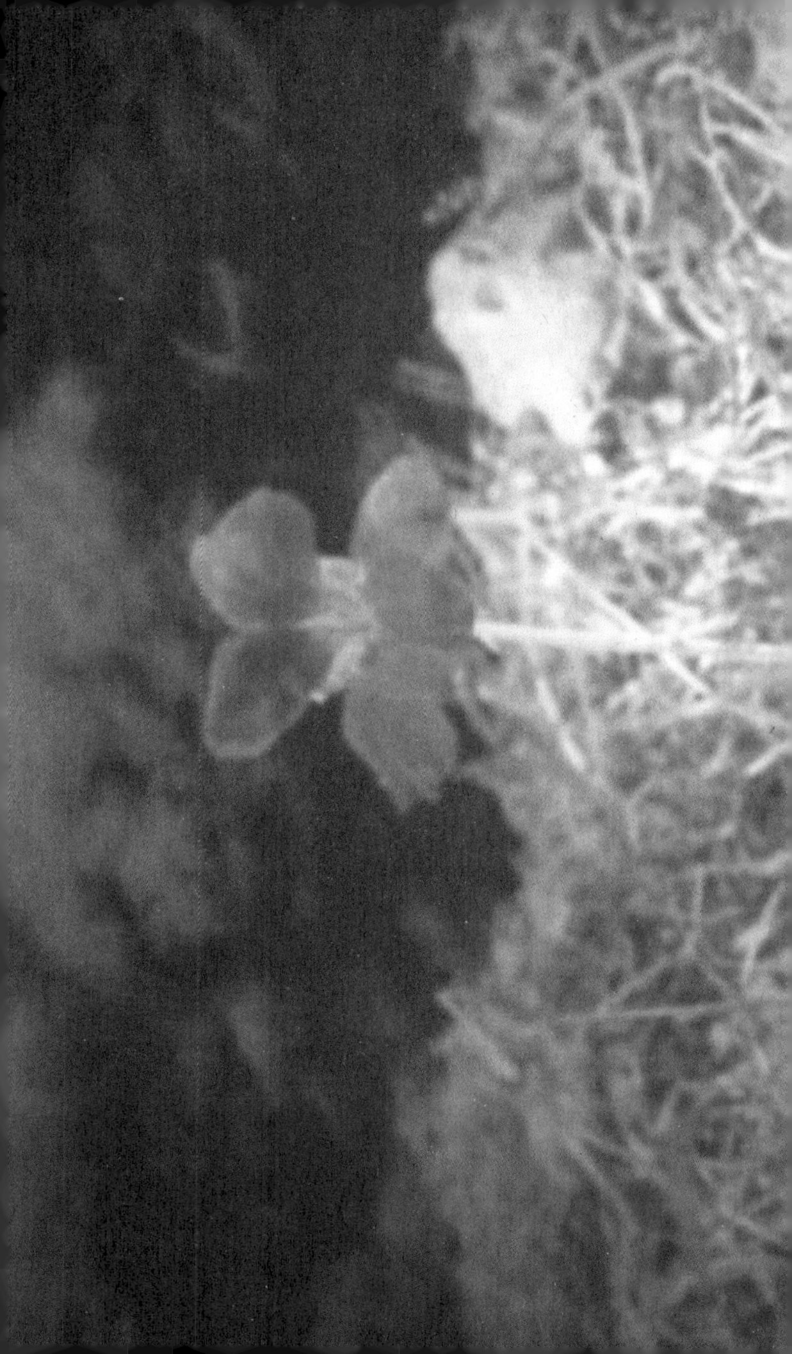

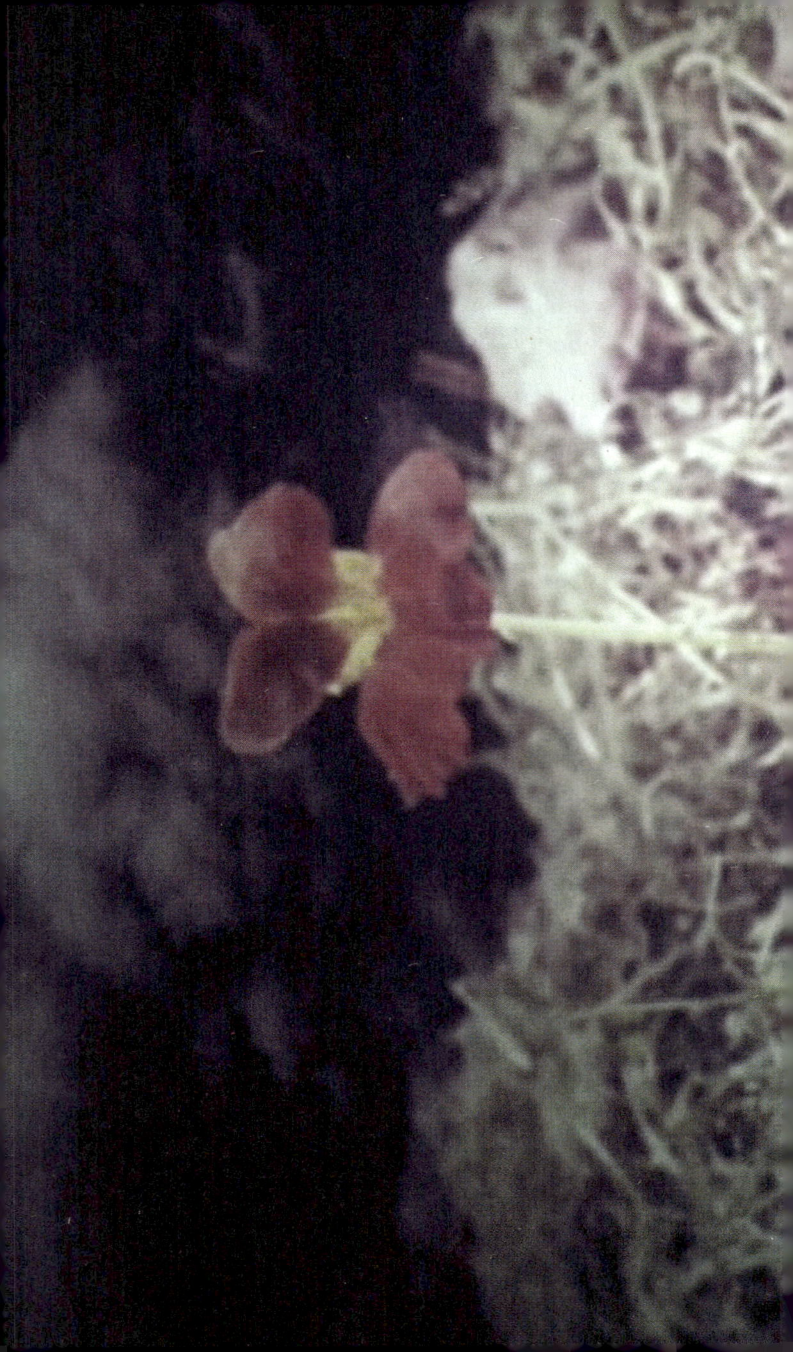

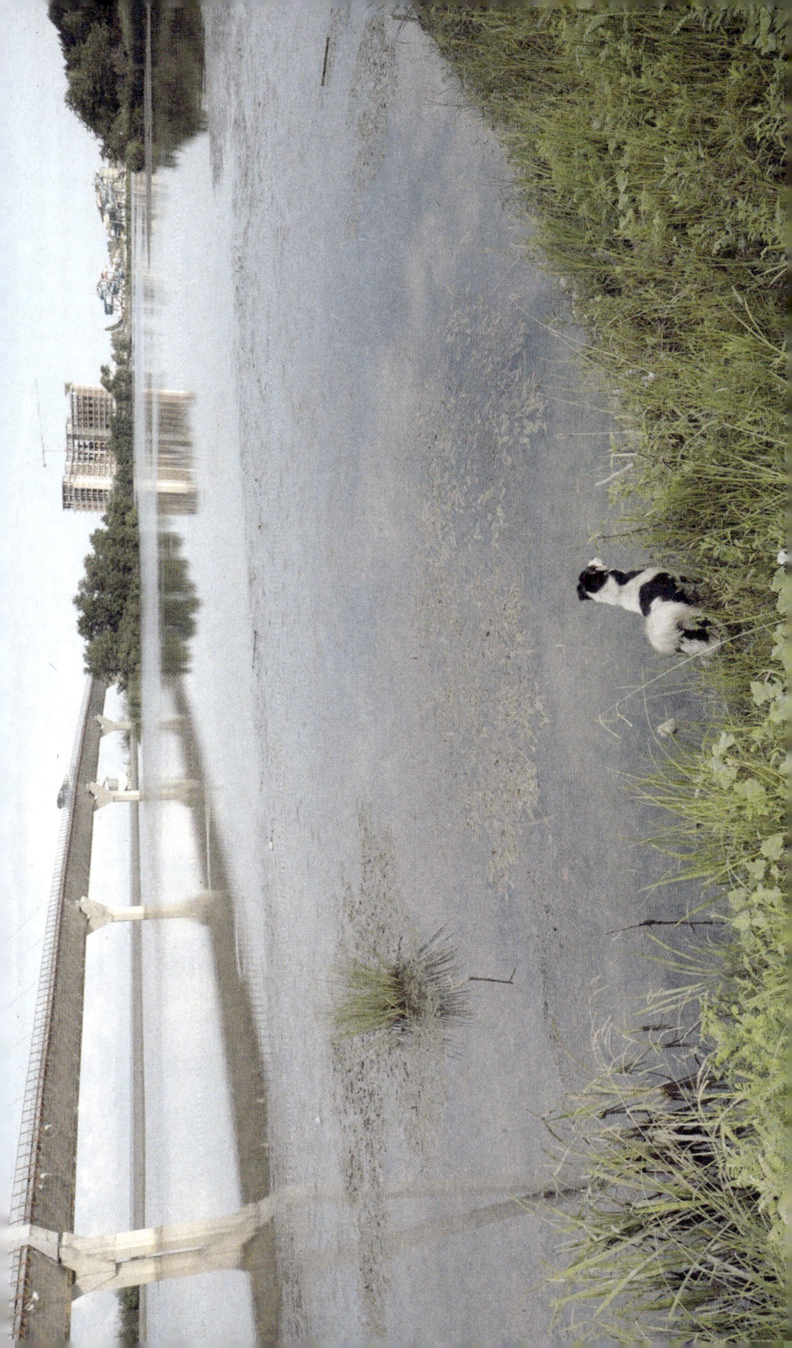

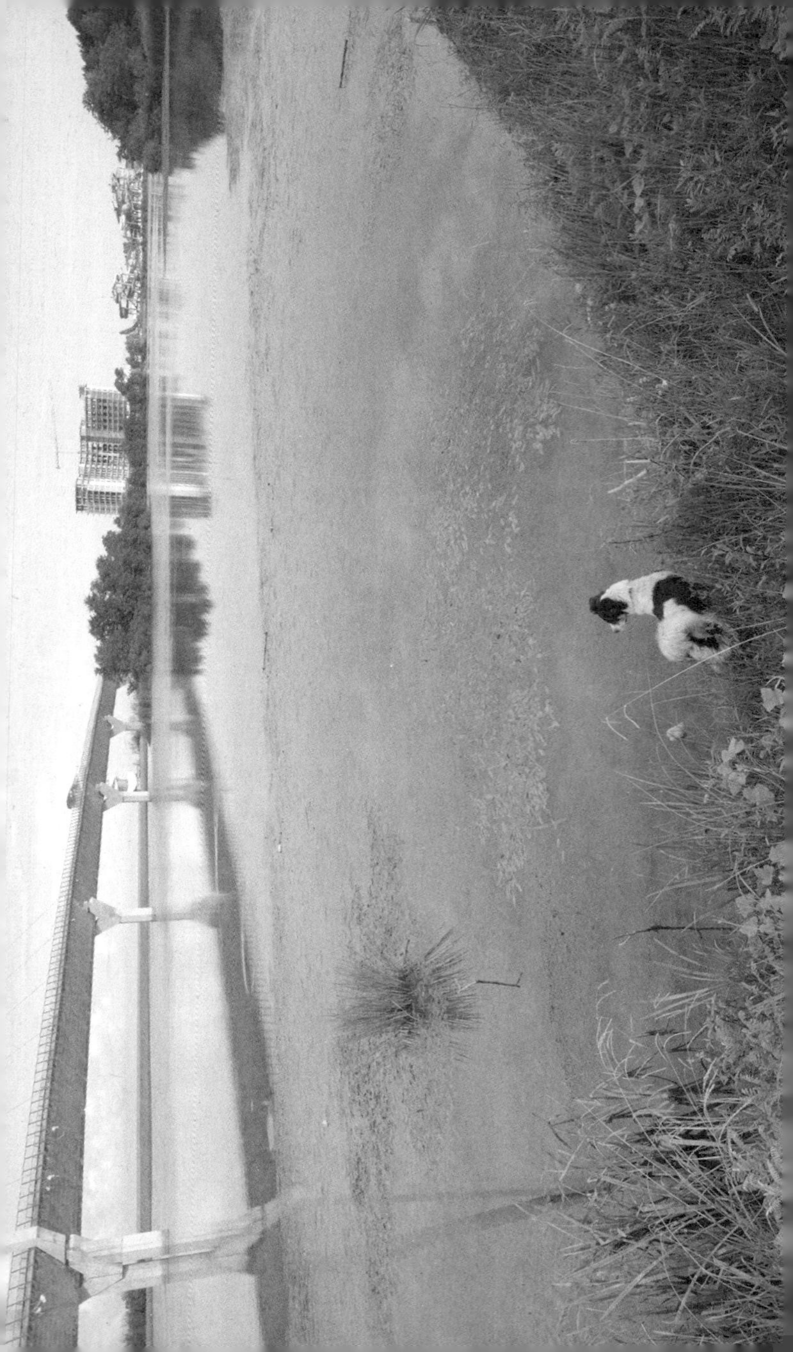

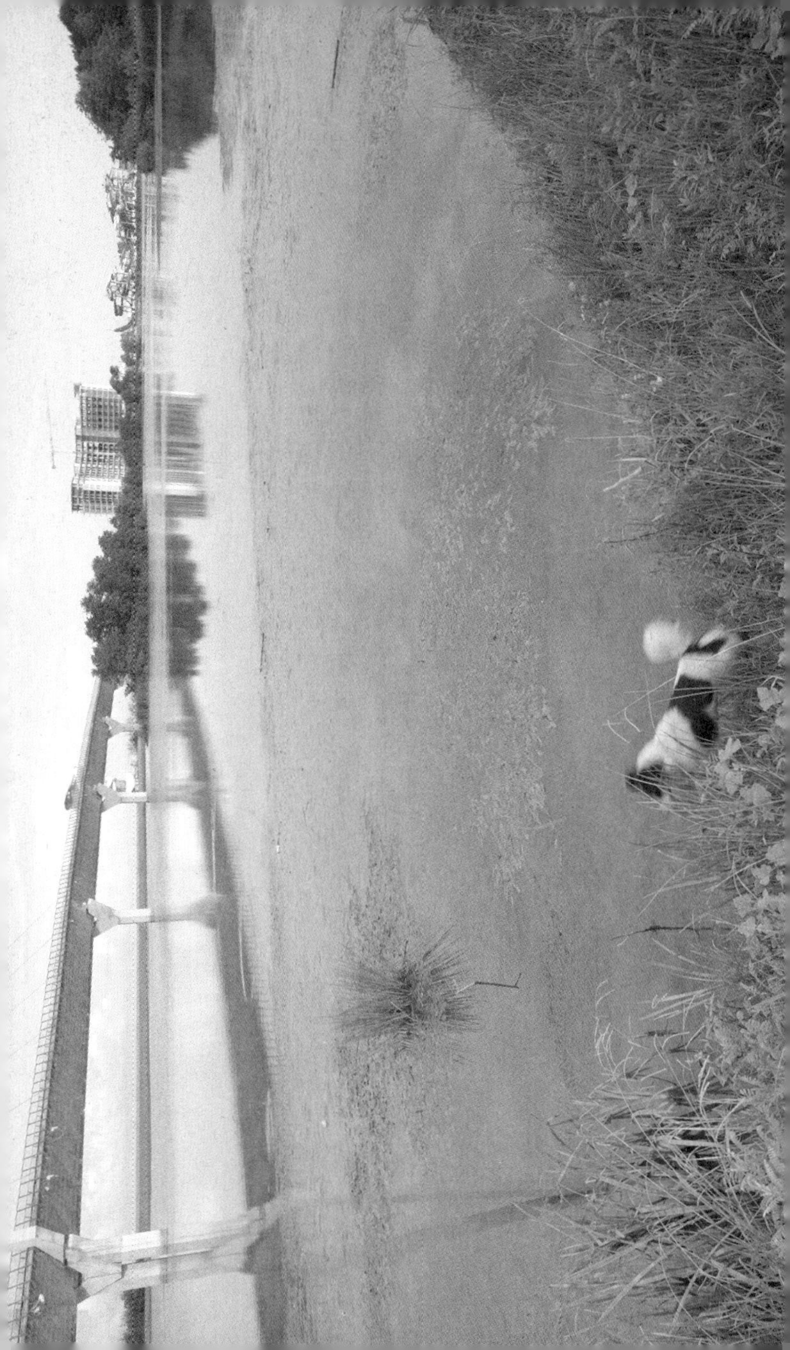

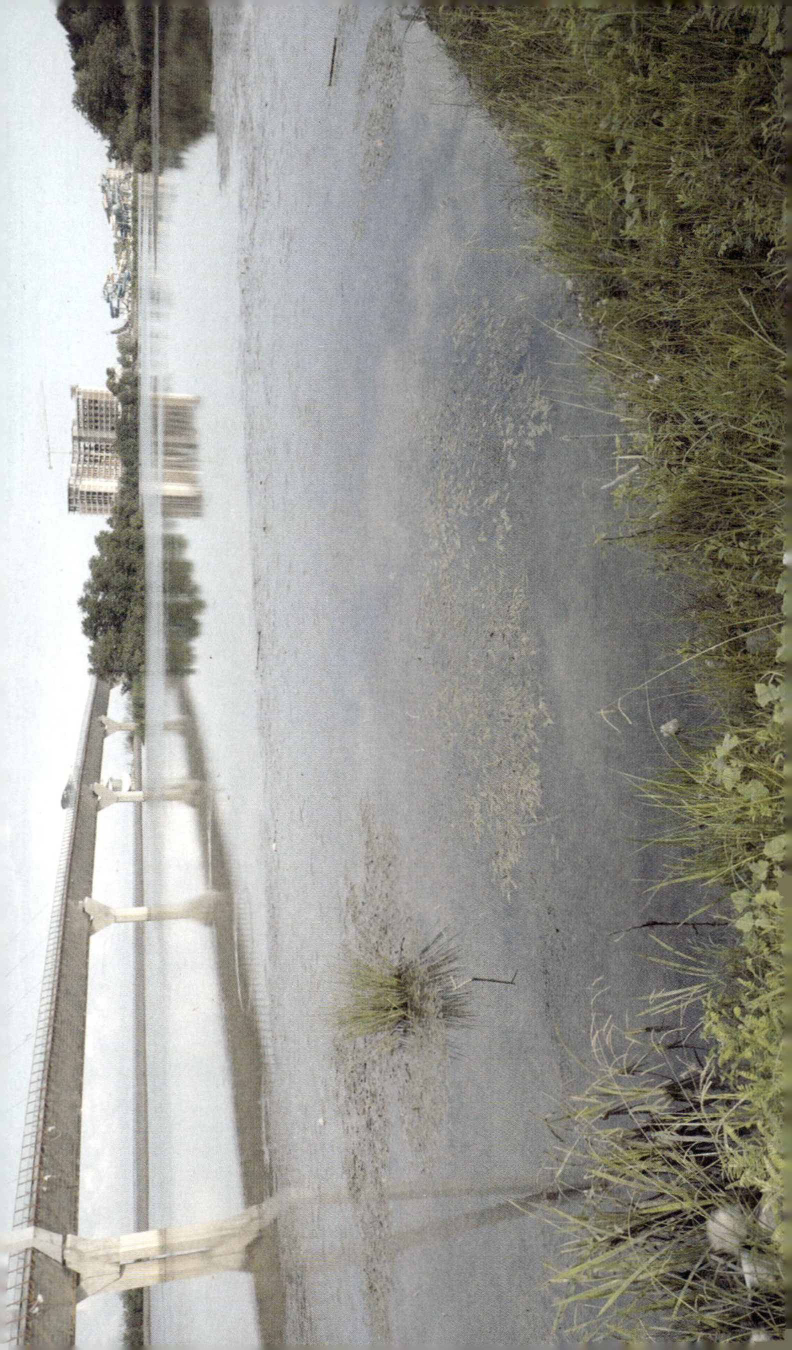

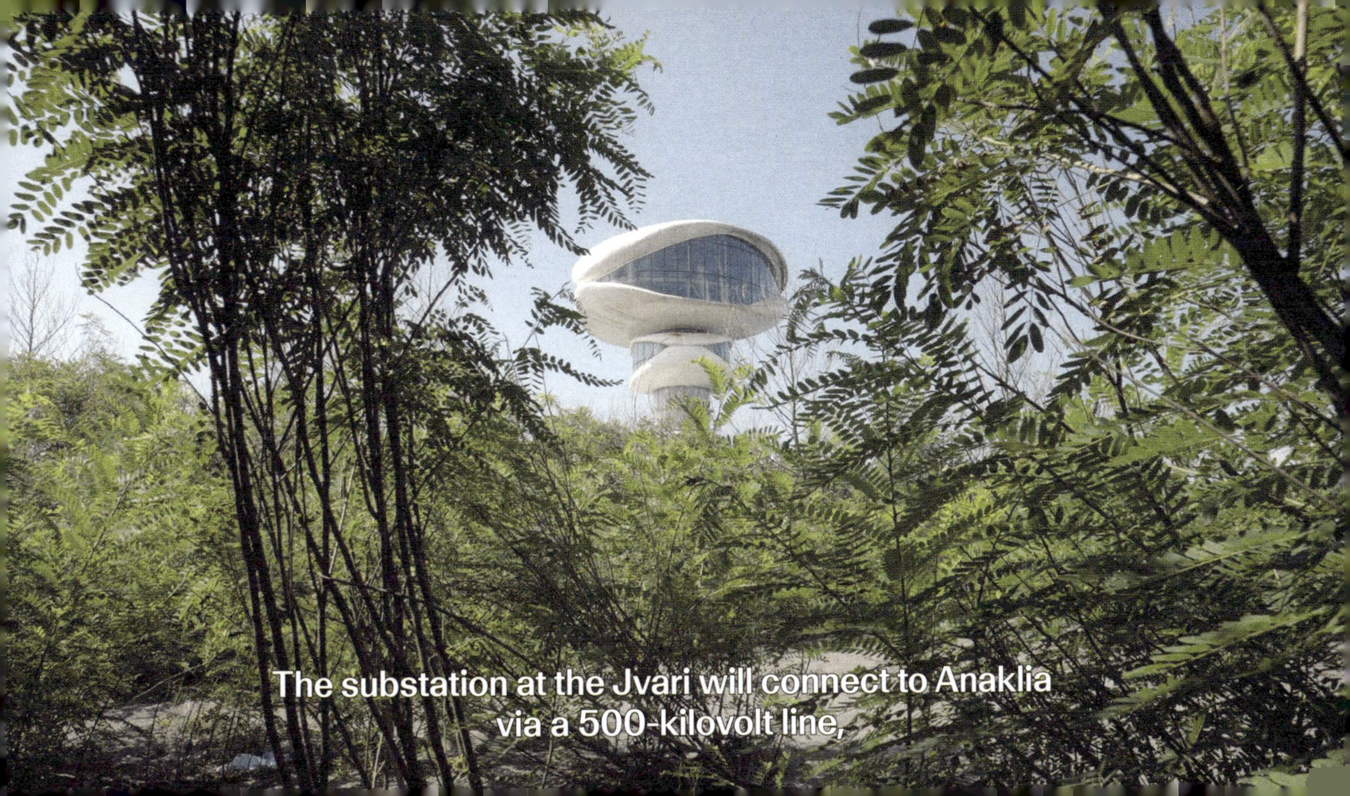
The substation at the Jvari will connect to Anaklia
via a 500-kilovolt line,

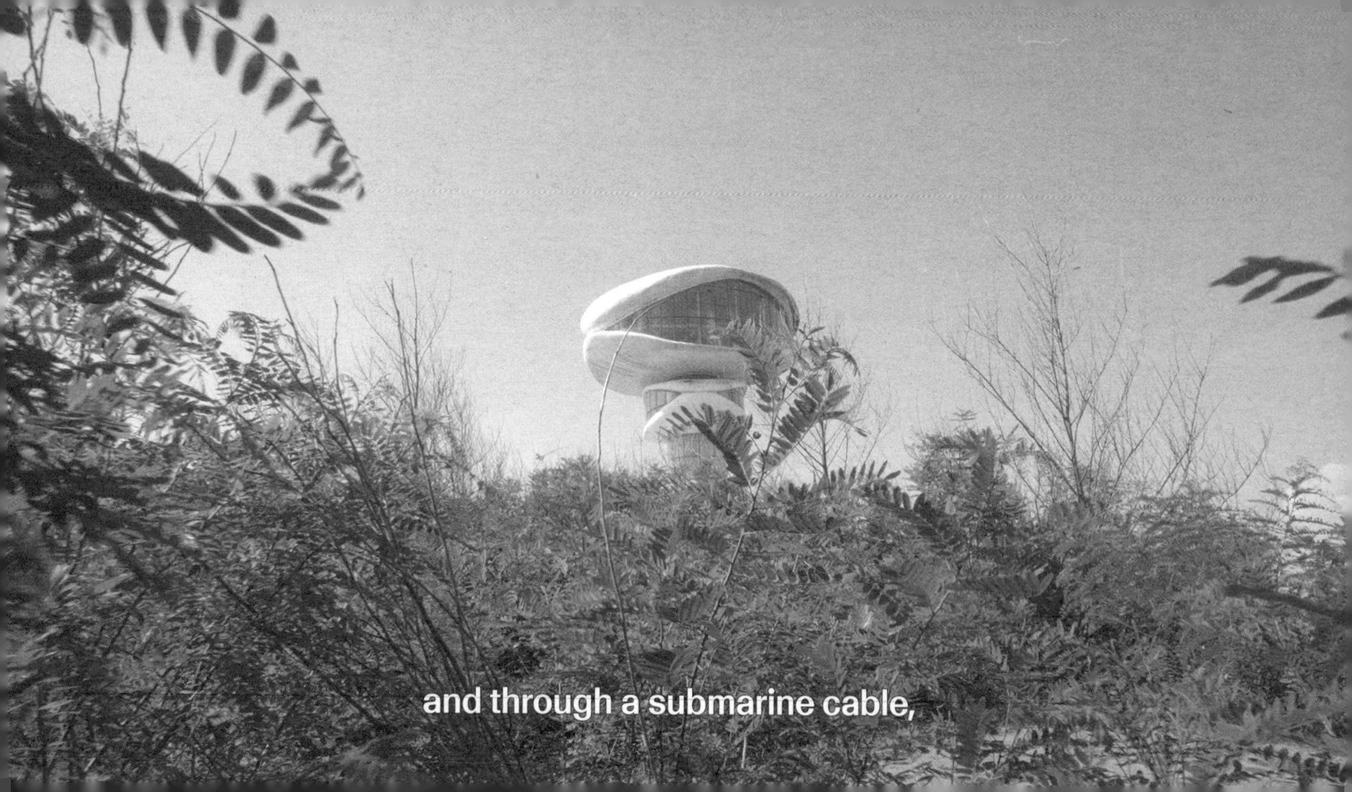

and through a submarine cable,

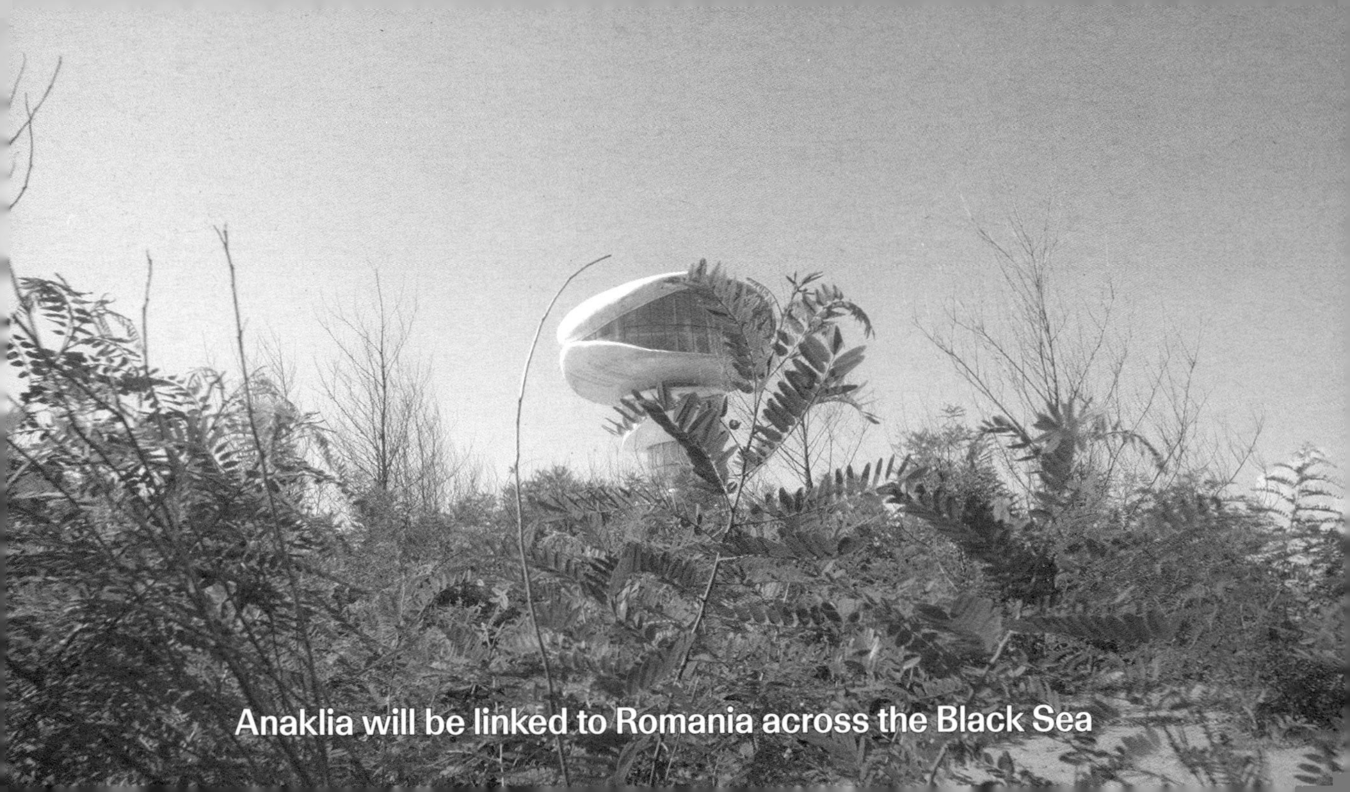
Anaklia will be linked to Romania across the Black Sea

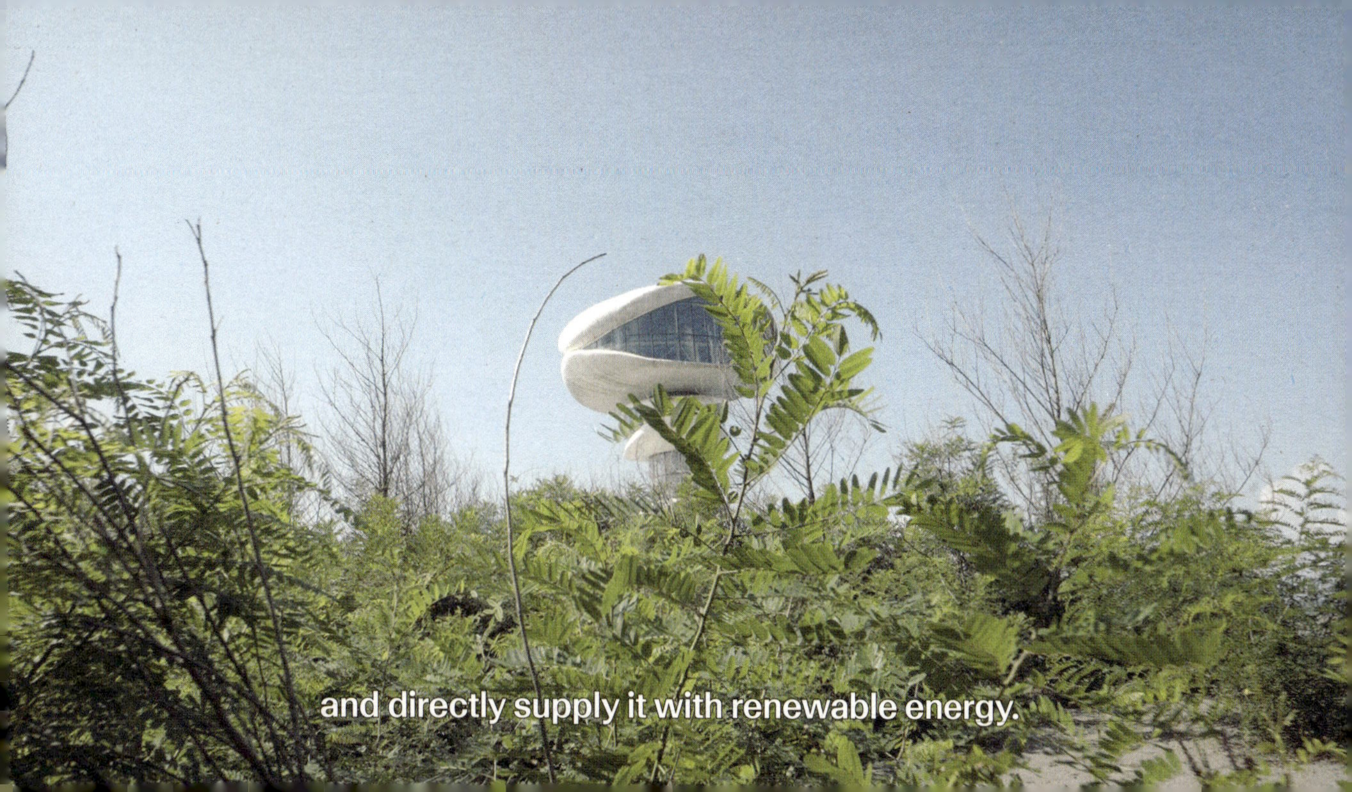
and directly supply it with renewable energy.

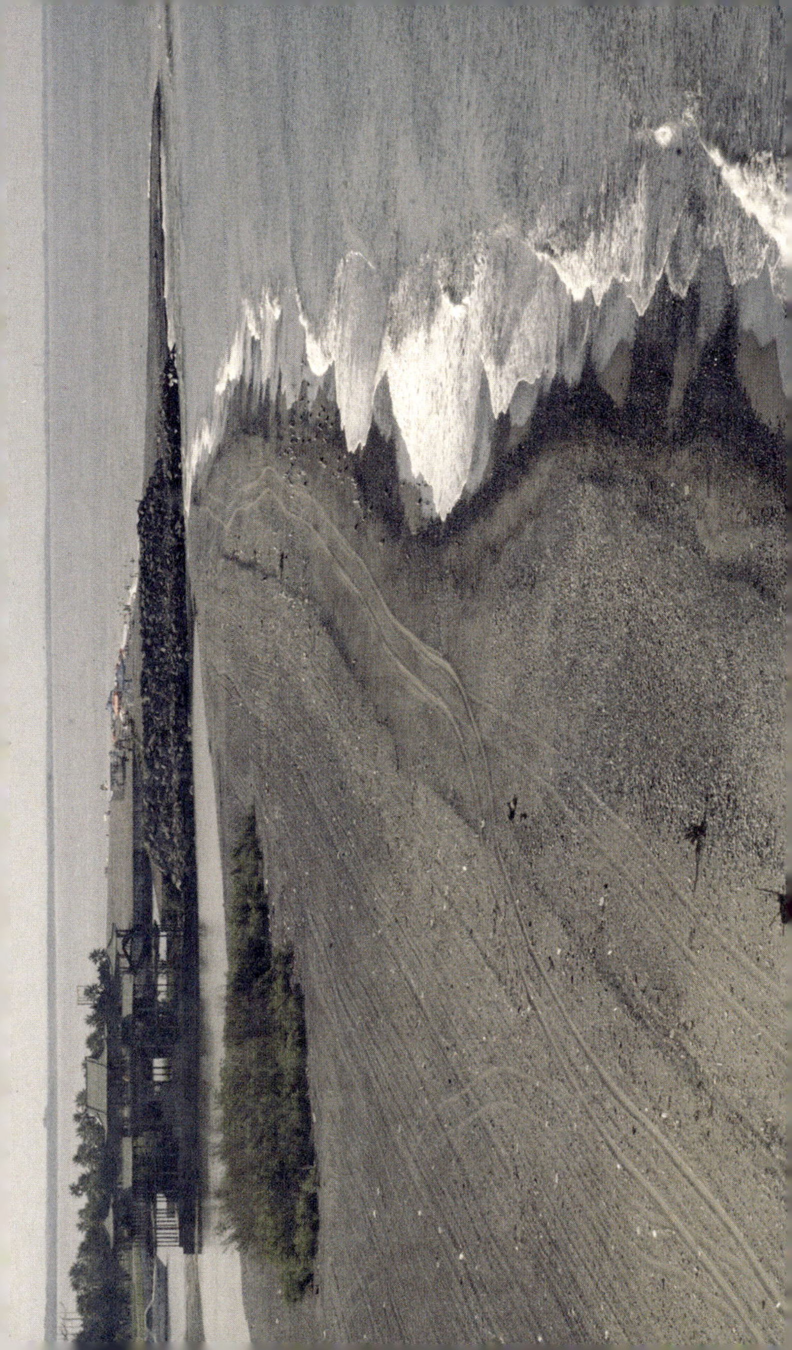

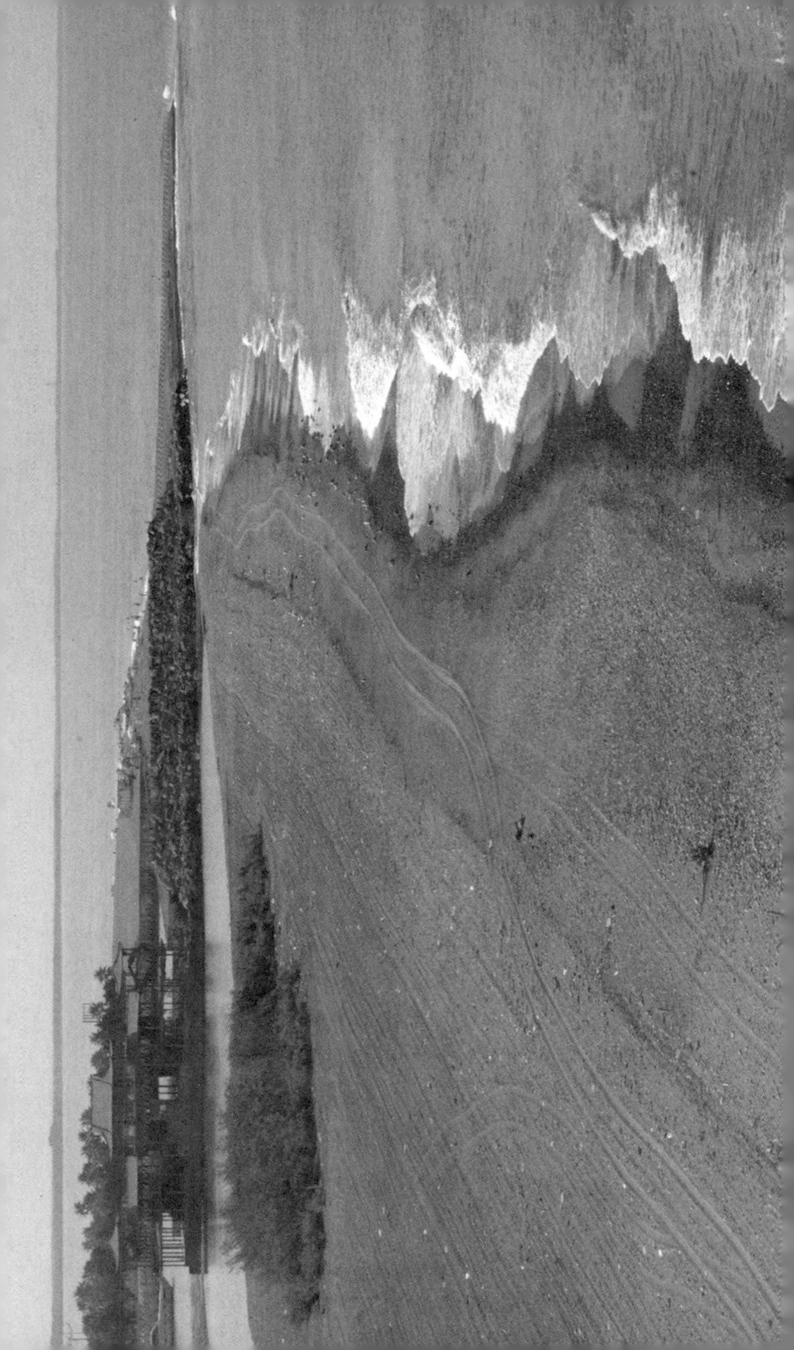

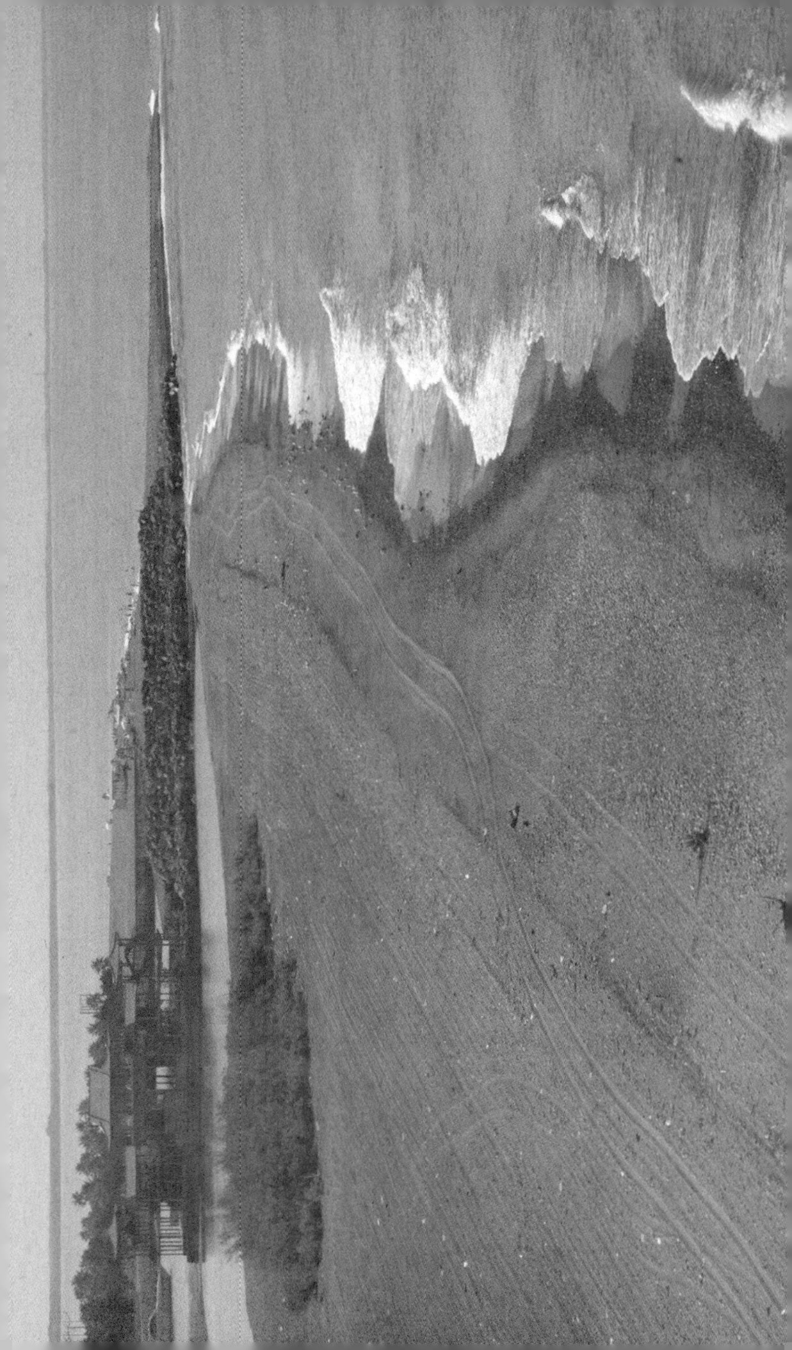

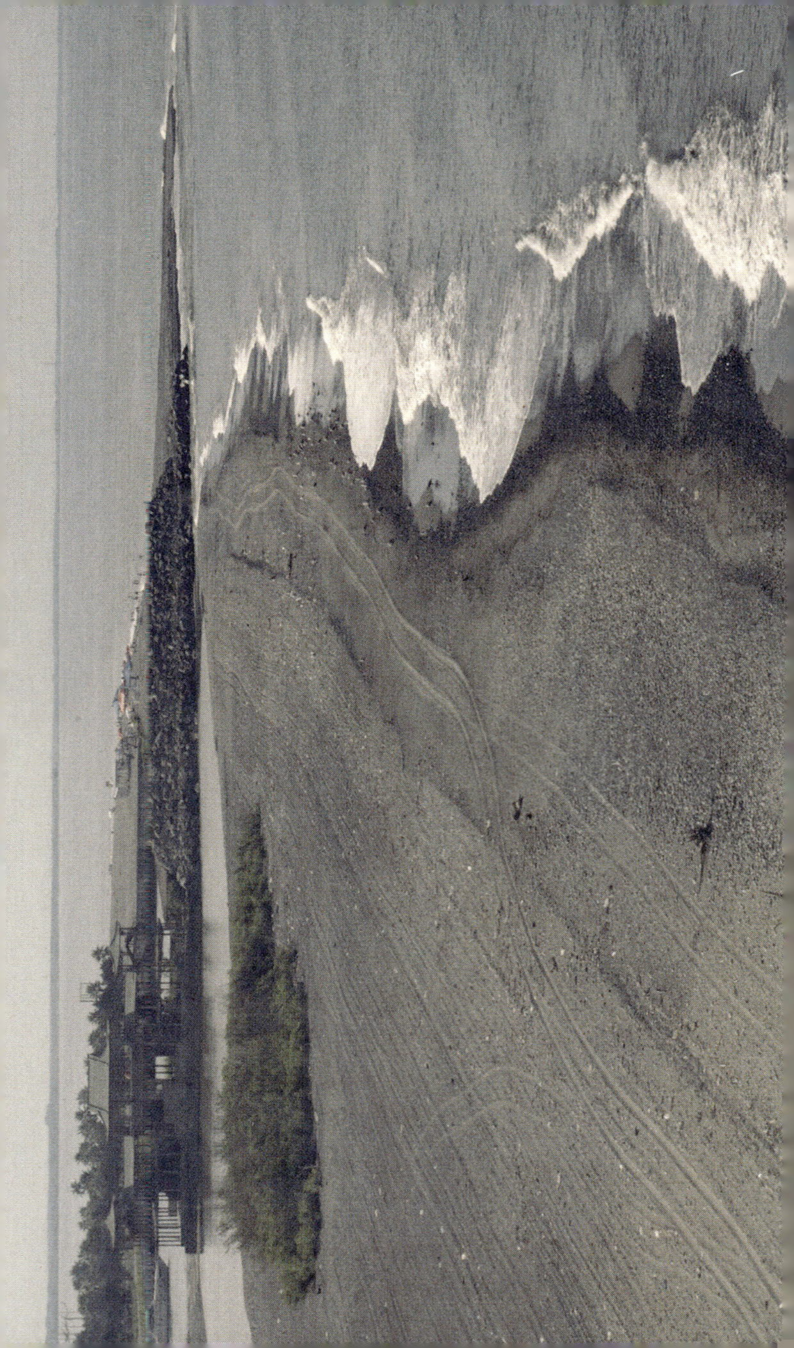

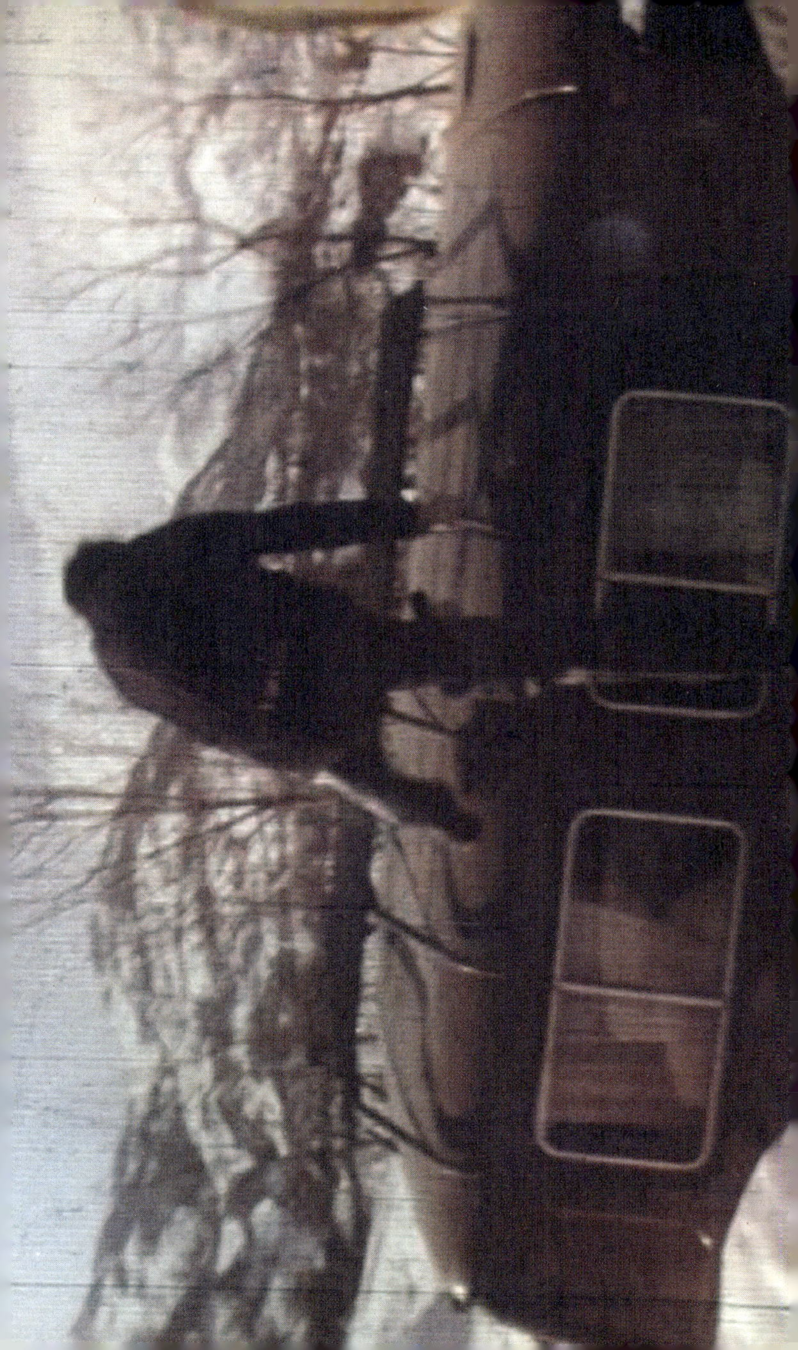

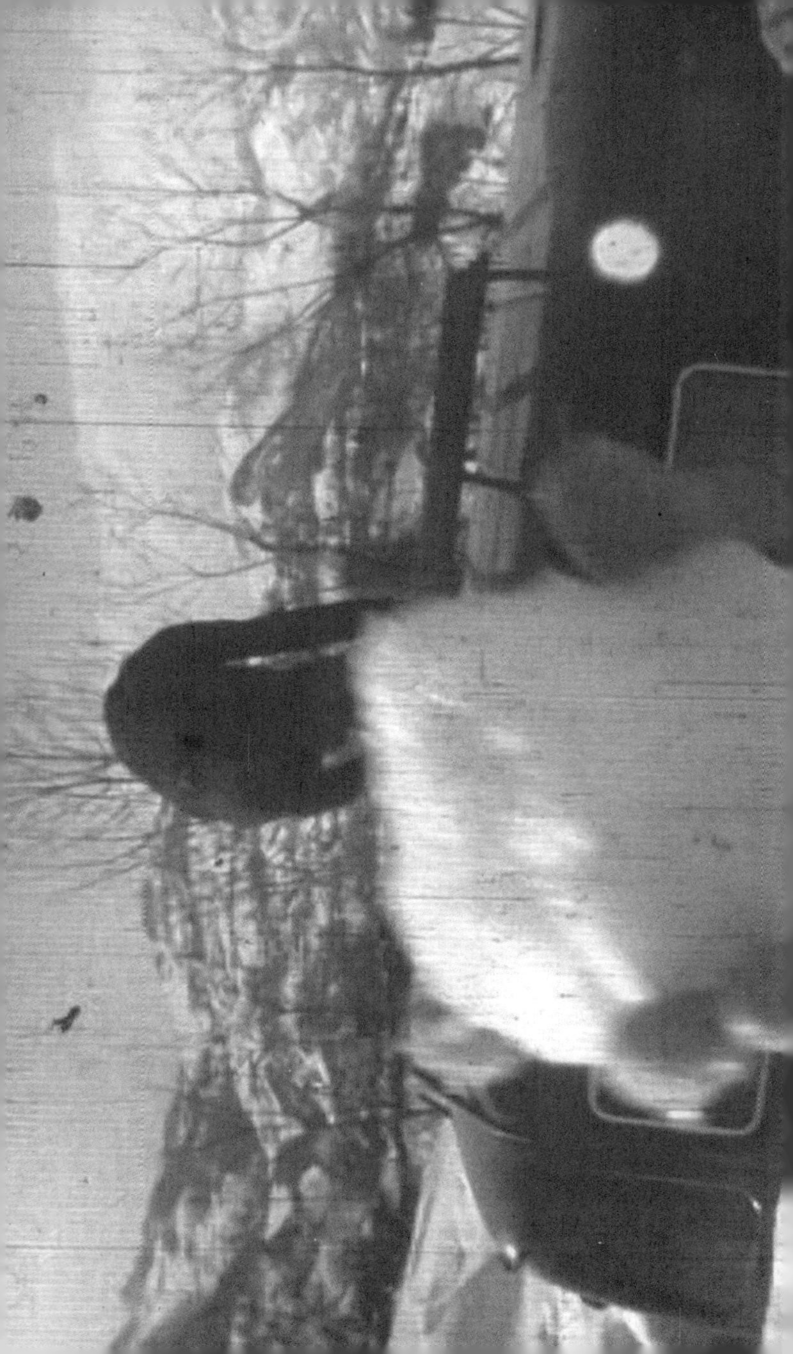

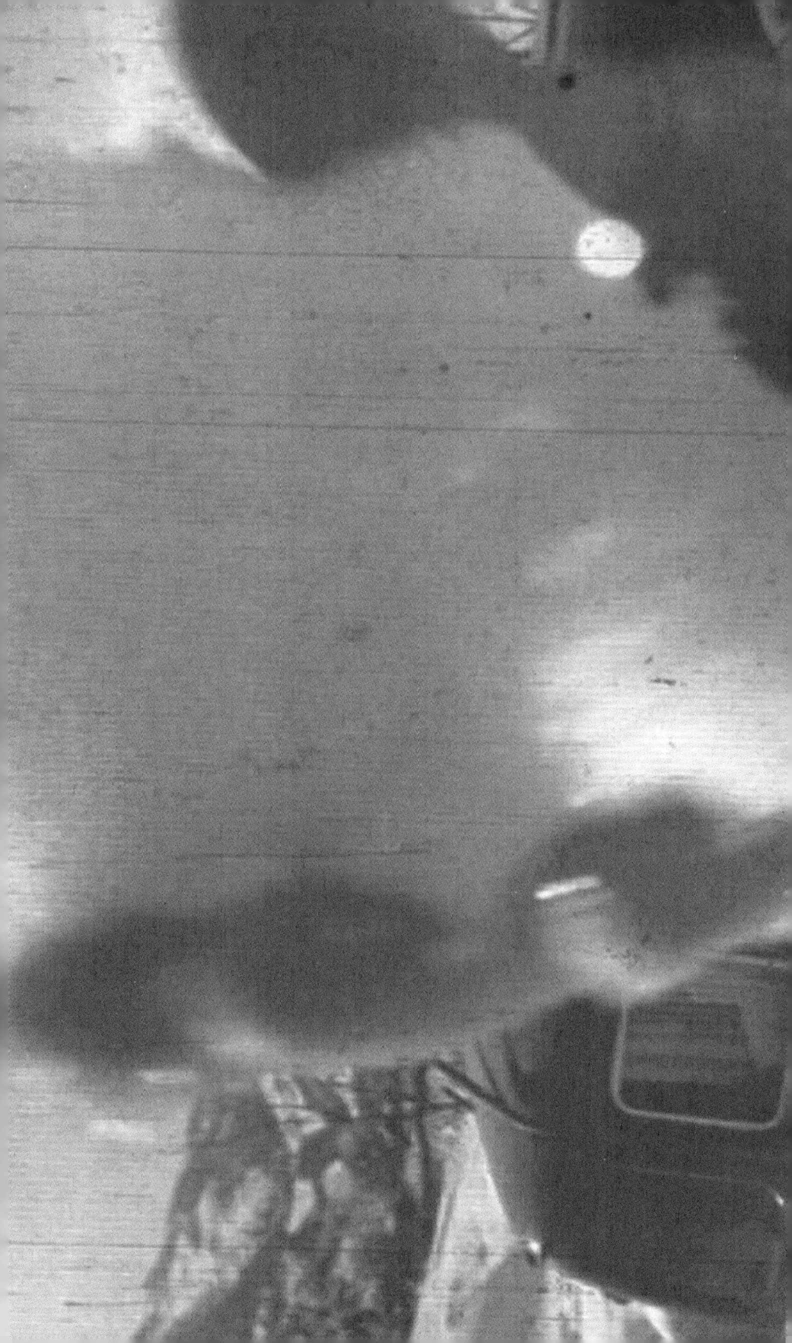

Rivers Shape Mountains

Mountains
become
Rivers[1]

Ifor Duncan

Imagine you are watching a plume of sediment as it is carried downstream by a river. The finest grains are lifted by the current and transported downstream in a state of suspension. Heavier aggregates ranging in size from pebbles to boulders are pulled along the riverbed at different speeds, simultaneously being eroded while cutting their way as they go. These aggregates are carried by water that has journeyed from melting snow and glaciers in high mountains. Driven by the force of gravity along an altitudinal path, these waters slowly yet dramatically rub, cleave, force, open, and fissure the folds and strata of their mineral and earthen surrounds.

As water cuts a path   rivers shape mountains

The carved riverbed returns to the surface in swirling shapes, eddies, roils and riffles. Each transient yet recurring shape is the negative of a boulder or a trapped branch on the bed below. The shapes formed on the river surface repeat themselves, even if differently each time. As a river erodes a mountain, the mountain gives the river its minerals and silts, resulting in an admixture of water and sediment.

Although material in form, I have long thought of these exchanges of flow and texture as a set of relations that have a metaphoric quality. While the river is not like the mountain and the mountain, in turn, is not like the river, they are, nonetheless, in a constant condition of becoming one another. And in this mutual becoming, the river and mountain are a metaphor for water and sediment—a sedimentary poetics.

Rivers Shape Mountains

As a river incorporates sediments it gains a distinctive colour   *mountains become rivers*

From this miraculous becoming, lifeworlds and belief systems are formed, as along the fertile banks of rivers communities organize themselves. Transported minerals feed into the nutrient cycles of water systems, supporting the plants and fish and other insects and crustaceans found there. These rich sediments are deposited along a river's course, following its seasonal pulsing between flood and drought.

Rivers not only carve their courses between banks but, through the deposition of alluvium, they also shape the biology of the plains and ecologies within which they flow and flood. The architect and planner Dilip da Cunha defines the invention of the river as a colonial project, and in doing so,

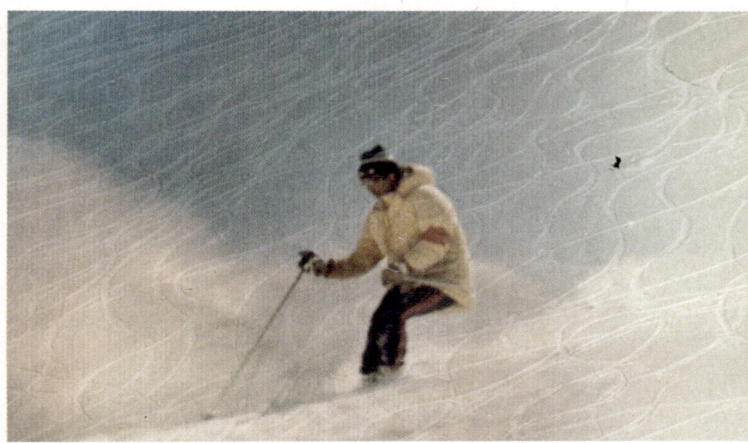

Film still. Tekla Aslanishvili, *The Mountain Speaks to the Sea*, 2024.

questions the boundaries defined by European geography—specifically, the division between land and water.[1] Building on the flood pulse concept in river ecology, the environmental historian Rohan D'Souza suggests that rivers are biological agents connecting "floodplains, wetlands, swamps and estuarine zones," maintaining the aquatic diversity of flora and fauna in the catchment.

> "Seasonal floods or pulsing regimes in particular [...] were crucial to connecting fluvial ecosystems and maintaining intricate biological webs. Rivers, in other words, were more than raging geological agents that sculpted landscapes through erosion and deposition."[2]

Writing in the context of the rivers of South Asia, D'Souza identifies that riverine ecosystems have

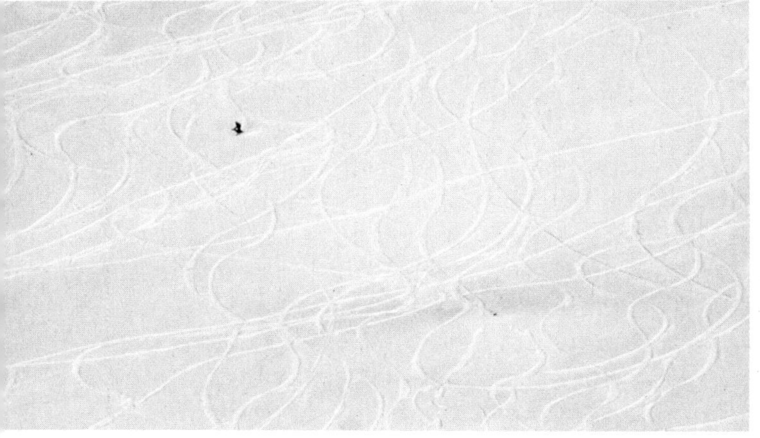

been devastated by forms of colonial manage-
ment that have broken the relationship between
river and territory afforded by the flood pulse.
Such conditions have political significance.

Riverine stories of the origins of ancient
civilizations, from Mesopotamia to Pharaonic
Egypt, are well known. Writing and thinking about
rivers necessitates framing such histories within
the physical and cultural use of water as resource,
source of knowledge, and belief system. These
histories of hydraulic cultures and civilizations, as
well as European colonial hydraulic projects, are
themselves grounded in exploitation of territory
and human life. The enslavement and the often-
fatal forced labour of populations working in the
mud brick factories, building levees and dam
structures, and working plantations on alluvial
plains, stretch from the river systems of the Nile,
to the Ganges, to the Mississippi.

I
THE FORCE FIELD OF
HYDROPOWER

Today, river systems are primarily transformed
by megadams: vast temples of extraction that
displace communities and devastate ecosystems beyond recognition. Visiting a megadam,
it is evident that the waters held back are no
longer rivers but something else. When a dam
stops a river's procession it breaks the mate-
rial-metaphorical relationality, or sedimentary
poetics, between lands, waters, and peoples.

It inserts new forms of relation between people and energy.

The vast curved sculptural forms of concrete, or impounded sloping earthen walls, and the flat steely surface of reservoir water are seemingly devoid of specificity. The dam holds back all those sediments flowing downstream and gathers them at its base; the unseen accumulating aggregates threaten to silt up the reservoir. The colours of the river afforded by the minerals specific to each waterway's sediments are lost deep down. The trapped decomposing biomatter, which deoxygenates and eutrophizes the water, turns it a luridalgal green.

"The weight of large reservoirs," writes Patrick McCully in the 2001 updated edition of his book *Silenced Rivers: The Ecology and Politics of Large Dams*, "is so great that they can trigger earthquakes". Hydropower has become so impactful in Earth processes that "geophysicists even estimate that the redistribution of the weight of the Earth's crust due to reservoirs may be having a very slight but measurable impact on the speed at which the Earth rotates, the tilt of its axis and the shape of its gravitational field".[3] This is the force field of hydropower, which not only shapes local processes but also introduces major shifts in planetary processes. The reservoir shapes geology in new and radically different ways.

Large hydropower infrastructures have long been featured as nation-building projects, particularly booming during post-colonial

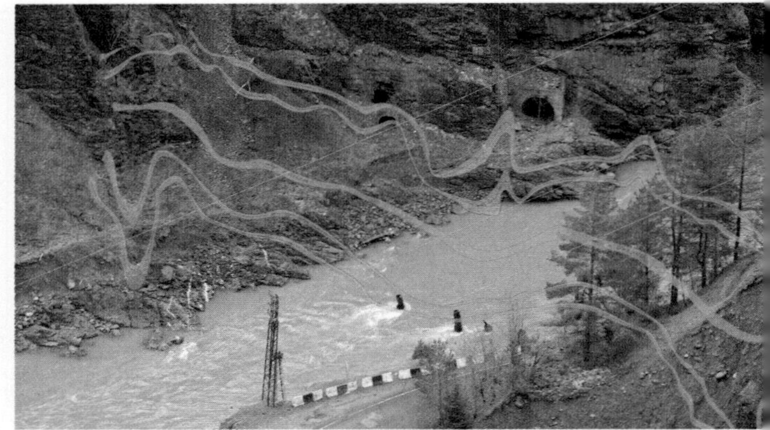

Film still. Tekla Aslanishvili, *The Mountain Speaks to the Sea*, 2024.

independence. Perhaps most famously, in 1954, the first Prime Minister of India, Pandit Jawaharlal Nehru, proclaimed the Bhakra-Nangal Dam to be a temple of national development: "Where thousands and lakhs [hundreds of thousands] of men have worked, have shed their blood and sweat and laid down their lives as well? Where can be a greater and holier place than this, which we can regard as higher?"[4] The modernist ideal faintly veils the violent and inefficient realities of the projects. Incredulity towards the temple ideal has been extensively explicated by Arundathi Roy, Rob Nixon, and Patrick McCully, who identify these huge embankments and concrete structures as floating or even false signifiers of modernity. Indeed, by 1958 even Indian Prime Minister Jawaharlal Nehru began to doubt the efficacy of megadams: "I have been beginning to think that we are suffering from what we may call a 'disease

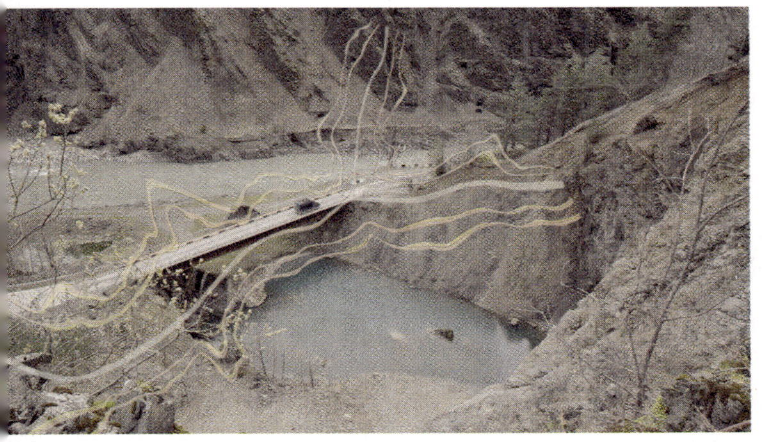

of giganticism.'"[5] Elsewhere, the Akosombo Dam, built in Ghana in the 1960s, flooded around 4 per cent of the country's landmass. When dams are of this scale they transform territories.

When a river becomes hydropower *so does the mountain*

Today, vast hydropower infrastructures continue to intervene in river systems, promising green transition and energy independence from foreign powers. This is critically explored in the film works by Tekla Aslanishvili which delve into the overlapping of time and territory in the context of Georgia's contemporary infrastructural transformations.

Opening with archival and contemporary footage of the snow-covered and cloud-shrouded peak of the Tetnuldi mountain, her two-channel video installation *The Mountain Speaks to the*

Sea (2024) situates the viewer amongst snow sports at the Hatsvali resort: gondolas, ski lifts, and skiers cutting tangled paths through powder snow. In the other channel, intrepid mountaineers cross a torrent via a rope bridge. Through the use of double exposure, the snowy slope becomes a picture plane for the archival image of the mountain's history.

Later, the two-channel double exposure places ghostlike figures of swimming fish in counterposition to the dam, contemporary images of trees or mountains form the backdrop for over-laid archival images of woodlands and mountain faces, and the churning of historic and contempo-rary waters are depicted beneath a vast rockface. By using this method, past and present become entangled in image form.

Aslanishvili's river/mountain story is one of interruptions, breakage, enclosure, and a set of metamorphoses that destroy ways of living through the building of new extractive worlds from the flows of the same rivers that cradled the old disappearing valley worlds. The video follows the spring thaw in the snowy peaks, along fog-shrouded streams, to steam peeling off forests, down towards dam projects in the canyons where the shadowy force field of extraction is felt most acutely. These are physical interruptions that figure as cornerstones of geopolitical contesta-tion, as well as new horizons of political suppres-sion and ecological devastation. Following the Mestiachala River, the sound of the small hydro-power dams Mestiachala 1 and 2 intermingles with what sounds like water flowing through rocks. The electricity generated from these dams enables new economies, such as power-draining cryptocurrency mining. The energy of the dam emerges from a history of political forces that feed new forms of financialization. Bitcoin becomes a mineral in digital form around which the contemporary river is organized.

Later in the film, Aslanishvili introduces Mikhail Kalatozov's 1930 documentary-fiction film *Salt of Svanetia*; a pioneering work of ethnographic Soviet Cinema about the construction of the Svanetia road, replete with the bare torsos of labourers breaking huge chunks of mountain into slates for roofing. From this archival moving image, Aslanishvili shifts to the Khudoni Hydro Power Plant, a dam partially built during the Soviet period, with expansion planned for the near future. The old diagram for the dam is overlaid onto contemporary shots of the mountain and river today. The moving image of past infrastructure merges into the present, creating a vision of a future dictated by infrastructure.

Fed by rivers descending from the melt of the Shkhara and Chalaadi glaciers, dams here metamorphose water into energy—a metabolism that transforms water's relation to the mountain. The shapes of the river are lost, as are the alluvial and social relations between mountain and plane that shape the contemporary nation-state. The film tells the story of interventions in the immediate social, economic, and environmental conditions, set against the backdrop of interlapping financial and geopolitical dynamics at play within legacies of Soviet Imperialism, present Russian aggression, as well as the EU and China's soft power pursuit of their own interests. In this context, the Georgian state's attempts to forge its own energy sovereignty through the production of megadams, obfuscates a whole other set of deterritorialized politics.

In another work titled *Scenes from Trial and Error* (2020), Aslanishvili's moving image practice disentangles how the intervention of an infrastructure or financial mechanism — such as the free port project of Anaklia — opens up new imaginaries of future markets and logistical horizons as a hub of global trade. This is a nodal point of what Evelina Gambino, who is also a contributor to this book, positions as a promised seamlessness of global trade that is itself replete with frictions.[6] Anaklia is also the planned site for

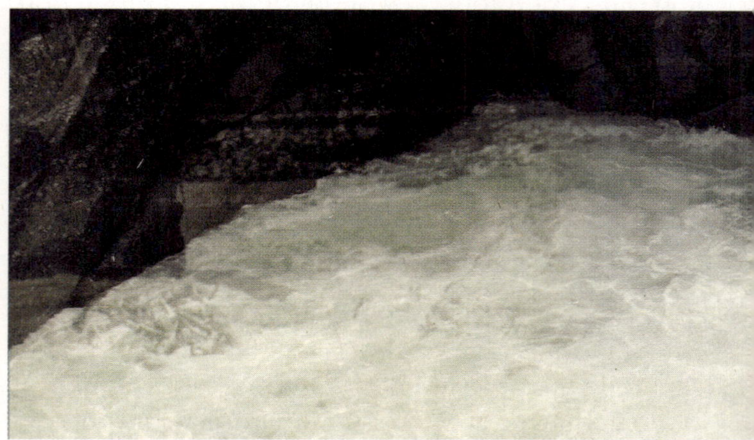

Film still. Tekla Aslanishvili, *The Mountain Speaks to the Sea*, 2024.

the Black Sea Submarine Cable Project, which would take energy extracted from the dams in the Caucasus Mountains into the deep sea to supply the EU. The project aims to connect the ecological devastation of mountain river valleys to the other end of the altitudinal scale in the form of imagined logistical infrastructures running along the bed of the Black Sea.[7]

The backdrop of Aslanishvili's work is a complex set of politics taking place over time, whereby the harnessing of energy from Georgian mountain rivers begins to eradicate the distinction between mountain and plane. James C. Scott has prominently identified the plane as the location of state formation, and the mountain as a "shatter zone" where autonomous communities form.[8] The politics of Georgia are organized around the relationship between mountain and sea, as it follows the communication of energy

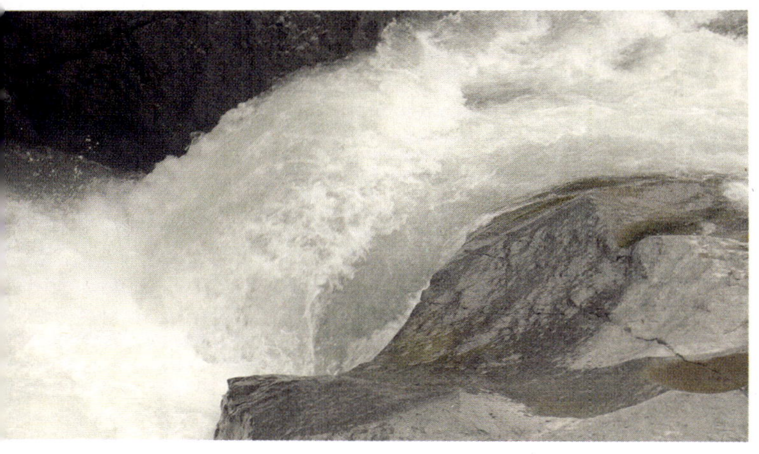

from its rivers and devastates the mountain and river communities. Hydropower transforms what was once a "shatter zone" into an extractable resource, inextricably connecting the mountain and planes in an attempt to consolidate a state under both internal and external threat.

II
RESISTANCE IN SEDIMENTS[9]

Elsewhere, in a very different context, I have considered the dual hope and despair that rivers represent through a specific reading of Édouard Glissant's 1958 novel, *La Lezarde [The Ripening]*.[10] In the novel, the Lezarde River is a central feature of the narrative about post-colonial self-determination. Glissant's novel depicts an election on the Antillean island of Martinique, which would decide whether it became independent or a department of France. The river is the focus of a plot to assassinate a French colonial agent, Garin, by Thaël, a young descendant of maroons who recently arrived from the mountainous interior upstream, where people who had escaped slavery in plantations had formed marronages (self-determined communities). Glissant treats the river in a way that both evokes the history of marronage and fugitivity transported from the mountains and reflects his disillusionment with Martinique's political condition. Under the guise of départmentalisation, the legacy of the plantation economy remained the focus of power on the island, trapping it in a limbo of ongoing colonialism. The polluted and canalized river is both symbolic and a consequence of the ongoing failure of emancipation and self-determination, and Glissant aligns the river's fate with the possibilities of an autonomous Martinican state. The Jamaican theorist, Sylvia Wynter, argues that the hope embodied by the river lies in its linkage between the mountains, the plains, and the sea:

> "Lézarde River provides the central millennial metaphor of hope and liberation (since it is the image of this river which links the mountain, as 'the repository of Maroon memories', with 'the unfettered sea' and therefore links the tradition of the Maroon repudiation of the plantation to a new future whose synthesis transcends both that gesture of refusal of, and the plantation slaves' submission to, the course of modern history)."[11]

The river has both a metaphoric and physical resonance in this mountain-plain relationship. The "Maroon memories" of the mountain are carried downstream by the river like alluvial deposits. Indeed, Glissant navigates both the metaphoric and real flows and stages of the river as a vital feature of the political landscape:

> "On the west, the torturous curve of the Lézarde tries to surround the town, then suddenly stops short, refuses such a role and, turning back to the east, runs past the sinister cane fields and gets lost in its delta.

> This channel is shot through with currents
> of filth; the river does not die a beautiful
> death. And yet it is beautiful enough when
> it comes rushing down from the highlands
> in the north, with the bright impatient blue
> of youth, the swirling rush of its beginning.
> Under the first rays of the sun, the river,
> caught in its meandering, seems to grow
> drowsy and like a prudent lady lies in
> wait, then suddenly it surges forward, like
> a people in revolt, shooting out first from
> one side and then from the other, soon
> gathering the foam deposited on its banks,
> grasping, avaricious like a factory owner
> inspecting his boilers closely, unwilling to
> leave behind either the flashes of blue or
> the yellow sediment."[12]

The river bears the traits of both the fugitives who escaped to the mountains, and the impending actions of the young revolutionaries. Difficult to control, the river shifts states as it meanders, refusing the exploitation of the plantation, before surging into flood with revolutionary energy. Thus, in Glissant's Antillean poetics, the captured river threatens to break from its restraints enforced by the oppressive concrete enclosures of ongoing colonisation.[13]

At the end of the novel the narrator, a stand-in for Glissant himself, is instructed to go to France with Michel, a young scholar, and write the story of the events in an alluvial style, that of the actual novel:

"Write it like a river. Slow. Like the Lézarde. With rushing water, meanders, sometimes sluggish, sometimes running freely, slowly gathering the earth from either bank. Like that, yes, picking up the earth round it. Little by little. Like a river, murky with secrets that it deposits in the calm sea ..."[14]

The story of their political actions is to take the form of the Lézarde itself; it is to be written like a river, with its changing tempos, accretions, insurgent energy, and alluvial opacity—in line with Glissant's conception of opacity developed in his later theoretical treatise *Poetics of Relation*.[15]

III
RIVERS BECOME HYDROPOWER

While addressing a very different history and present, Aslanishvili's moving image practice engages with a state and a people caught in a struggle for self-determination. *The Mountain Speaks to the Sea* focuses on Georgia's embattled river systems to tell a similar story of disillusionment with past and present, mixed with a fear for the future. Waters and their over-exploitation are also entangled with the contestation of national self-determination, the threat of regions being annexed or becoming autonomous—like the de facto state of Abkhazia—and the colonisation of land by the logistical mega-projects of global trade. All the while, like the rivers, resistance to these projects is violently suppressed.

Rivers Shape Mountains

In *A State in a State* (2022) the change of railway
gauges that takes place in Georgia is a technical
object around which an entire substate/commer-
cial zone emerges, replete with its own postal
service. The railway and its changing gauges
between East and West become the location at
the geopolitical border where resistance organizing takes place. A mini and semi-autonomous
state is formed around a seemingly simple technical apparatus—but one with a plethora of political
unfoldings including railway unions that show
solidarity by preventing the transportation of
arms to Russia.

 When a dam is a political device, however,
the wall and turbines act to both destroy existing
communities and make new economic worlds.
The territory changes, new communities emerge
to support the upkeep of the dam, and the corporations behind the dam become the patriarchs of
the valley, displacing and replacing populations
under the aegis of the metabolism of water. Here
the river is not so much redrawn as submerged
deep in the reservoir. The river disappears and is
consigned to the memory of the community who
once knew it. When it returns and runs freely it
comes with devastating effects—like after the
flash floods in Chuberi in 2018, with the admixture of mud left behind on all surfaces.

 What agency does a river have in the
context of large geopolitical and infrastructural
processes? Are the river/mountain's sedimentary
poetics lost? Or have they been harnessed for
alternative forces that shape tectonic plates,

displace populations, and perform the devastation of extraction?

The power of hydropower floods, seeps, and grips an entire territory, reshaping it in its image. As megadams hold the territory, they produce new economies—a new hydropower world. Just as it is challenging to locate the thresholds between river and mountain, once hydropower disrupts this relationship, it is also difficult to locate where the impact of the dam ends in a process where rivers become hydropower.

Rivers Shape Mountains

1	The title emerges from thinking alongside the artist filmmaker Solveig Qu Suess and her forthcoming moving-image work *Holding Rivers, Becoming Mountains*, 2024.

2	Dilip da Cunha, *The Invention of Rivers: Alexander's Eye and Ganga's Descent* (Philadelphia: University of Pennsylvania Press, 2018).

3	Rohan D'Souza, "Event, Process and Pulse: Resituating Floods in Environmental Histories of South Asia," *Environment and History* 26, no. 1 (2020): 43.

4	Patrick McCully, *Silenced Rivers: The Ecology and Politics of Large Dams* (London: Bloomsbury, 2001), 7.

5	Jawaharlal Nehru, *Jawaharlal Nehru's Speeches. Vol. 3, March 1953–August 1957* (New Delhi: Publications Division, Ministry of Information and Broadcasting, Govt. of India, 1958).

6	McCully, *Silenced Rivers: The Ecology and Politics of Large Dams*, 20–21. 1953–August 1957 (New Delhi: Publications Division, Ministry of Information and Broadcasting, Govt. of India, 1958).

7	Evelina Gambino, "The Georgian Logistics Revolution: Questioning Seamlessness Across the New Silk Road", *Work Organisation, Labour & Globalisation* 13, no. 1 (April 2019): 190–206.

8	I have been discussing the relationship between hydropower and the underwater cable with Tamara Keller for her Masters project at the Centre for Research Architecture (Goldsmiths, London). I am also aware of this condition through the work of Tekla Aslanishvili and Evelina Gambino.

9	James C. Scott, *The Art of Not Being Governed: An Anarchist History of Upland Southeast Asia* (New Haven, CT: Yale University Press, 2009), 7.

10	Passages from this section are adapted from a previous article I wrote which resonated in unexpected ways with *The Mountain Speaks to the Sea*. Ifor Duncan, "Fugitive Rivers: Maroon Ecologies and Édouard Glissant's *La Lézarde*," *Green Letters* 27, no. 1 (October 2023): 92–108. I also write about the geopolitical importance of river sediments in my collaborative article: Ifor Duncan & Stefanos Levidis, "Median line: A century of border violence and the alluvial geopolitics of the Evros/Meriç/Maritsa River border," *Area* 00 (2024). Available from: https://doi.org/10.1111/area.12961

11	Édouard Glissant, *La Lézarde [The Ripening]*, trans. Michael Dash (London: Heinemann Educational Books, 1985).

12	Sylvia Wynter, "Beyond the World of Man: Glissant and the New Discourse of the Antilles," *World Literature Today* 63, no. 4 (Autumn 1989): 638.

13	Glissant, *La Lézarde*, 32.

14	Beverley Ormerod, *An Introduction to the French Caribbean Novel* (London; Kingston; Port of Spain: Heinemann, 1985).

15	Glissant, *La Lézarde*, 175.

16	Édouard Glissant, *Poetics of Relation*, trans. Betsy Wing (Ann Arbour, MI: University of Michigan Press, 1997), 190.

A State in a State

47:00'
Georgia, Spain, Germany
2022

Director and Editor	Tekla Aslanishvili
Research and Script	Tekla Aslanishvili, Evelina Gambino
Music	Ani Zakareishvili, Nika Pasuri
Cinematography	Nikoloz Tabukashvili, Tekla Aslanishvili
Typography	Dato Simonia
Field Recordings	Viktor Bone, Teona Rekhviashvili
Sound Mastering	Irakli Shonia
Color	Sally Shamas

Produced by the Han Nefkens Foundation with support from the Fundació Antoni Tàpies; Museum of Contemporary Art and Design, Manila; Jameel Art Centre, Dubai; NTU CCA, Singapore; and WIELS, Brussels. Supported by the Berlin Senate for Culture and Europe.

A State in a State is an experimental documentary film that follows the construction, disruption, and fragmentation of railroads in the South Caucasus and Caspian regions. It examines railways as the technical materialisation of fragile political borders that have re-emerged after the collapse of the Soviet Union.

Revolving around scenes of waiting and delay that constitute cargo mobility, the film reads the optimistic narratives about the New Silk Road against the grain. It observes how the iron foundation of connectivity can be used as a weapon of exclusion and geopolitical sabotage.

Along the same lines, other forms of sabotage are deployed by workers to disrupt the political violence. Looking at historic and current practices of resistance *A State in a State* explores the potential of railroads for building a different, infrastructural consciousness and the lasting, transnational kinship among the people who live and work around them.

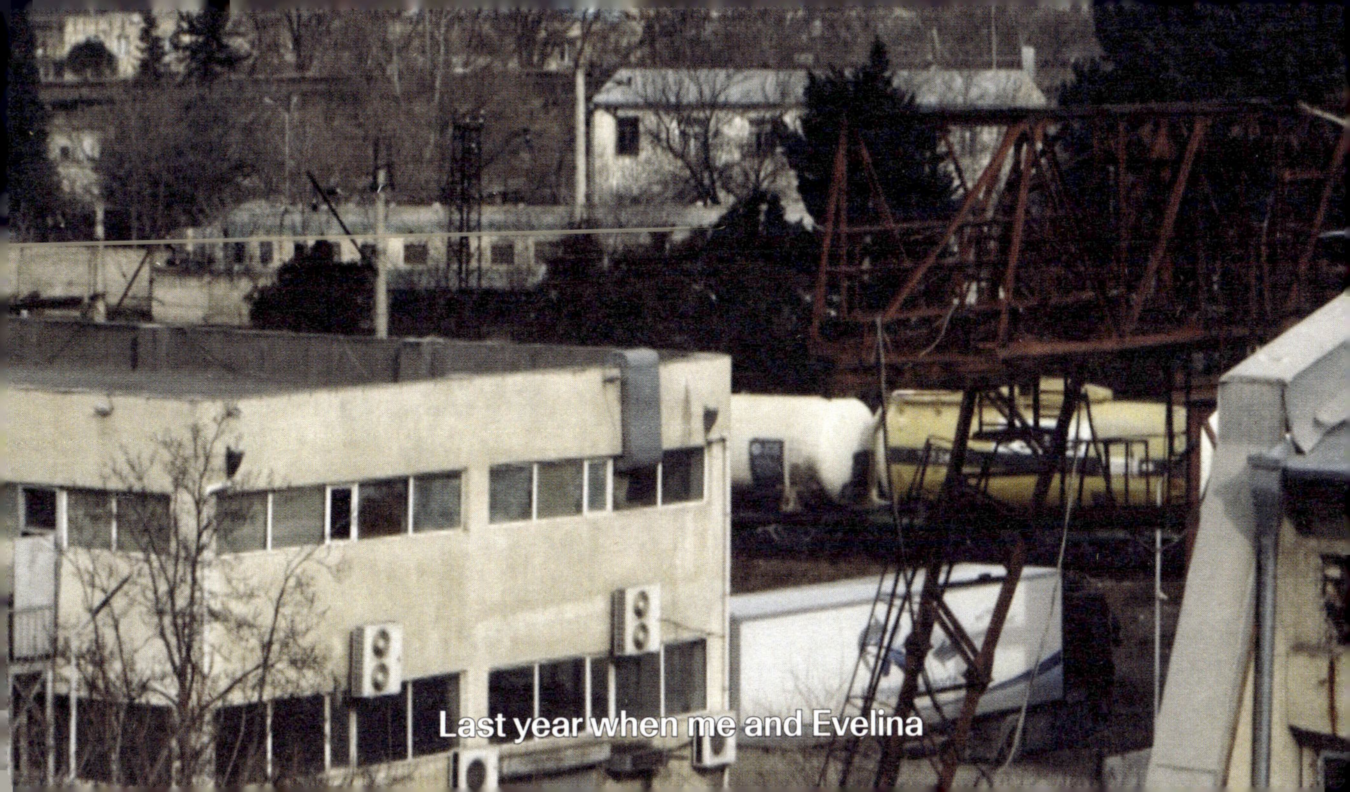
Last year when me and Evelina

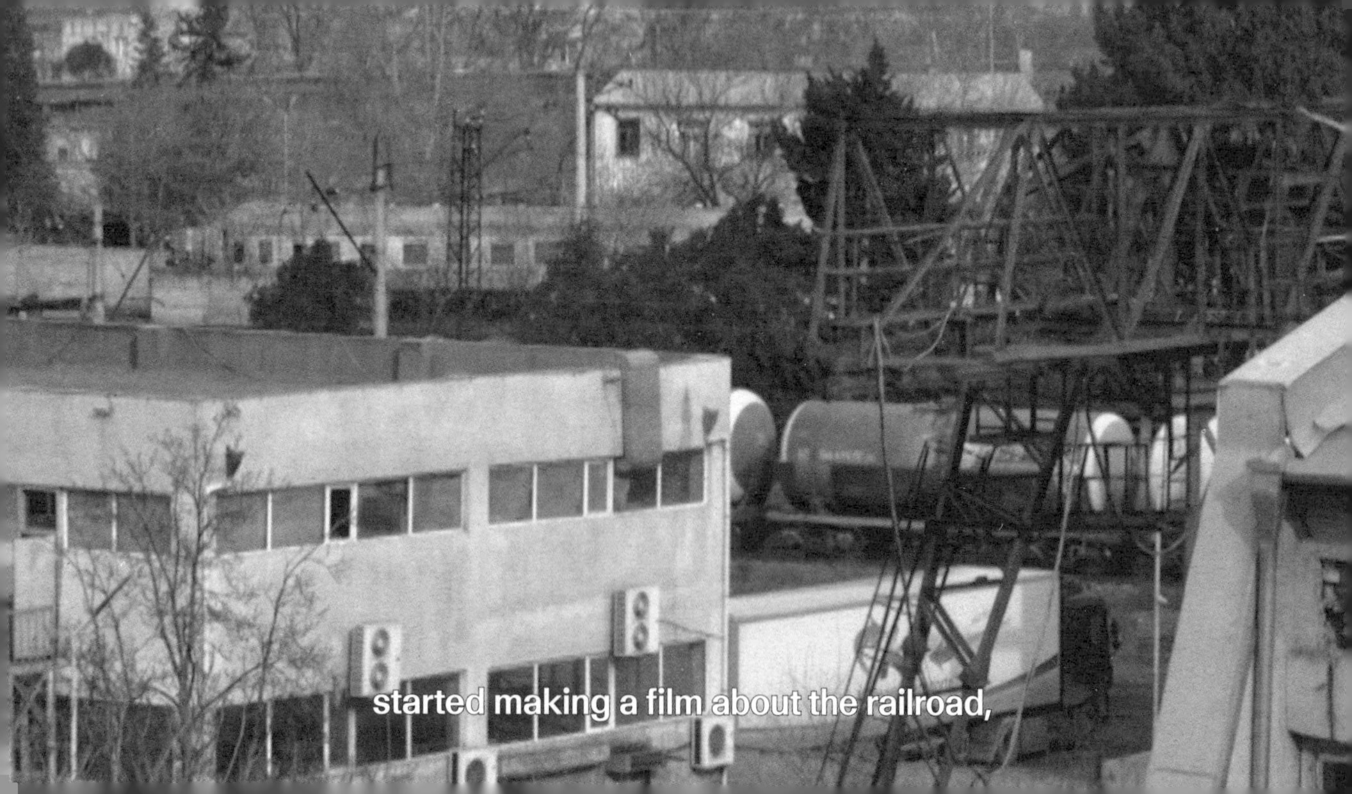
started making a film about the railroad,

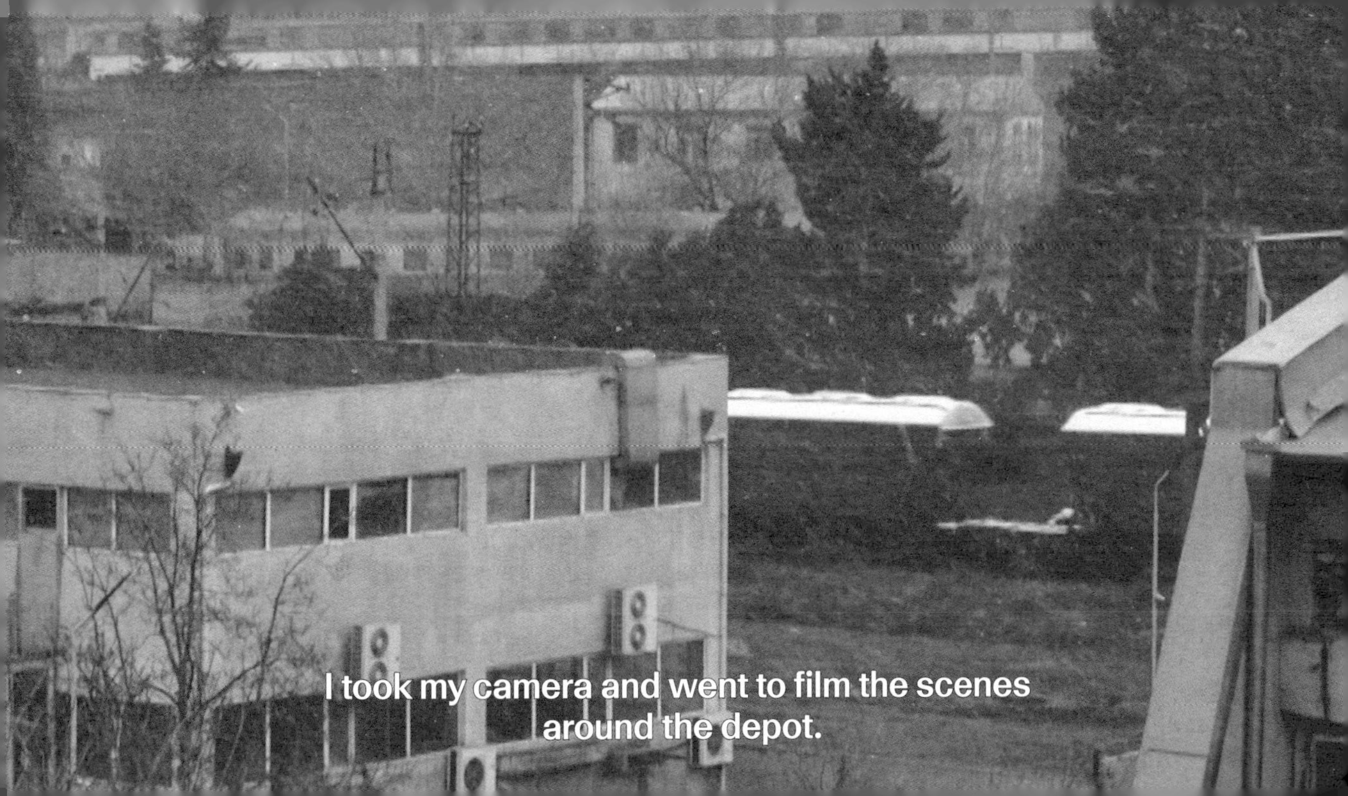
I took my camera and went to film the scenes around the depot.

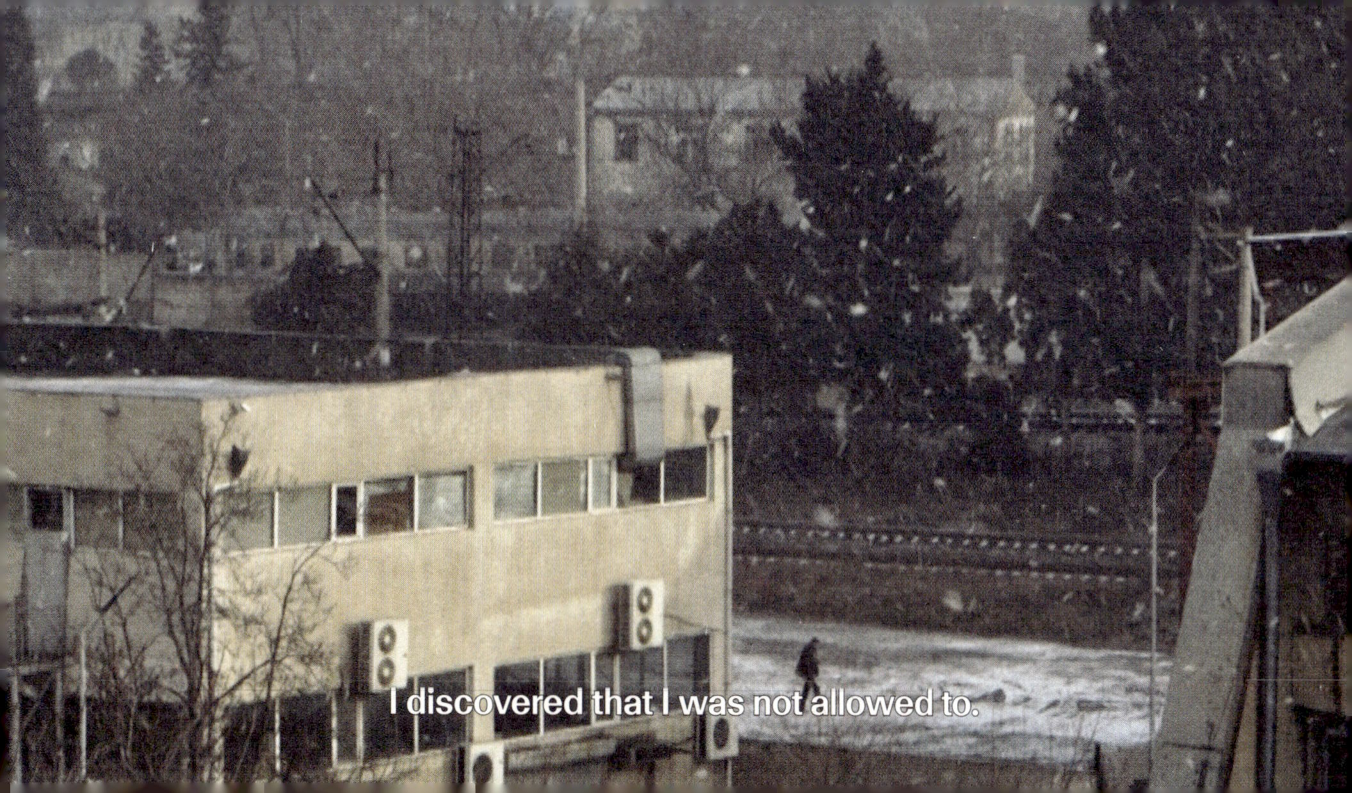
I discovered that I was not allowed to.

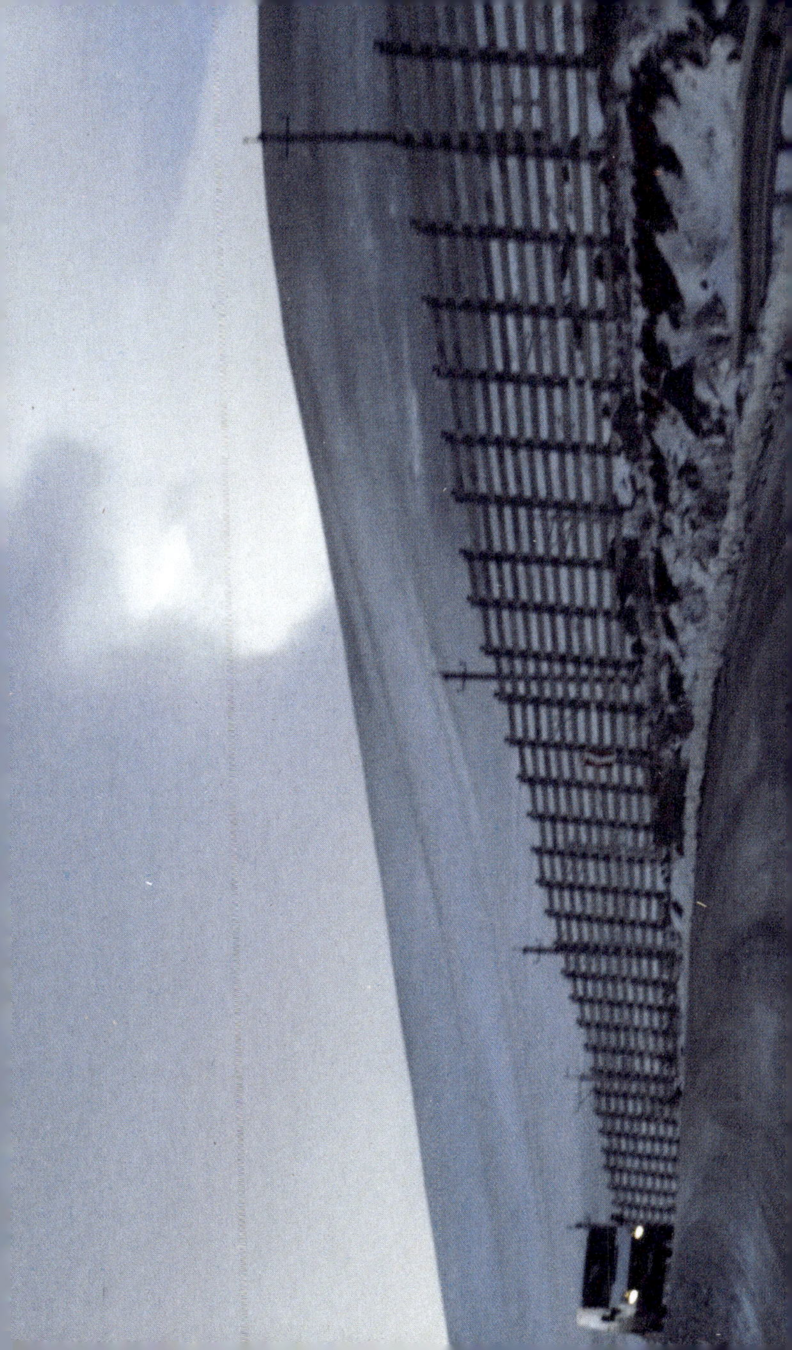

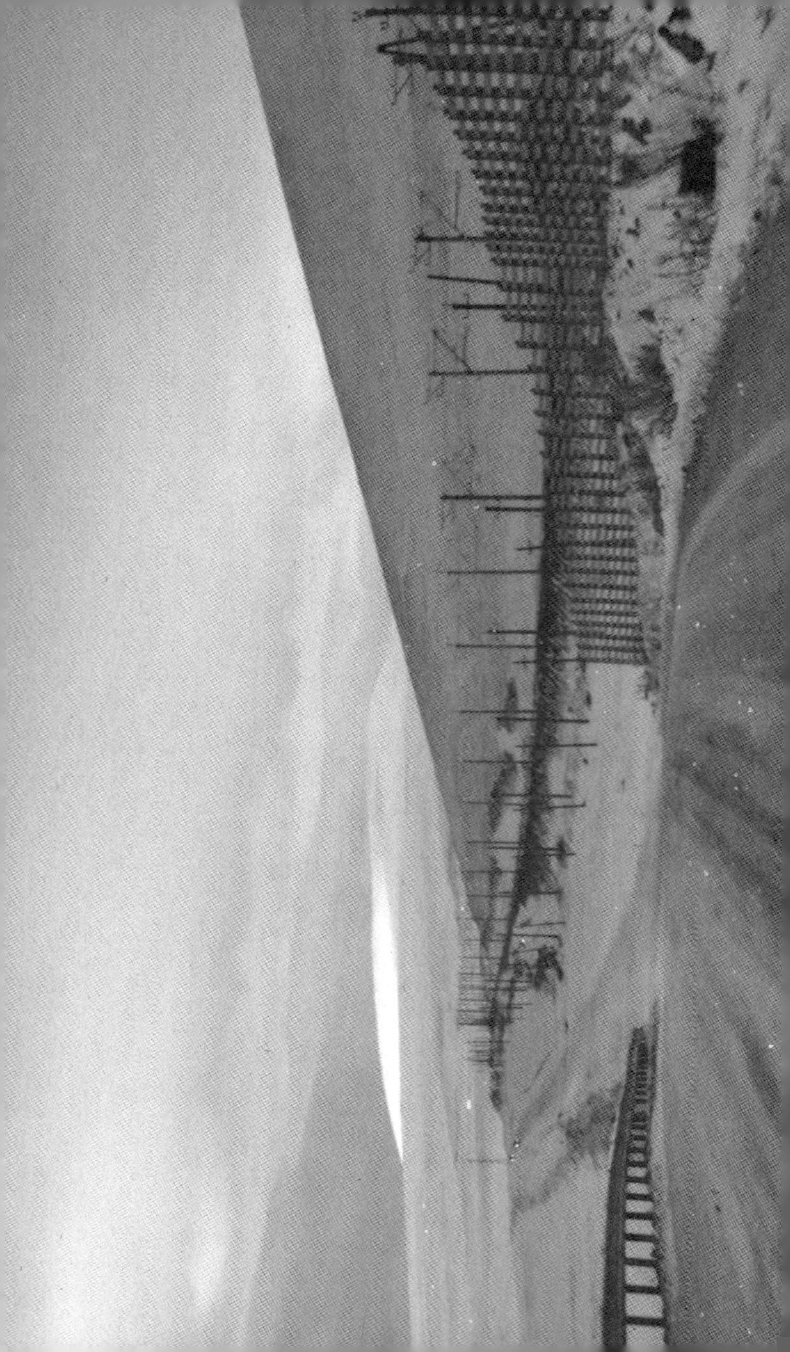

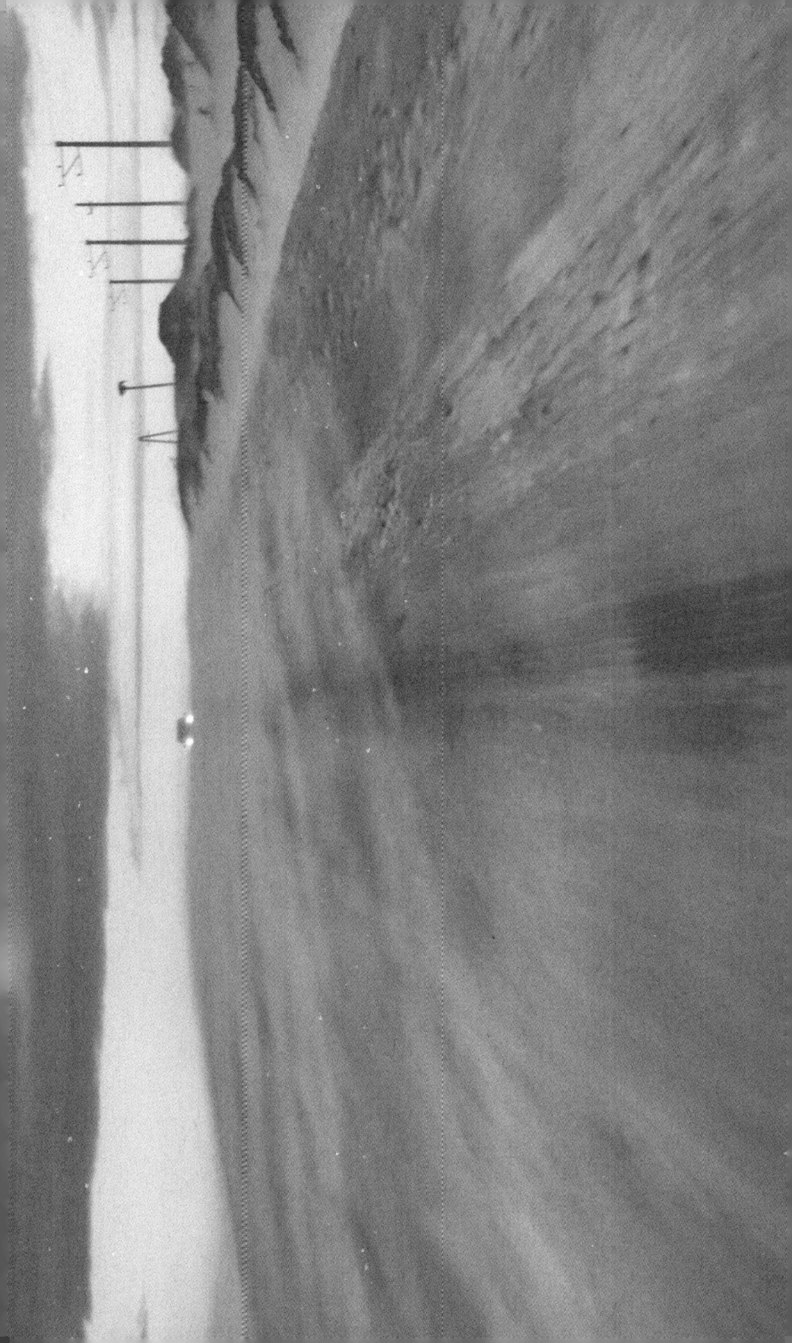

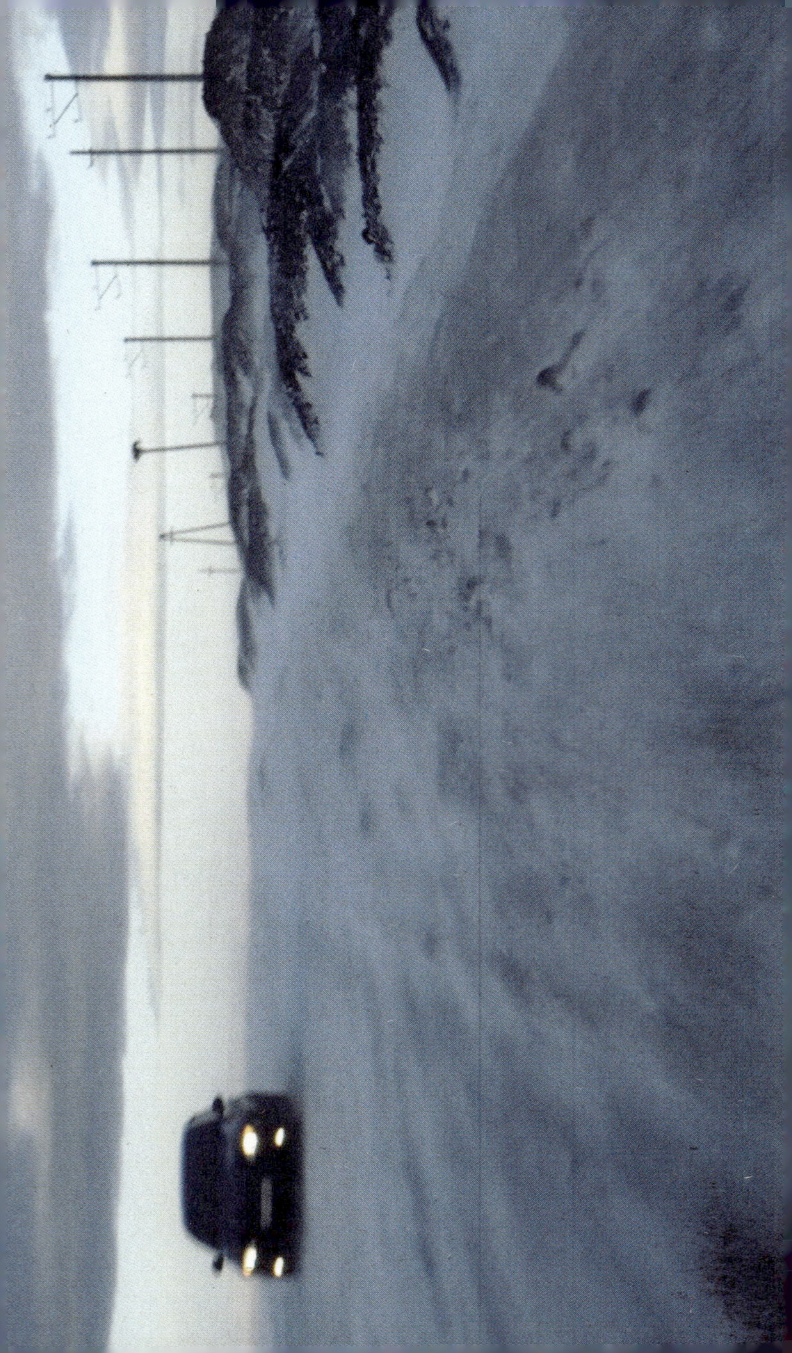

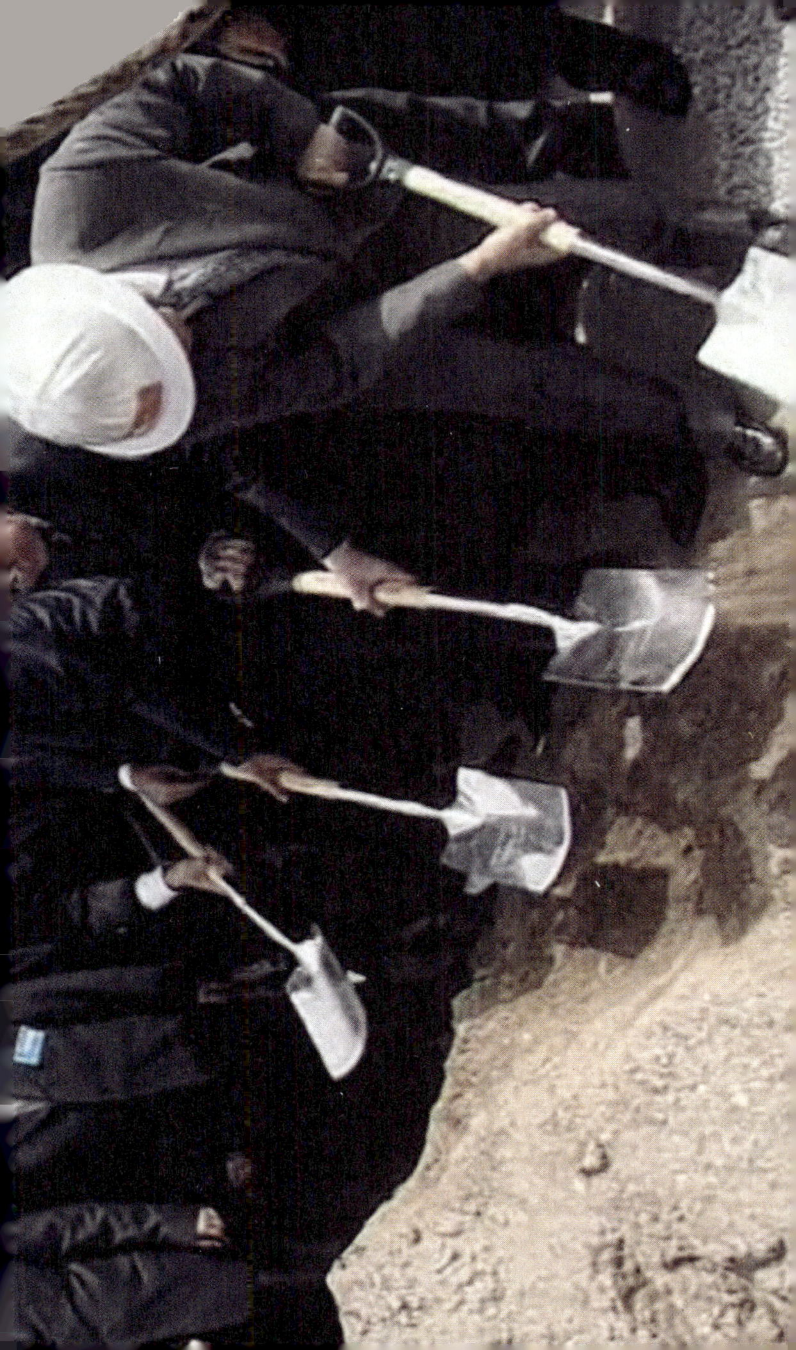

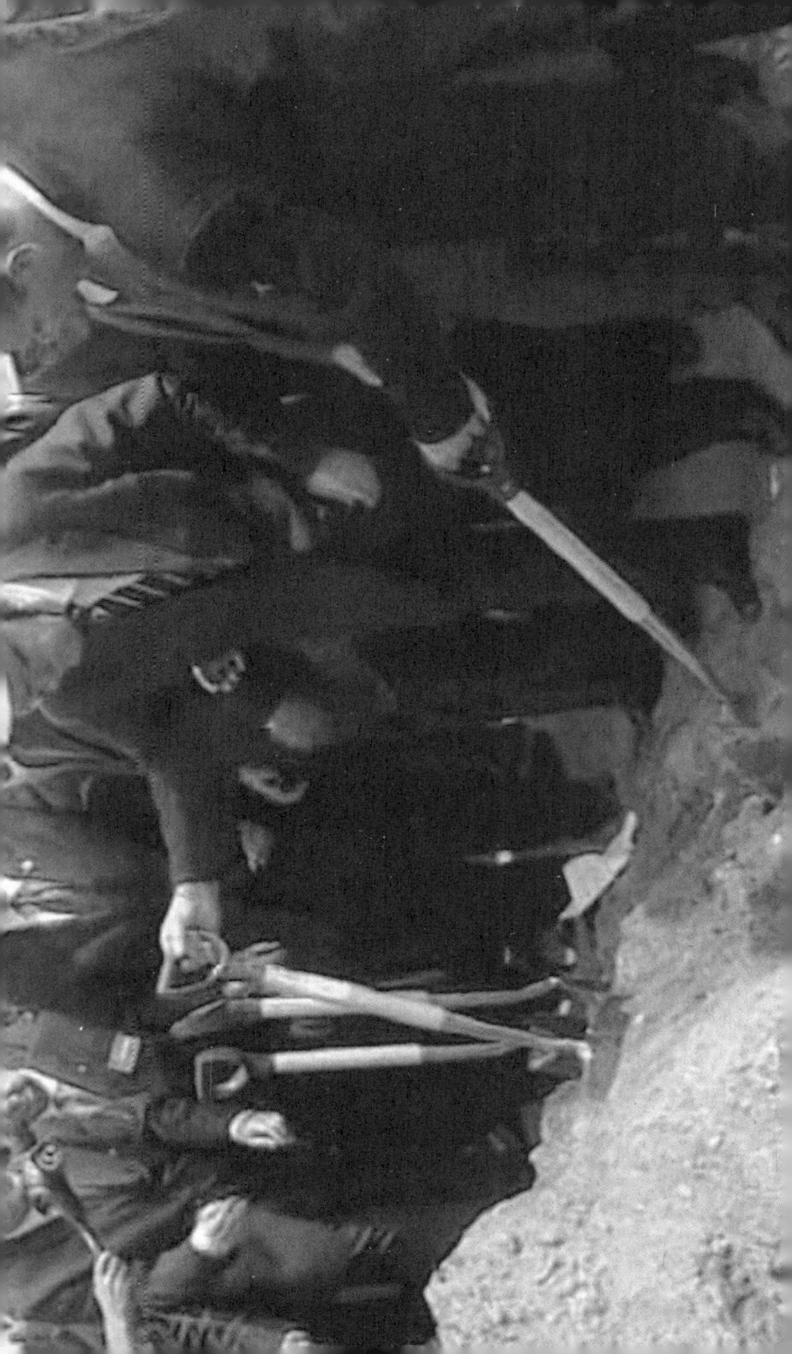

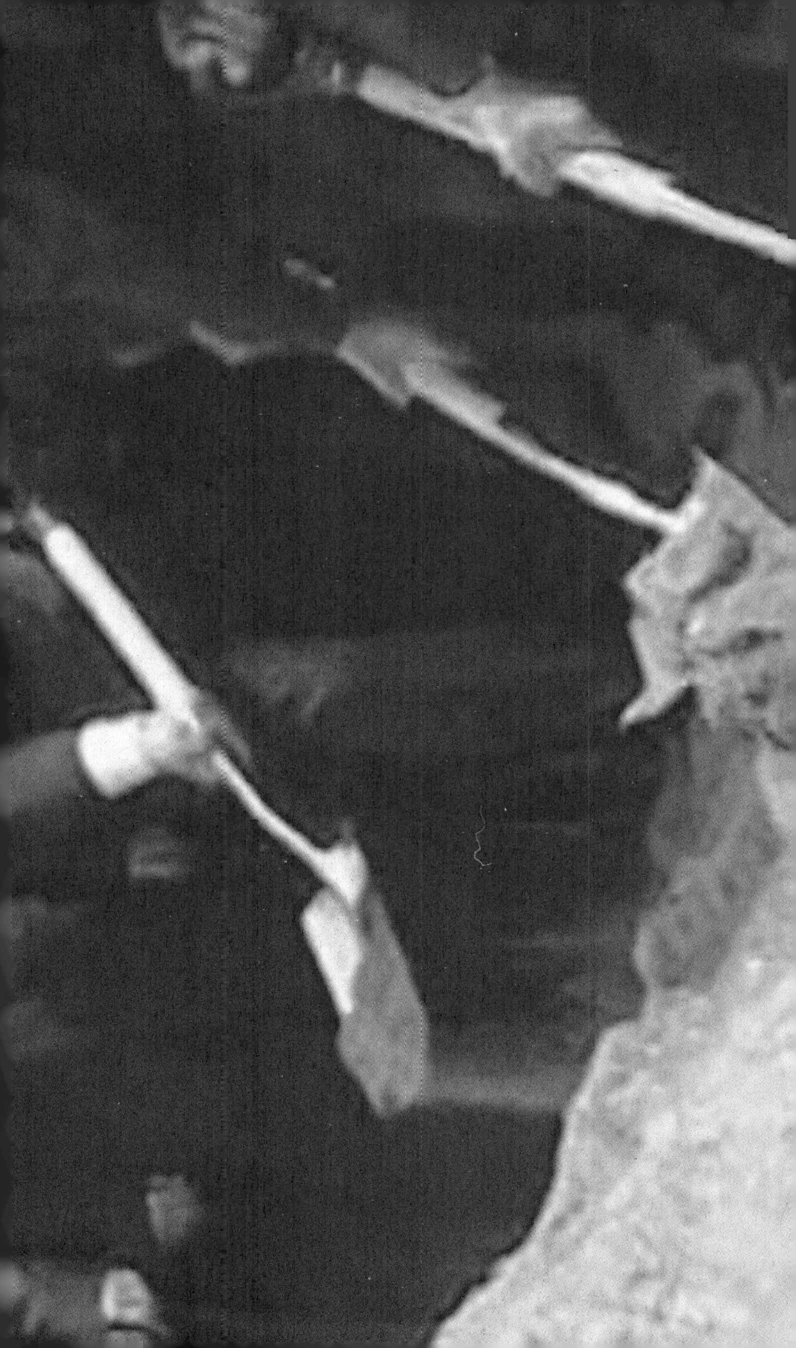

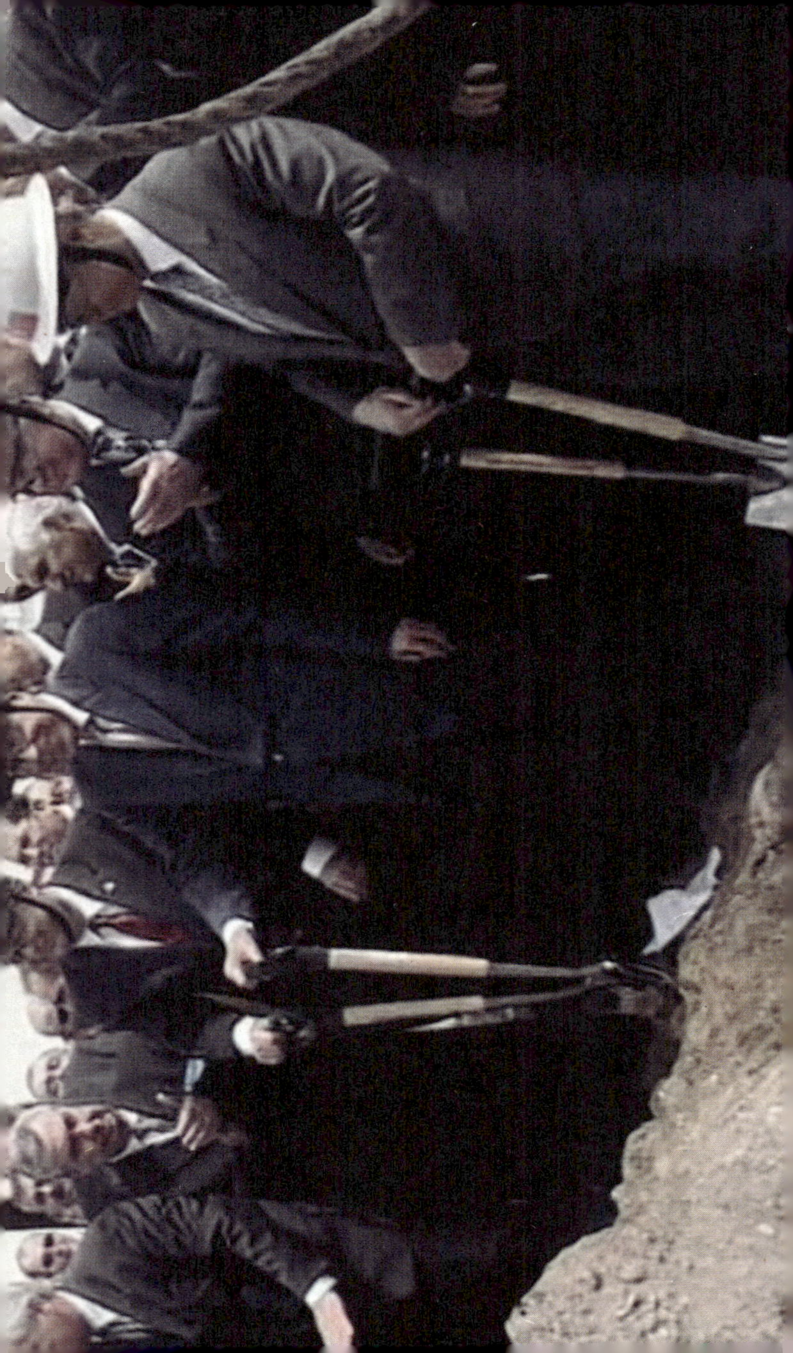

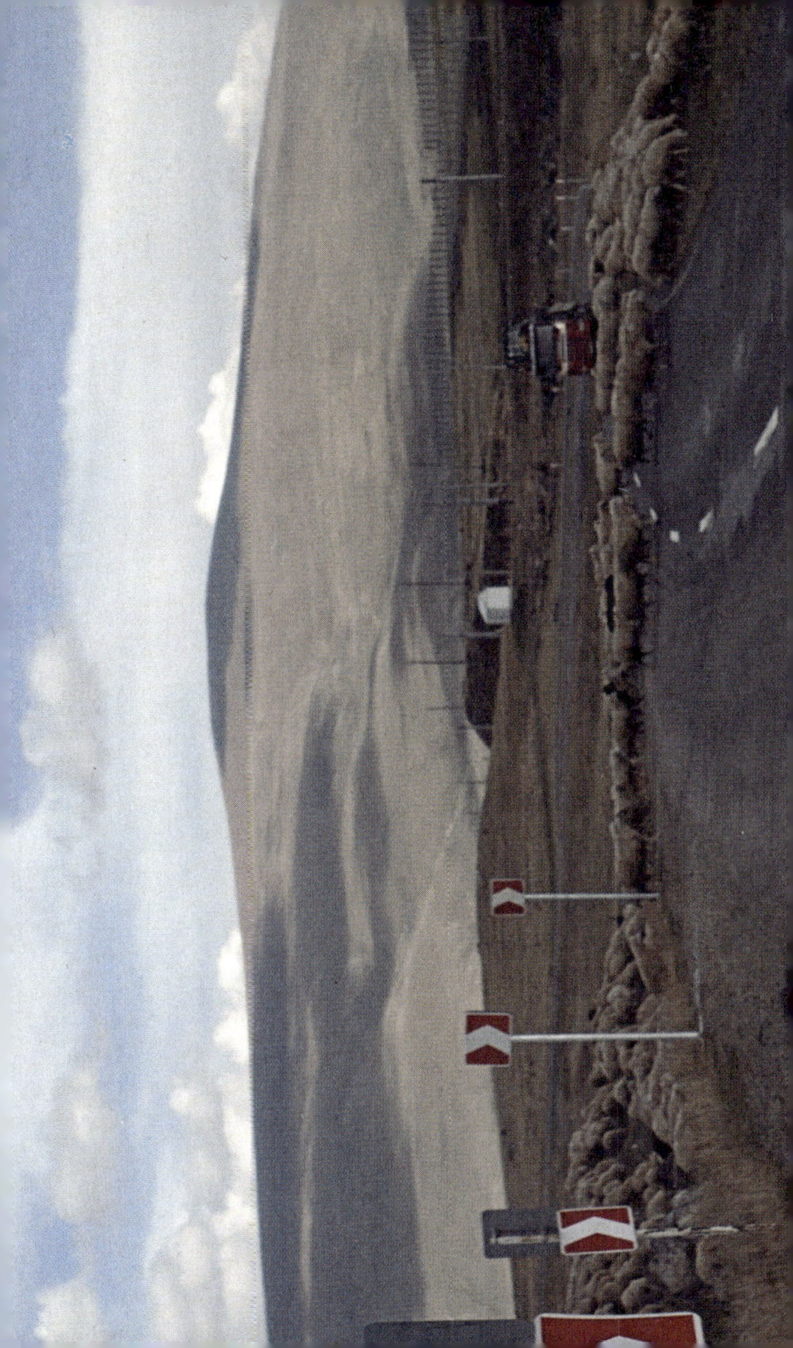

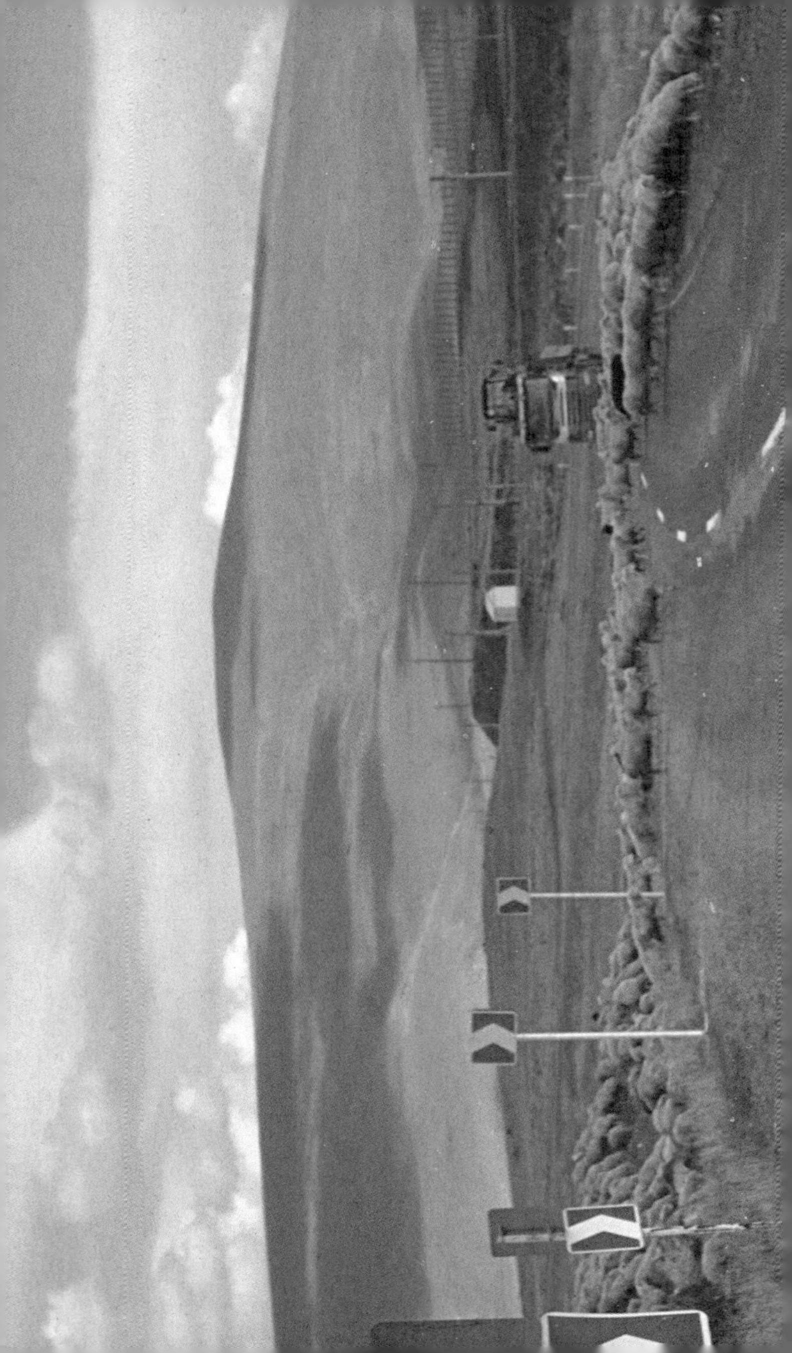

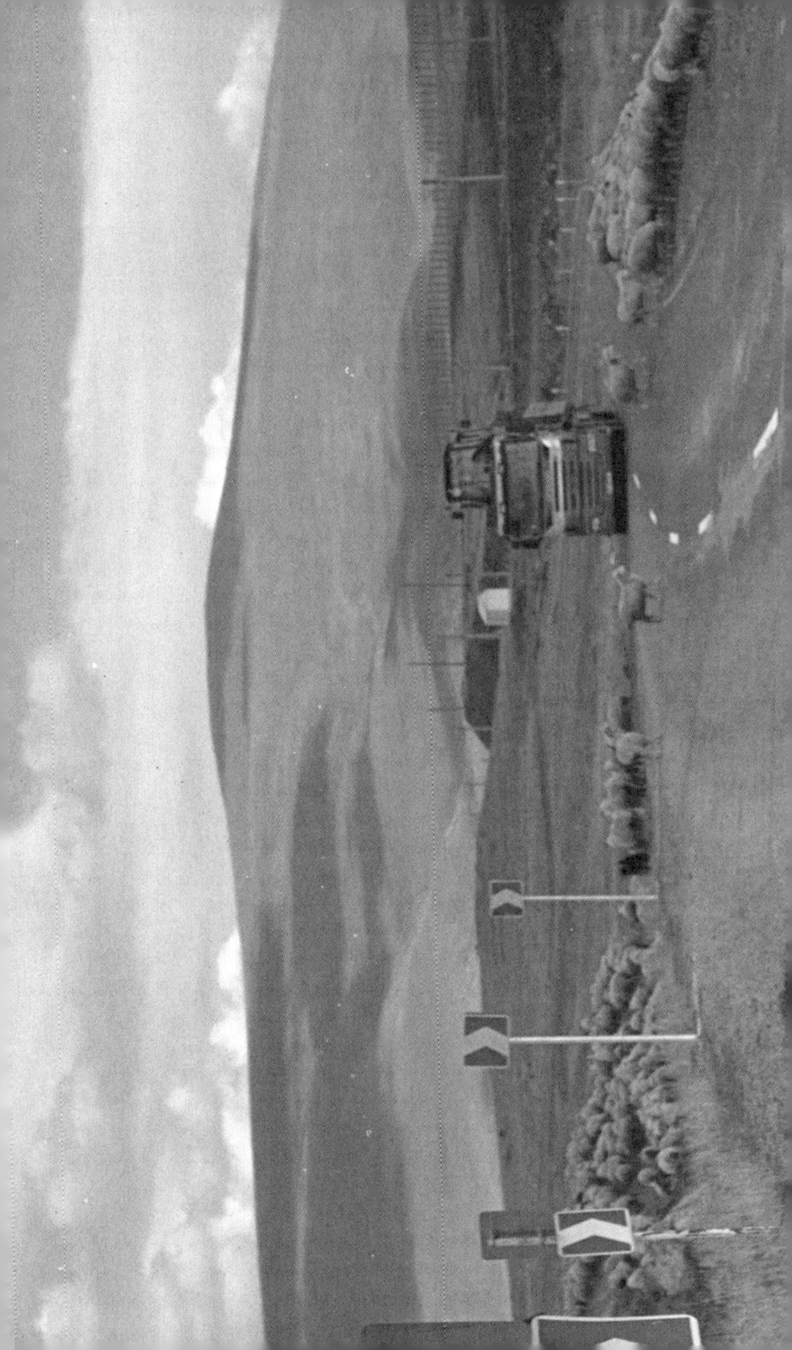

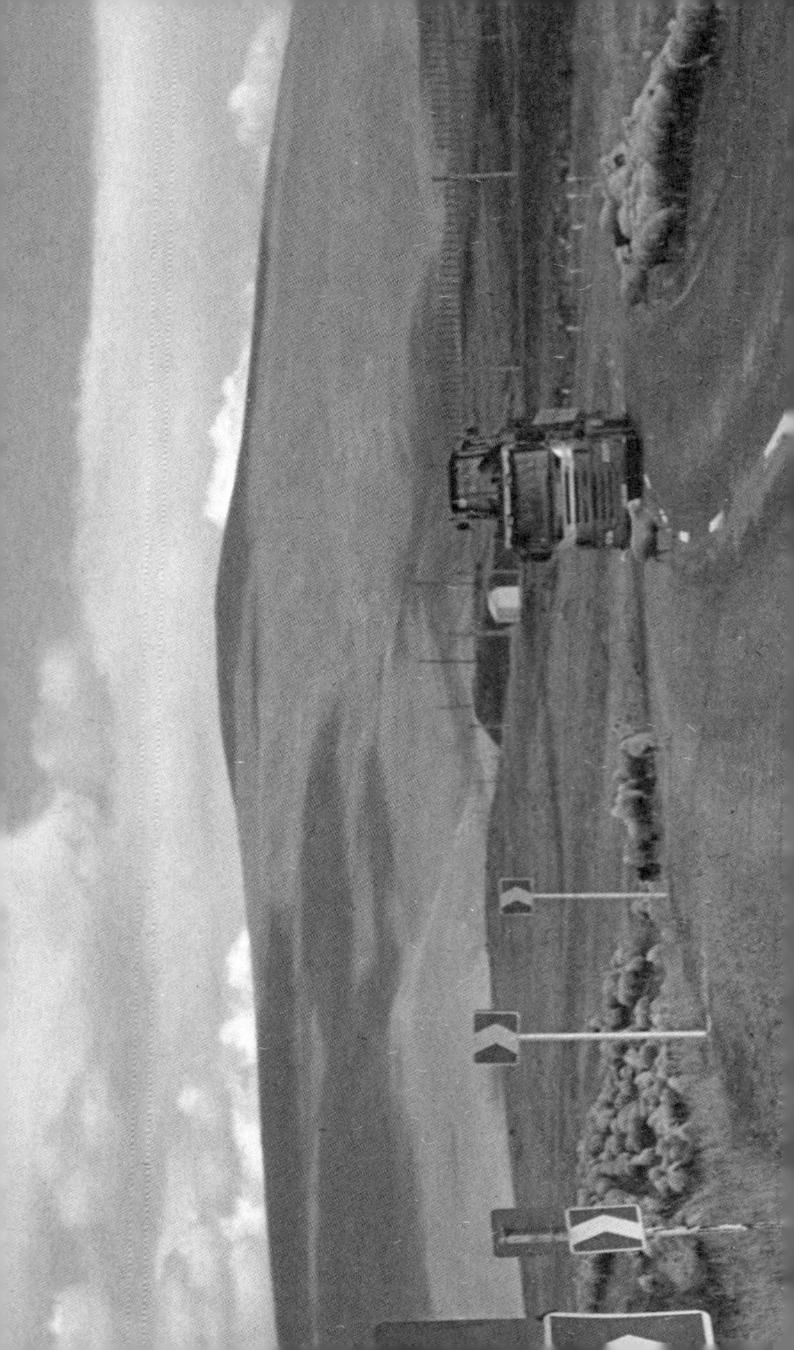

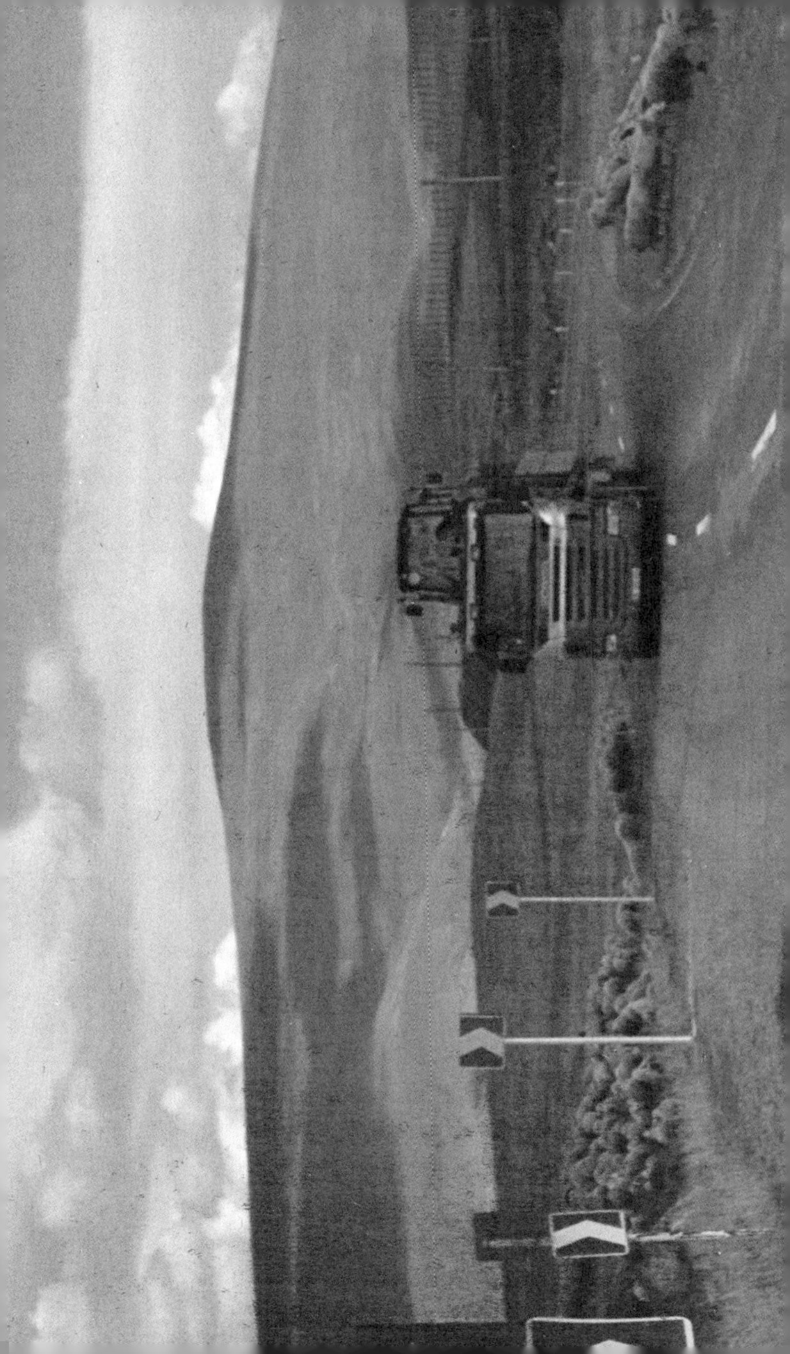

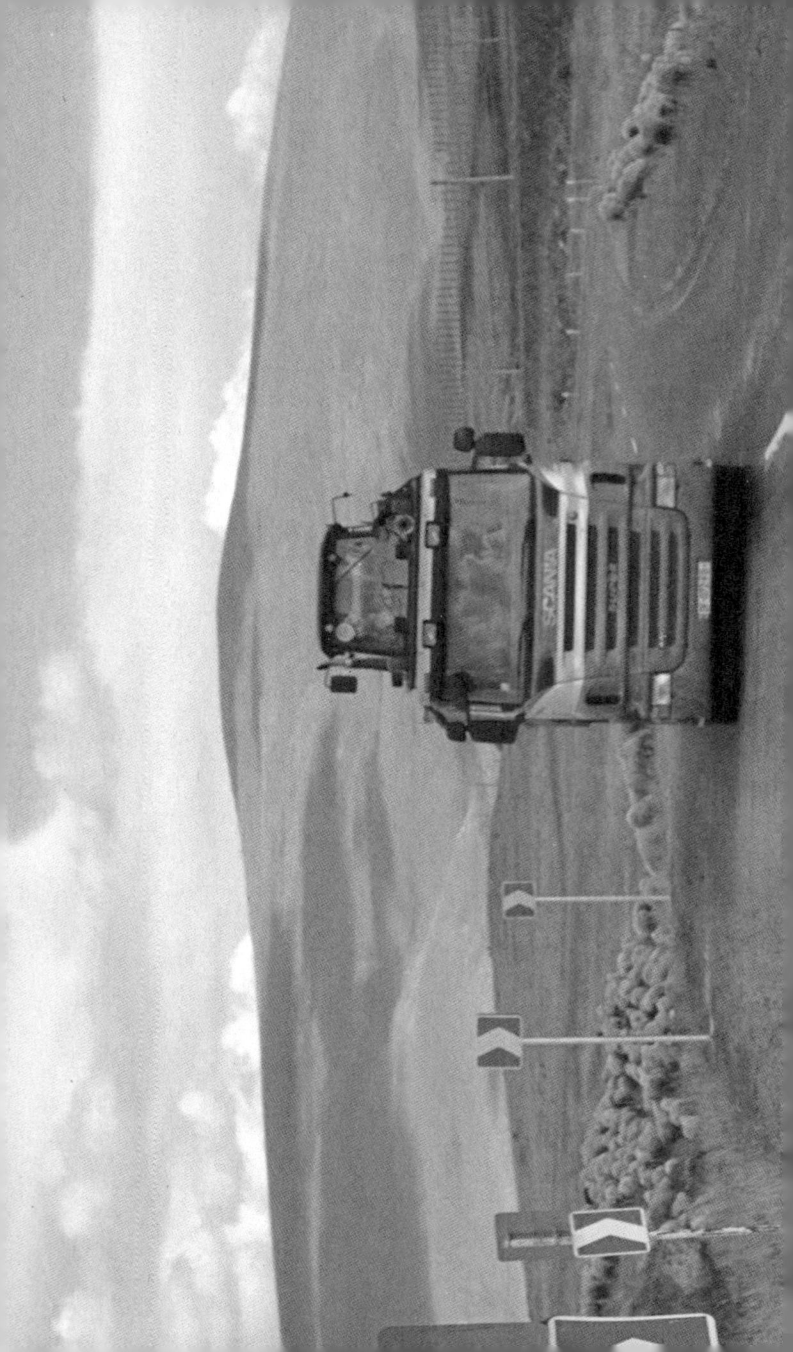

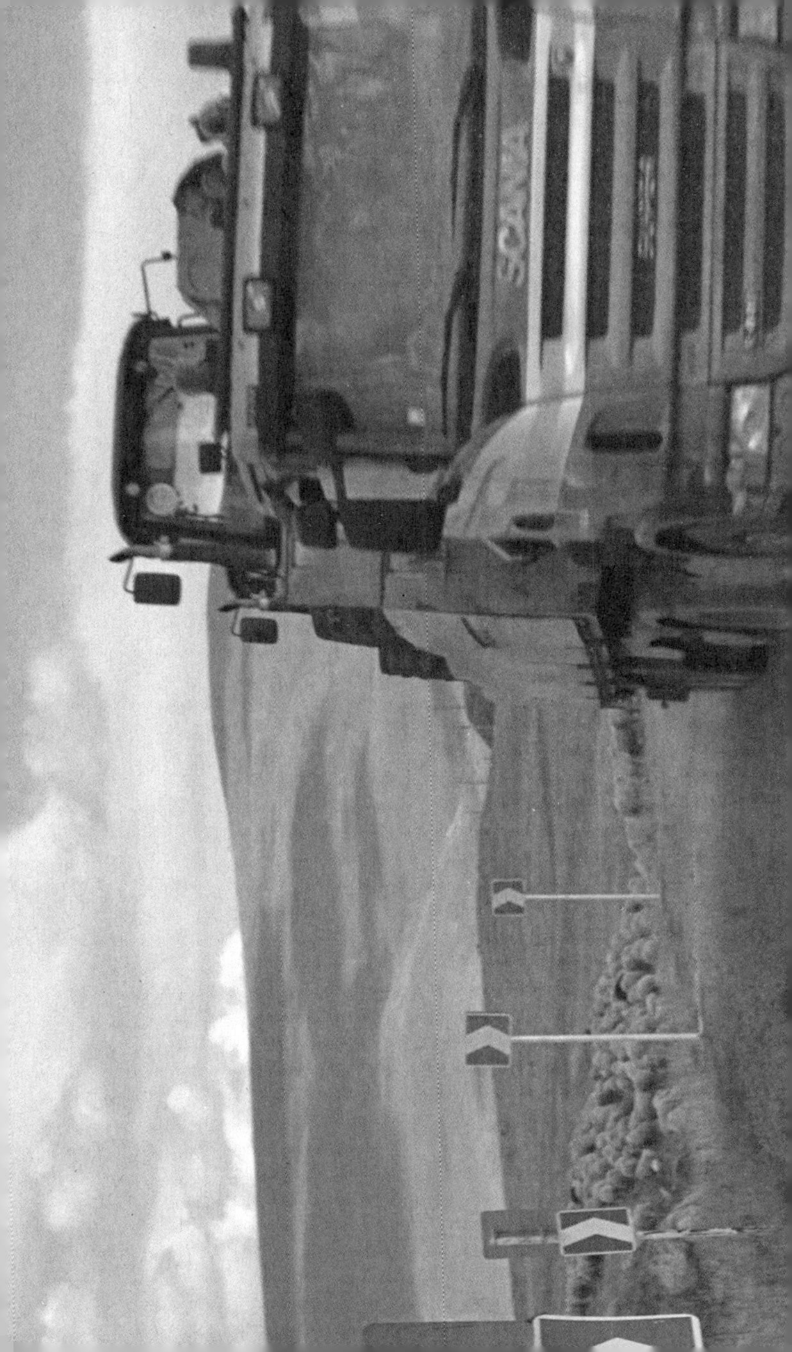

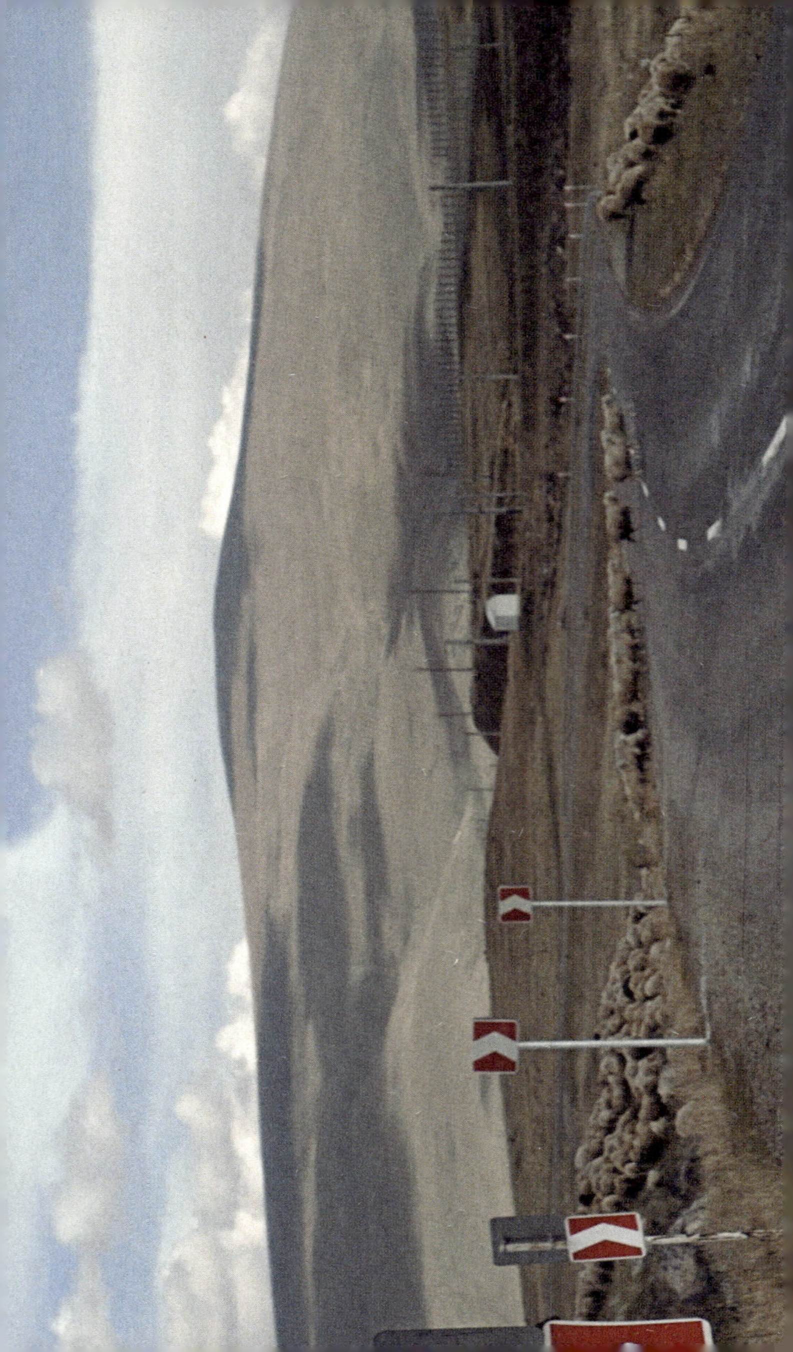

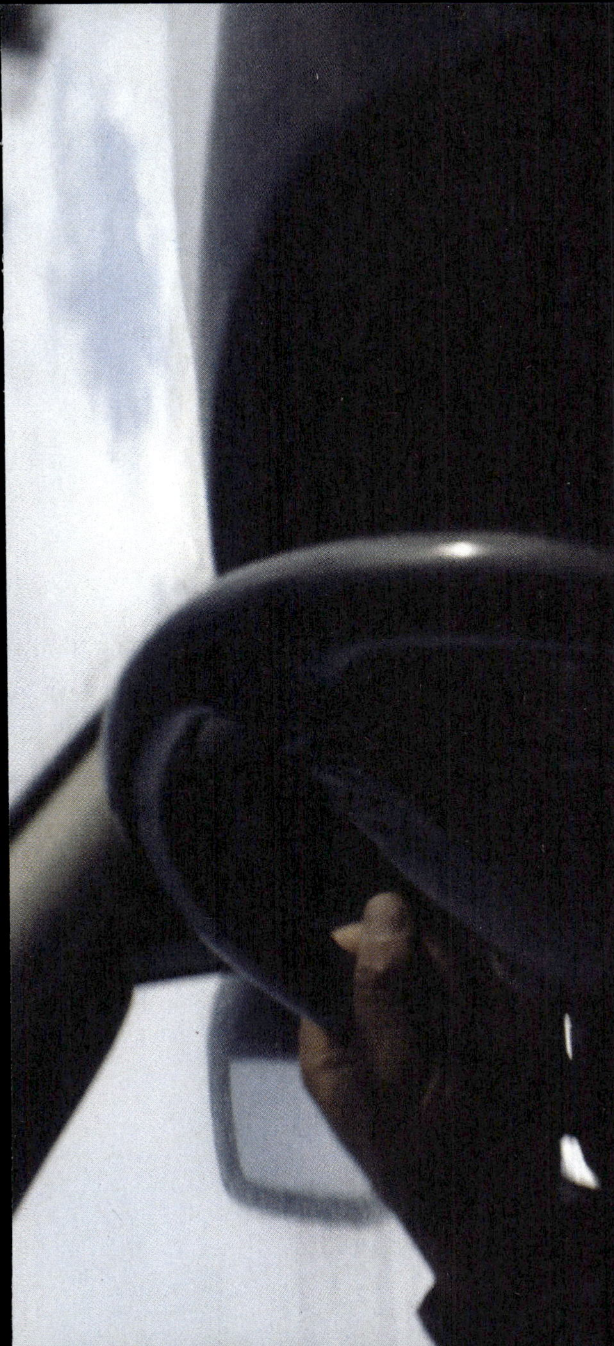

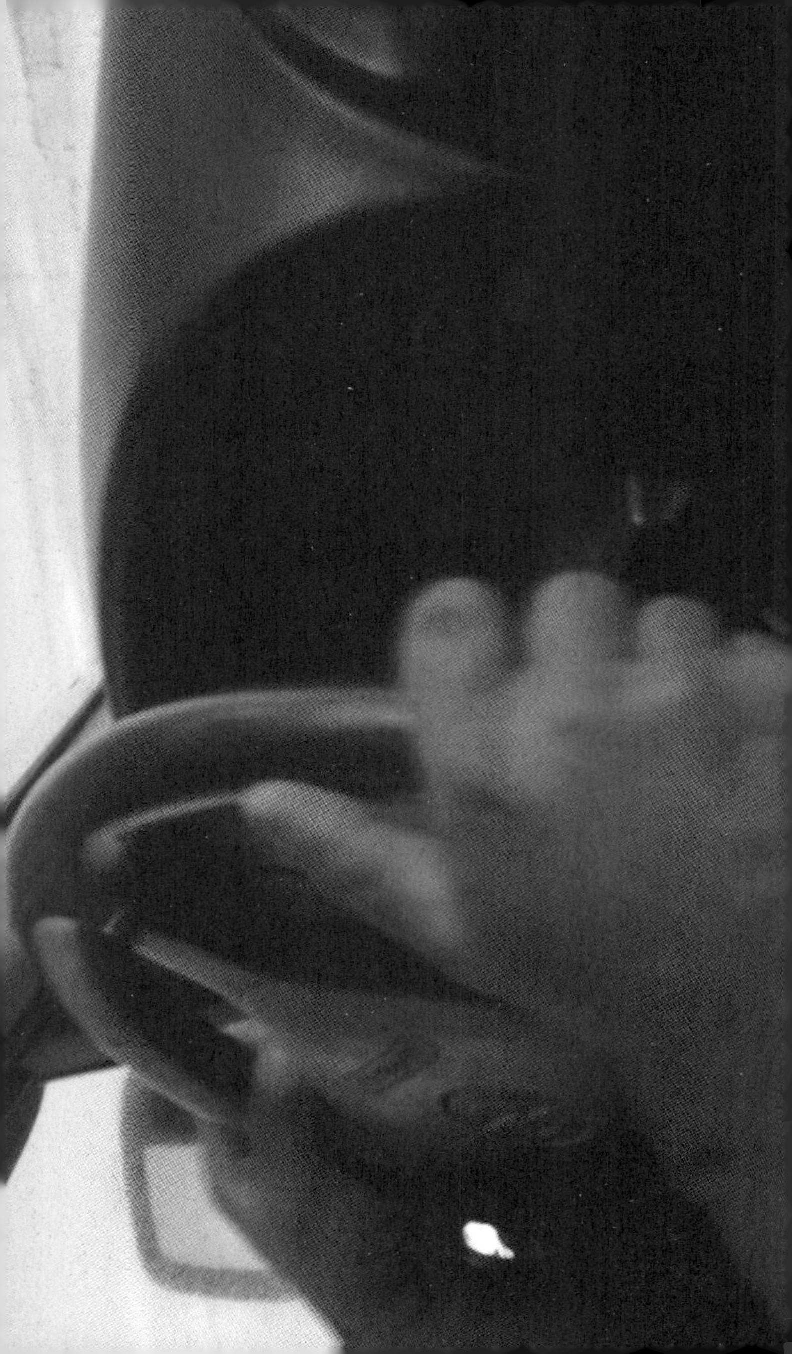

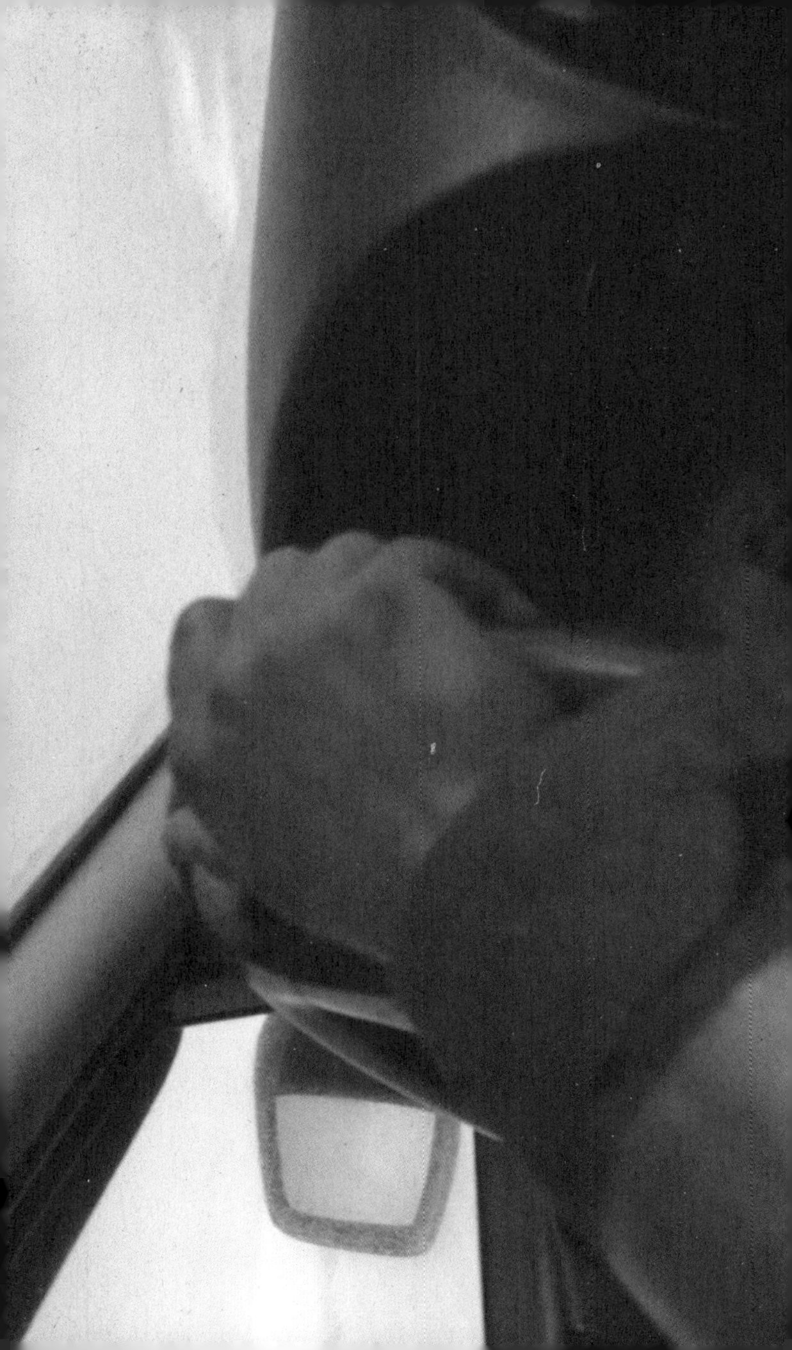

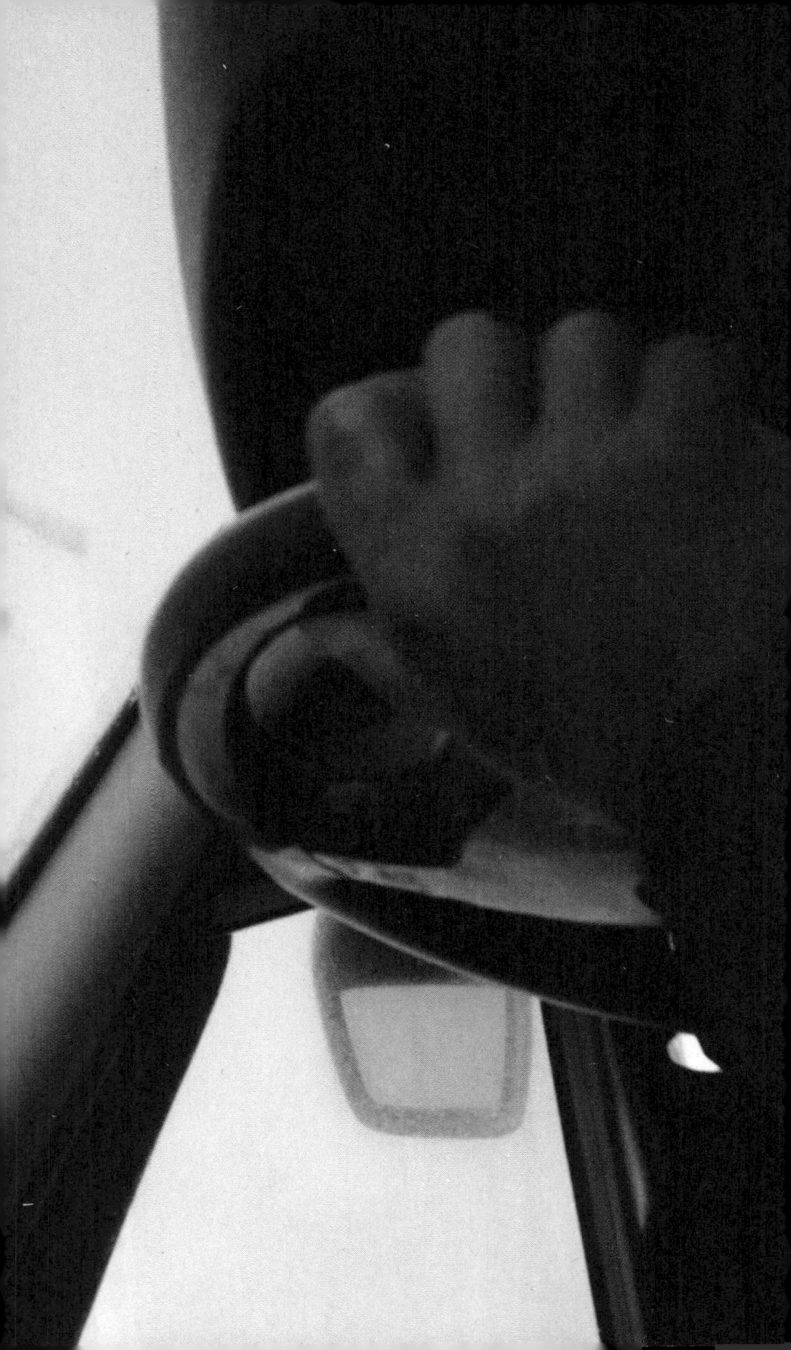

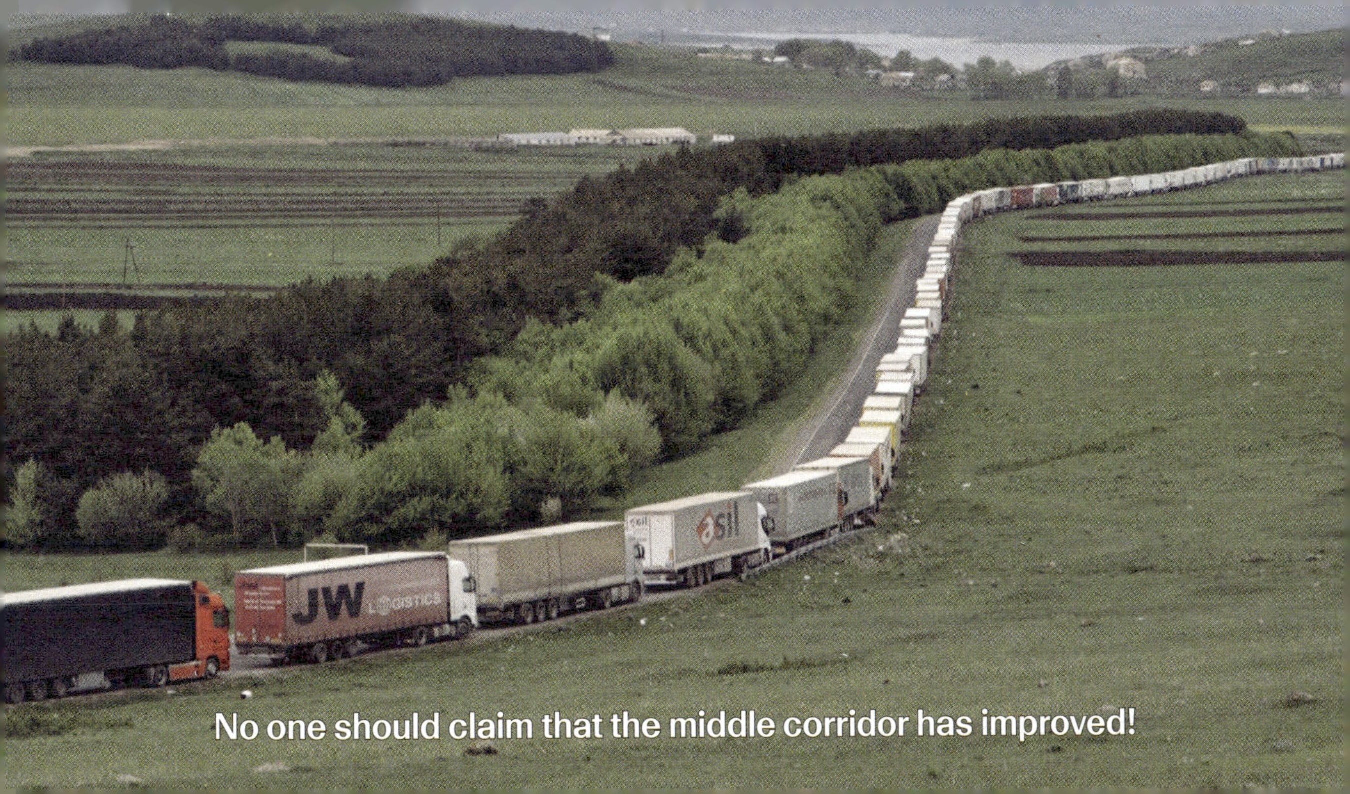
No one should claim that the middle corridor has improved!

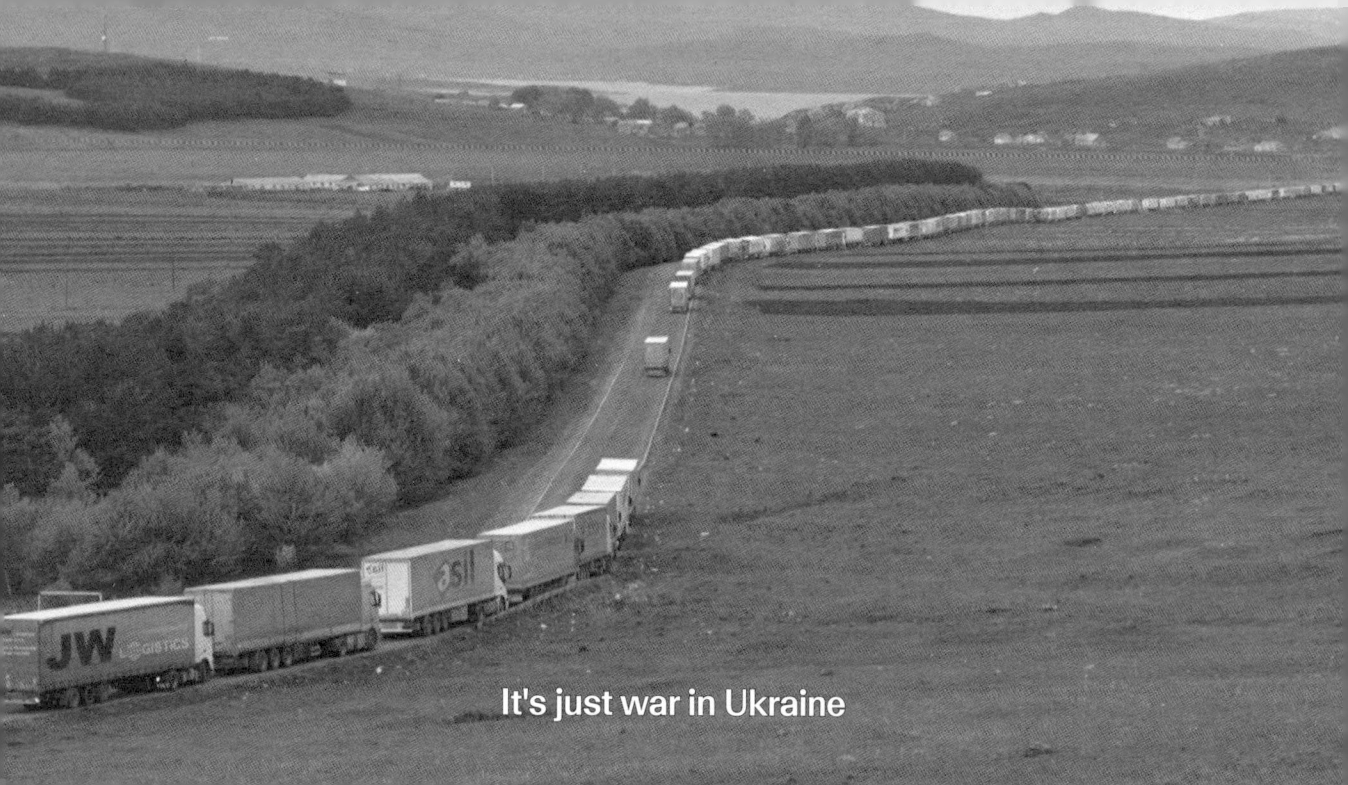
It's just war in Ukraine

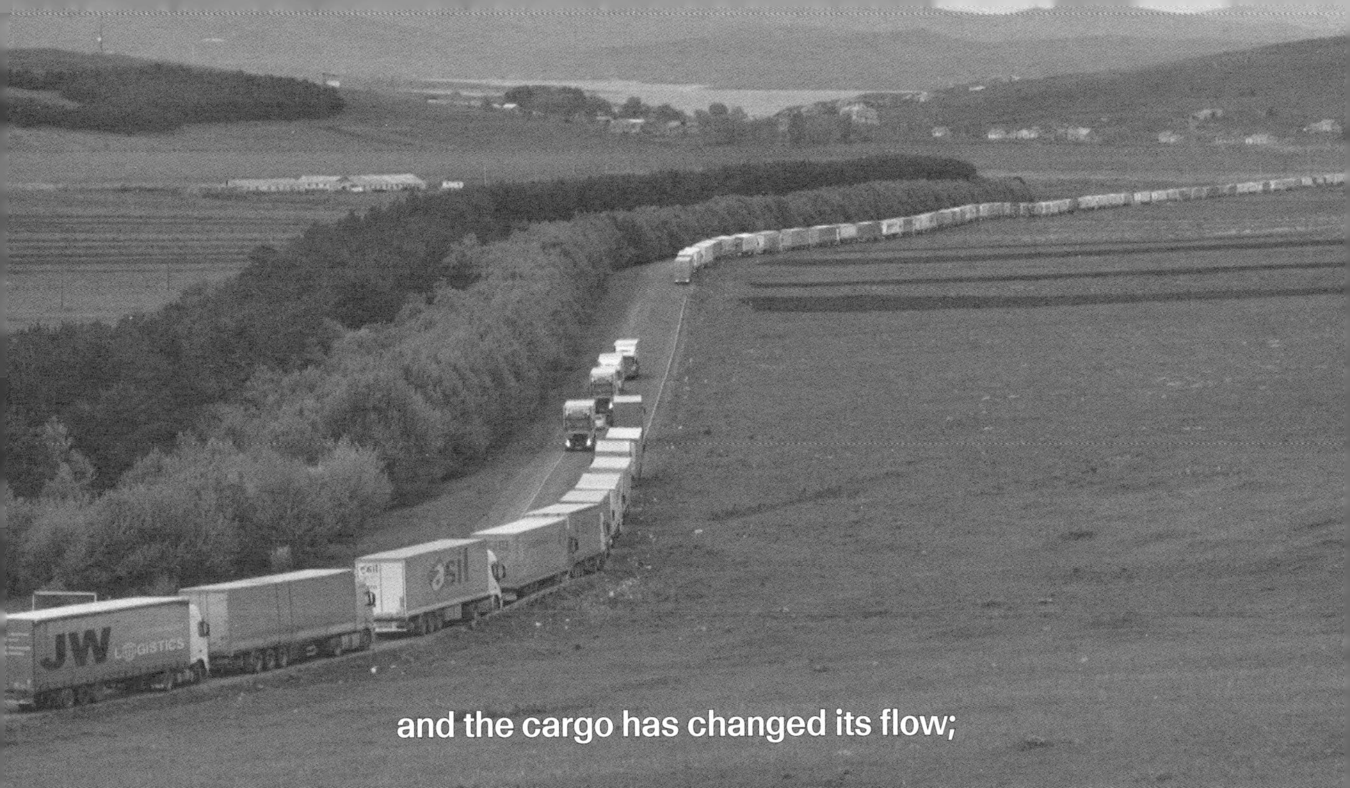

and the cargo has changed its flow;

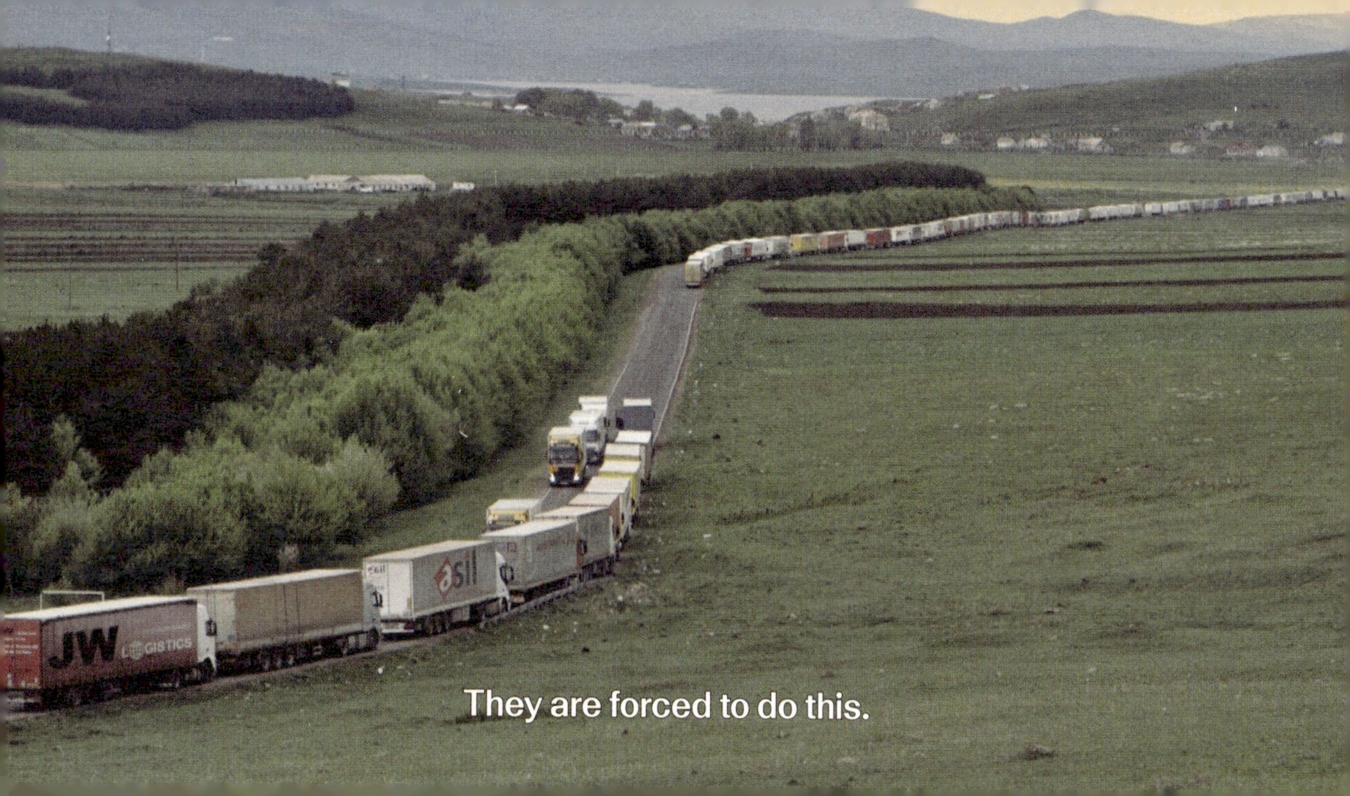

They are forced to do this.

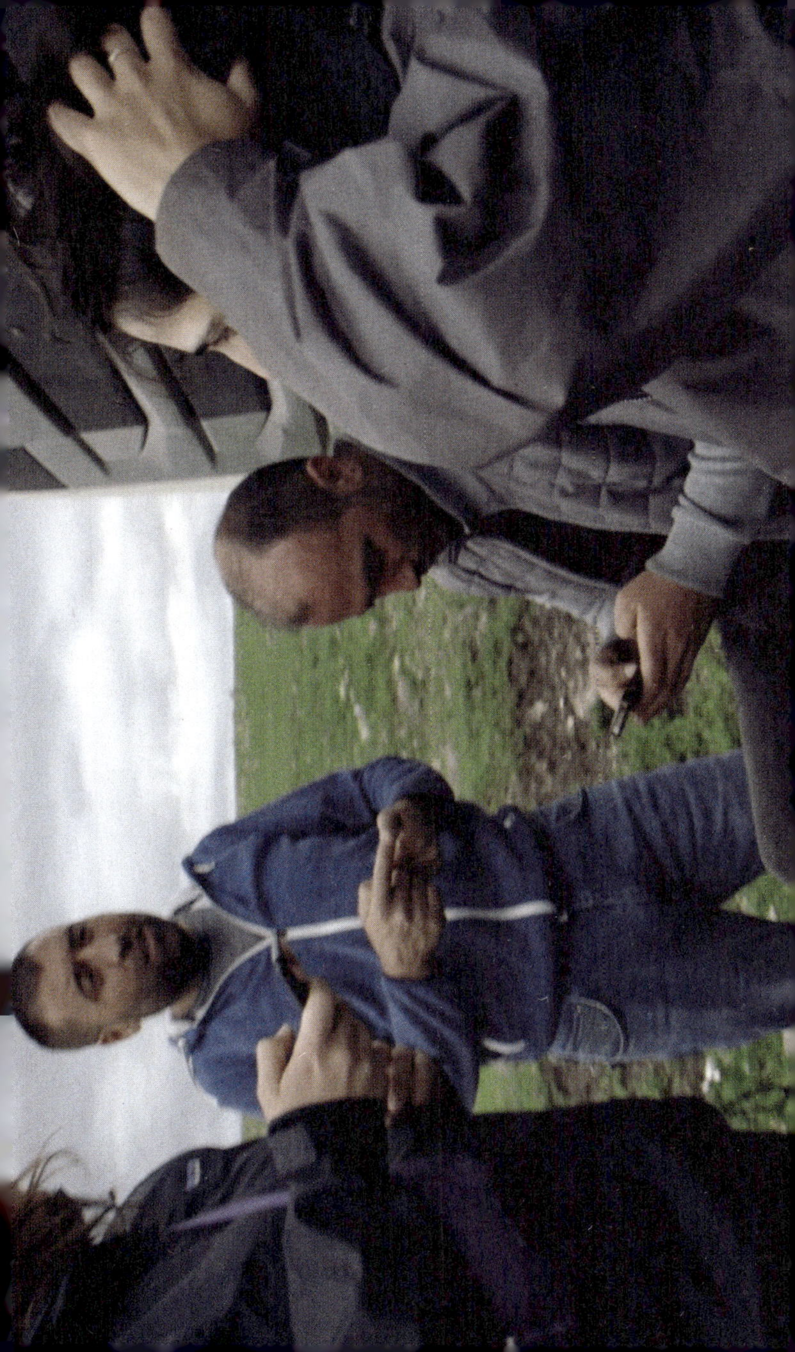

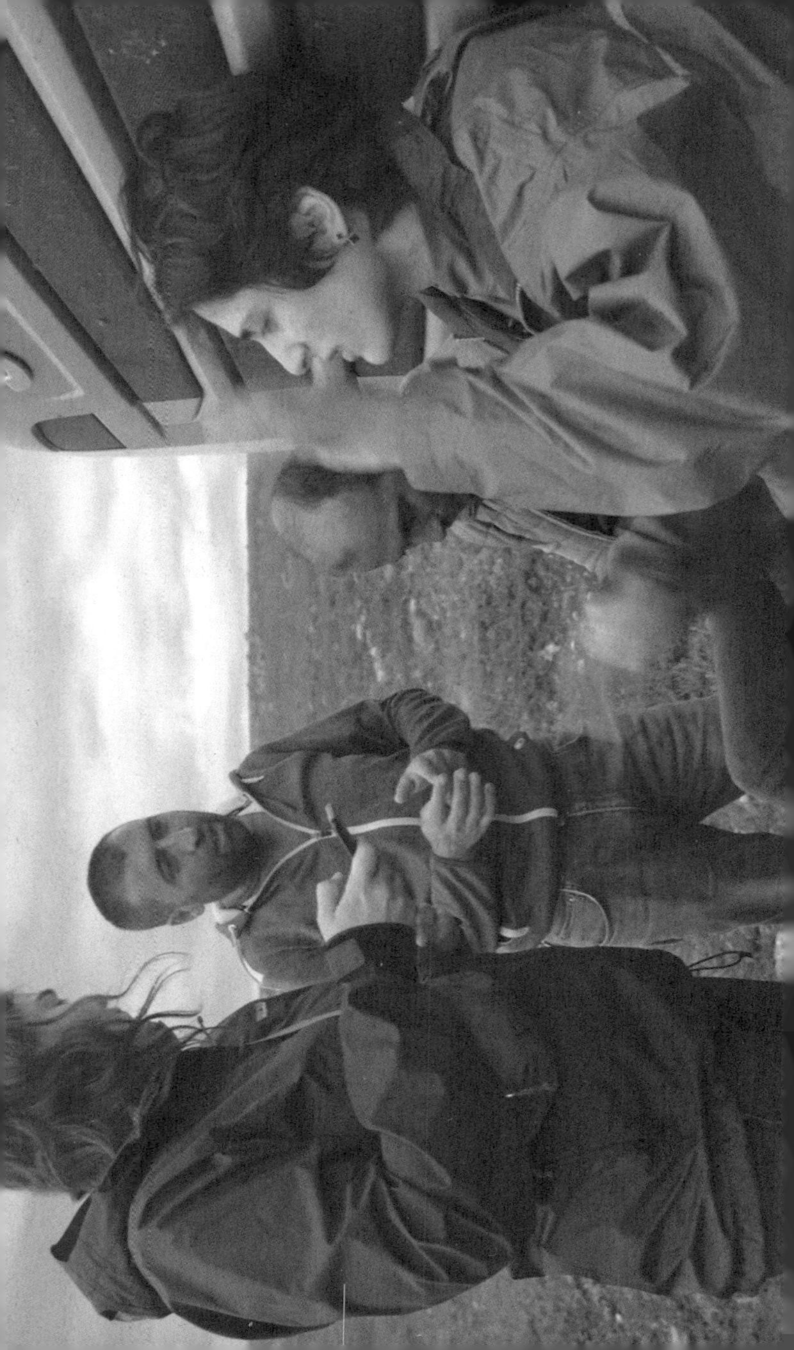

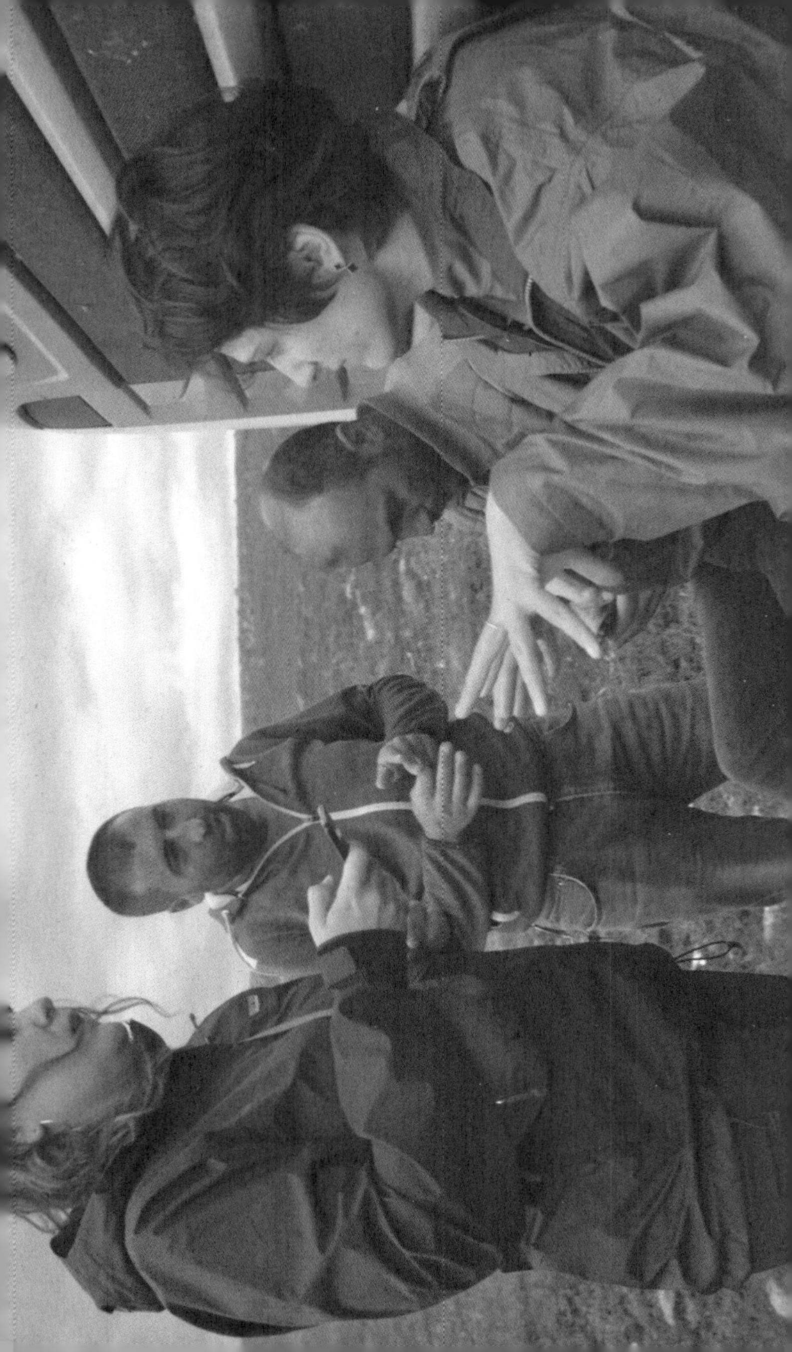

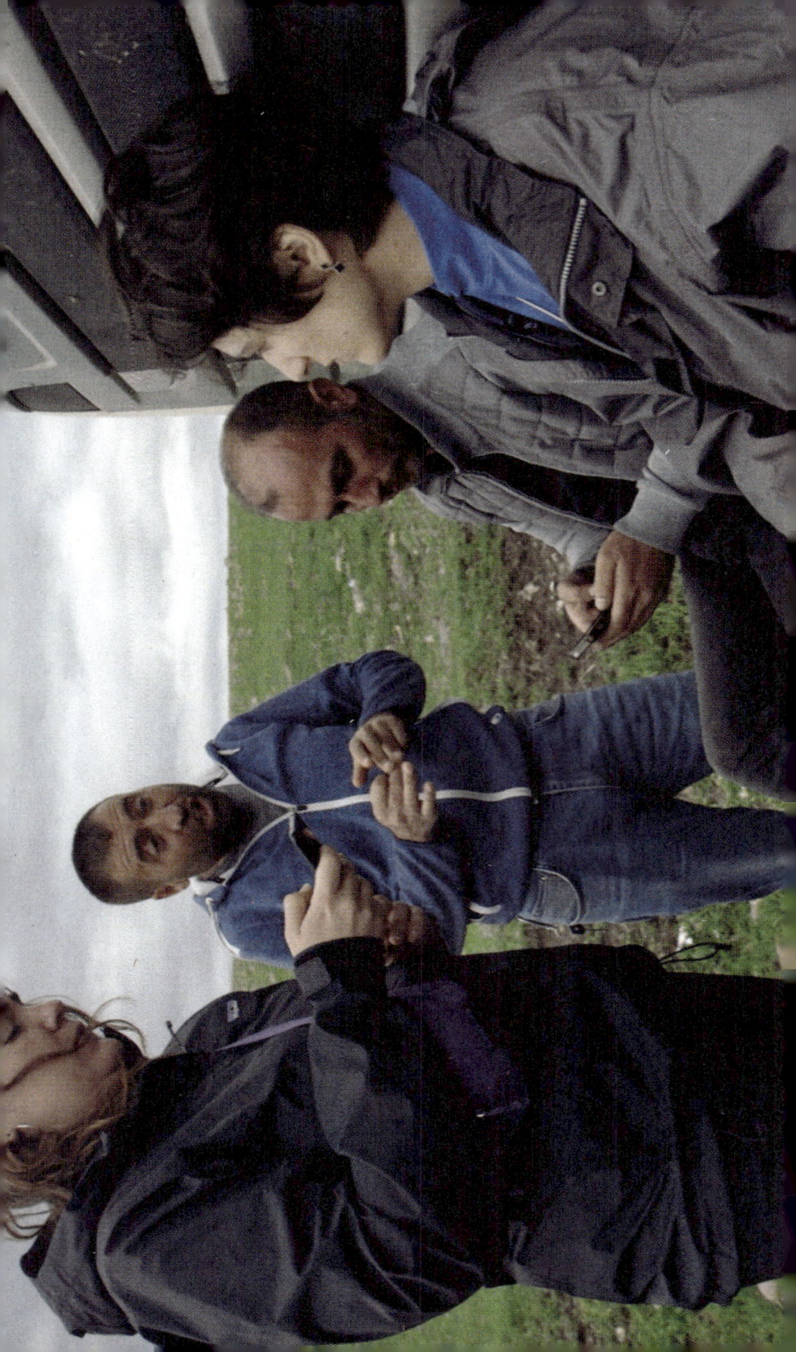

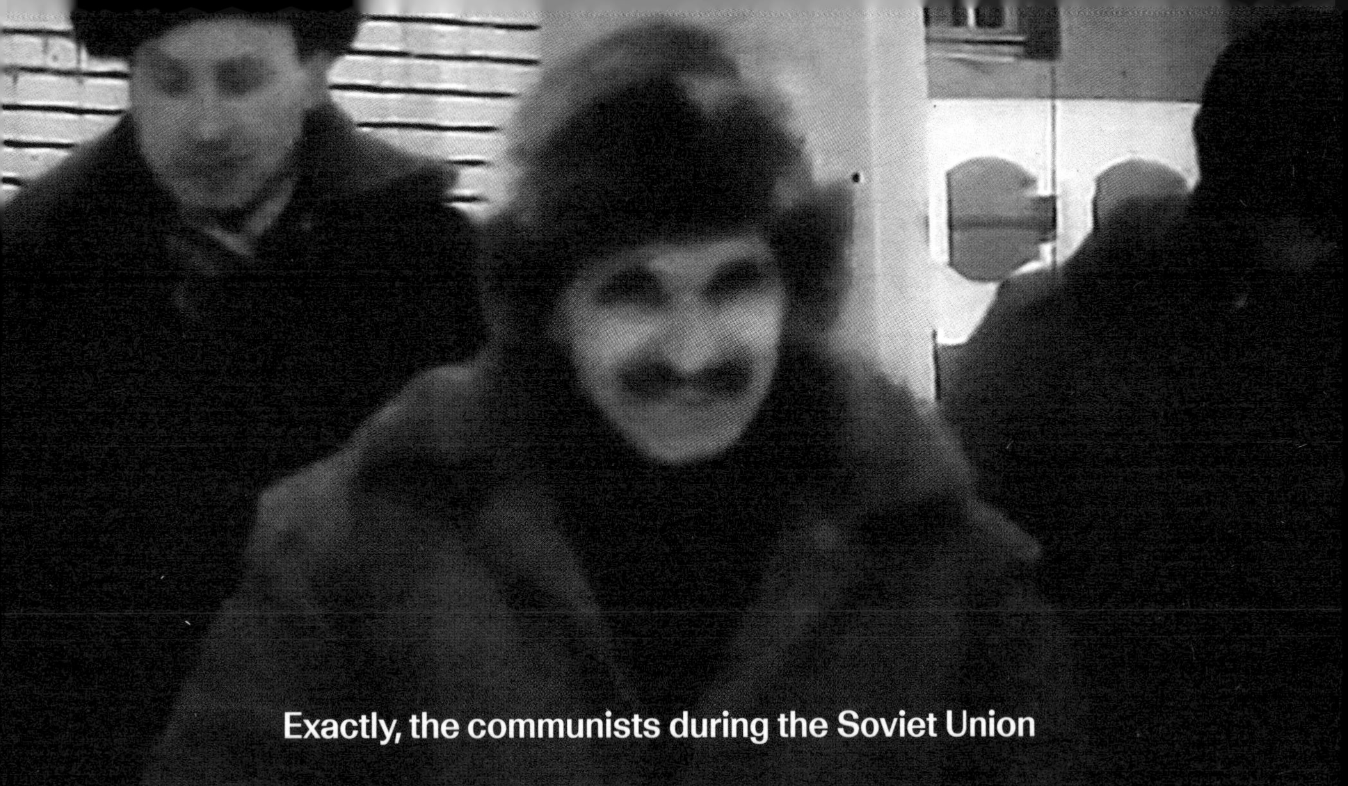
Exactly, the communists during the Soviet Union

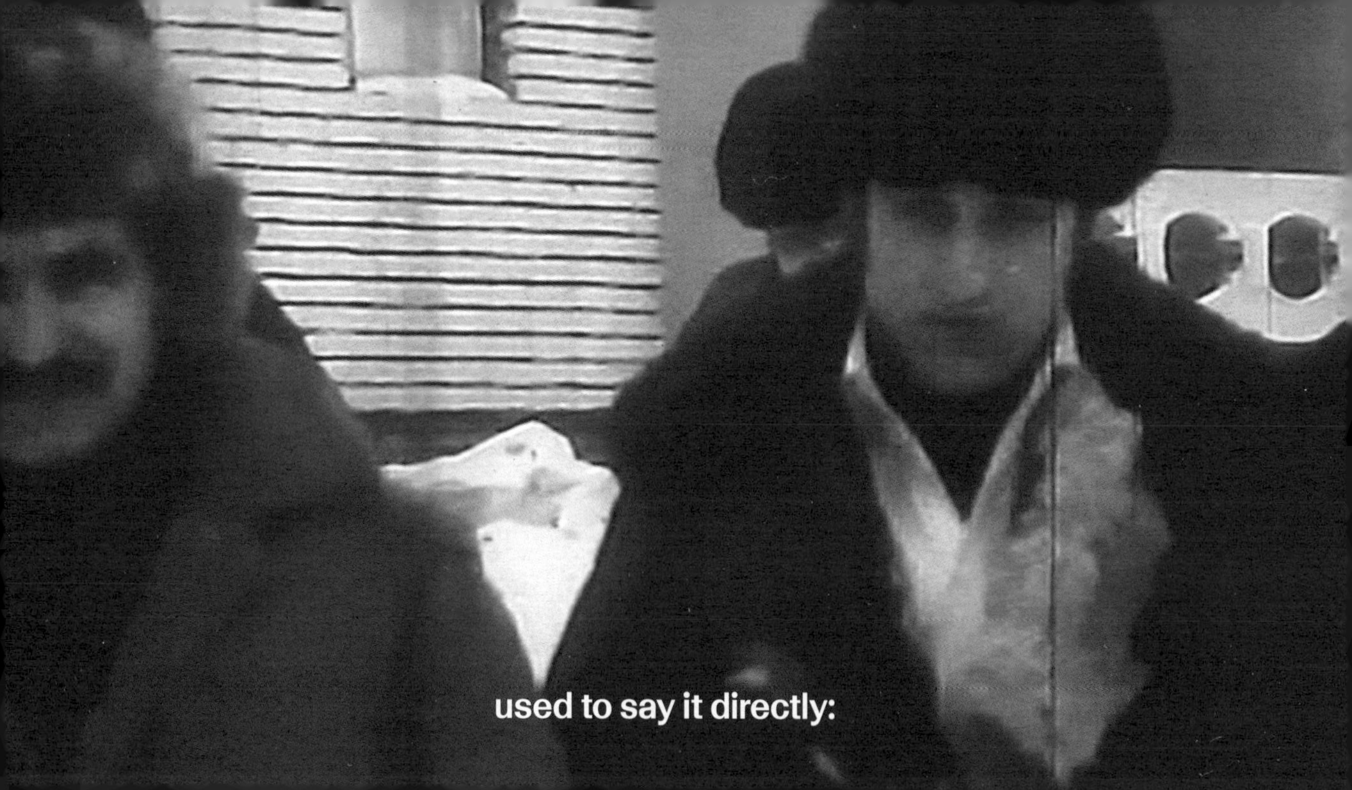

used to say it directly:

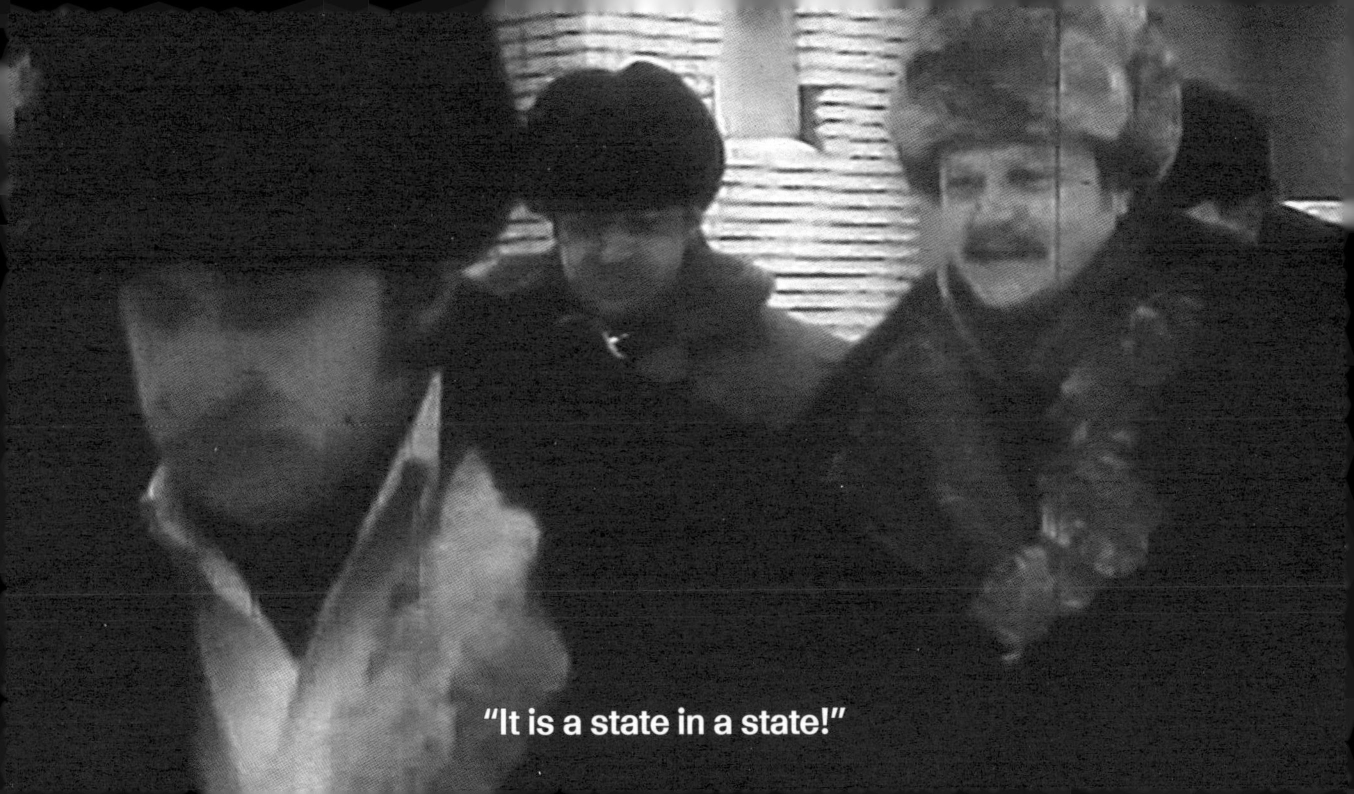
"It is a state in a state!"

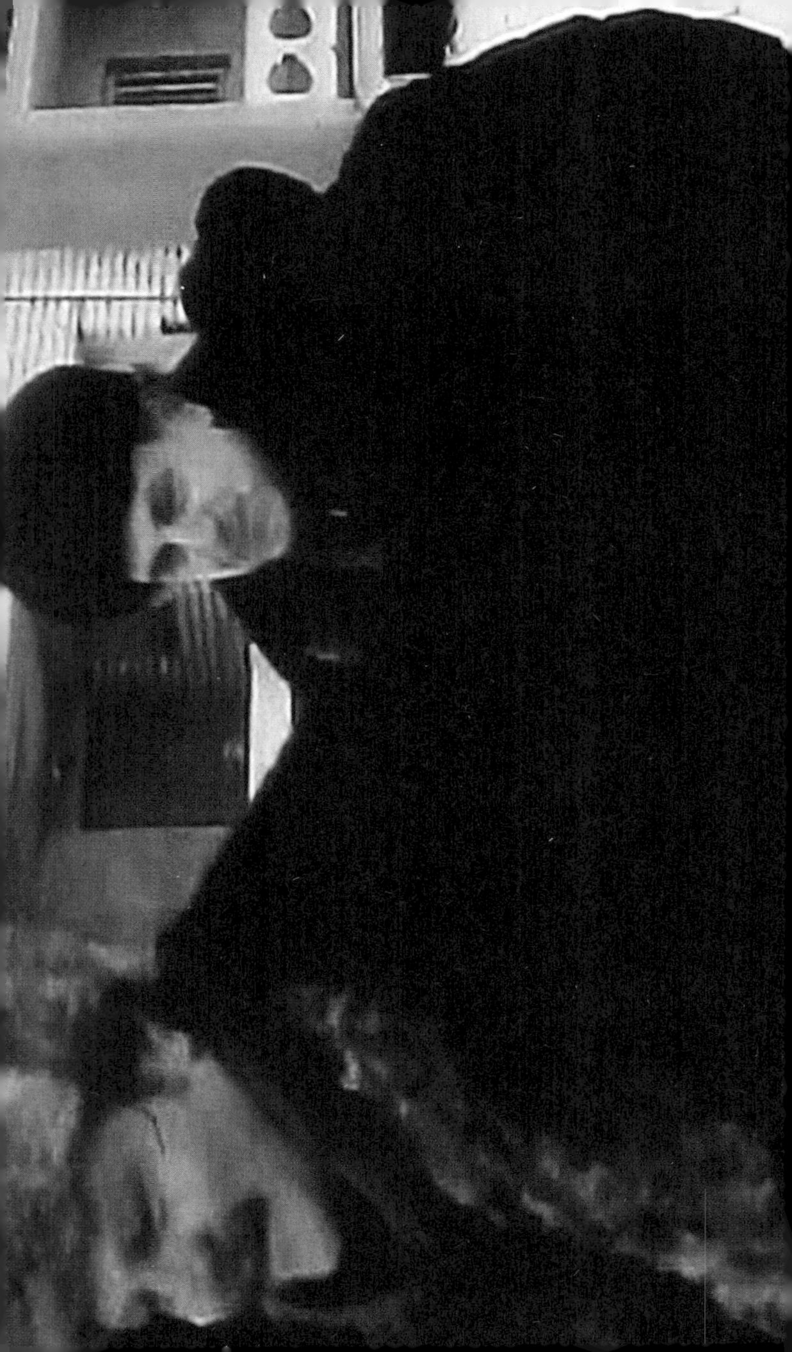

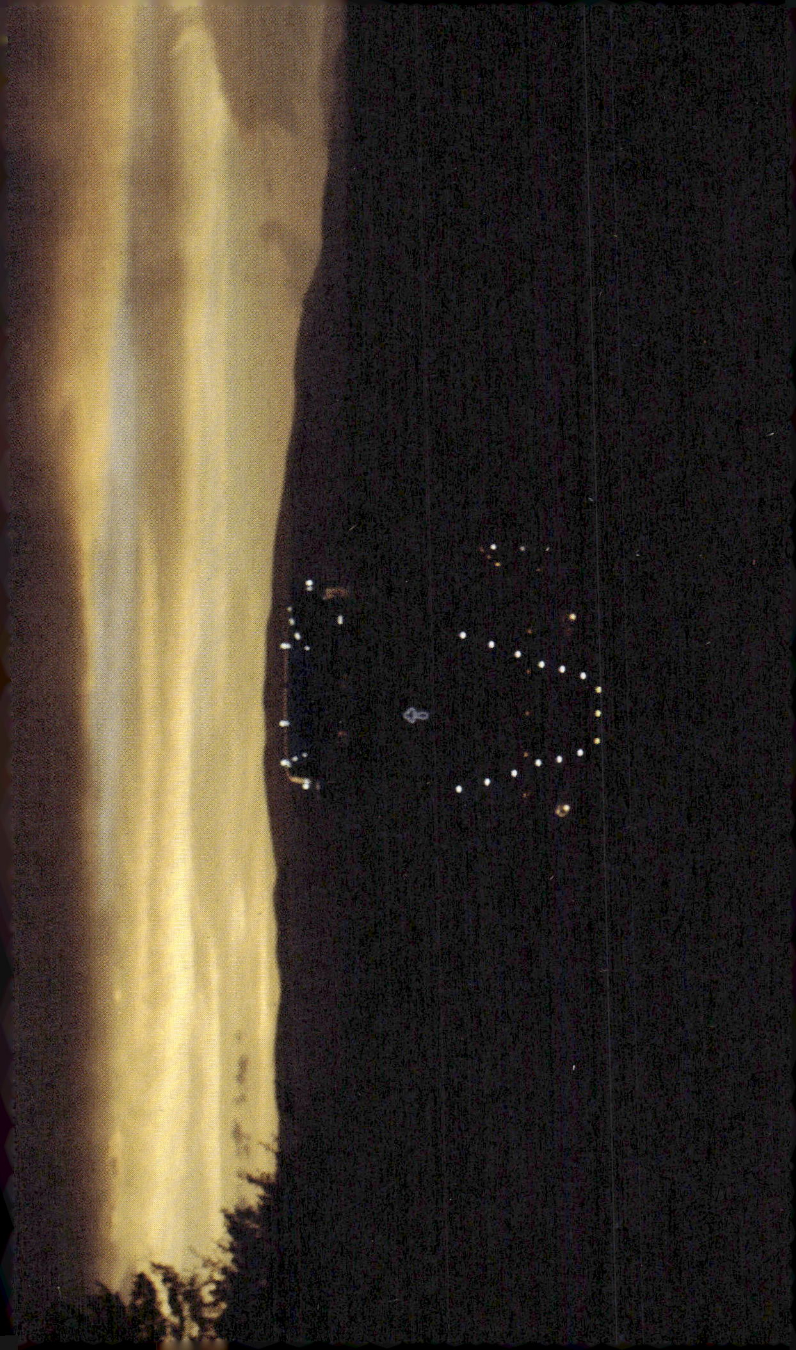

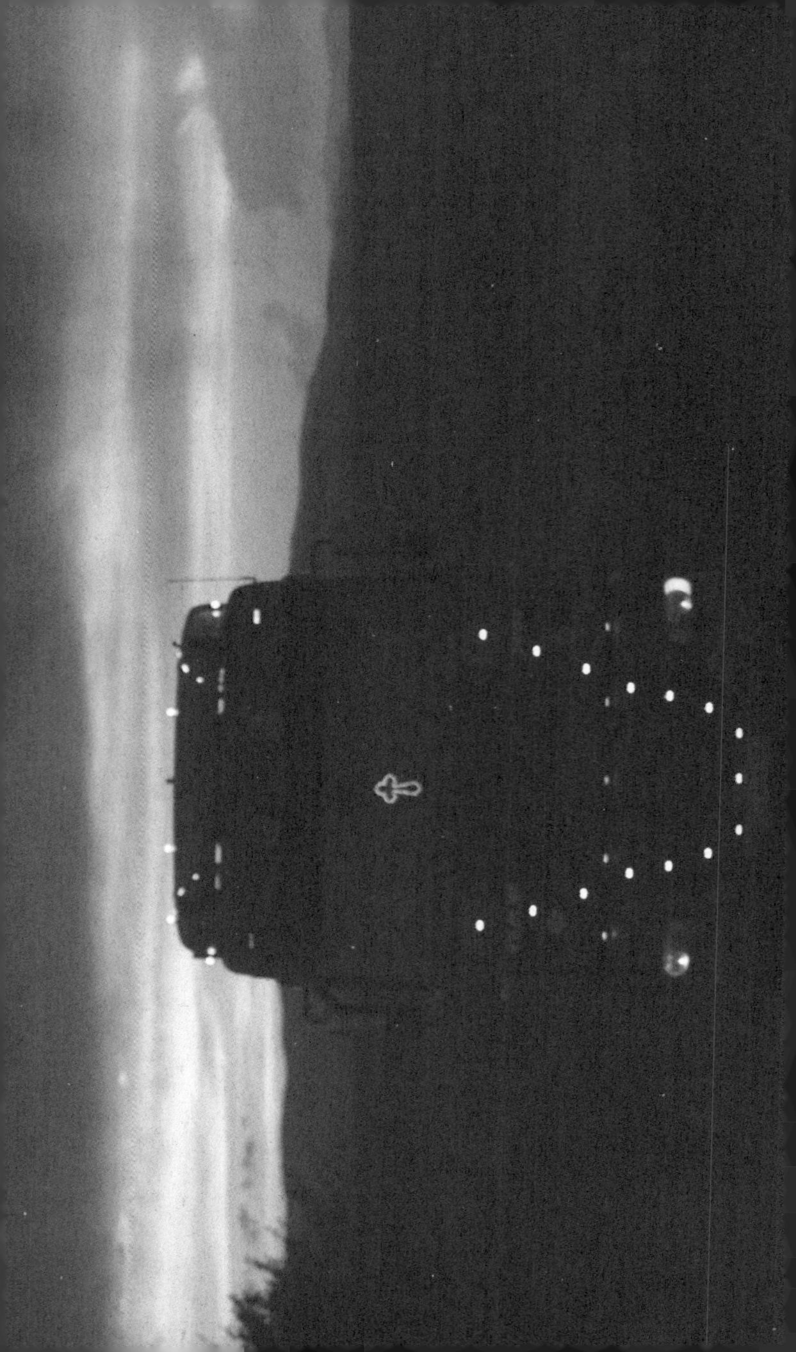

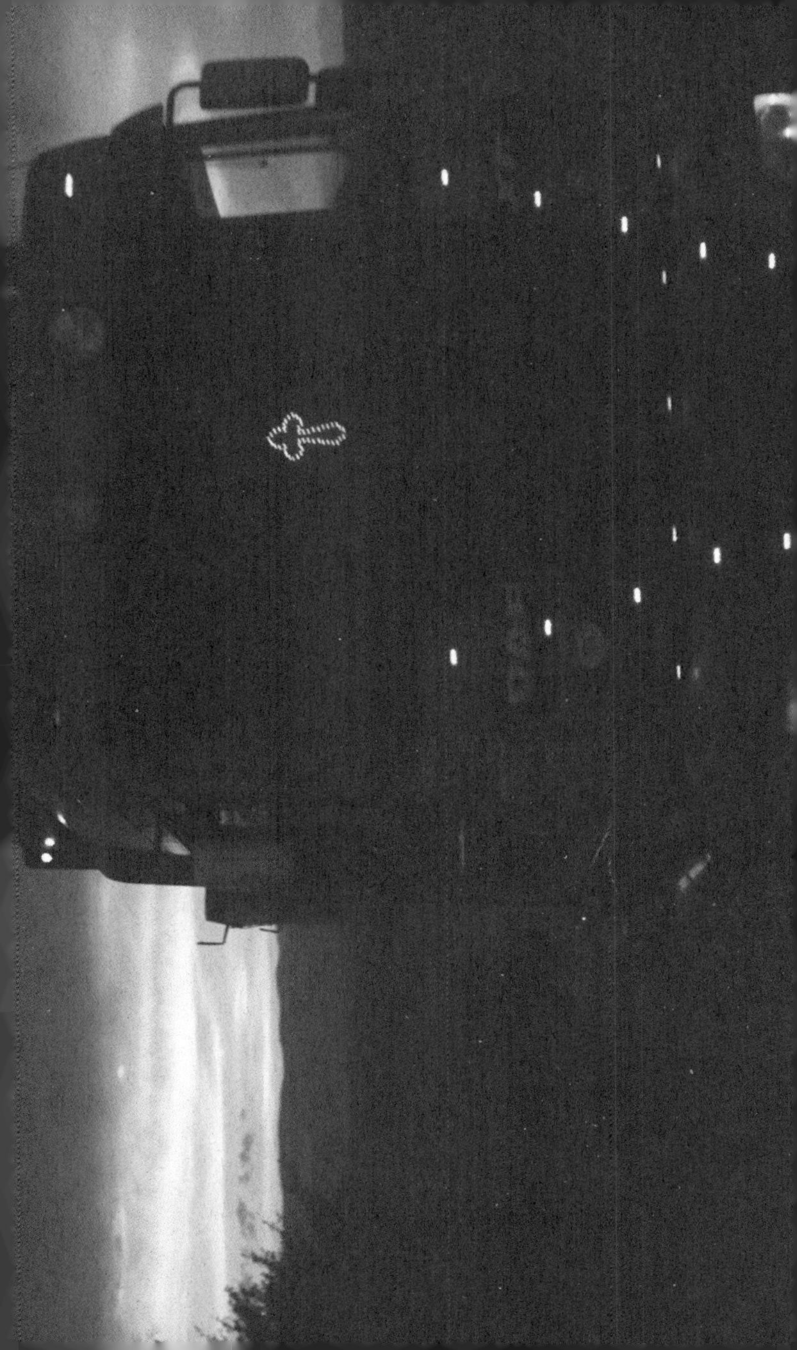

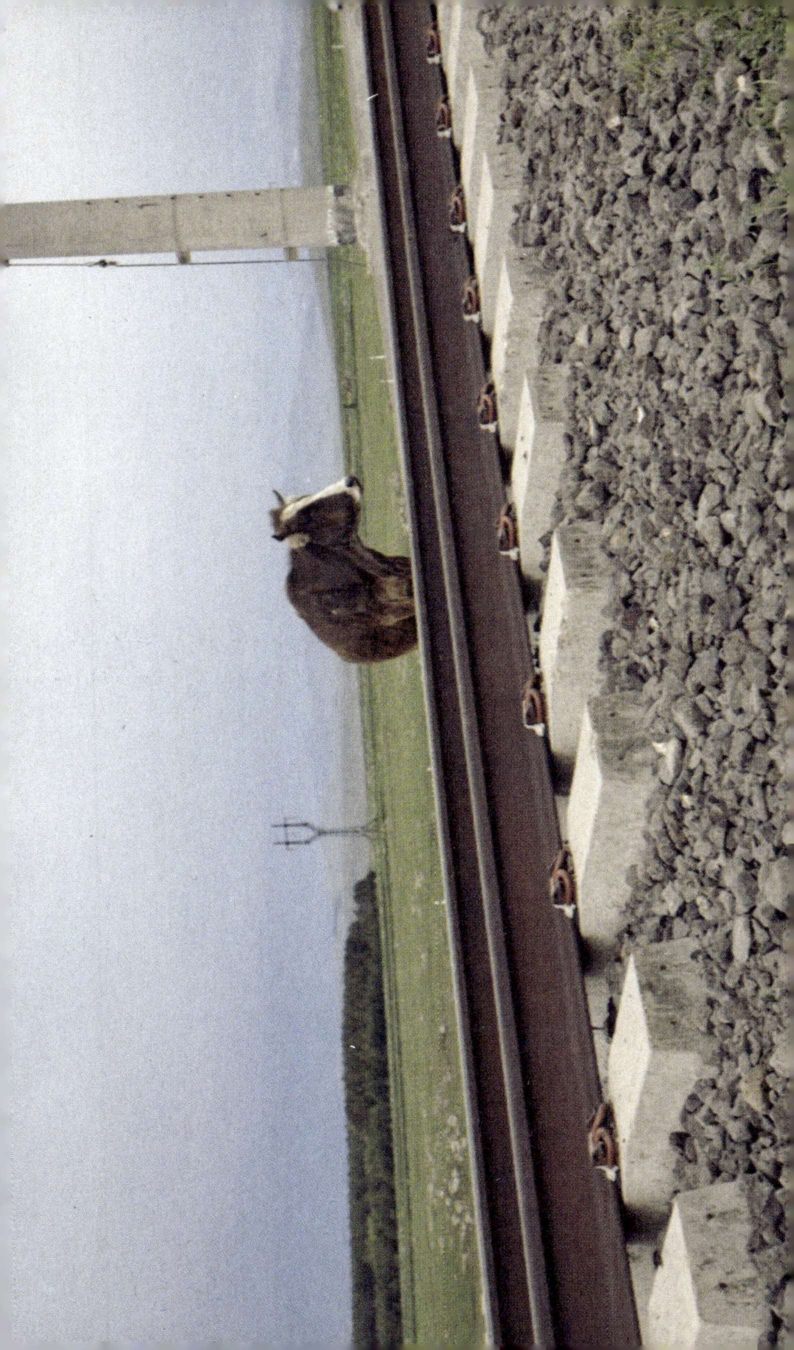

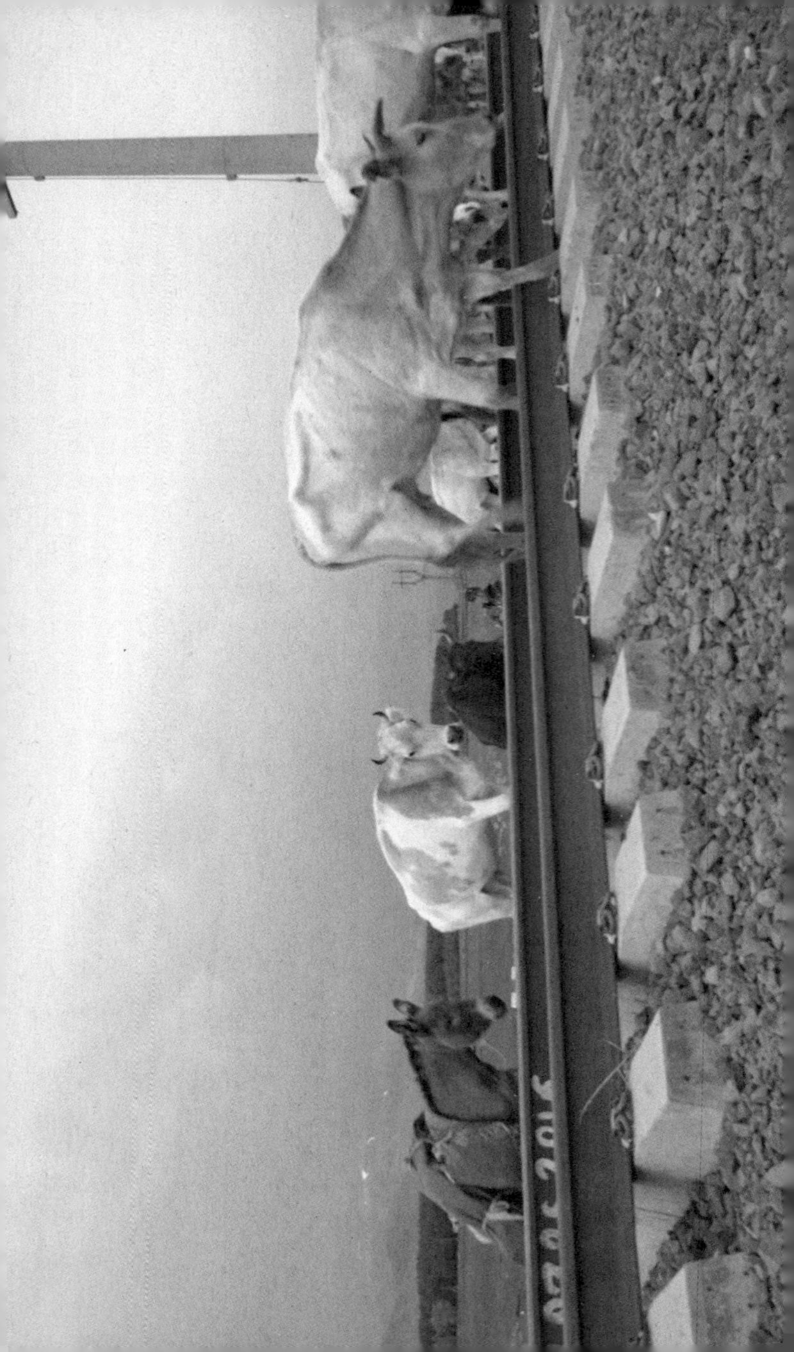

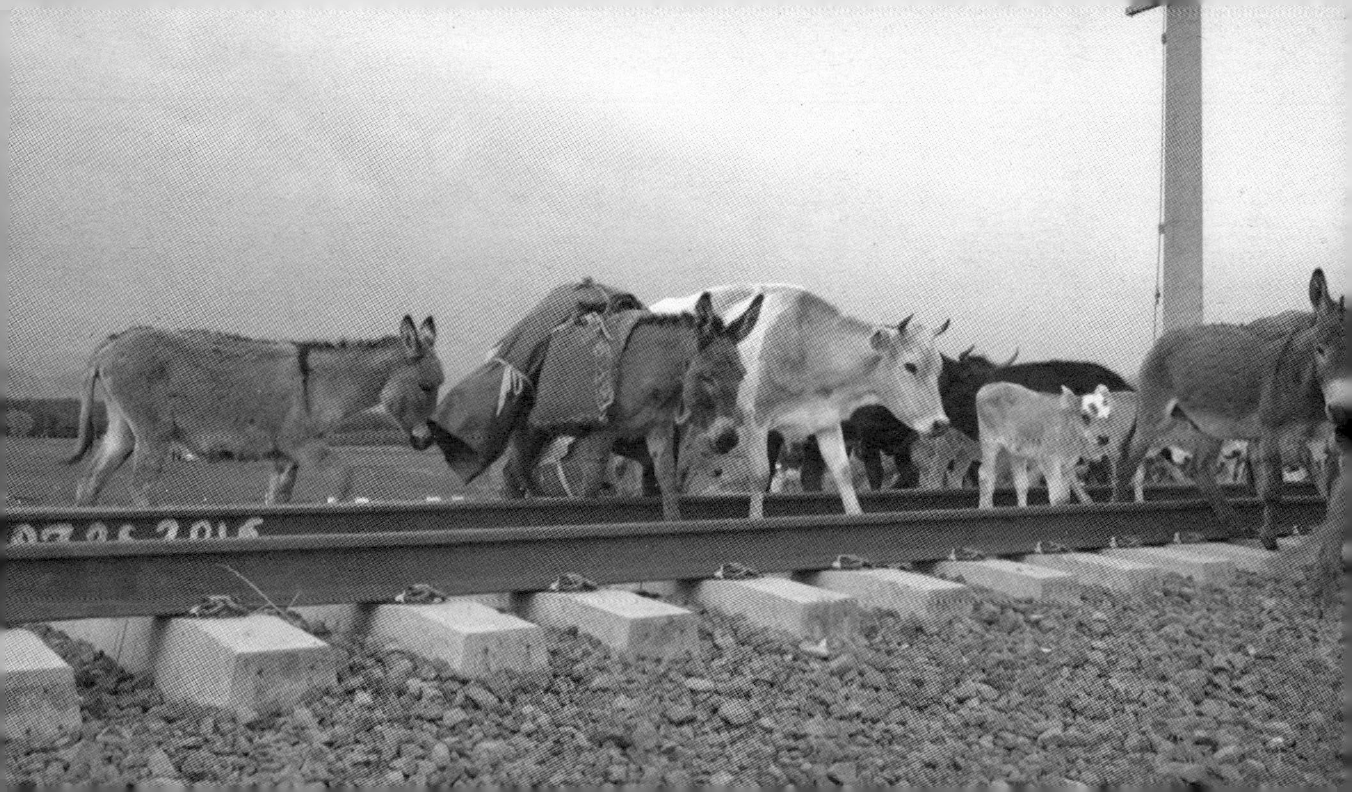

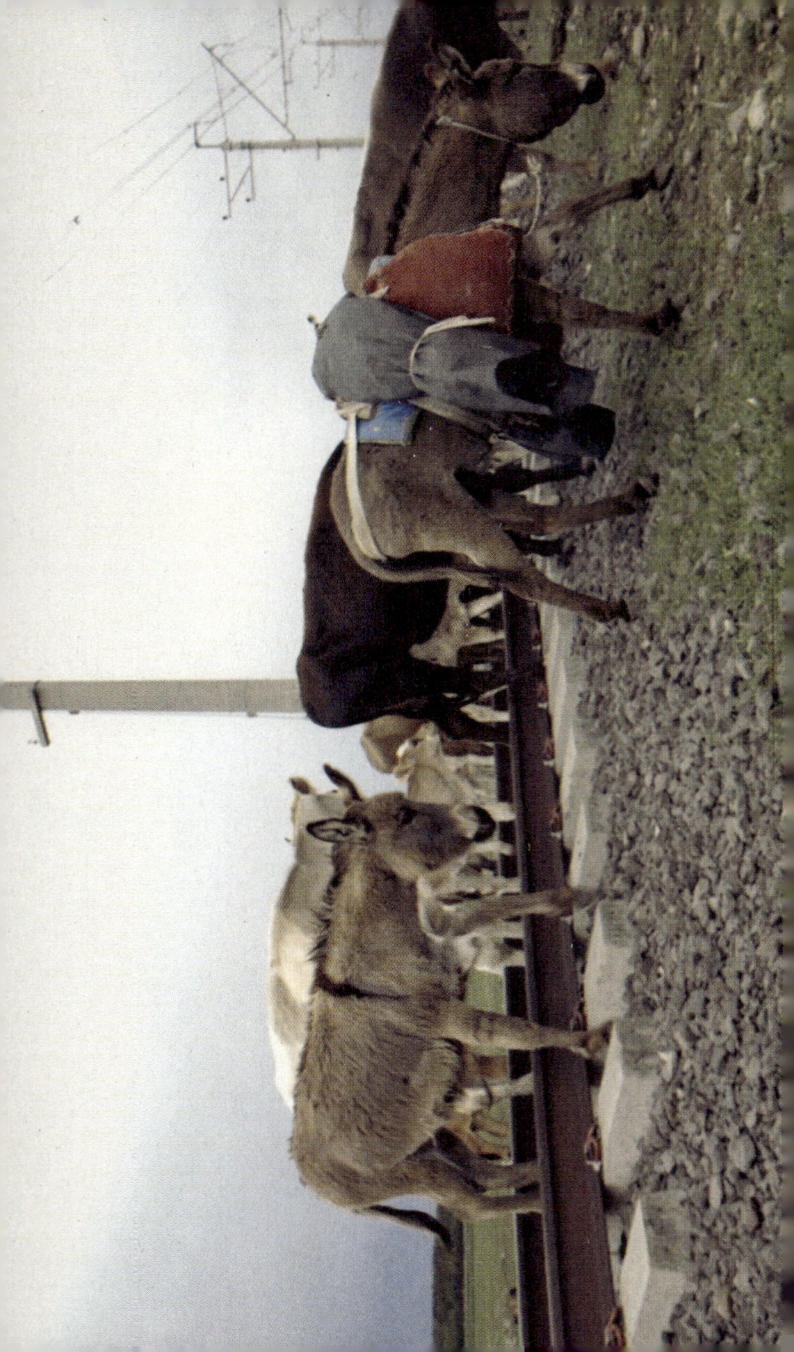

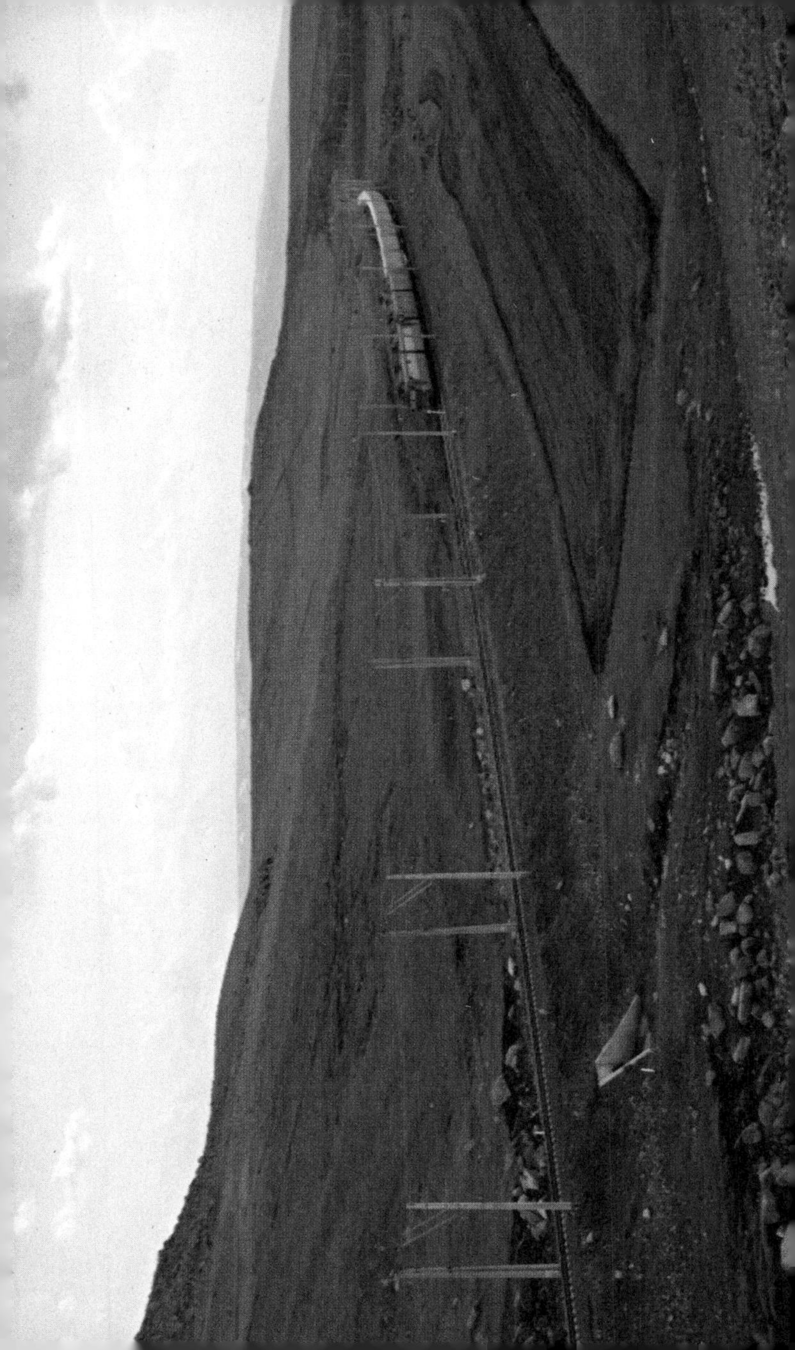

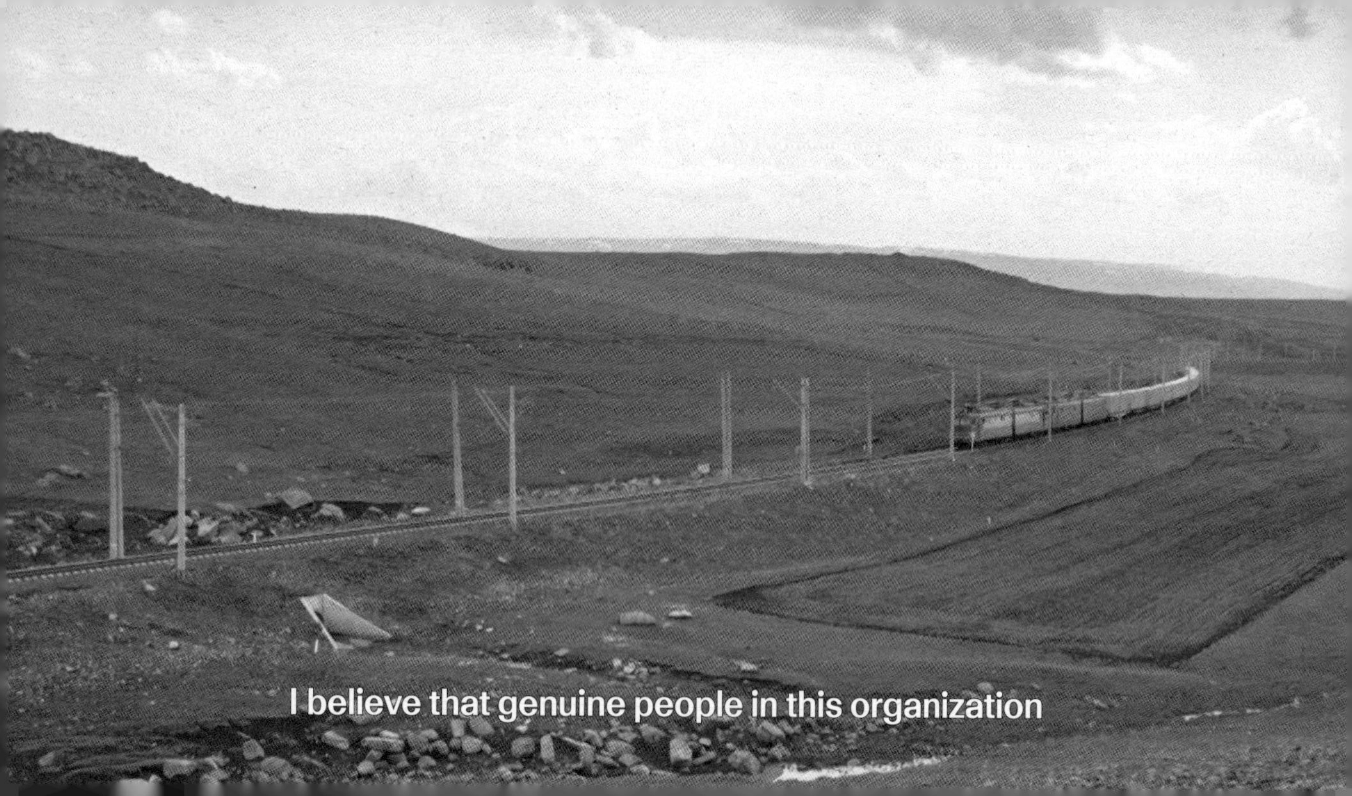
I believe that genuine people in this organization

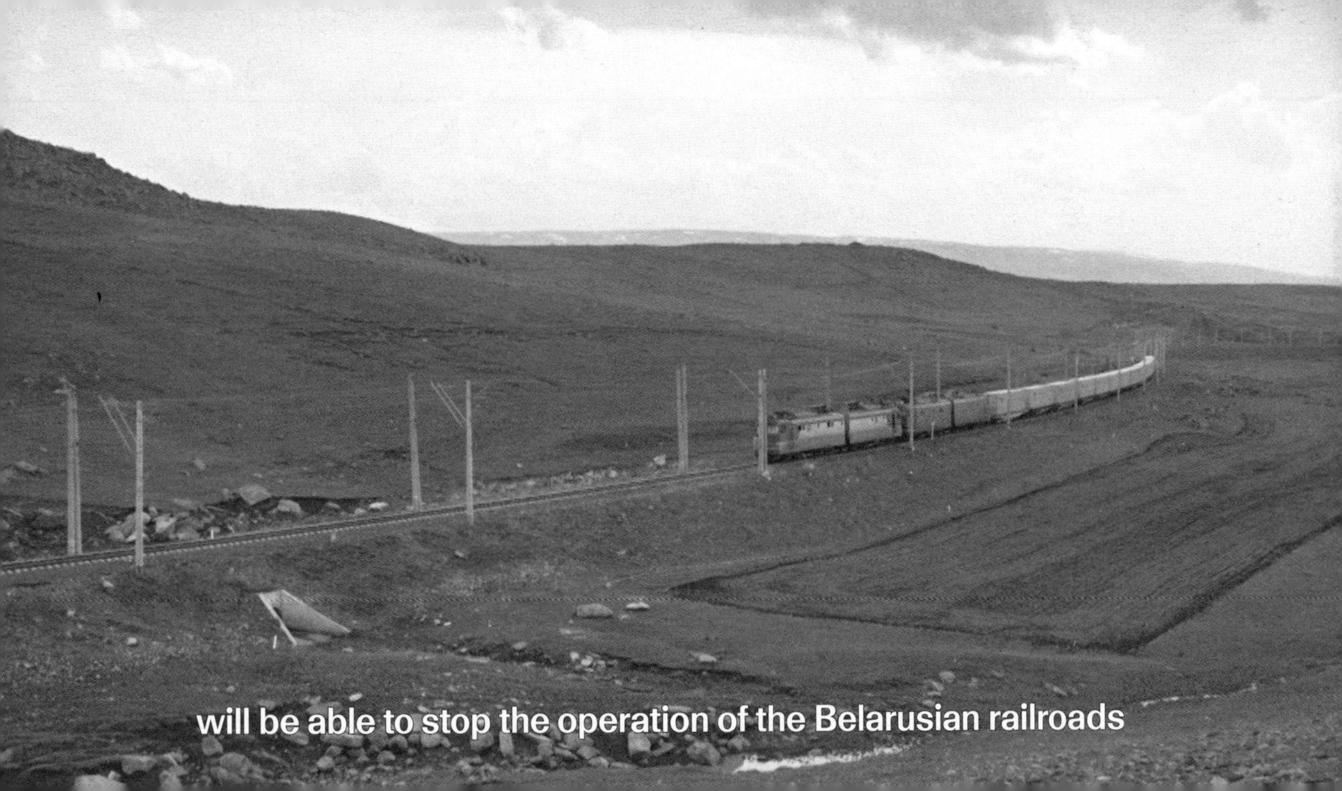

will be able to stop the operation of the Belarusian railroads

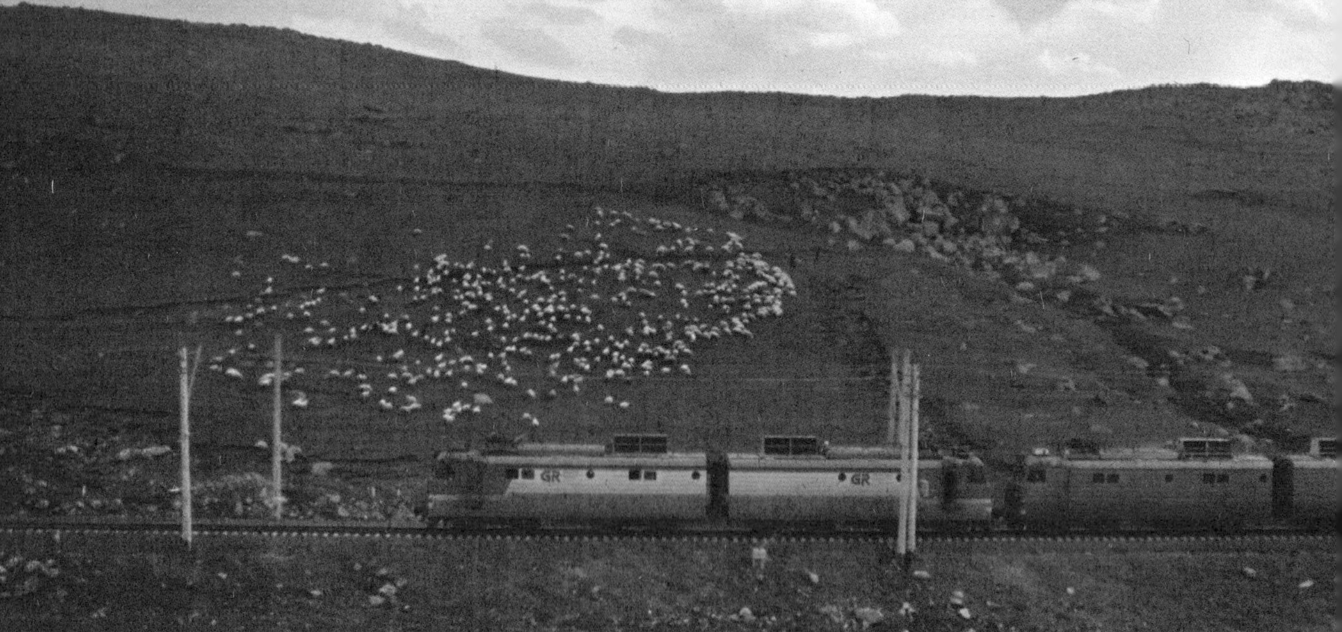

in the direction of transporting Russian troops to Ukraine.

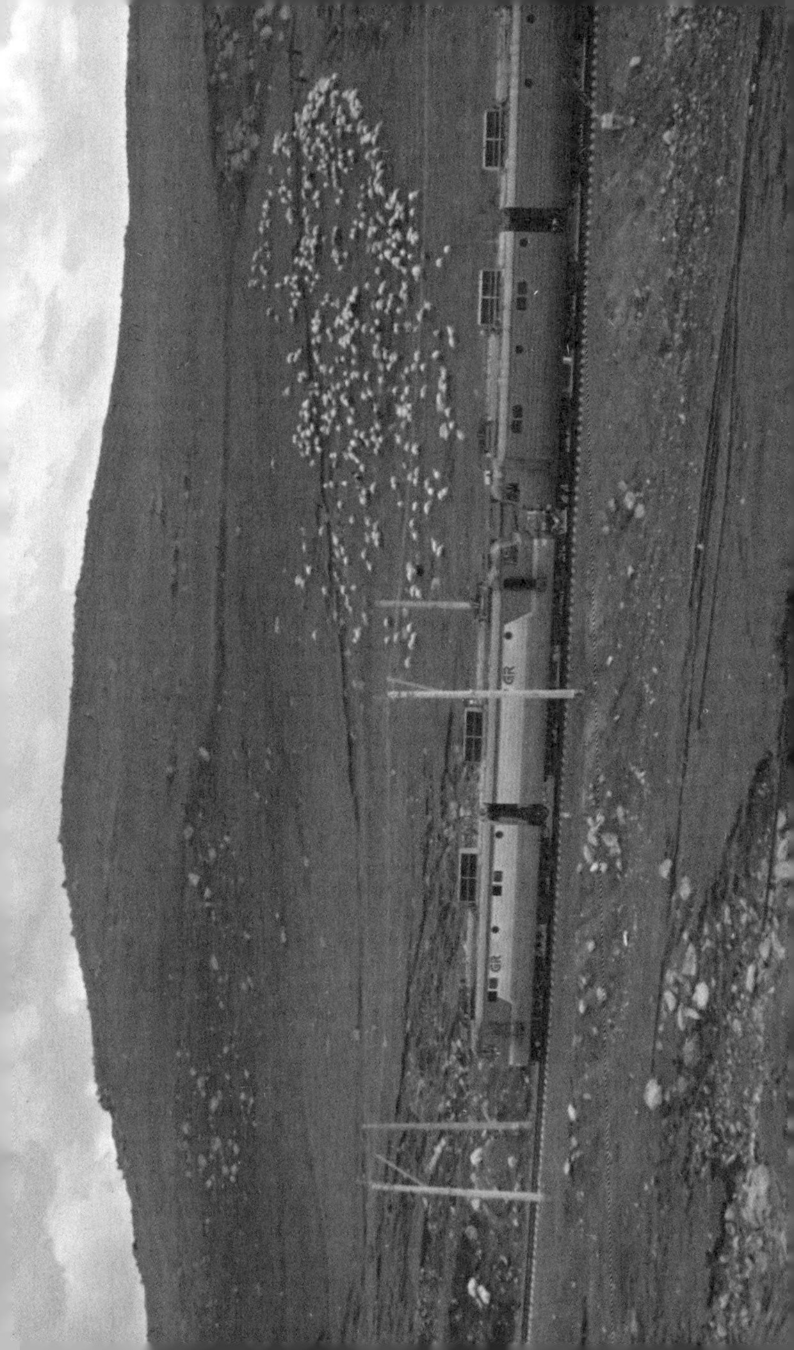

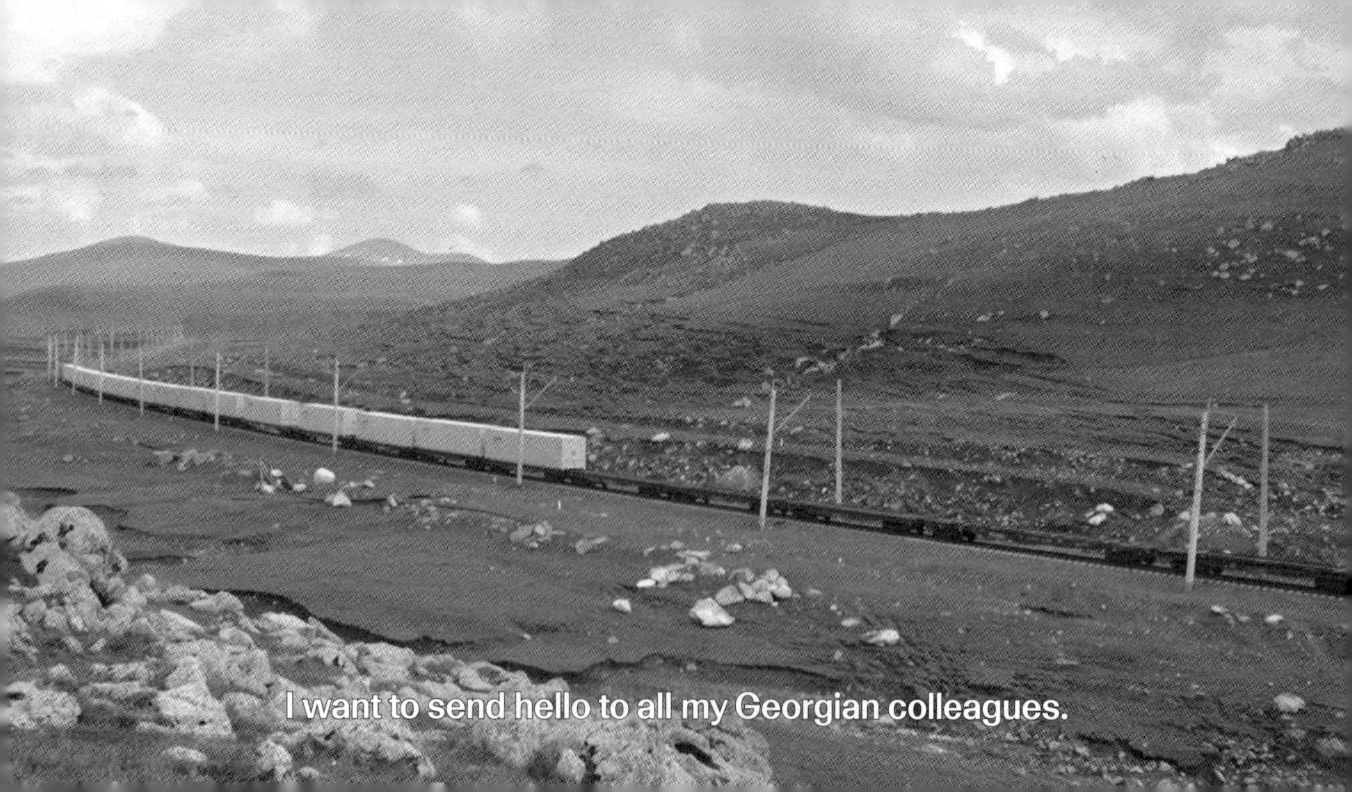

I want to send hello to all my Georgian colleagues.

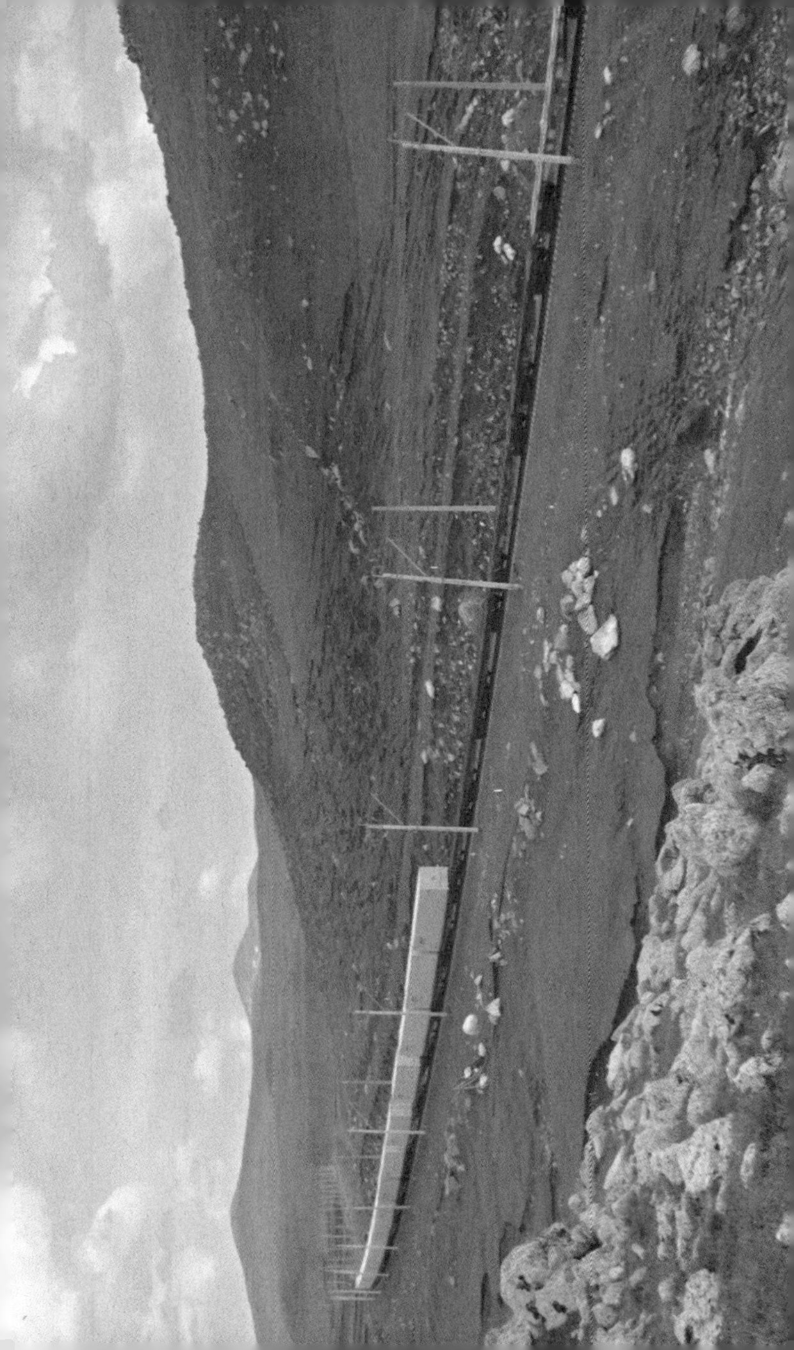

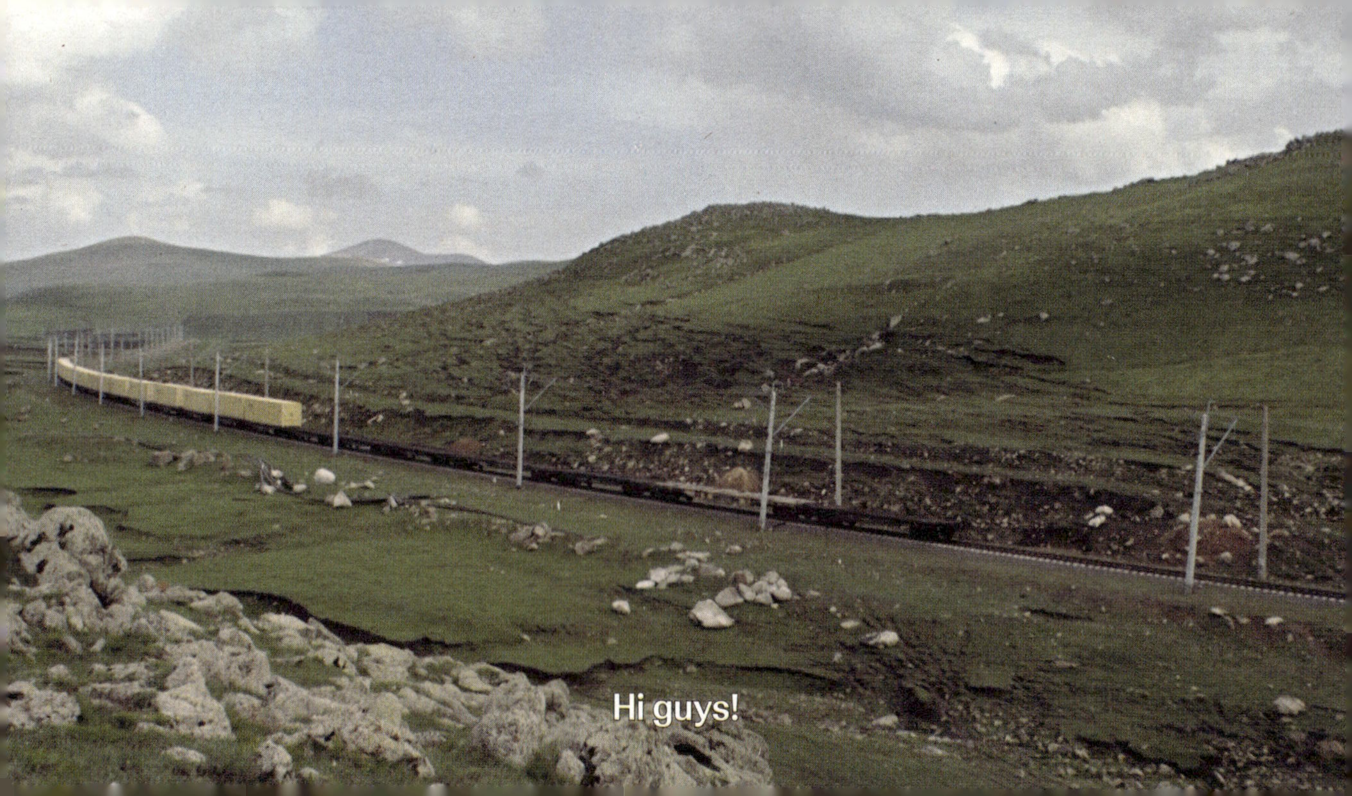
Hi guys!

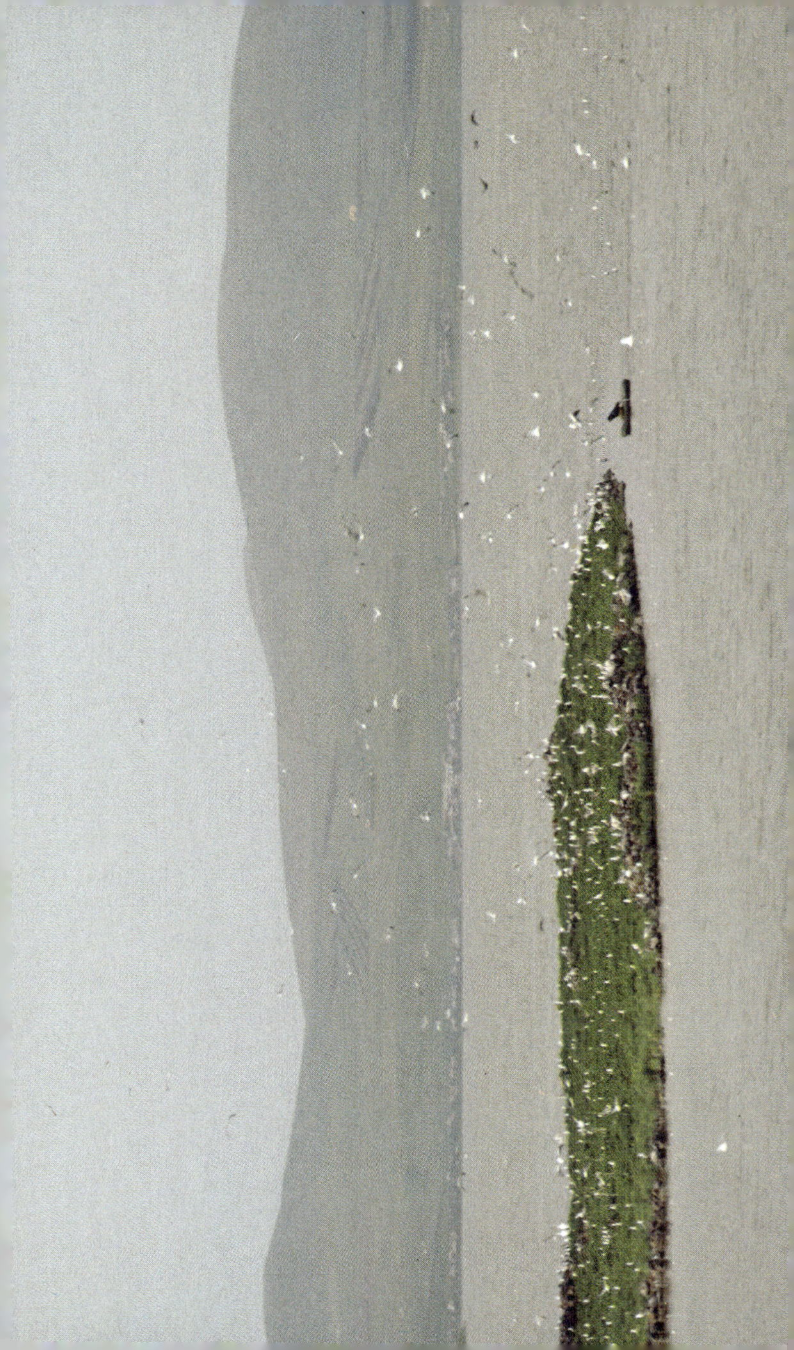

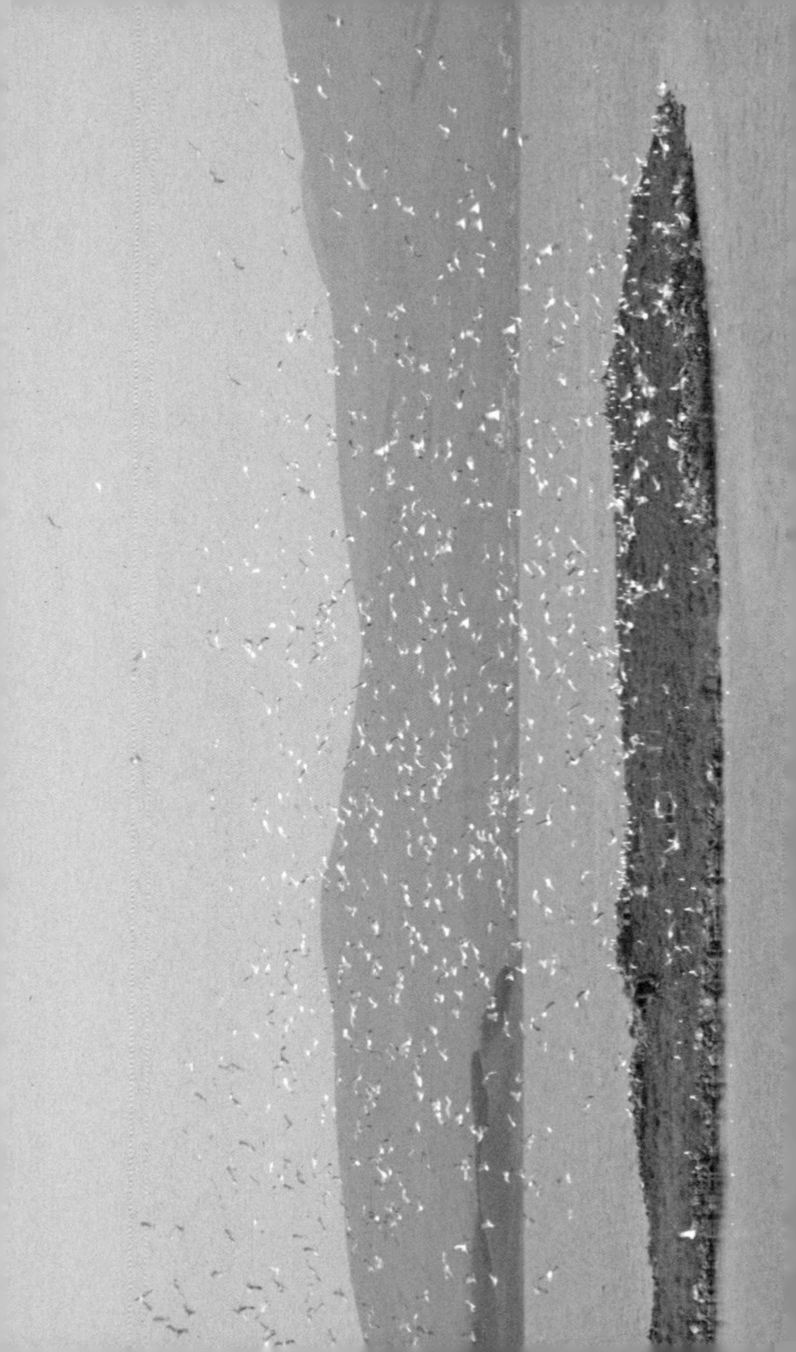

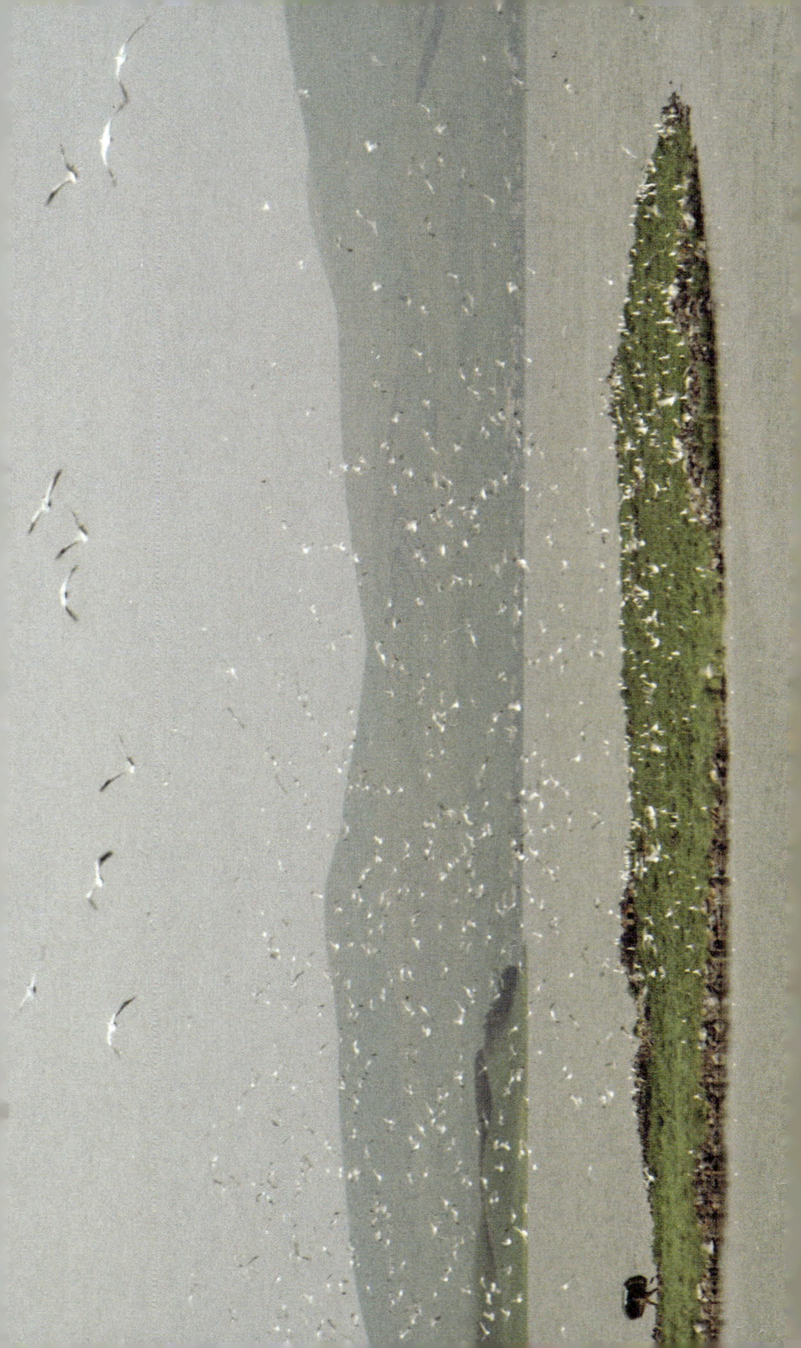

Economies of Delay

A conversation between

Tekla
Aslanishvili,

Evelina
Gambino

and

Timothy
Mitchell

TA, EG   Dear Timothy, thank you very much for accepting this conversation. Firstly, we would like to talk about your work around infrastructures and time. And then we would like to move on to discuss the specific material politics of different infrastructures. We are particularly interested in the questions around infrastructural sabotage that you explored in your book *Carbon Democracy*.[1] Starting with infrastructure and time: in one of your recent essays, you say that "infrastructures work on time."[2] Could you start by explaining what you mean by that, please?

TM

The phrase deliberately plays with the idea that infrastructure's purpose is to be efficient and punctual: to work on time. This is particularly true of infrastructures that are moving goods or people. Railways and other kinds of infrastructure of communication seem to promise efficiency and predictability, but I was interested in taking that notion in a different direction. It's often the case that the moving of goods, people, ideas or communication is the justification for a project where the actual purpose that project is serving is different. One of the most common differences is when an infrastructure is built to serve a financial goal. Or put another way, often what infrastructures are trying to move is finance, even though the vehicle for doing that might be a pipeline or a railway or some other large infrastructure project.

So, my interest is to make a point about the workings of finance and infrastructure and indeed capitalism. We've inherited a very 19th-century view of capitalism as being something fundamentally rooted in the production of things and of the transformation of the material world through a productive process that, of course, involves labour. But there's another way of thinking of capitalism. Capital itself is not something fundamentally rooted in a productive process, but rather based in a relationship to time and, in particular, on an ability to extract resources from the future. That view of capitalism puts not the factory or production at the centre, but credit and the creation of credit. Credit being a way of promising a future stream of payments or constructing a way to have a future stream of payments and then finding a way to profit off that future stream in the present.

This sounds all very abstract so it's probably easier to give a concrete example. In the 19th and early 20th centuries, railway entrepreneurs created durable infrastructure projects that promised long-term revenue. Railways, lasting for decades, allowed entrepreneurs to sell shares in future revenue, making that revenue available in the present. This led to the rise of the joint-stock company. The joint-stock company was a way not so much of raising money for a project, but of selling the project's future income. The future income is acquired at a discount because the value of a share is discounted to reflect the delay in acquiring future income. The other side of this is that the burden of paying back that price in full in the future is carried by the users of the infrastructure, the passengers, those who pay for freight, those who work to run the infrastructure, and so on. All their costs, prices, and wages will carry the burden of paying back this discounted income.

Once you think of large infrastructure projects as ways of organizing future flows of revenue, and understand them as being associated with financial technologies that make that future revenue available in the present, then the purpose of the infrastructure can no longer be seen as moving goods or ideas or people, but as moving these financial instruments, of moving these flows of finance. This is different from the standard way of thinking about finance. From this perspective, finance has to be understood in terms of the material arrangements that have to be built to make profitable access to the future possible.

So, in contrast to the common sense notion of working on time as being efficient and timely, the point is that infrastructures work on time differently because they don't make things more rapid, but are capable of stretching time. And it's that very ability to technically build out a kind of stretched-out future that becomes critical to the usefulness or success of an infrastructural project.

TA   This relation to the future is relevant
        to the infrastructures we have studied.
        Interestingly, our current project focuses
        on a railway—the Baku-Tbilisi-Kars line
        (BTK)—which is funded by Azerbaijan.
        We have observed how it 'works on
        time' in a similar way to what you just
        described: rather than bringing things

together, in time and in space, economic value is generated through a form of delay. Akhalkalaki, the site where the new BTK station was built, acquired importance because of the delay caused by a mismatch between the size of European and former Soviet tracks. The presence of this technological border allows a number of profitable operations to be performed on this site. We are often told that logistics relies on the pursuit of seamless connectivity, but what we have observed is that delay is sometimes as desirable!

TM

The case you're dealing with is unusual and interesting for that reason, especially when considering the role of the state. In some ways, if you look at the whole history of large-scale infrastructure and other long-term financial projects that gave rise to the joint-stock company, historically, the state wasn't the exception. Both because originally corporations had to be authorised by the state and were seen as quasi-public bodies, and because in some ways they mirrored or mimicked the powers of the state. This is because they had this exceptional control over the future, through monopoly rights over a certain route and the powers of raising revenue that was similar to the power of taxation.

Corporations were state-like bodies and this fact has been completely forgotten in the 21st century whereby corporations become something called 'the private sector' and are seen as the opposite of the state. Historically, they weren't. And even beyond that, prior to the kinds of infrastructures we're talking about here, the one institution that could tax the future and acquire income from the future reliably was the state. And that's why, historically, the rise of finance, in the form of large-scale banking, was about providing credit to a state. In the case of a state-funded railroad, of course, the population that will pay the taxes will pay for this railroad.

Now, when it's in the hands of the state, one hopes that it is therefore serving a public and collective purpose and that in the future everyone will benefit from this investment. But as you show, unfortunately, this is not always the case. So even when a project is state-funded, you are right to observe that it still relies upon the ability to construct something over a long-term future and the ability to tax that future.

EG   And of course, this brings into focus the uneven ways in which this future is discounted and partitioned...

TM

The point you make about delay and slowing down, I think that's really interesting because it shows that the battle is over where the slowdown should happen. Of course, historically with the building of the first railways when the routes were being decided, this was, and still is today, related to the enormous increase in land values that

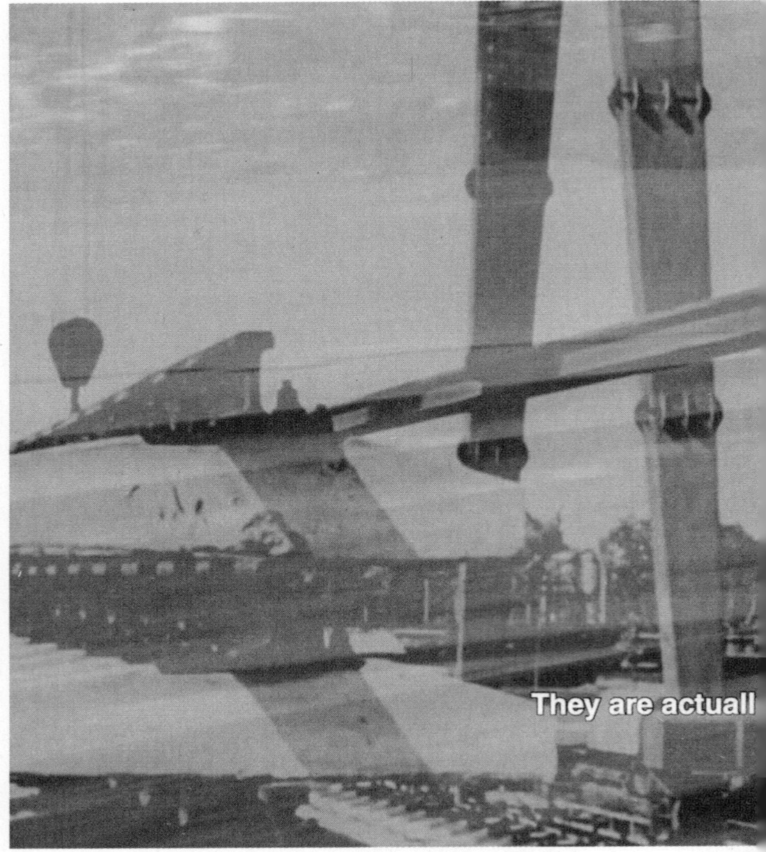

Film still. Tekla Aslanishvili, *A State in a State*, 2022.

accompanied the laying out of any route. So a lot of the battle wasn't to make the railroad productive, it was to persuade investors or a state to get involved in supporting a railroad because all the money would actually be made on the side. And this money would tend to be made at the points of delay or slowdown.

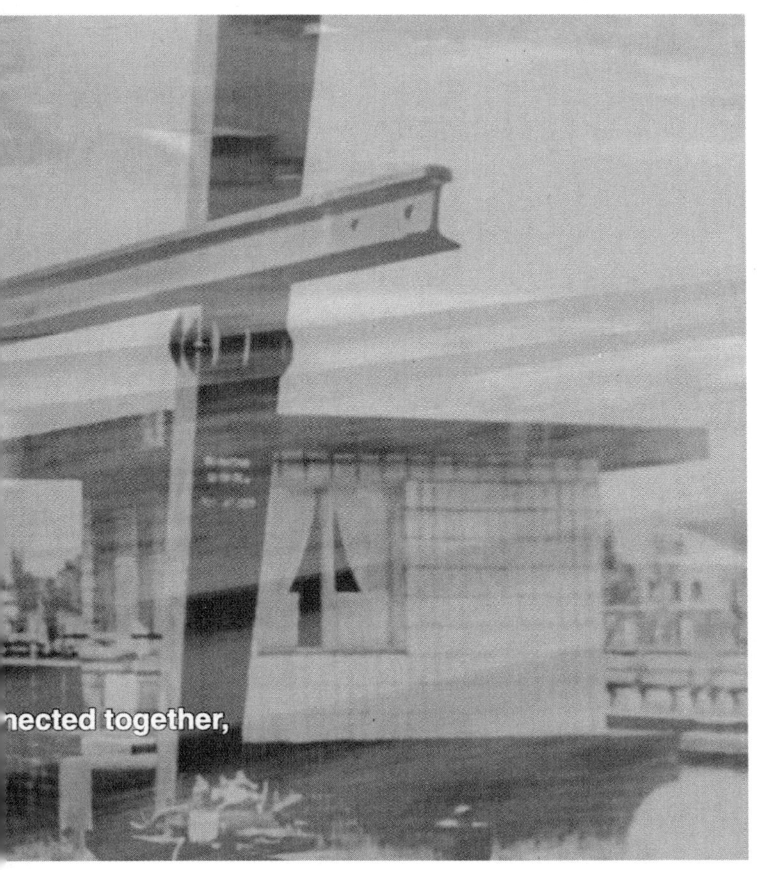

In other words, wherever, for example, a station was being built, that was a point of delay and slowing down. And that's where suddenly you had a concentration of opportunities for making money on the side.

And this is a particularly poignant case of it because of the change in gauge. So there's both the money to be made out of the cost of that interruption, as well as the larger world that is built around it. But in a way, any infrastructure project that's built around moving goods, people, and liquids has these points of transit and transformation where one modality switches to another. The battle is often over the siting of those points of transition. It's the delay involved that is going to be the source, as you say, of interest.

EG   This is funny because when we started working on this project, we thought that this was a disadvantage. By observing the railway and talking to people we learned that this was not the case. But this also brings us to a central point that you make, which is that railways or infrastructures in general are 'time machines of sorts'. And we think that this is a generative way to think about infrastructure. Studying the railway, we observed a whole set of temporalities generated by infrastructure, including forms of waiting, abandonment, and stillness.

TM

What you're suggesting, which I like a lot, is that there are so many different temporalities that accompany the building of an infrastructure project and that the project is as much as anything about those temporalities. Thinking about forms of waiting, delay, or stillness can help us read the history of infrastructure against its grain.

Infrastructures are often connected to the standardisation of time. But as soon as you have a structure of temporality, one that is commonly associated with a pattern of predictability, then you've got the possibility of delay because things don't always work out. And you've got entirely new ways of experiencing delay that wouldn't have been there before you'd constructed a framework of predictability. Delay is experienced in contrast to that expectation.

This also applies to the example I gave at the beginning. The stretching out of time and profitable delay afforded by infrastructure are not just isolated things, they are very much worth thinking about in connection with forms of speeding up or efficiency. They work together! The promise of speeding up is what attracts speculative finance—but what speculative finance wants is the stretching out of time.

TA Thinking specifically about the BTK and its politics, I wanted to zoom into the issue of political control and exclusion, and its relation to the temporalities we have discussed. This railway is clearly not just a tool for profitably binding different times and spaces together, but for causing disconnection—bypassing Armenia and connecting Turkey and Azerbaijan through Georgia—and interestingly both political and economic promises are attached to this disconnection. Does this tension resonate with your own work?

TM

Yes, it appears that in the context of the relationship between Georgia and Azerbaijan over the railway, the infrastructure is a sort of materialised stake in the territory. I think that infrastructure introduces the concept of security. It's not necessarily the case that there's a problem with security first and then you seek ways to solve it, but that infrastructure itself helps constitute a form of vulnerability around which you can then promise security. Infrastructures are expensive, highly technical and, we have seen, profitable and strategic objects, therefore their presence comes to be associated with a need for securitization. There are endless discussions of the vulnerability of pipelines and, of course, there were moments and times in which an infrastructure, a pipeline or anything else, would be vulnerable to forms of protest and disruption. But what then becomes possible is to make self-evident the need for security even though the actual vulnerability is limited.

When the Suez Canal was built in the 1860s, it was soon used, in 1882, to justify the British occupation of Egypt. What I'm getting at is that the threat to an infrastructure project is often something that is constructed as part of a larger political project around it. Most of the language around infrastructure assumes that security is an issue, instead of asking who gets to define what security is, and whose security we're talking about. And this gives the state, in particular, the ability to frame itself as an organization required for the security of infrastructure.

EG   Yes! I think that some projects in Georgia are emblematic of this production of infrastructural vulnerability. Take, for instance, the Baku-Tbilisi-Ceyhan (BTC) pipeline, which runs parallel to the BTK railway. If you remember, the BTC is featured in the 007 film *The World Is Not Enough* where it is portrayed as a site of potential warfare that must be protected. Shevardnadze, the second president of Georgia who commissioned this infrastructure, very knowingly played with these narratives and constructed the pro-Western identity of Georgia around Georgia's willingness to make this pipeline pass through its territory. The idea was that this pipeline would be a kind of materialised bond with Western countries at a time in which Georgia was actively searching for its post-Soviet identity.

But I think this discussion moves us very well to the question of infrastructural politics. One of the things that has brought Tekla and I together in our work is a shared understanding that infrastructures materialise a specific kind of politics, which is inscribed on and derived from the material relations that make up infrastructural networks. And this is obviously a thread that runs through all your books, especially in *Carbon Democracy*.

The argument I was developing in *Carbon Democracy* is concerned with the difference between coal production and oil production, and the ways in which coal production created multiple opportunities for disruption, sabotage, and, through that, forms of democratic political claim. With the production of oil, although attempts were made to use infrastructures in the same way, it was much less successful. So, in general, the difference in the transition from coal to oil was that, during the height of dependence on coal in the late 19th and early decades of the 20th century, coal was the only source of carbon energy, of fossil fuel energy, and it tended to be used for industrial purposes very close in proximity to where it was produced. Therefore if you could shut down the coal fields and simultaneously organize industrial action along the railways that carried the coal, it meant that from the key sites where coal was produced and used you could shut down an entire economy. It was the first time in history that you could have what could be called a general strike.

With oil production, that was so much more difficult because largely oil was discovered in places far from the centre of coal production. Therefore, unlike coal, it was not being used close to where it was produced. Oil was mainly used in parts of the world already industrialised using coal. So this huge gap opened up between where the energy was being produced, particularly in places like the Middle East and the Caspian Sea, and where it was being used. That gap made it much harder to build political alliances and even interruptions to supply between the place of production and the place of use. There's also the fact that oil was a liquid, transported mainly by tankers rather than by rail, and you could easily shift to supplies from other sources, and so on.

Actually Baku—where the train you have been studying starts—was the exception to this story because despite being an oil centre, it acted more like a coal centre. Strikes in the oil fields became central to the revolutionary moment of 1904–1905. Baku belonged more to the coal age. In fact, the oil produced in Baku at the turn of the century, when Azerbaijan was part of the Russian empire, was being used like coal. It was being used to fuel trains principally, and also to power the use of steam boilers in industry. So, it was much more like the situation of coal, and therefore, in shutting down the Baku industry, one had that a kind of political potential that resembled the revolutionary potential historically associated with coal production, rather than the later history of oil production.

EG This is interesting for us because the BTK is a re-routing of the original railway that was built by large oil producers to connect the oil fields with the ports of Poti and Batumi in the Black Sea, which were also sites of major uprisings during the 1905 revolution. And railway workers were building bridges between the two sites

of this extractive network. In our interviews with workers who used to work
on this line, this infrastructural class
consciousness remains alive in some
ways. Several of the workers said that
the railway was in many ways 'a state in
a state'. This definition indicates the role
of infrastructure as a space of relations,
organization, and also solidarity between
workers on a transnational scale. Do you
have some thoughts about this specific
politics of the railway?

TM

I think it's a wonderful example and a really helpful
way to think about this whole question of political
consciousness and class consciousness. I didn't
really spell this out so much in my book, but what
I was trying to get at is that once you focus on the
infrastructure, you have a better way of thinking
about something like political consciousness.
Consciousness doesn't have to be something
floating at some separate level of culture, that has
to build its own sphere of operation. It's built into,
encouraged, and made possible by that shared
work on a railroad and it's not just because people
abstractly share a common kind of experience;
they are connected together because the thing
itself has to work as a connected system. Political
possibilities arise, as you're saying, from that
knowledge of the connected system and how
you can interrupt and break down its connections.
So in both its normal working and in moments of

political organization, it's the connectedness of the system that is constantly present. Therefore, you don't have to worry about explaining the development of consciousness as a separate problem.

Thinking via infrastructures is a better way to write about problems of consciousness and therefore problems of class.

TA   Yes, definitely. I'm also thinking about the potentialities of the identity that is grown on the infrastructural body. And how it often works against the grain of dominant narratives. The projects we have observed are depicted as the key to a new interconnected future, but, as we discussed, they often disconnect and dispossess. But if we zoom in on certain territories, we can see a different kind of connectivity made of historical infrastructures and of the human relations that travel along them. A sort of human and material chain that runs across these territories. When I interviewed people in Armenia, for instance, they were very emotional and told me about the different times in which Turkish workers provided help and support to Armenian workers, including after the blockade enforced by the Turkish state. Or how after the major earthquake that destroyed the city of Gyumri in Armenia in 1988, Georgian railway workers came faster than the ones coming from Yerevan. These acts of solidarity also happen in the present, like when in the aftermath of the full-scale invasion of Ukraine, Belarusian workers sabotaged their own trains to slow down the movement of Russian troops attempting to reach Ukraine from Belarus. I think that by looking at these examples you can see their relevance for thinking about political possibilities of organization and solidarity beyond the nation state.

TM

I think this technical connected togetherness that you're finding out about through these railways is absolutely fascinating. And precisely as you say, it's not about a national consciousness, it's about a consciousness that, like the railways, crosses these borders. And the more you can have these kinds of conversations and explorations at a particular point along the route, or engage with a particular kind of expertise, the more it is possible to bring into view a kind of politics that politicians don't want to talk about. And, you know, I think that's important.

Timothy Mitchell

1   Timothy Mitchell,
*Carbon Democracy: Political
Power in the Age of Oil* (London:
Verso Books, 2013).
2   Timothy Mitchell,
"Infrastructures Work On Time,"
e-flux, January 2020, https://
www.e-flux.com/architecture/
new-silk-roads/312596/
infrastructures-work-on-time/.

Scenes from Trial and Error

30:00'
Georgia, Germany, The Netherlands
2020

Director and Editor	Tekla Aslanishvili
Featuring	Ketevan Bochorishvili, Nikoloz Japaridze, Evelina Gambino, Orit Halpern
Cast	Alika Yorshia, Giga Izoria, Bacho Khasia, Zaza Kiria
Cinematography	Nikoloz Tabukashvili
Music	Mzia Arabuli, Gogi Dzodzuashvili
Sound & Music Editing	Nika Pasuri
Field Recordings	Irakli Shonia
Visual Effects	Viktor Bone
Color	Delfina Mayer

Supported by the Digital Earth Fellowship / Hivos and Elsa-Neumann-Scholarship (NaFöG).

Scenes from Trial and Error maps data-driven urban planning strategies, as well as myths, financial speculations and errors that accompany today's global infrastructural politics, through the lens of a seemingly insignificant real estate project of Anaklia city port on the shores of the Black Sea in west Georgia. By exploring the awkward landscapes and architectural frictions that have emerged on-site over the last decade, the film observes how the operational logics of large-scale infrastructural investments, and even mistakes—which the fantasies of technologically managed smooth urban life inevitably contain—are being manifested in the design of peripheral geoengineering projects. Through artistic and scientific collaborations with international researchers, the film positions itself at a distance from actual events and speculates about possible scenarios of development from a future perspective.

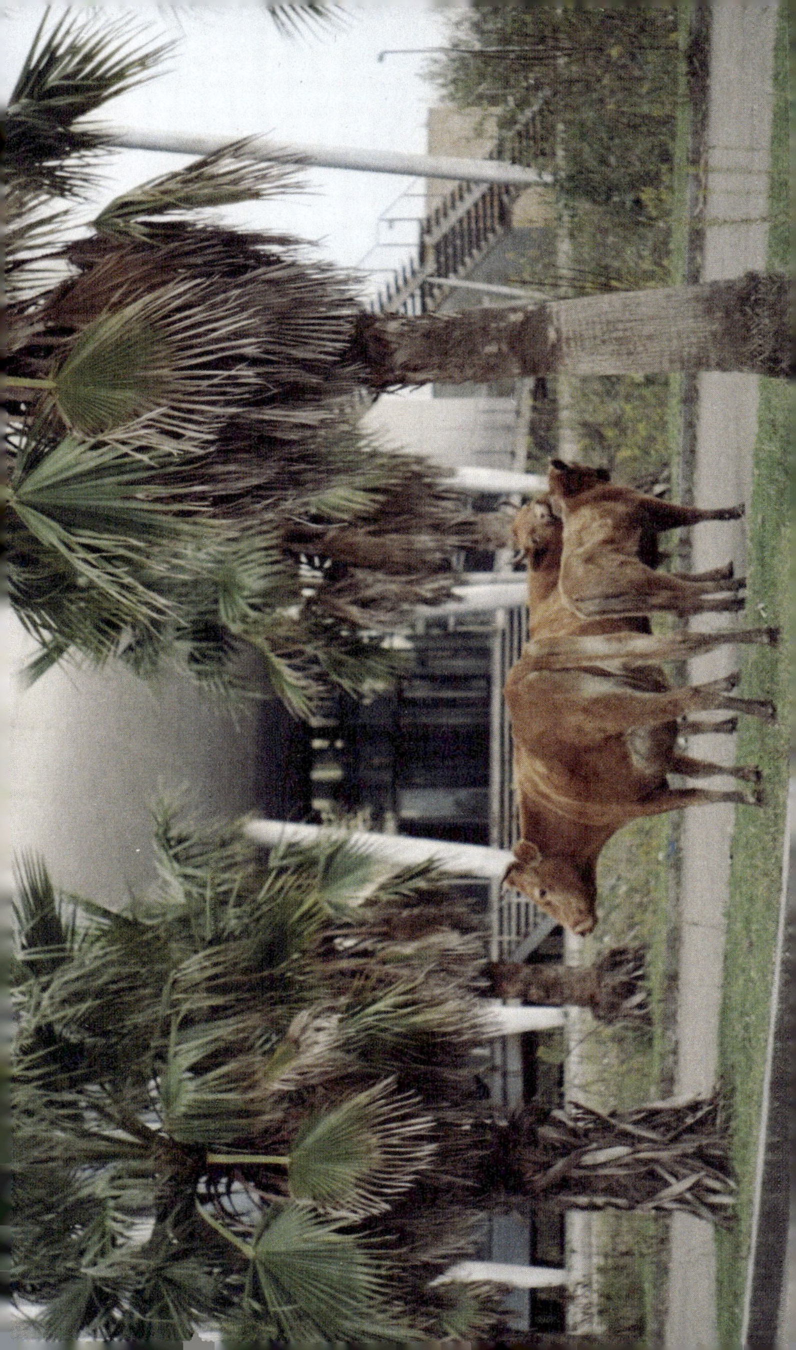

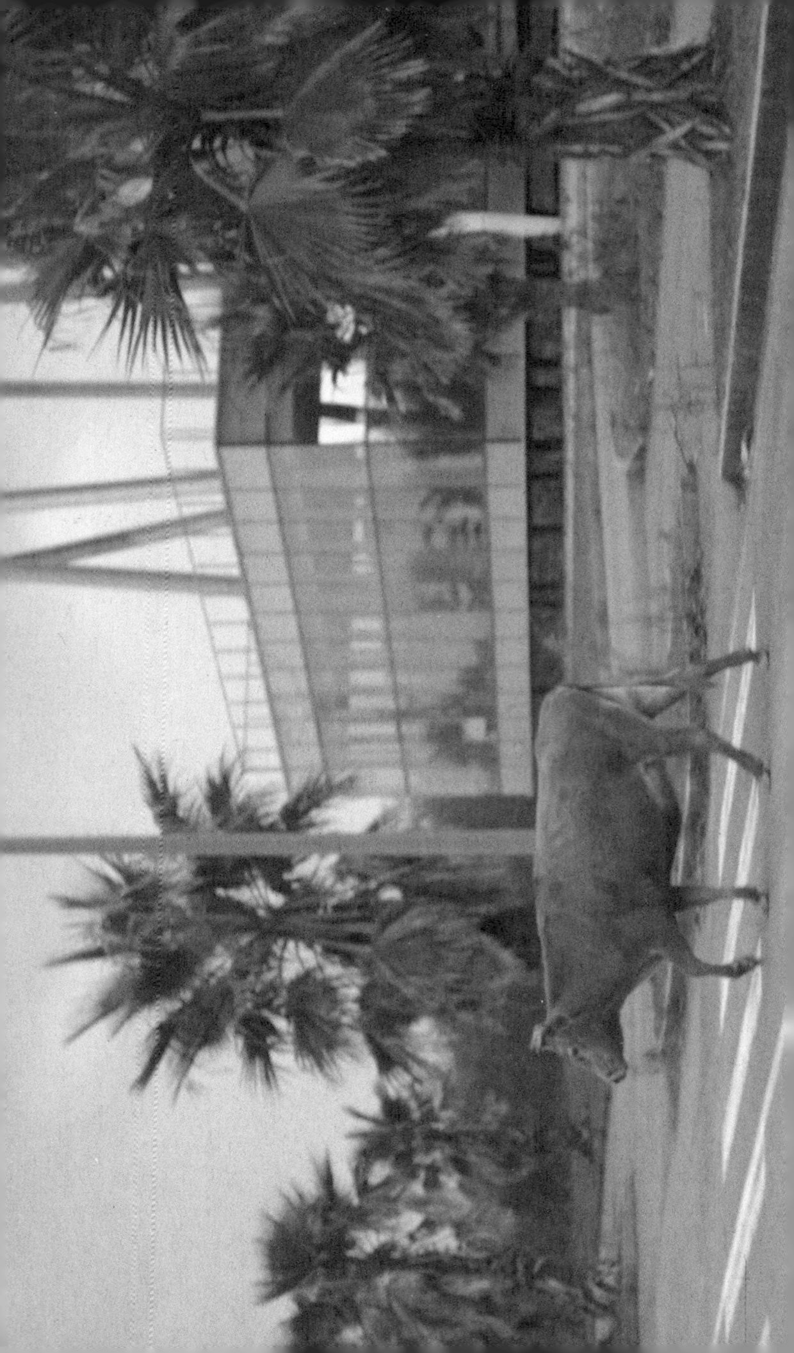

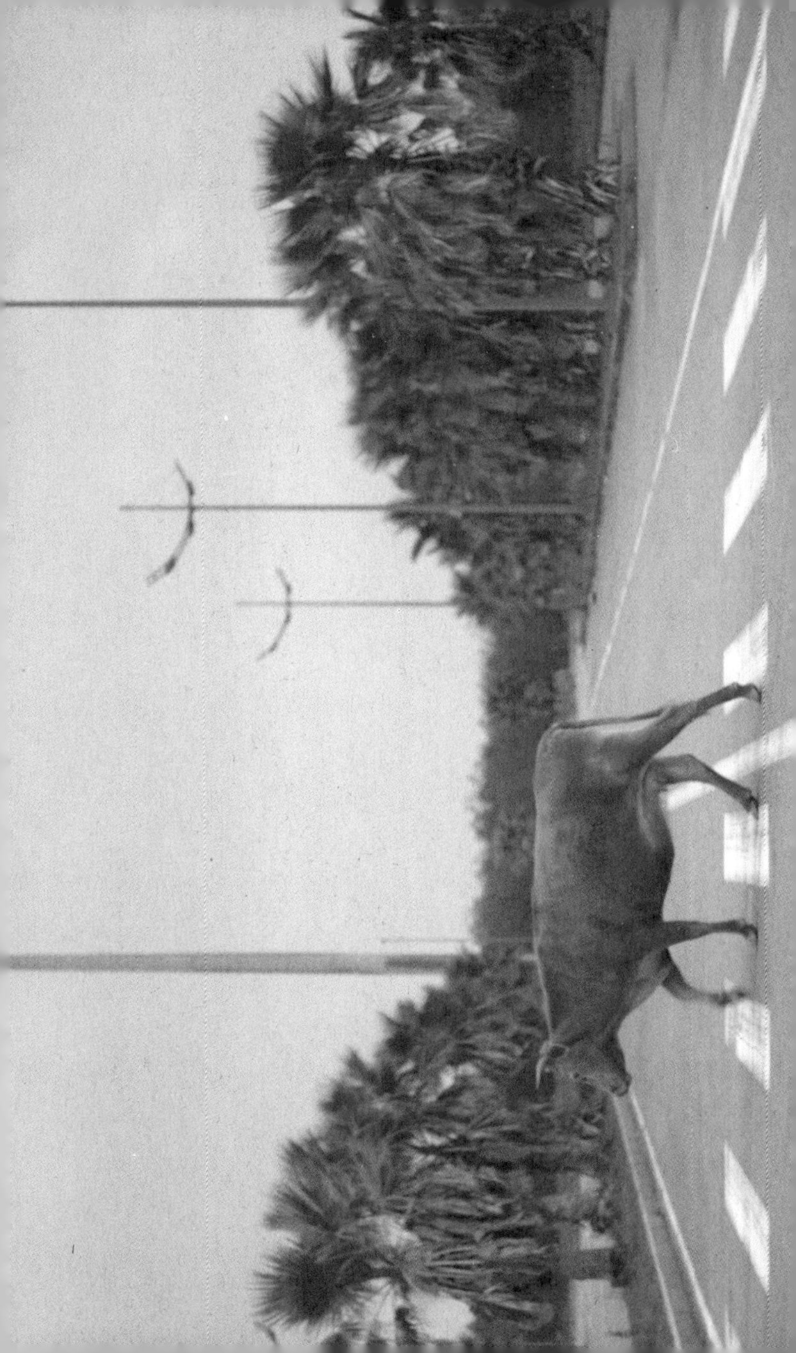

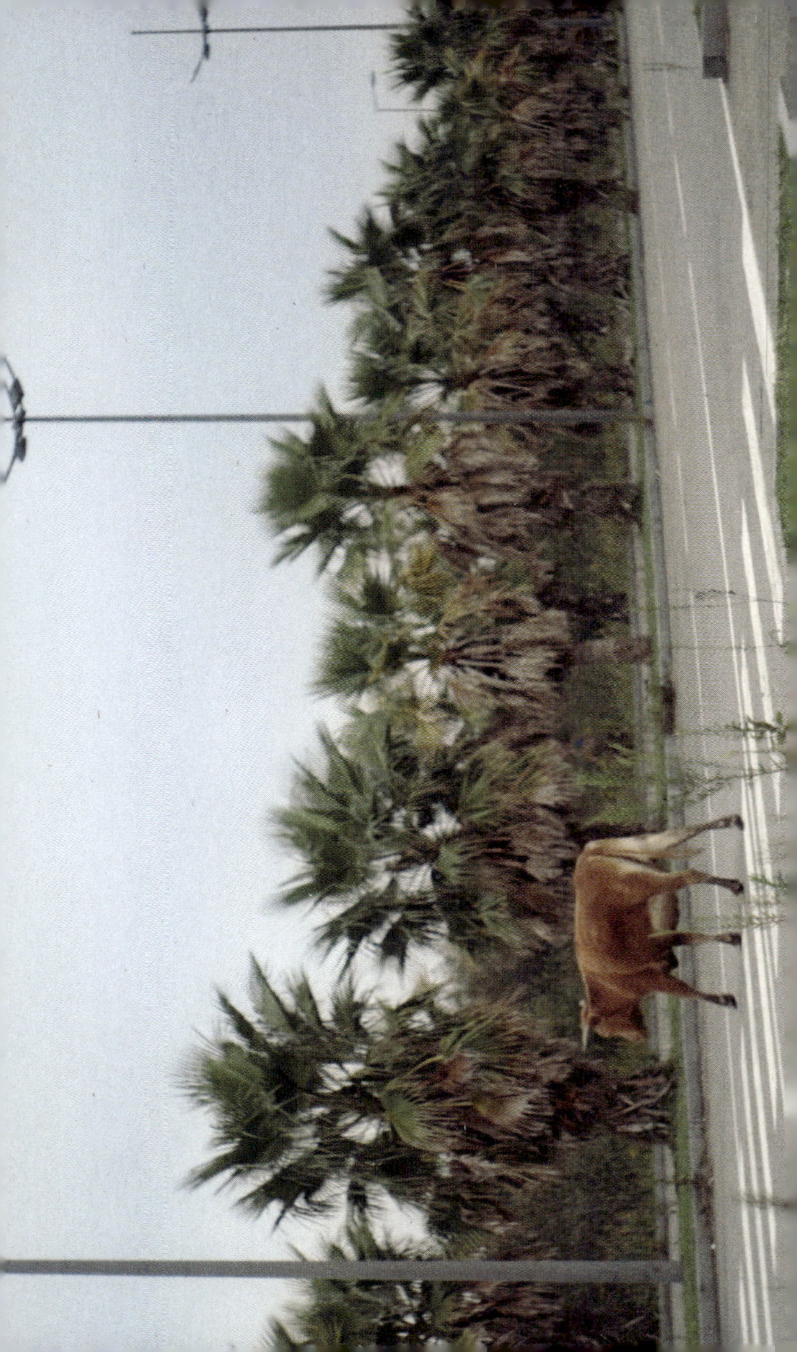

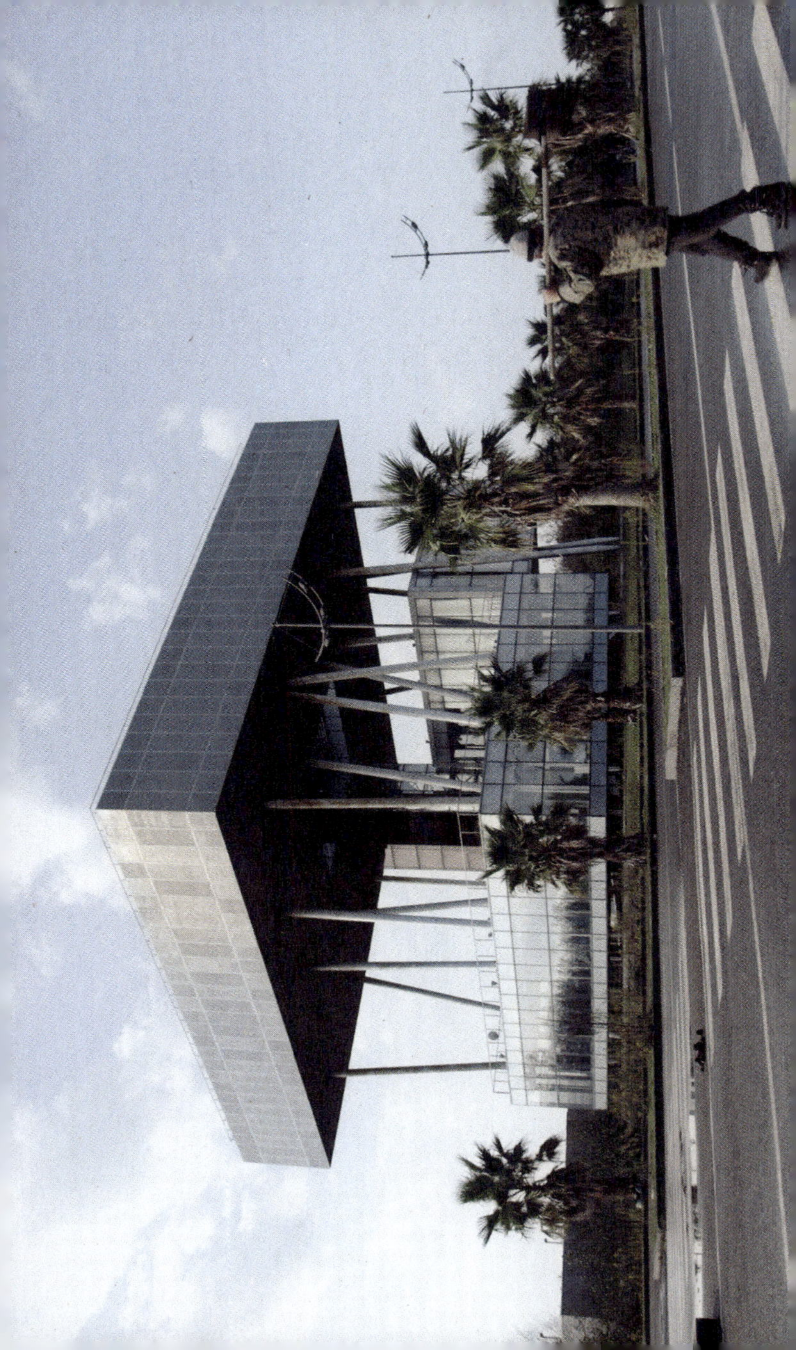

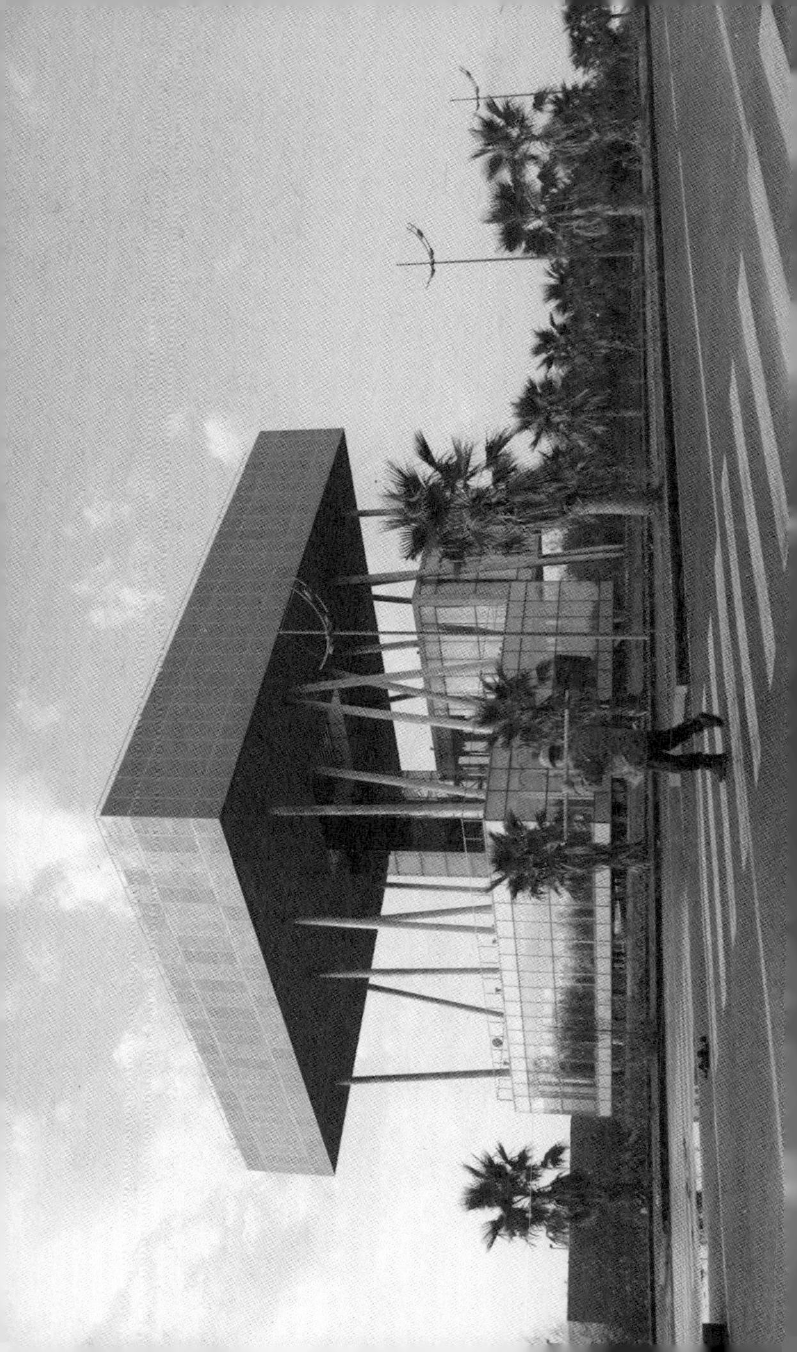

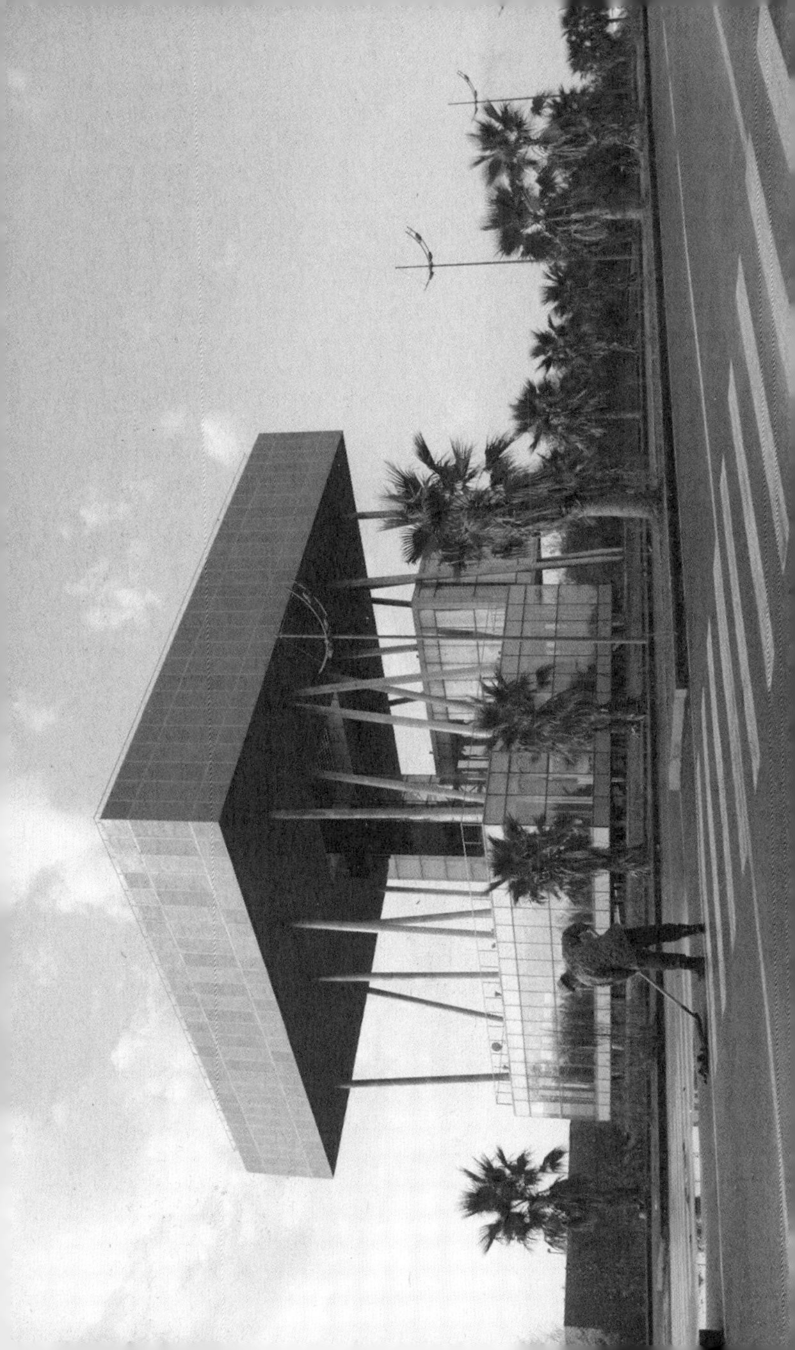

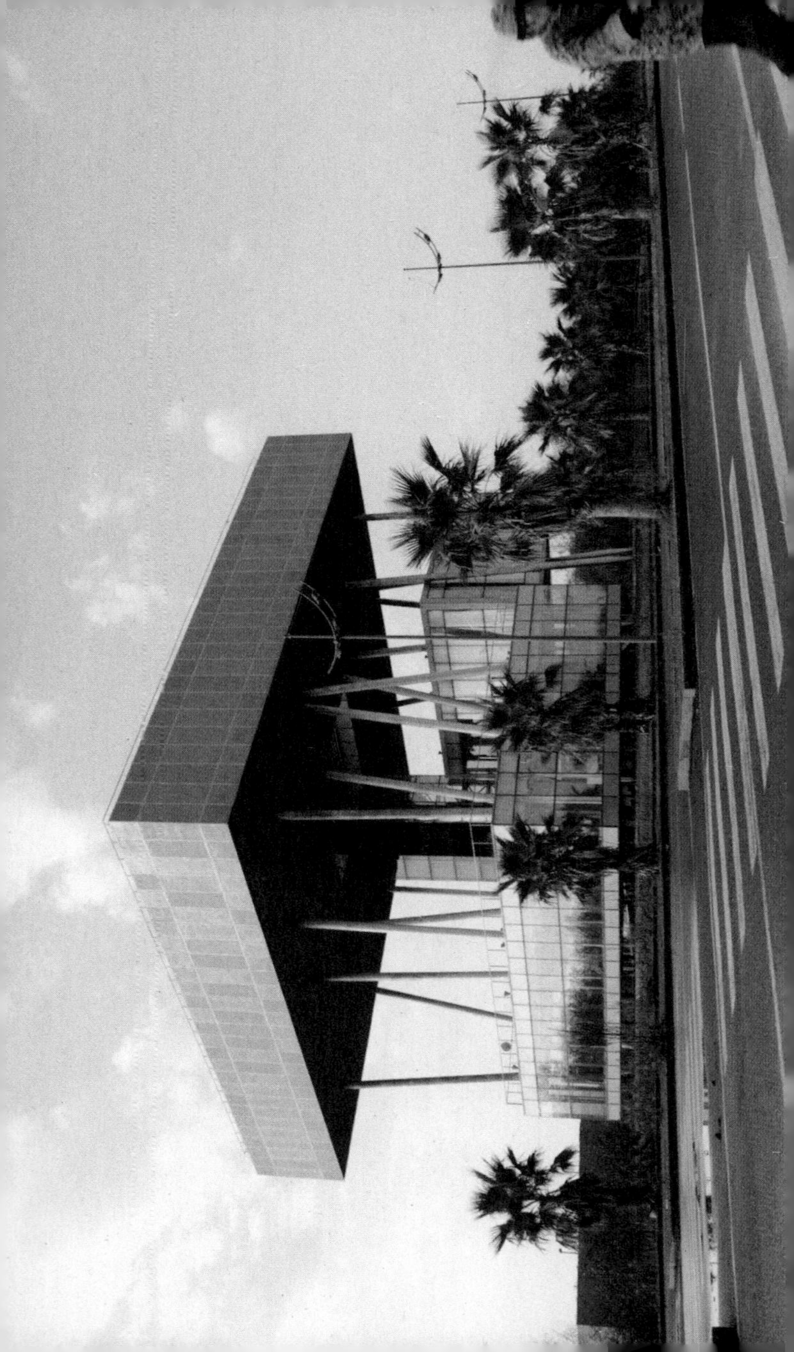

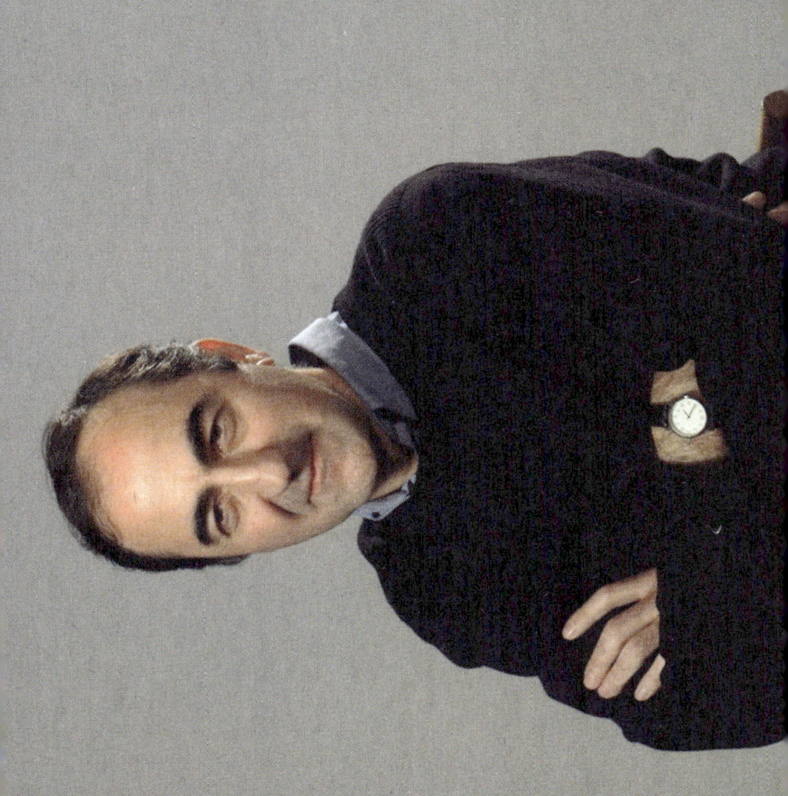

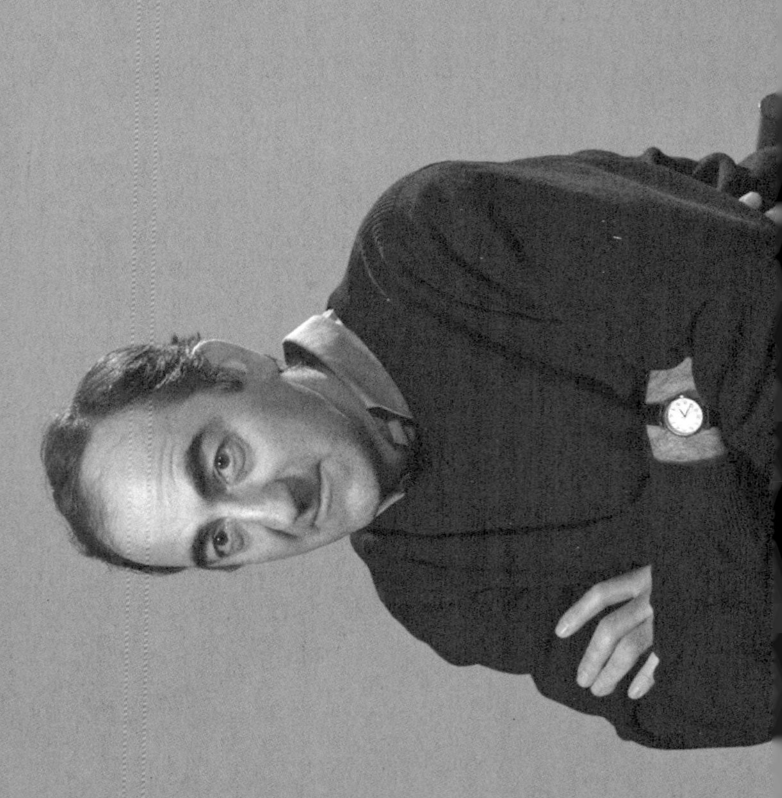

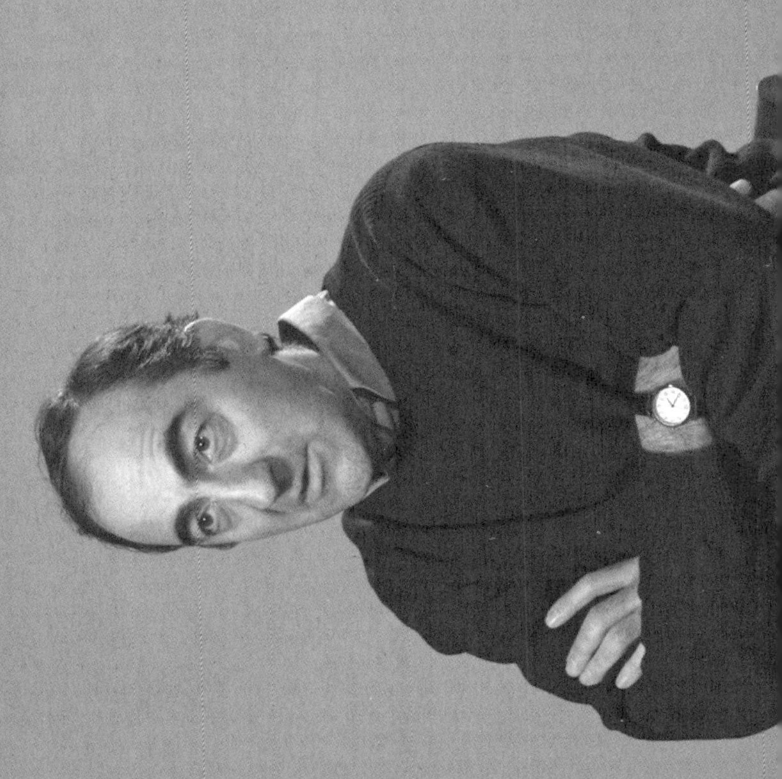

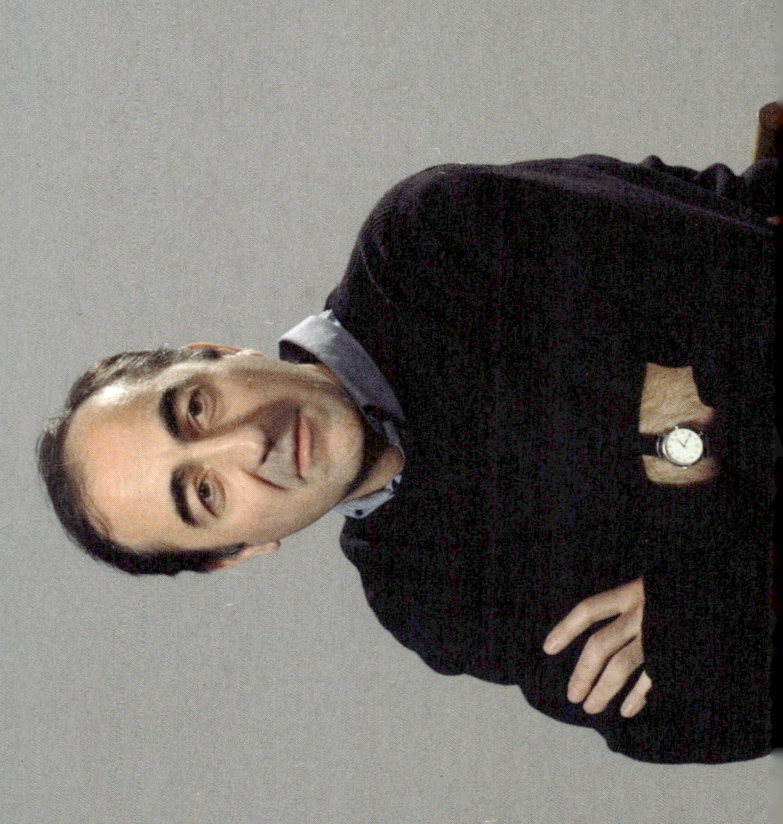

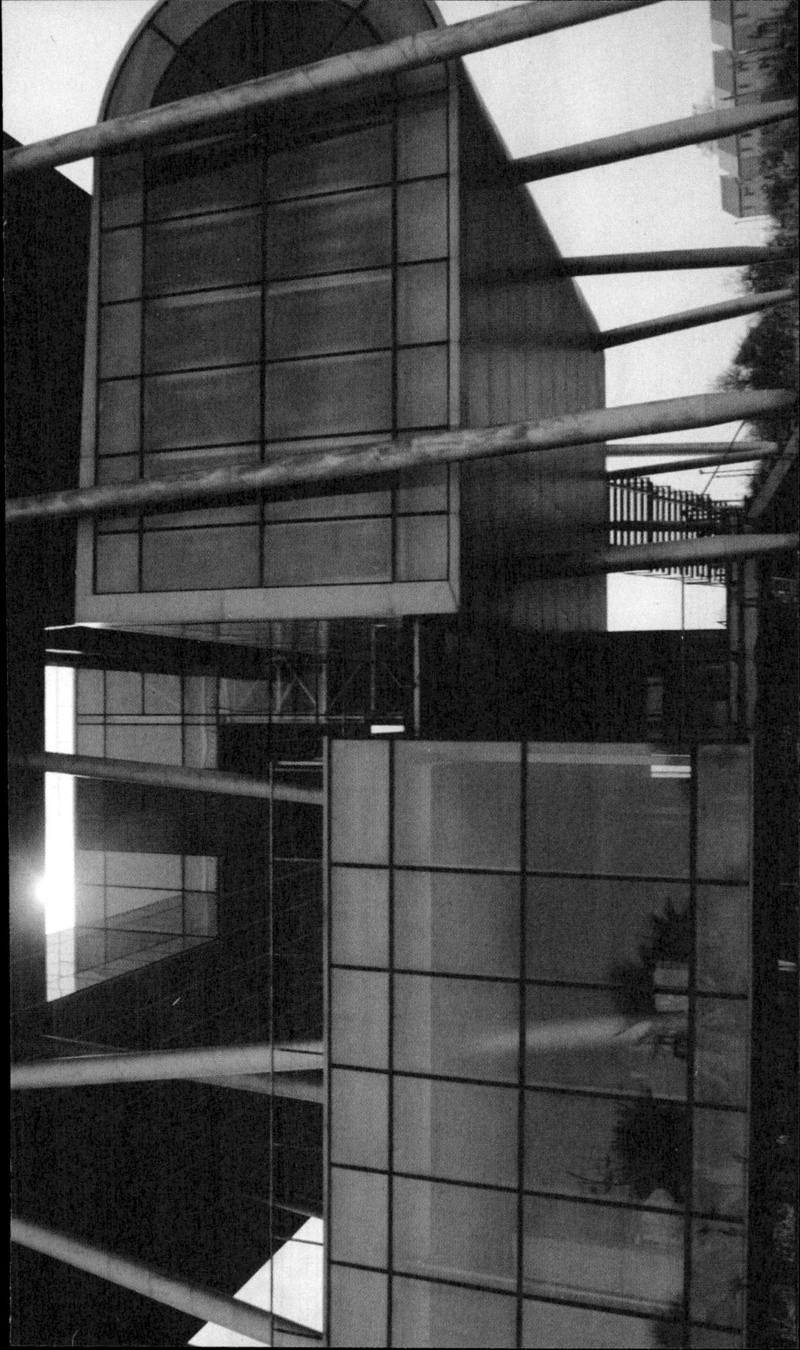

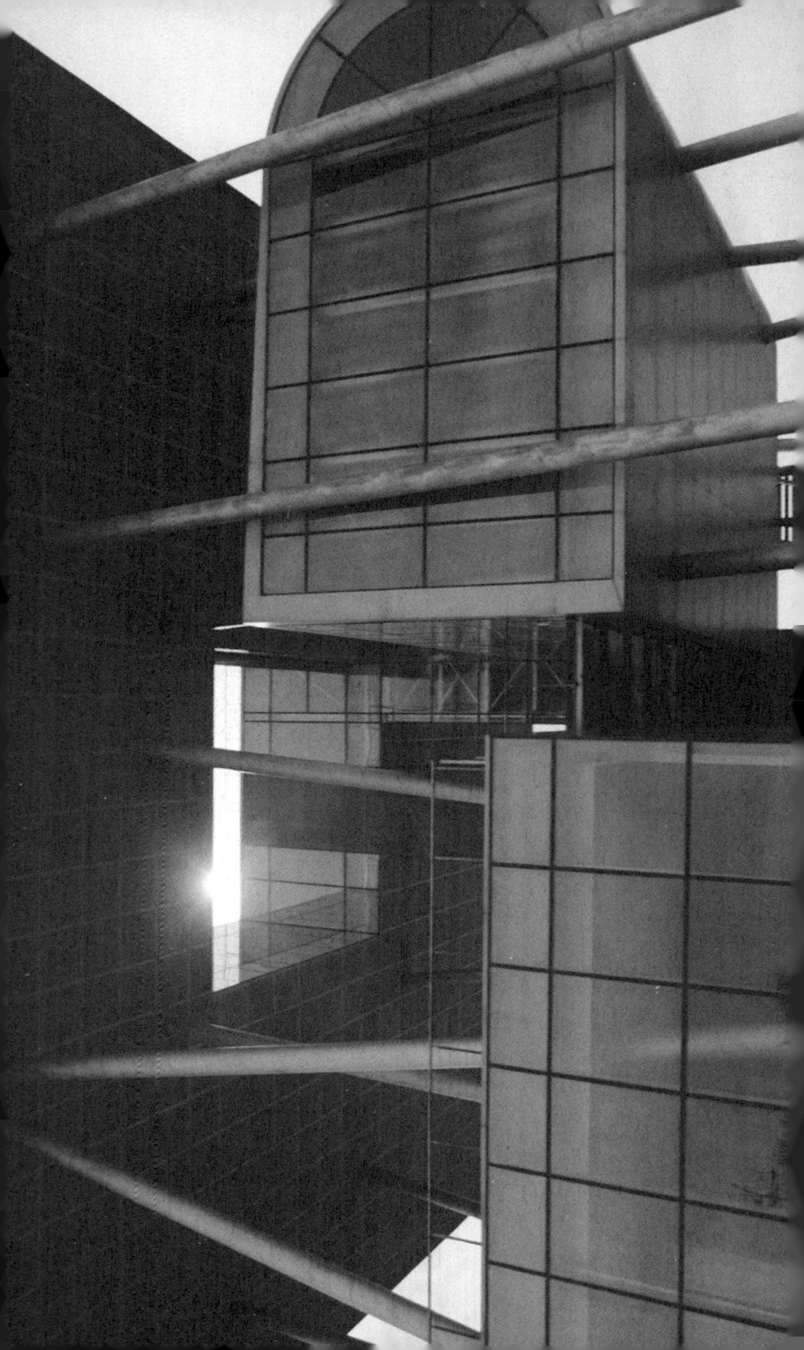

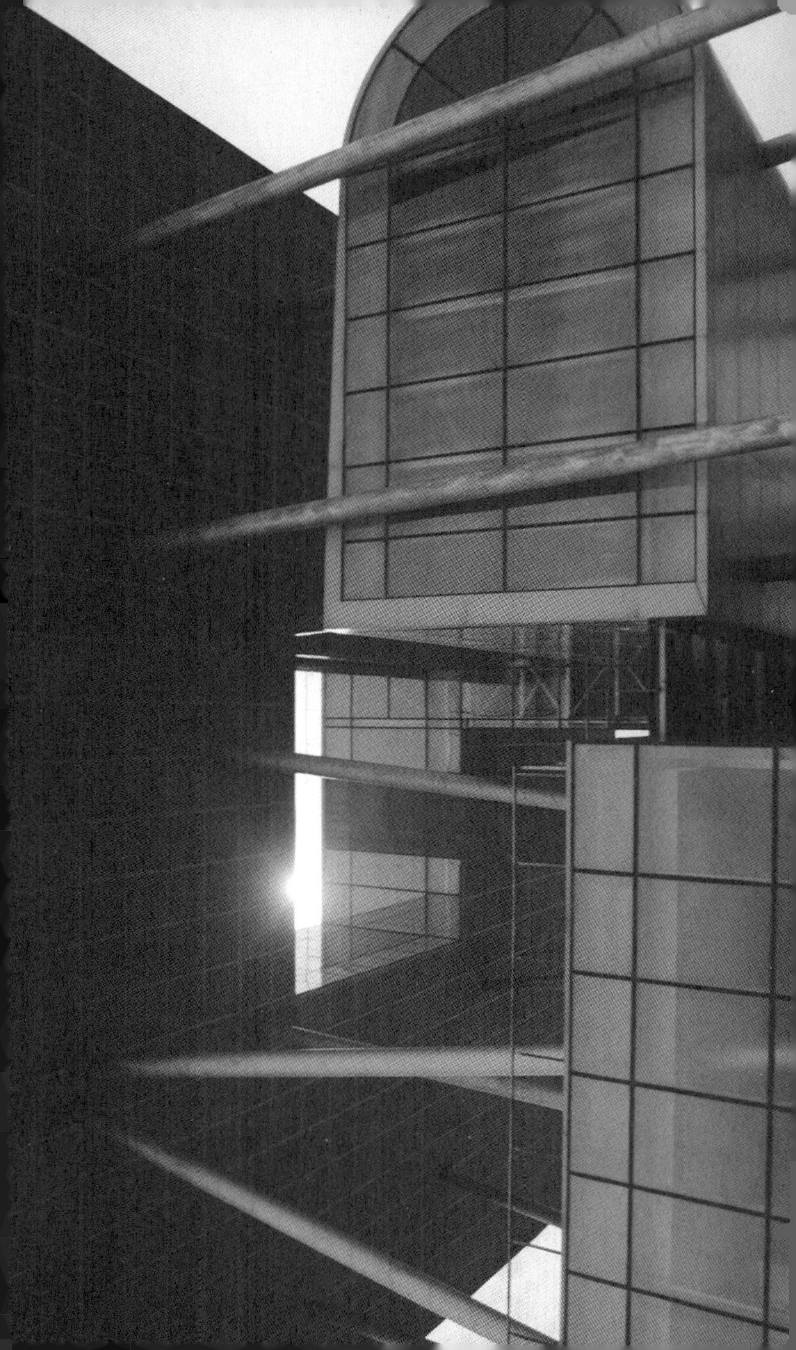

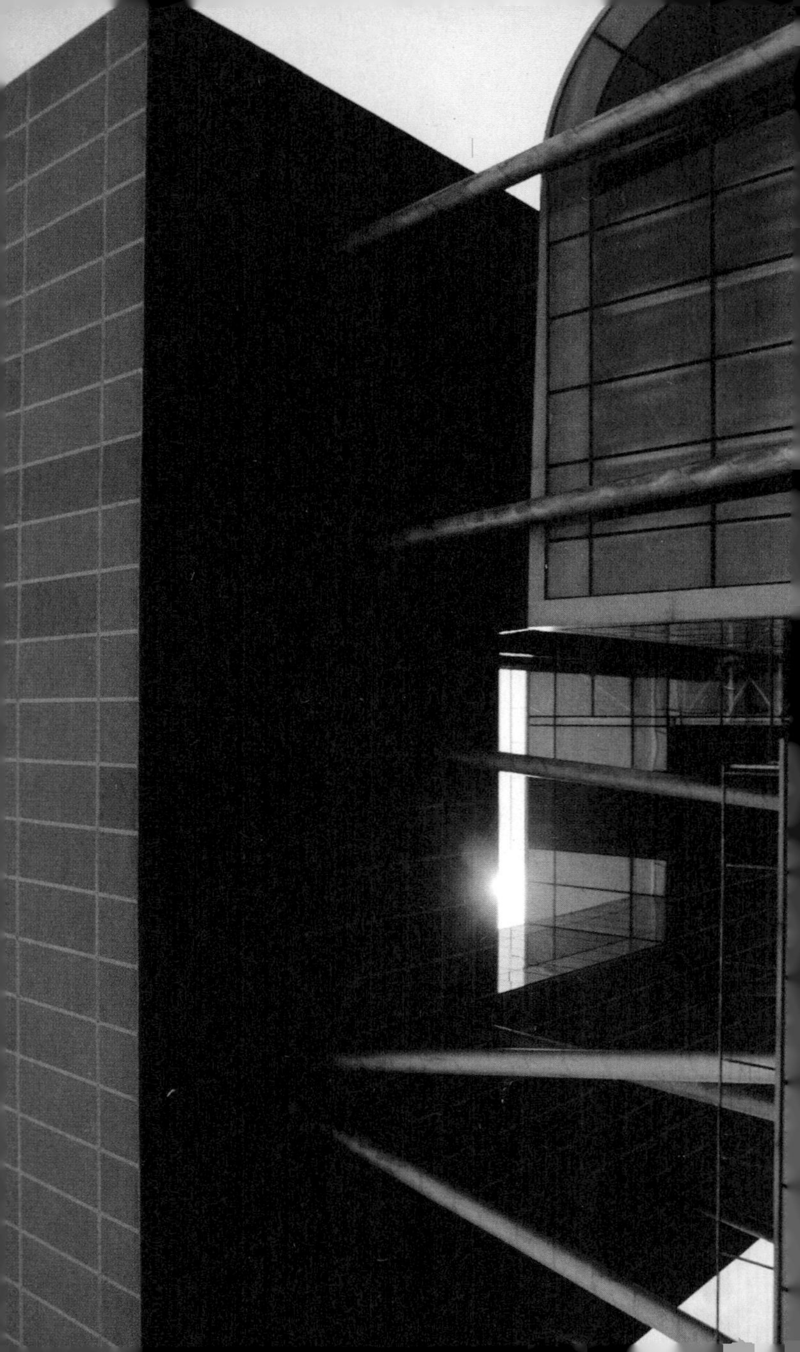

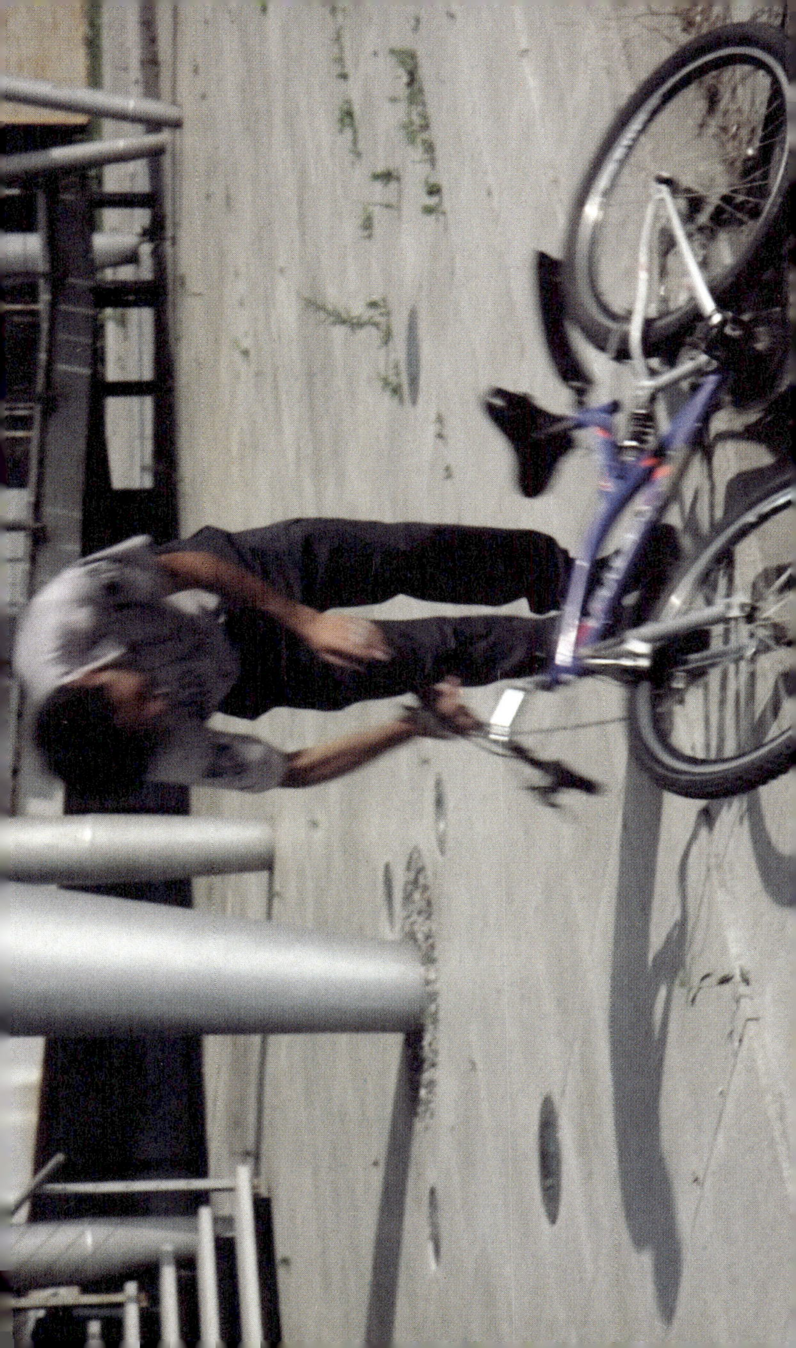

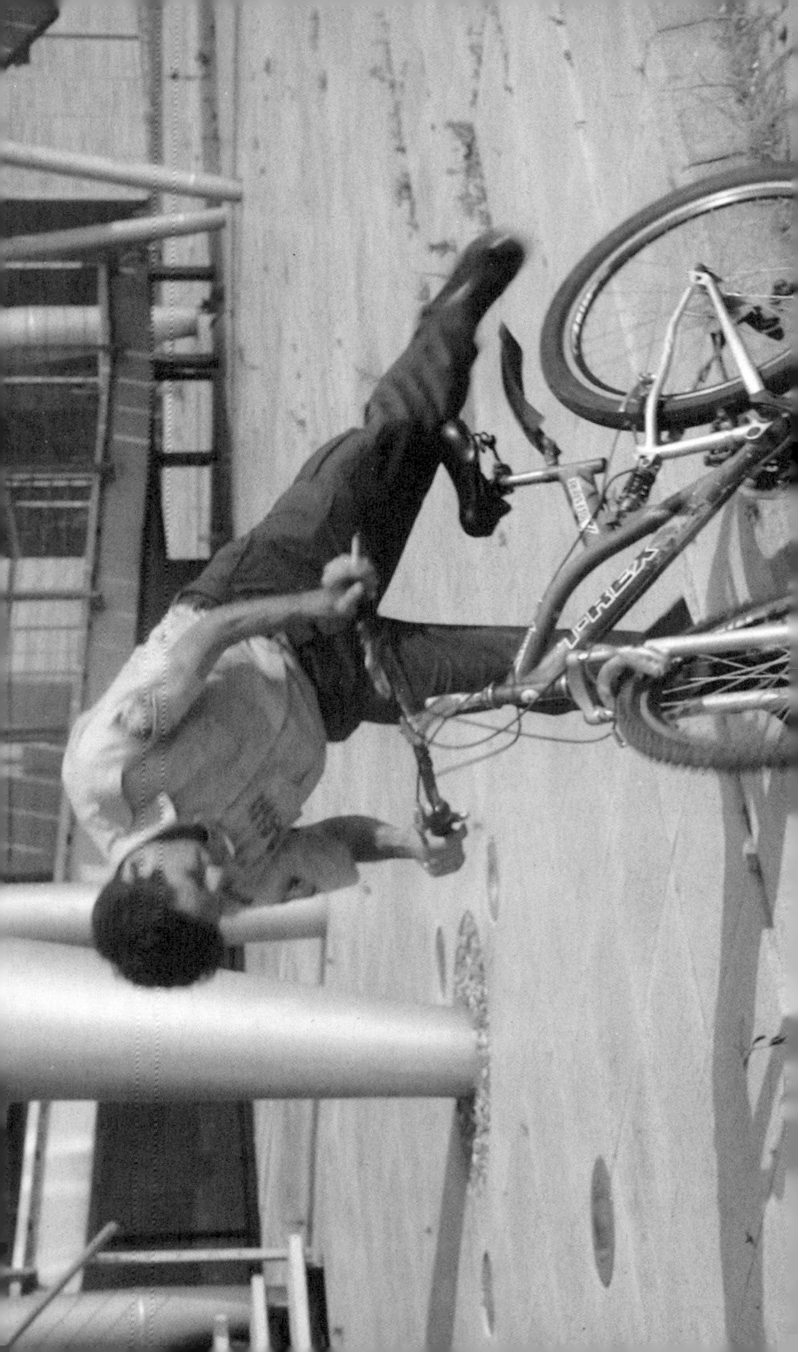

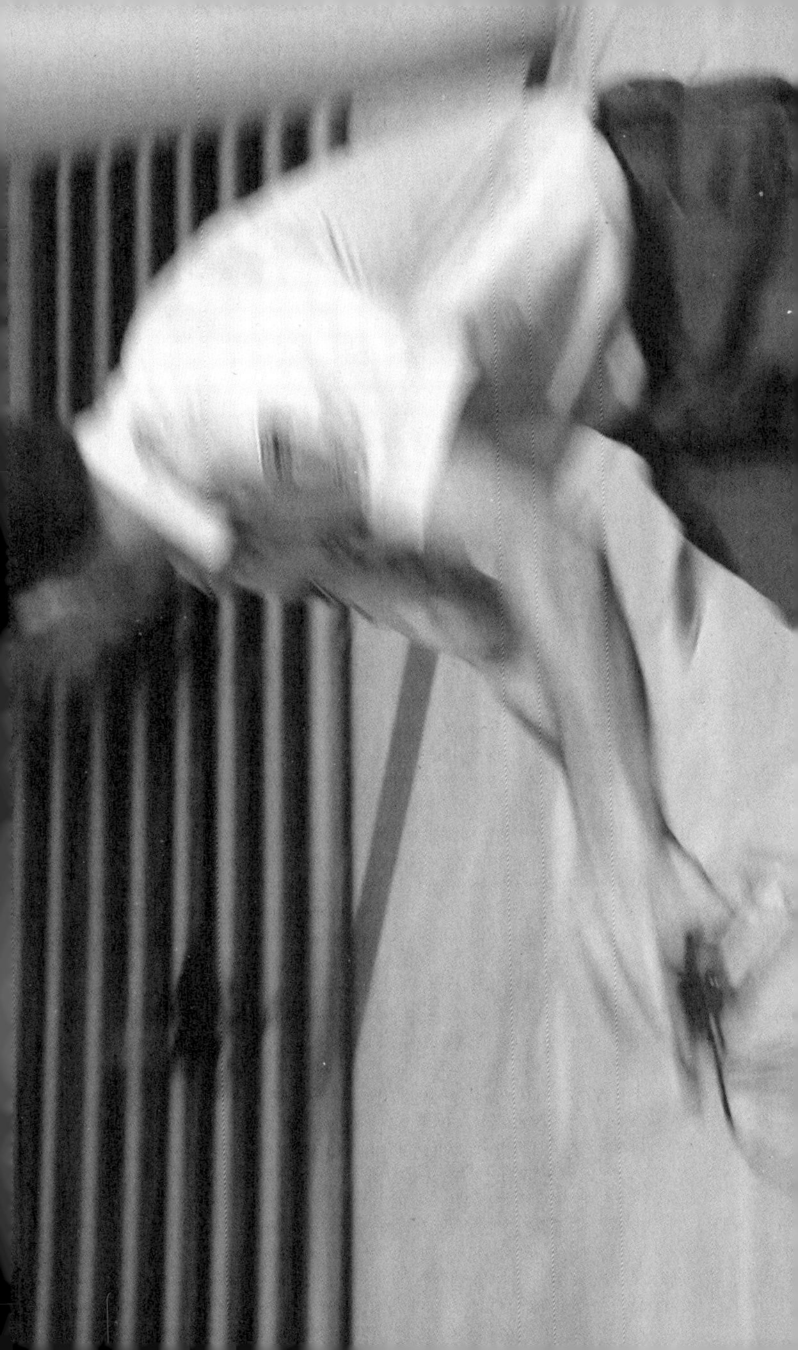

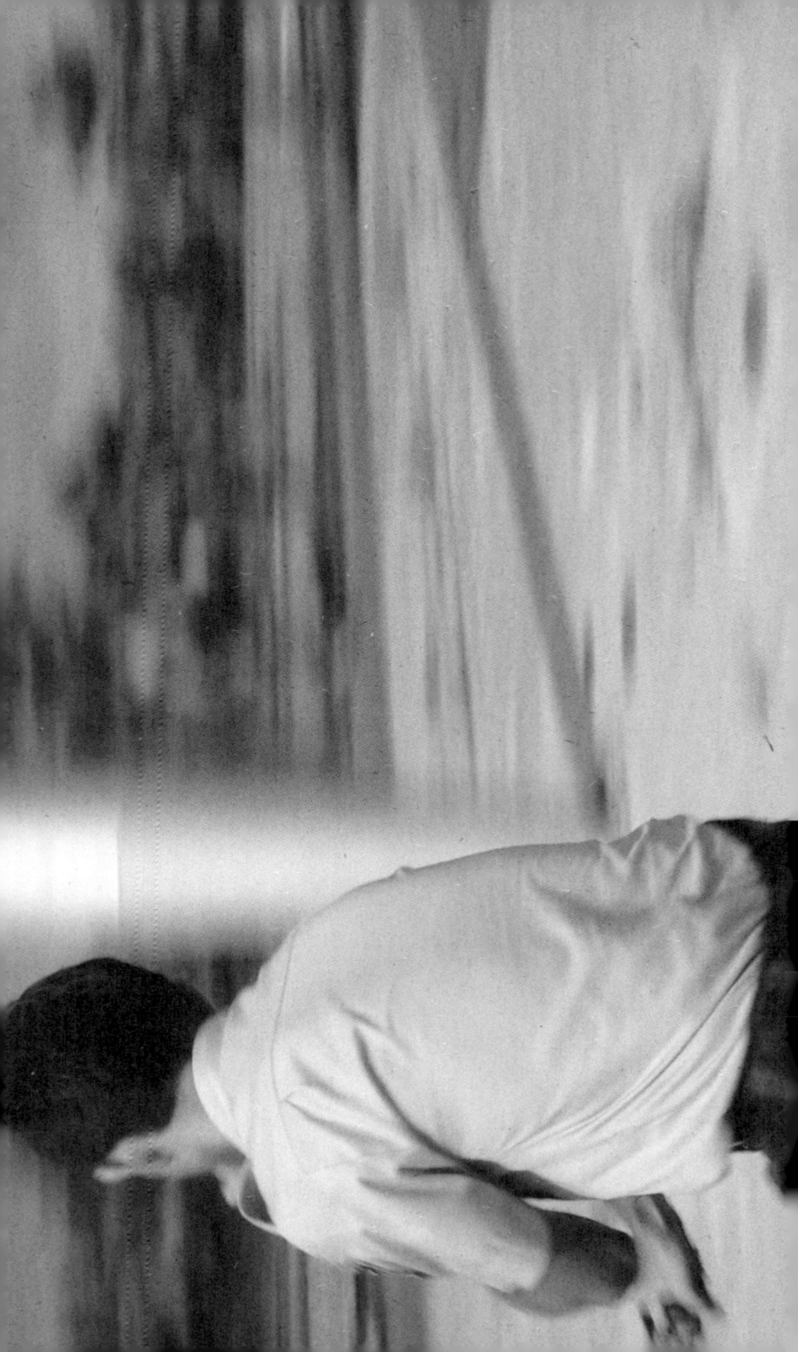

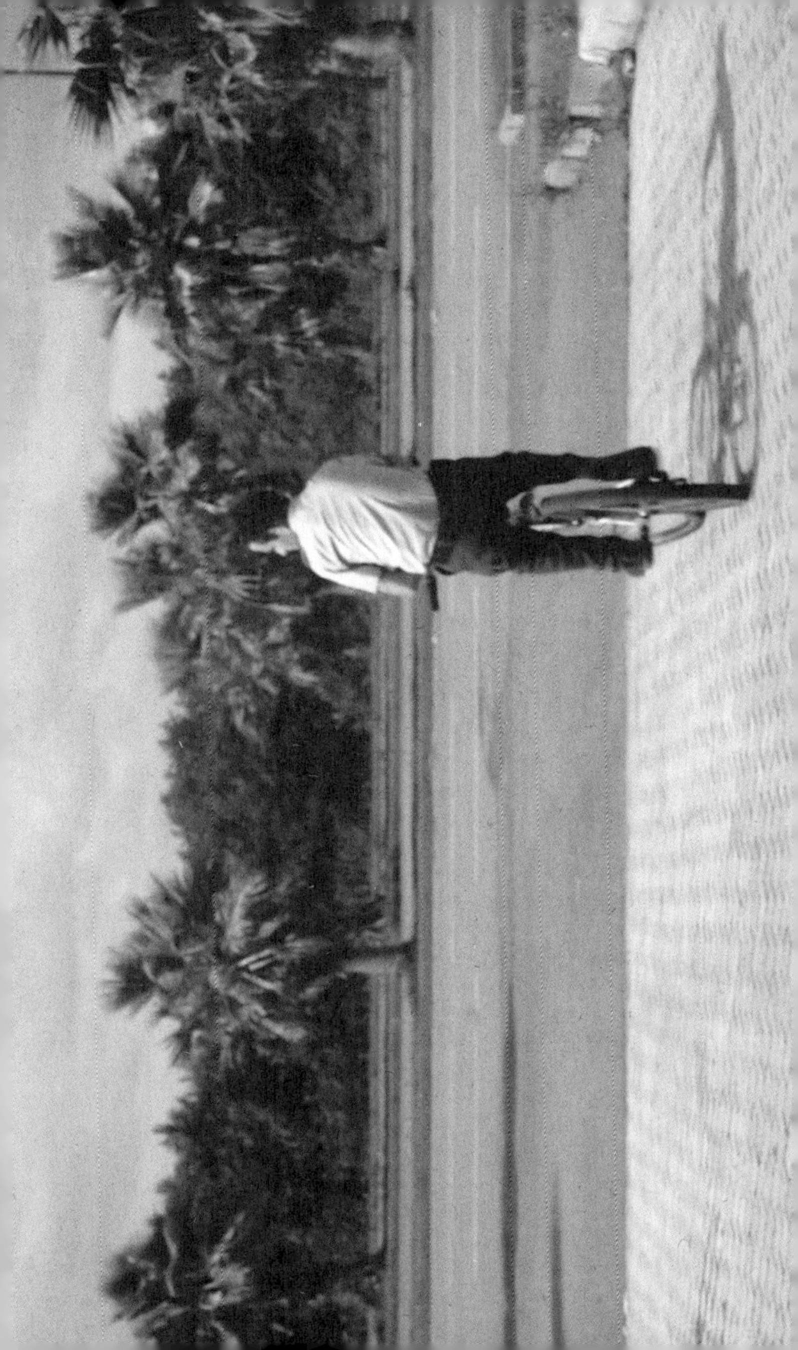

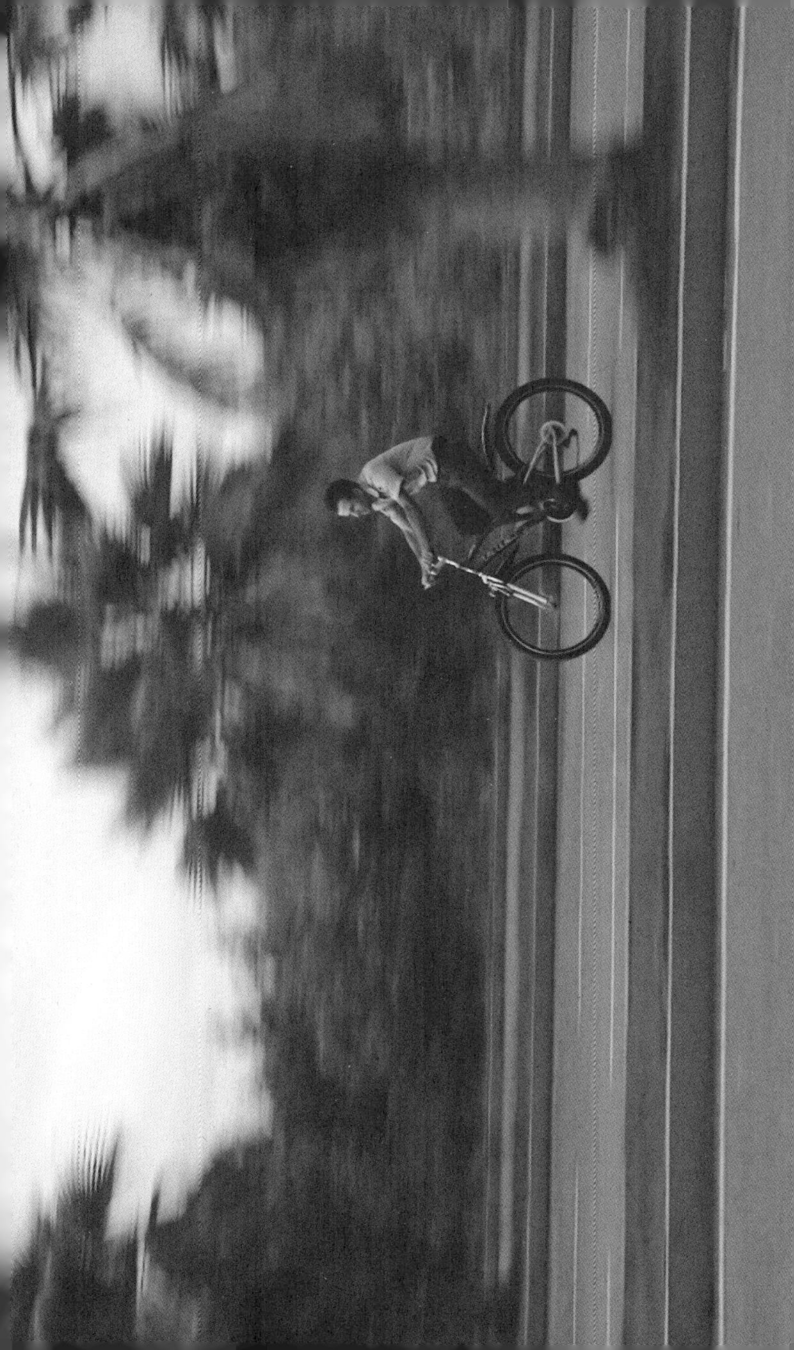

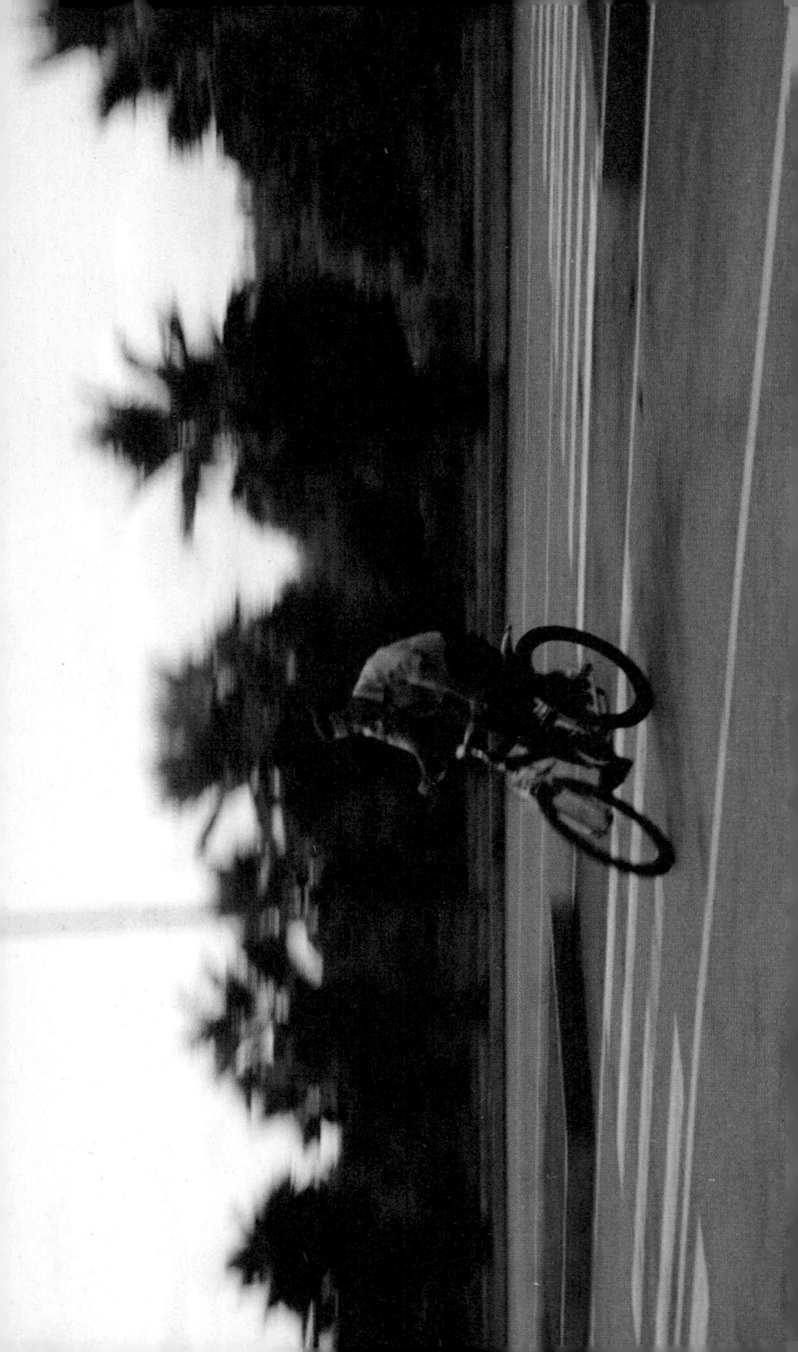

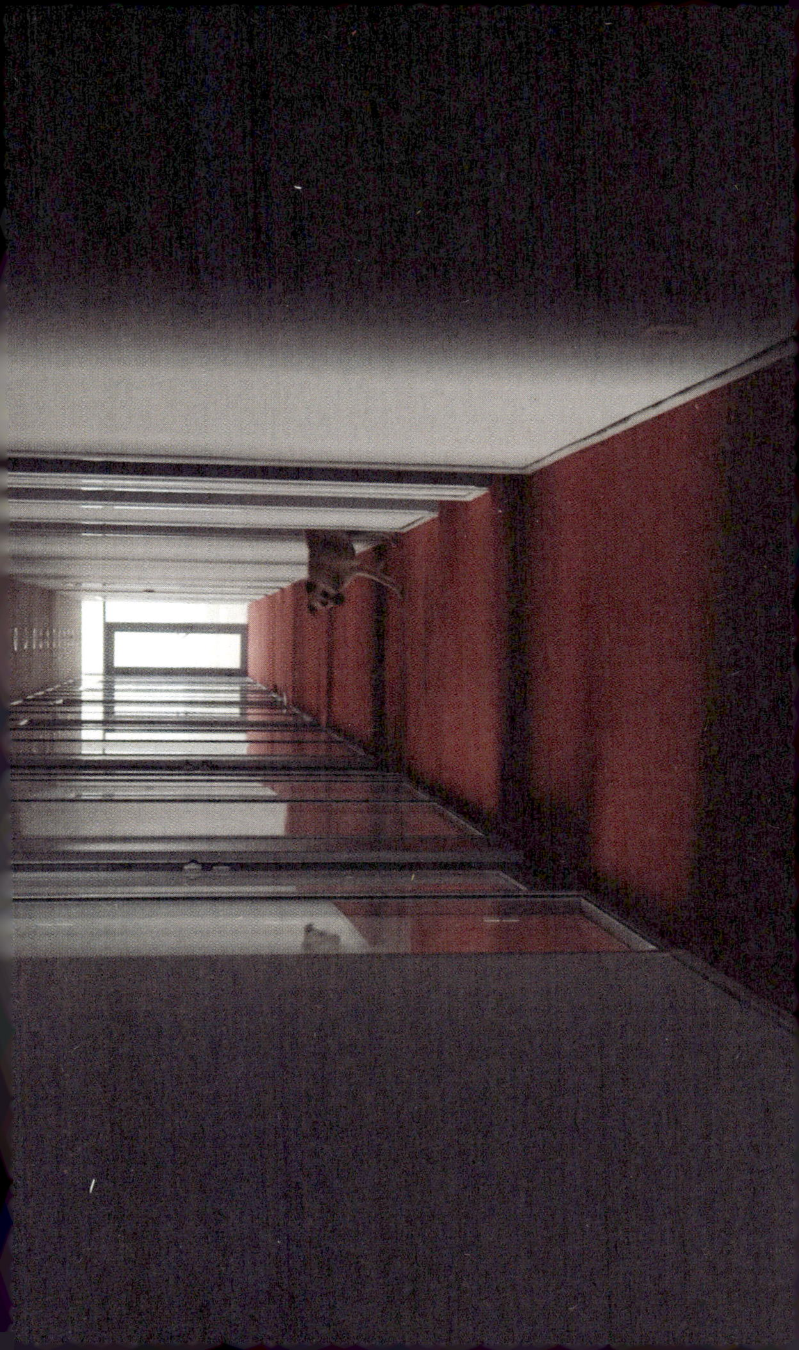

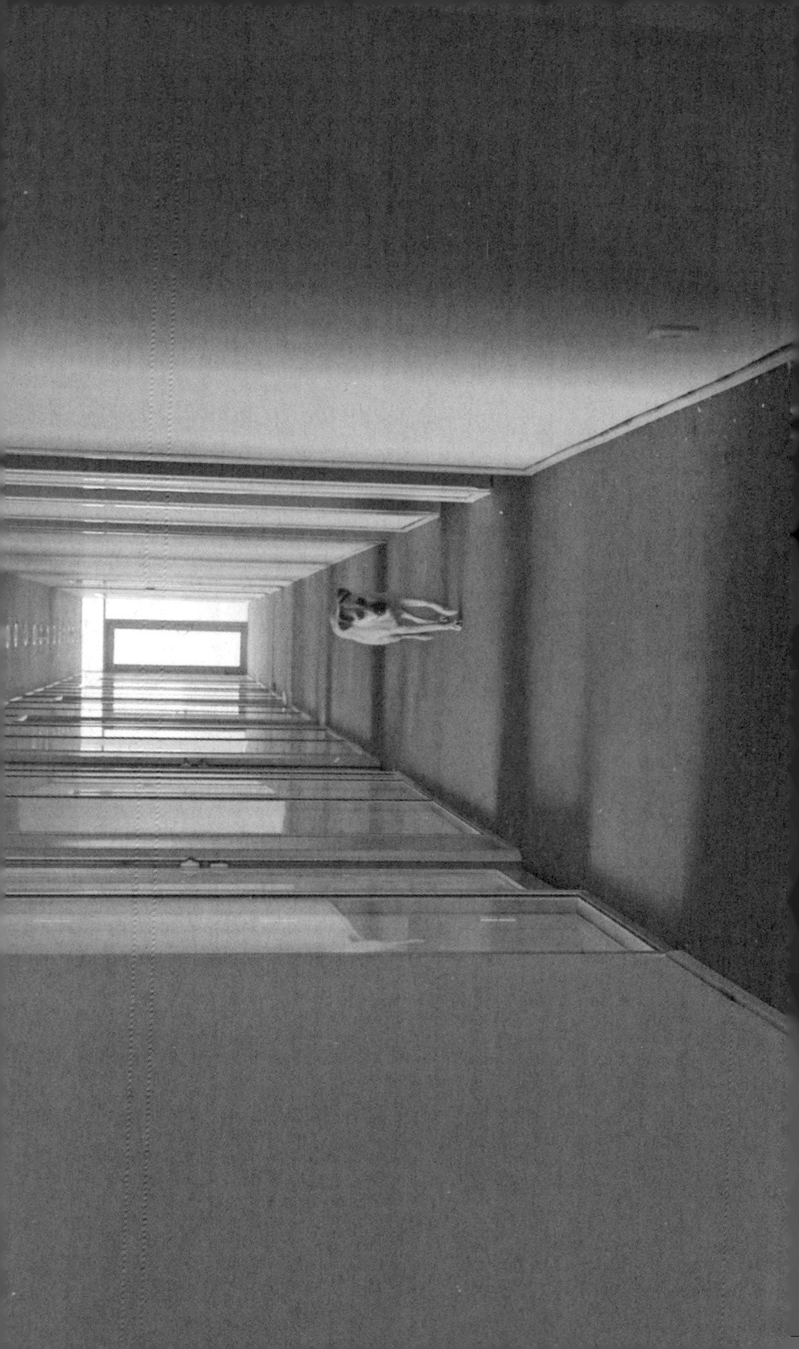

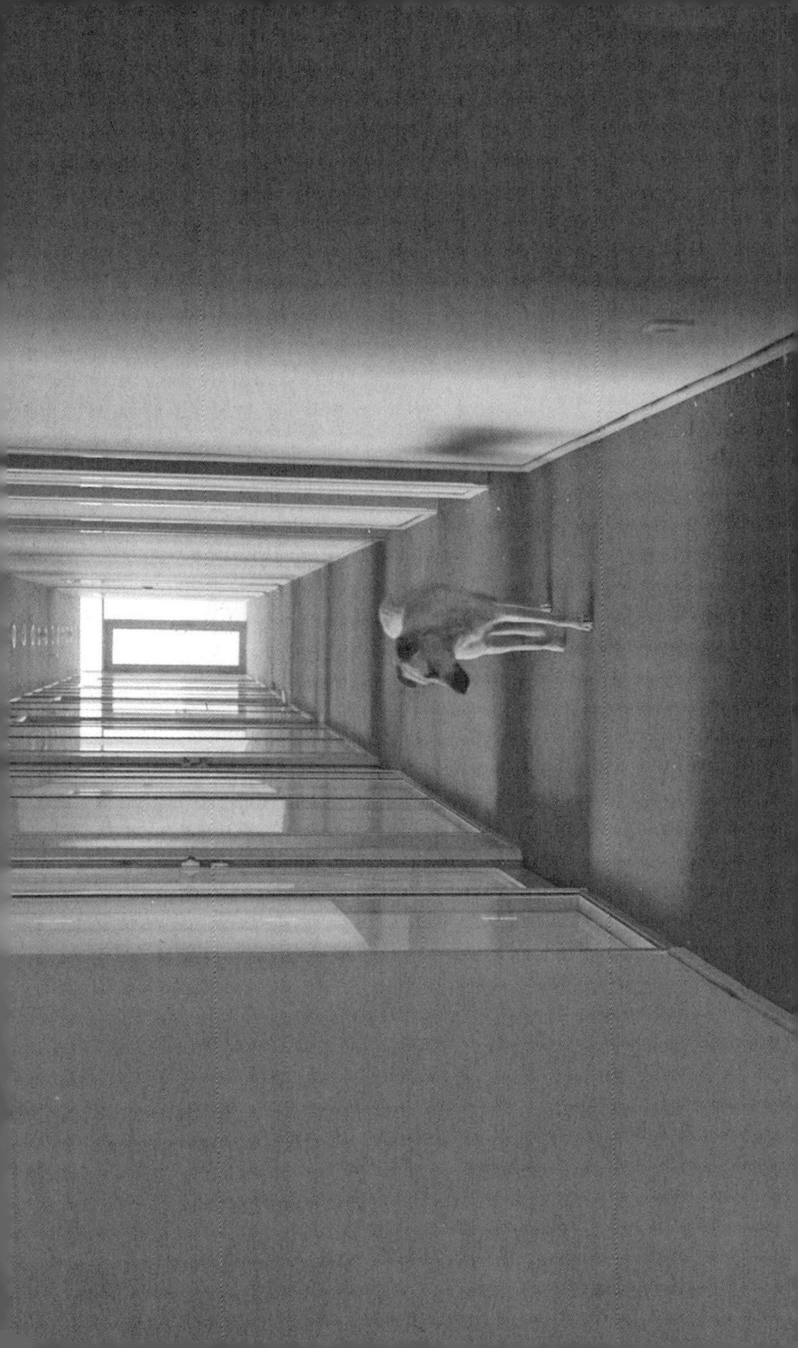

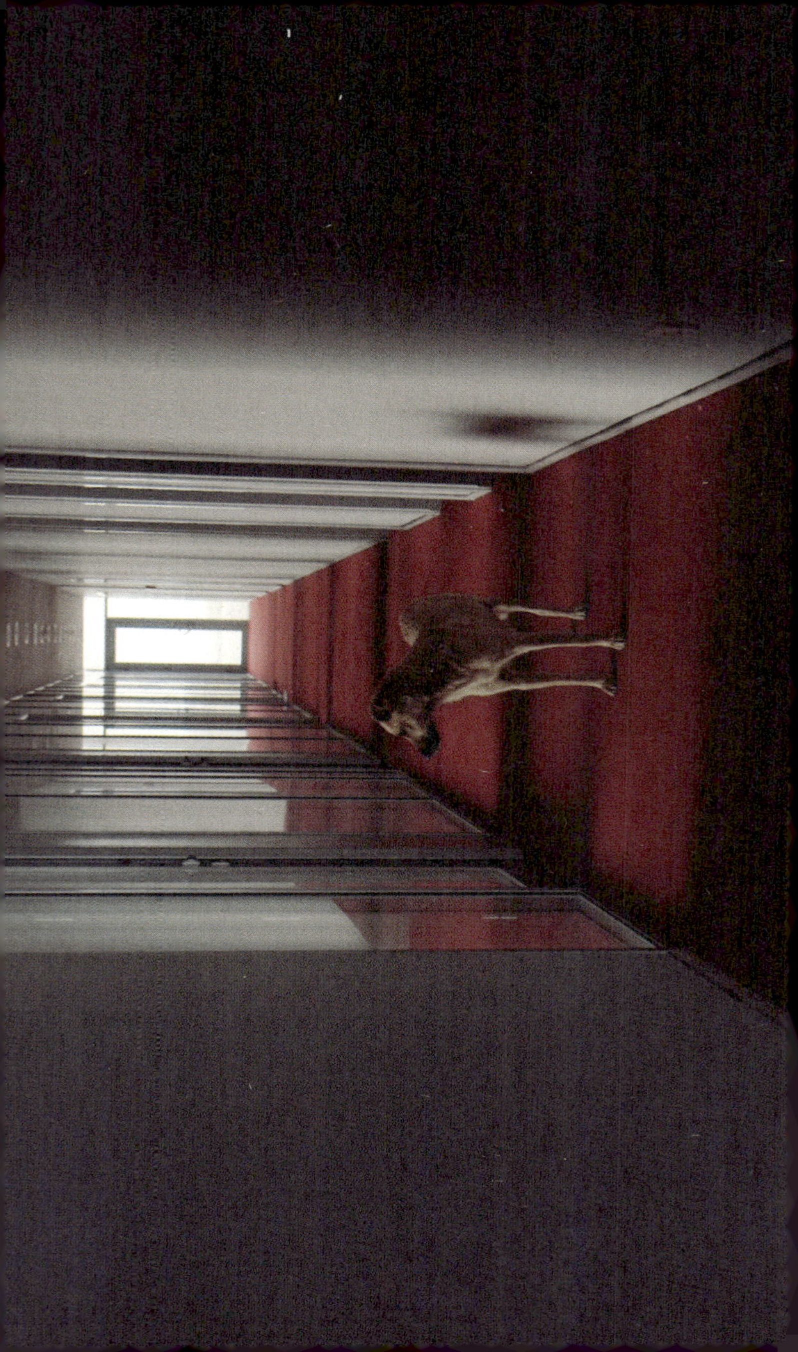

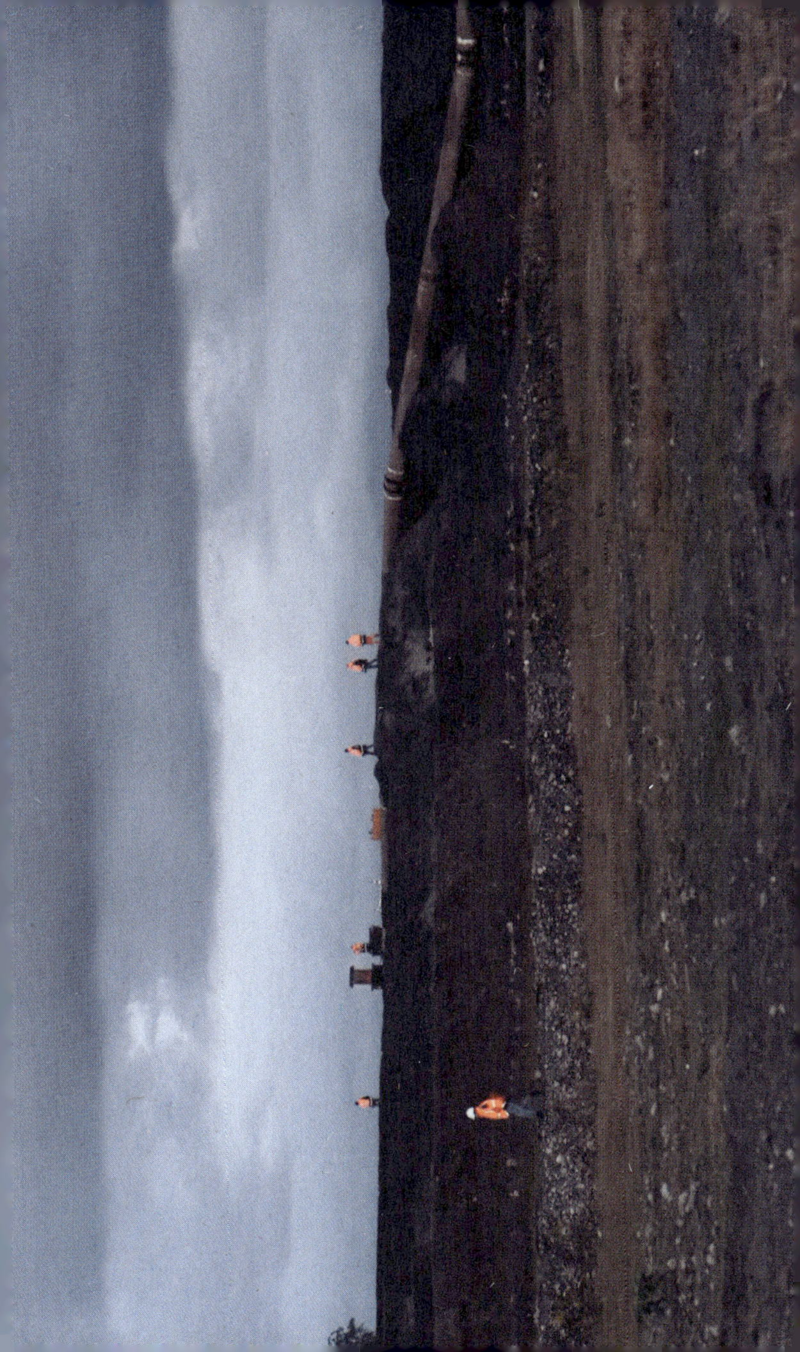

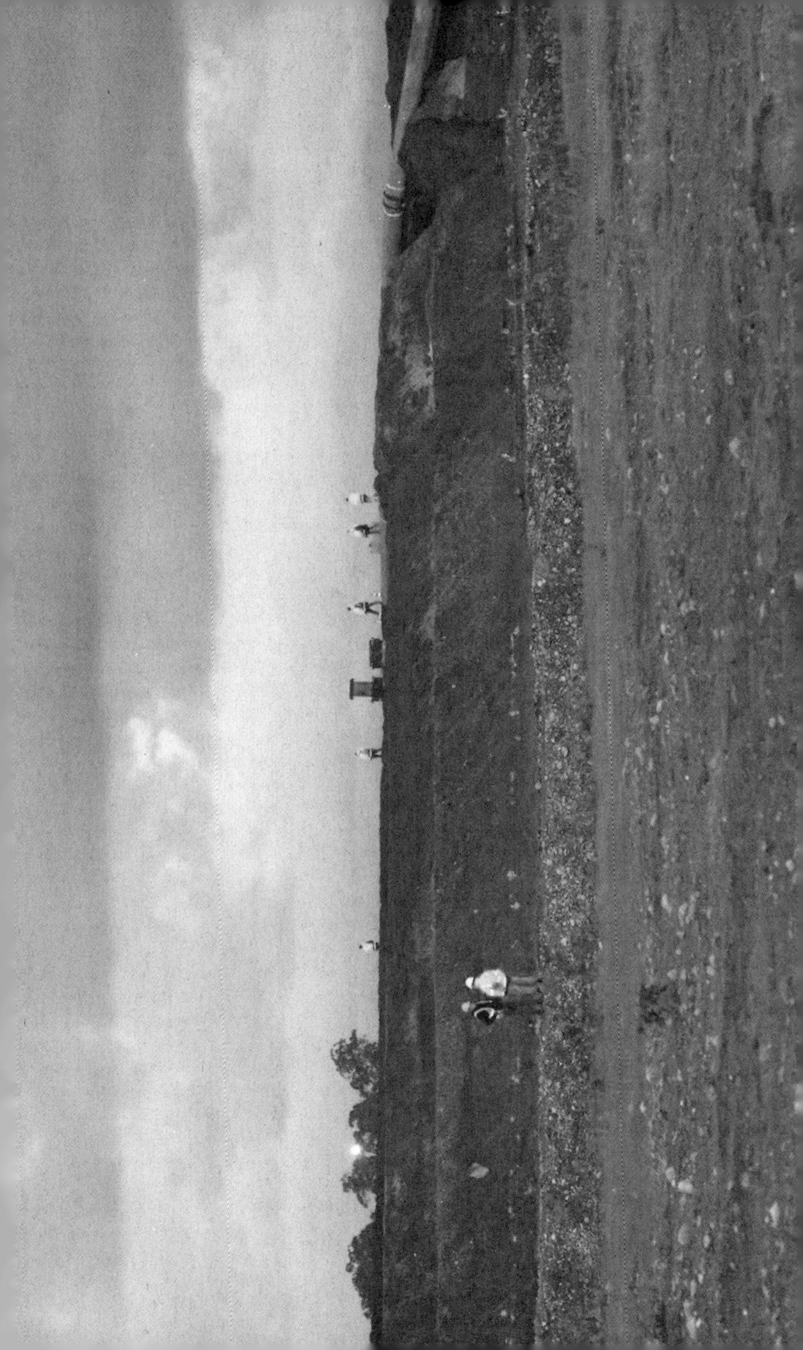

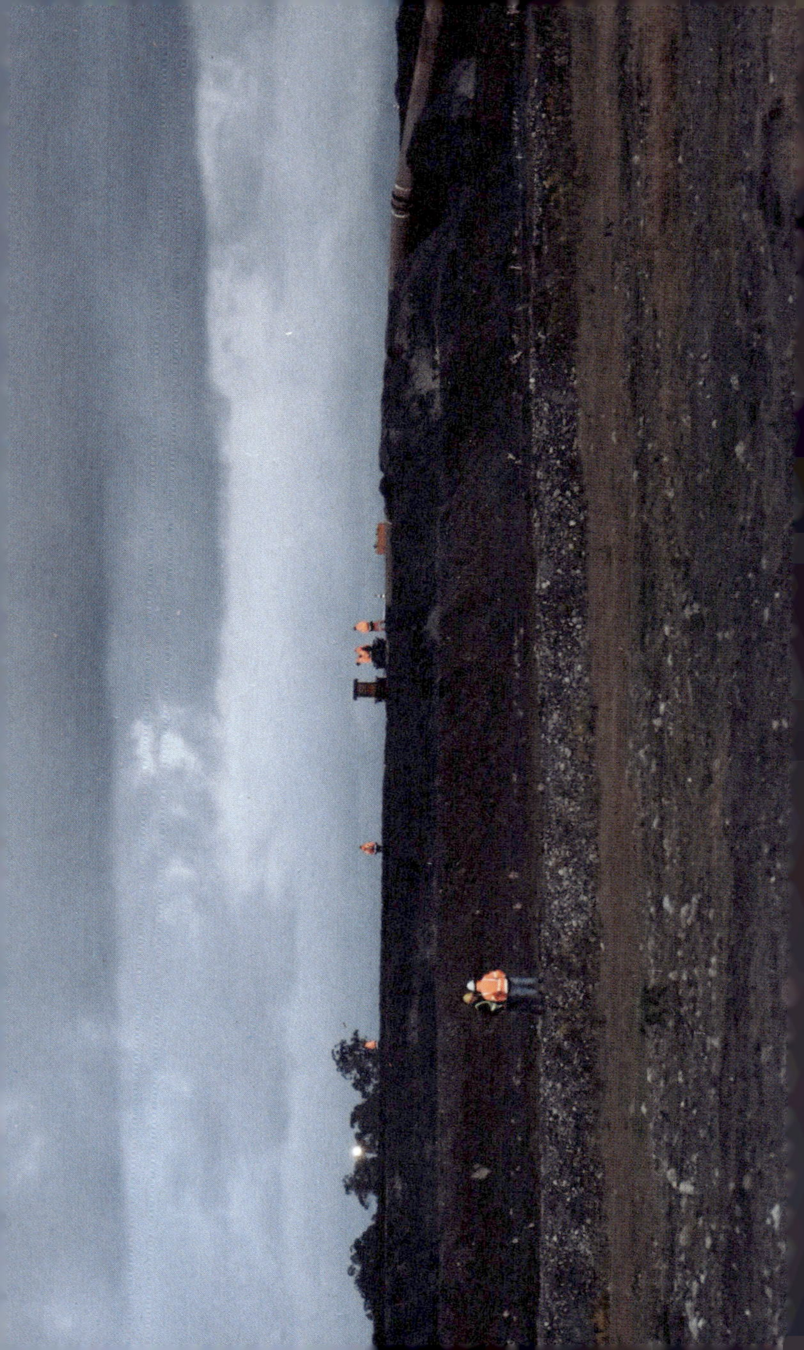

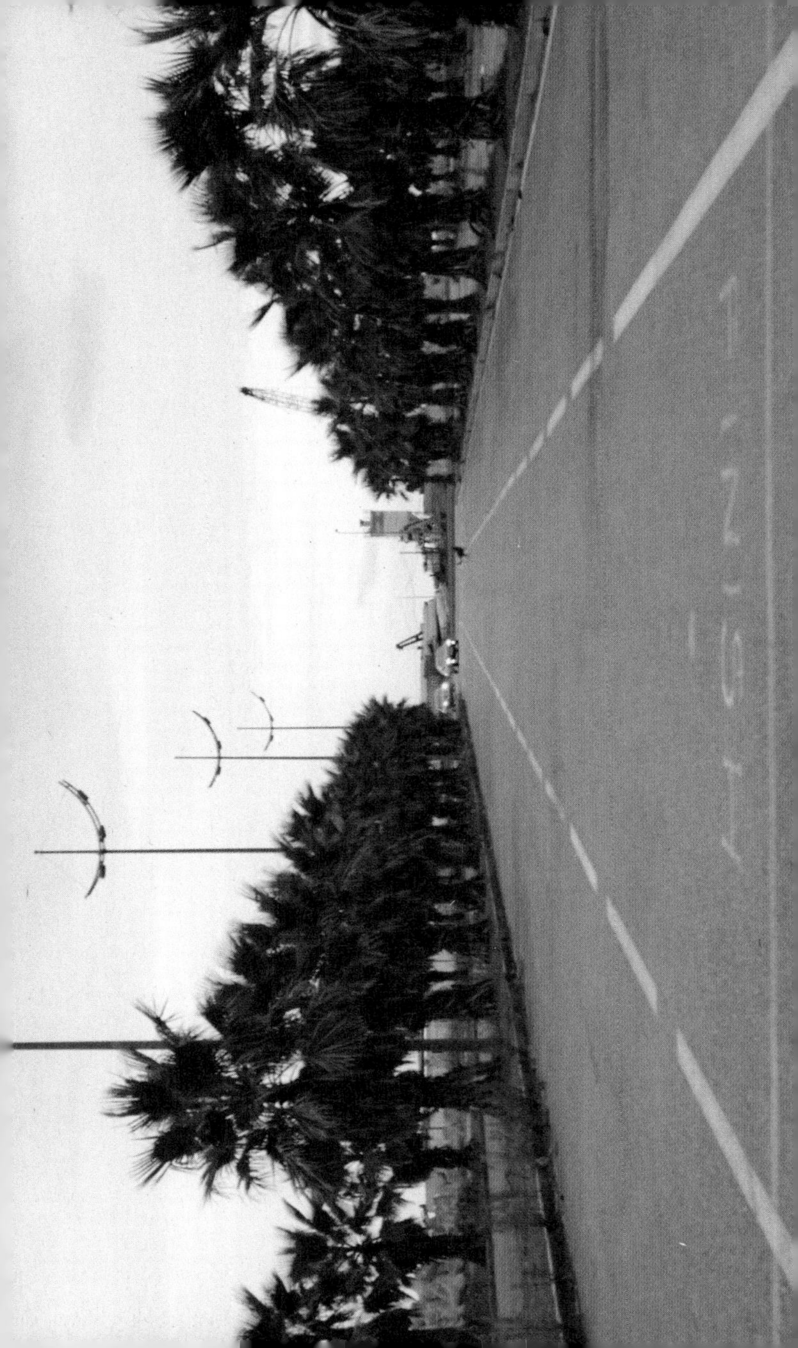

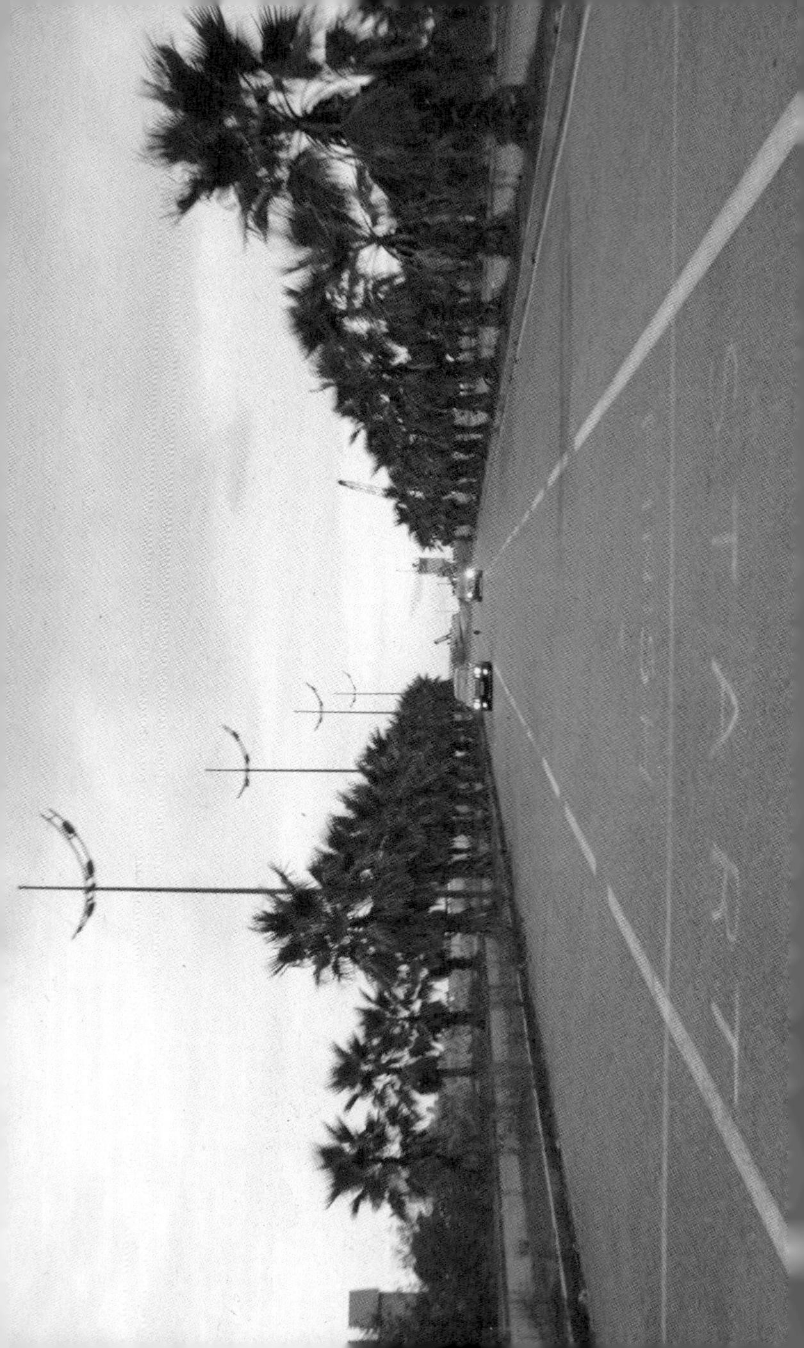

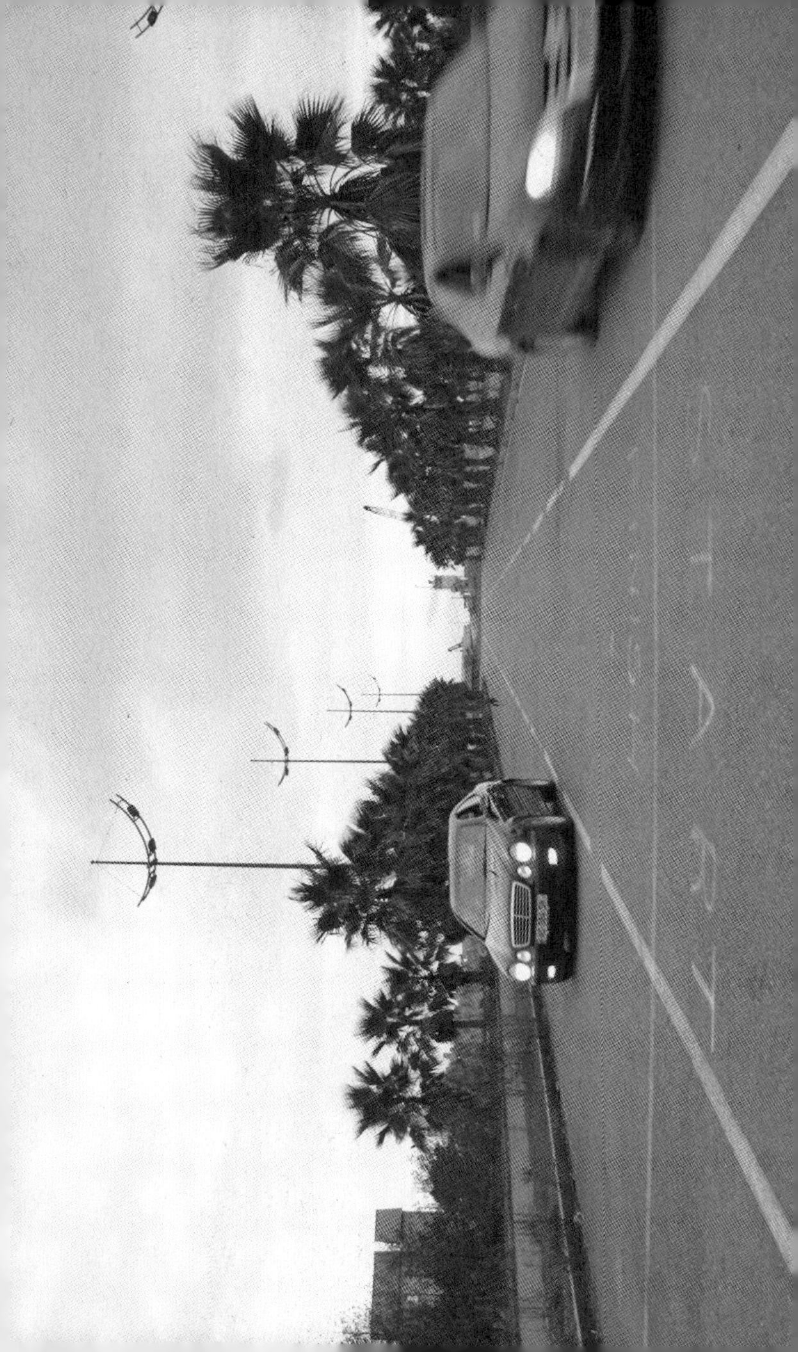

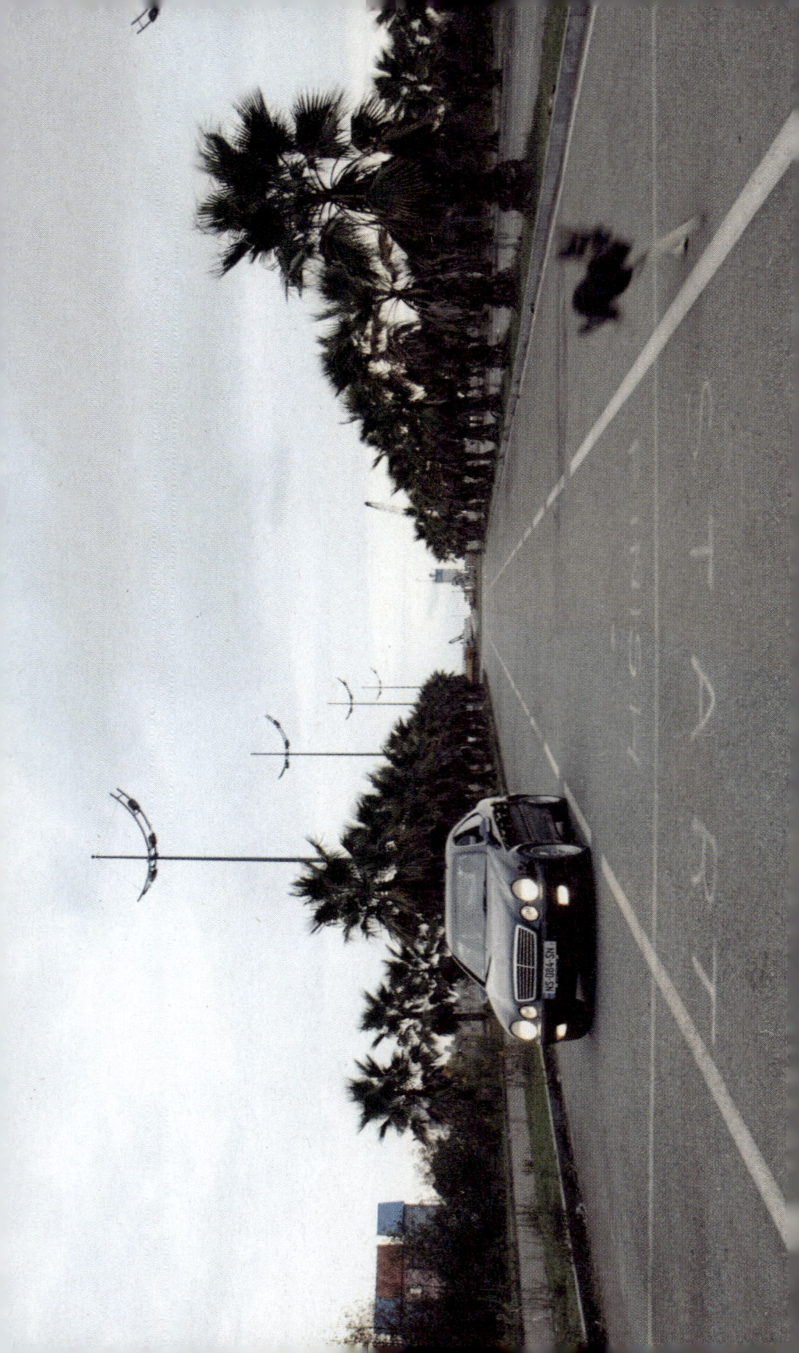

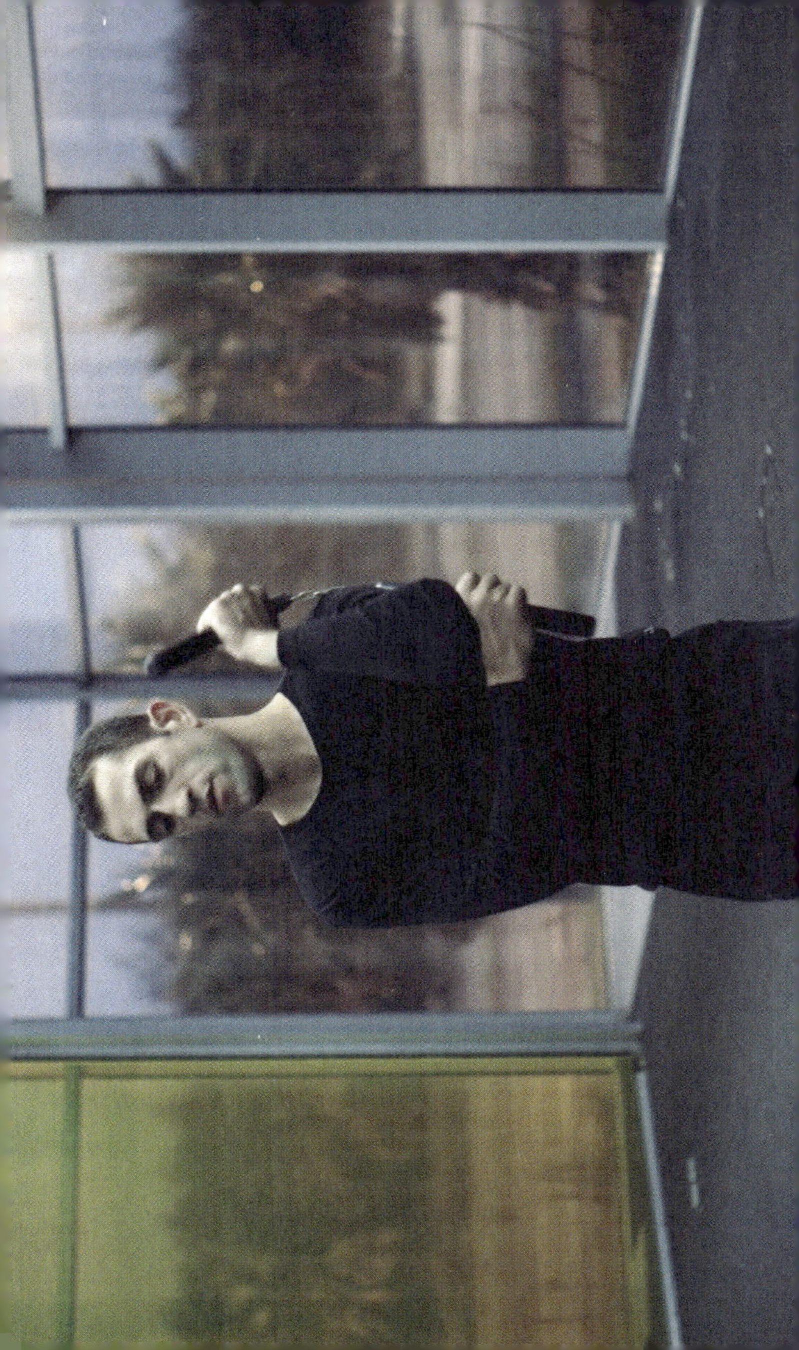

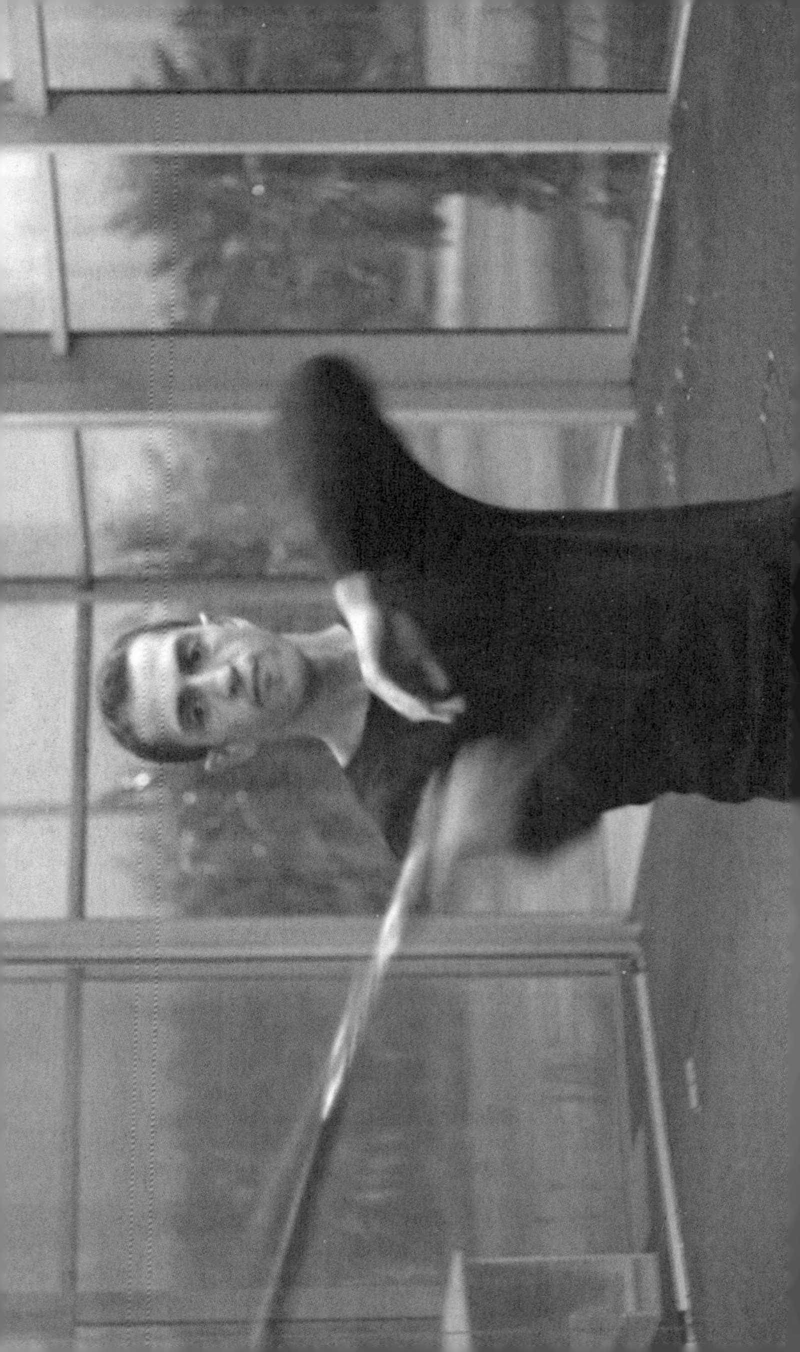

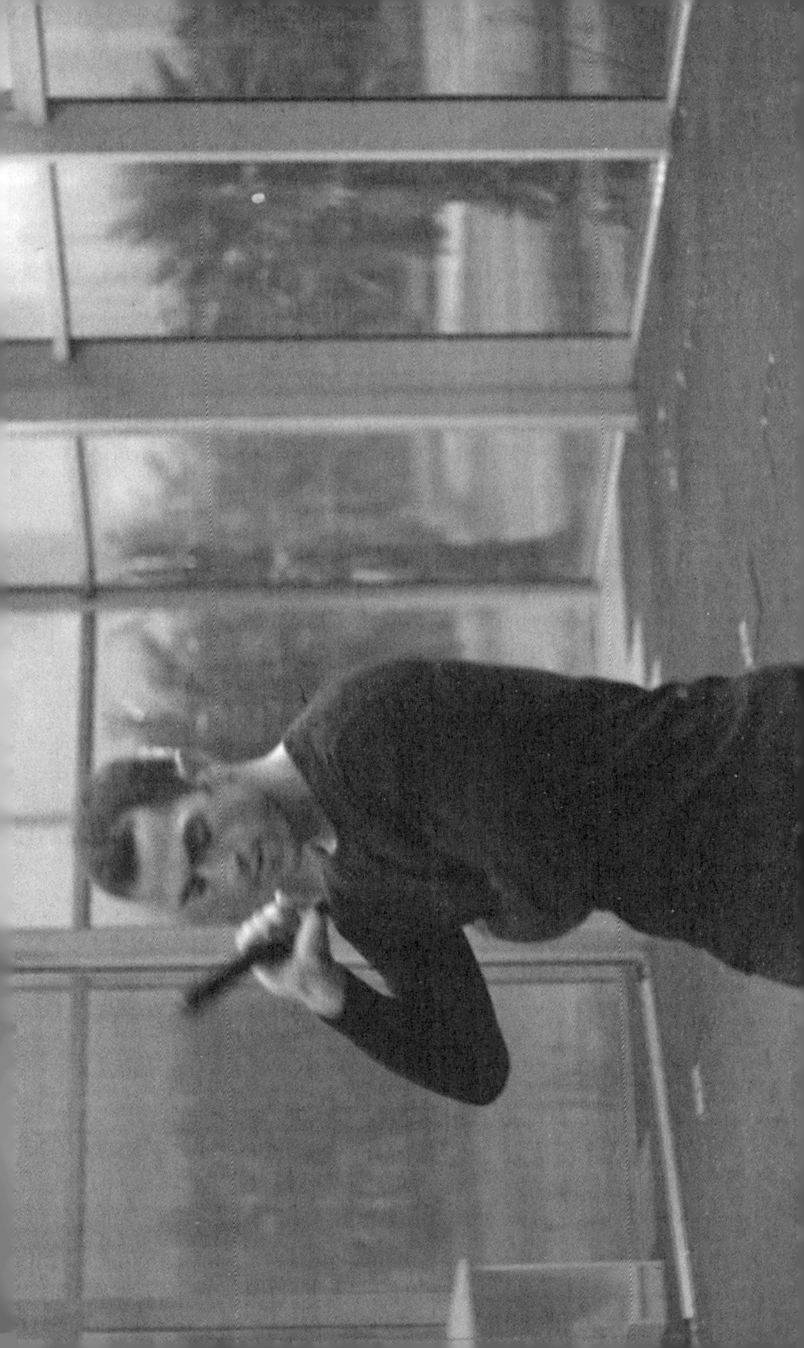

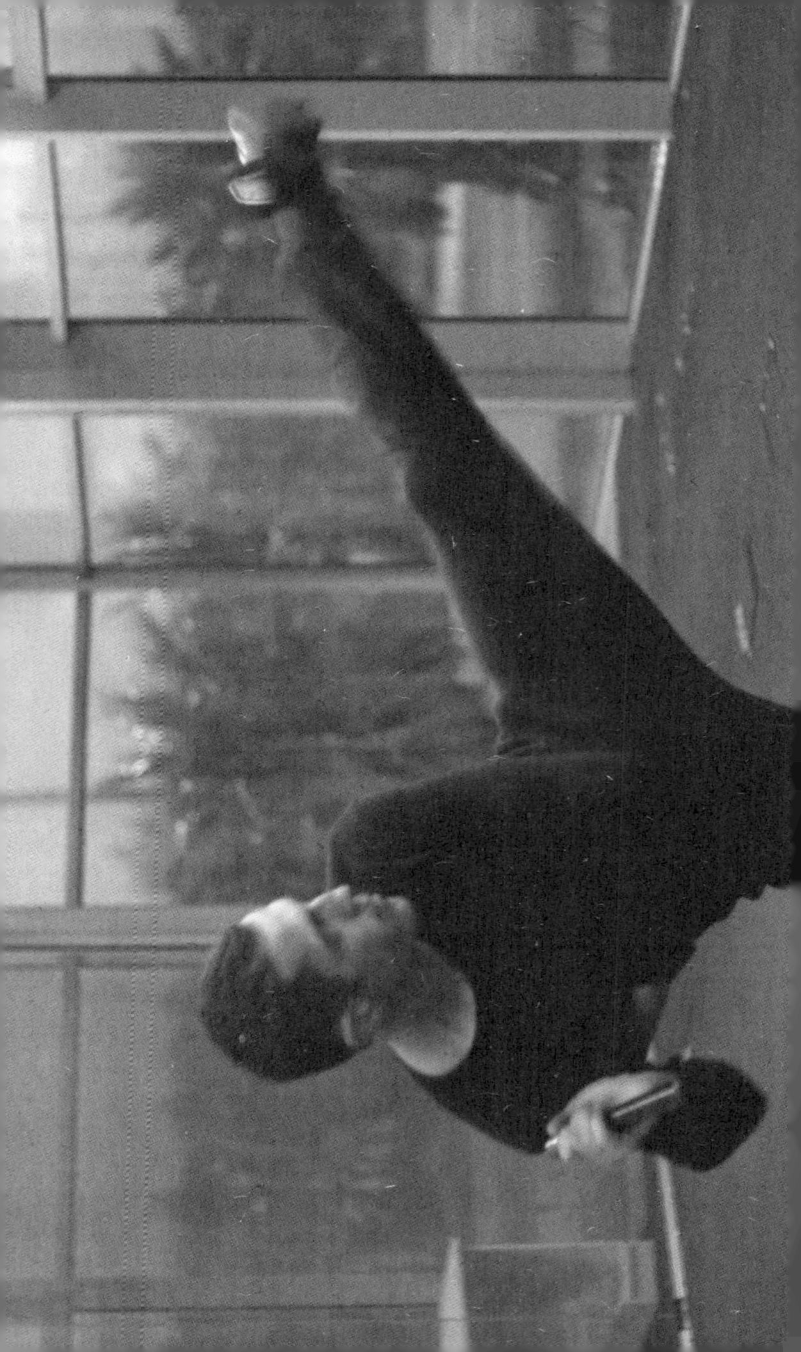

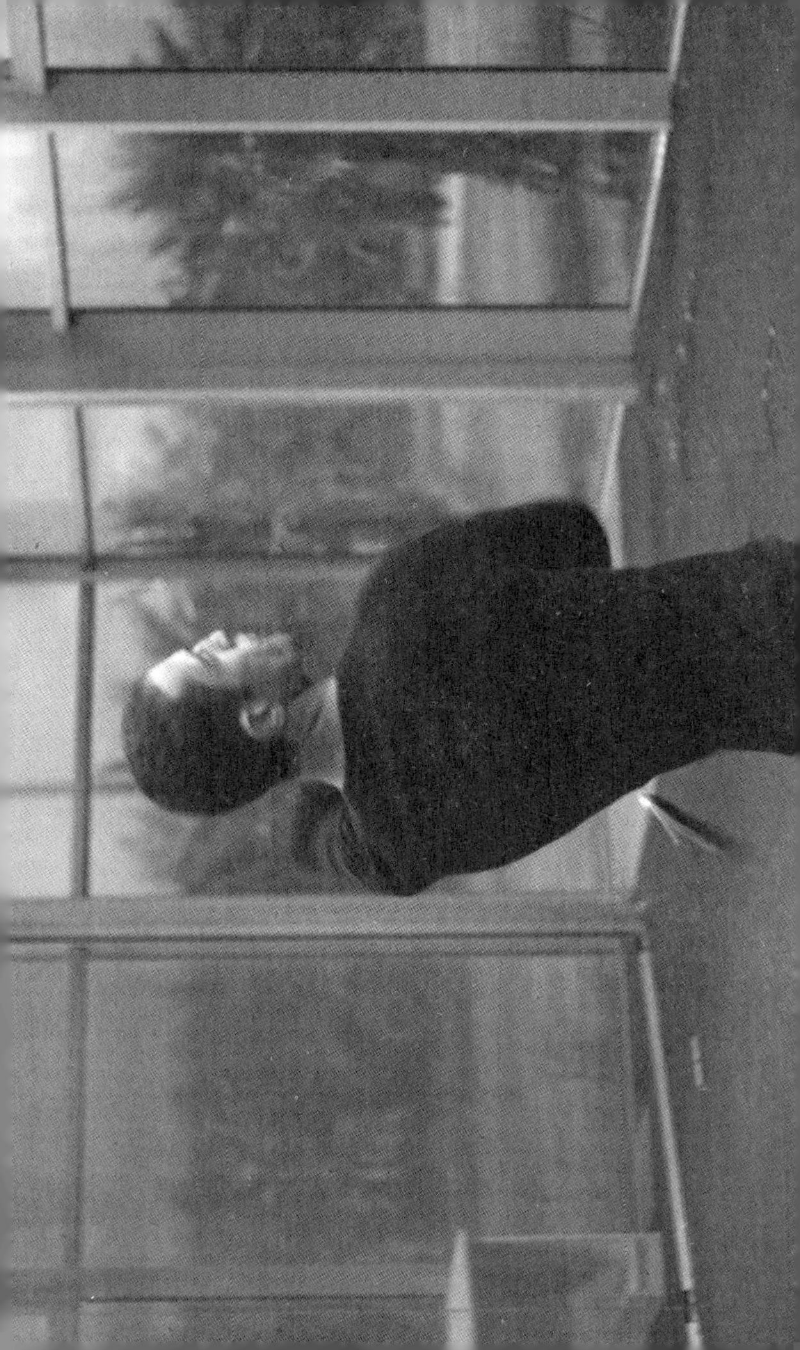

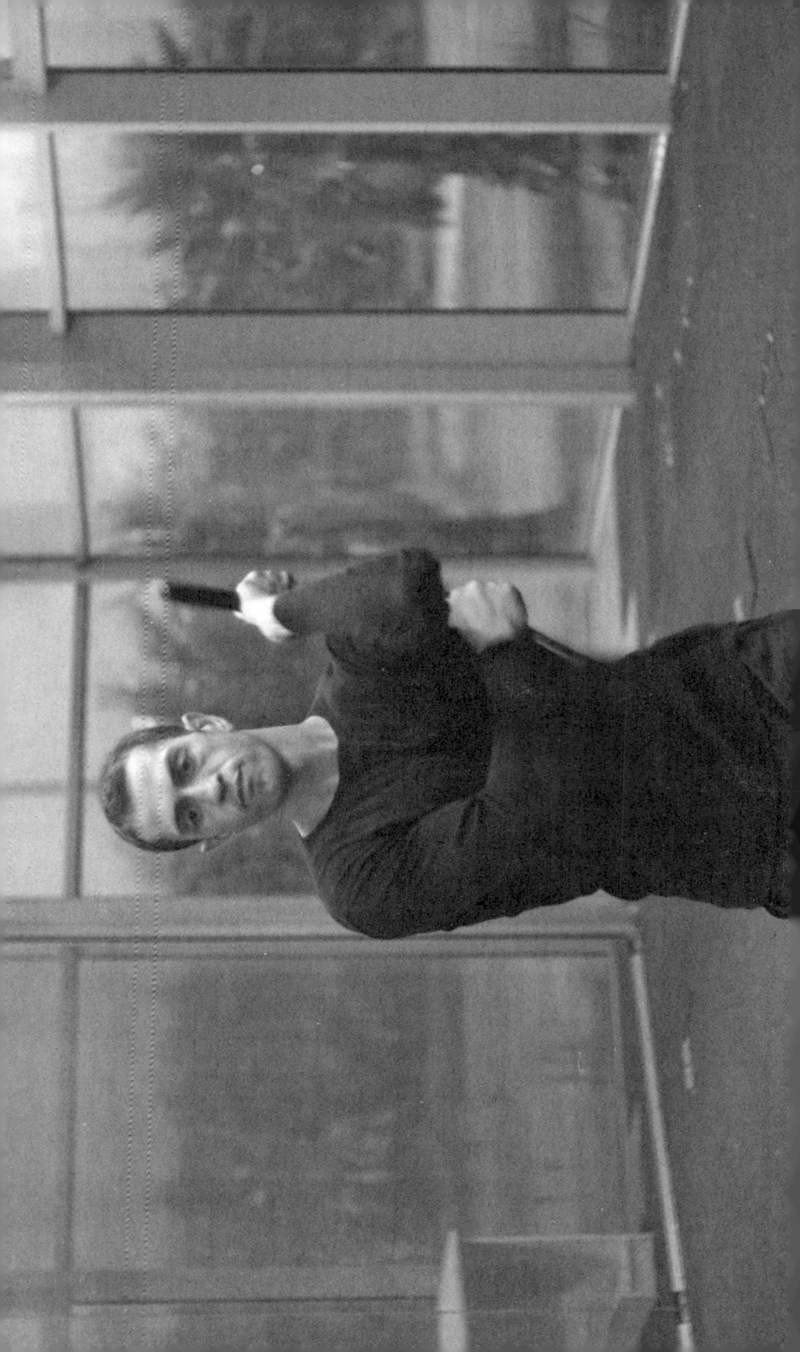

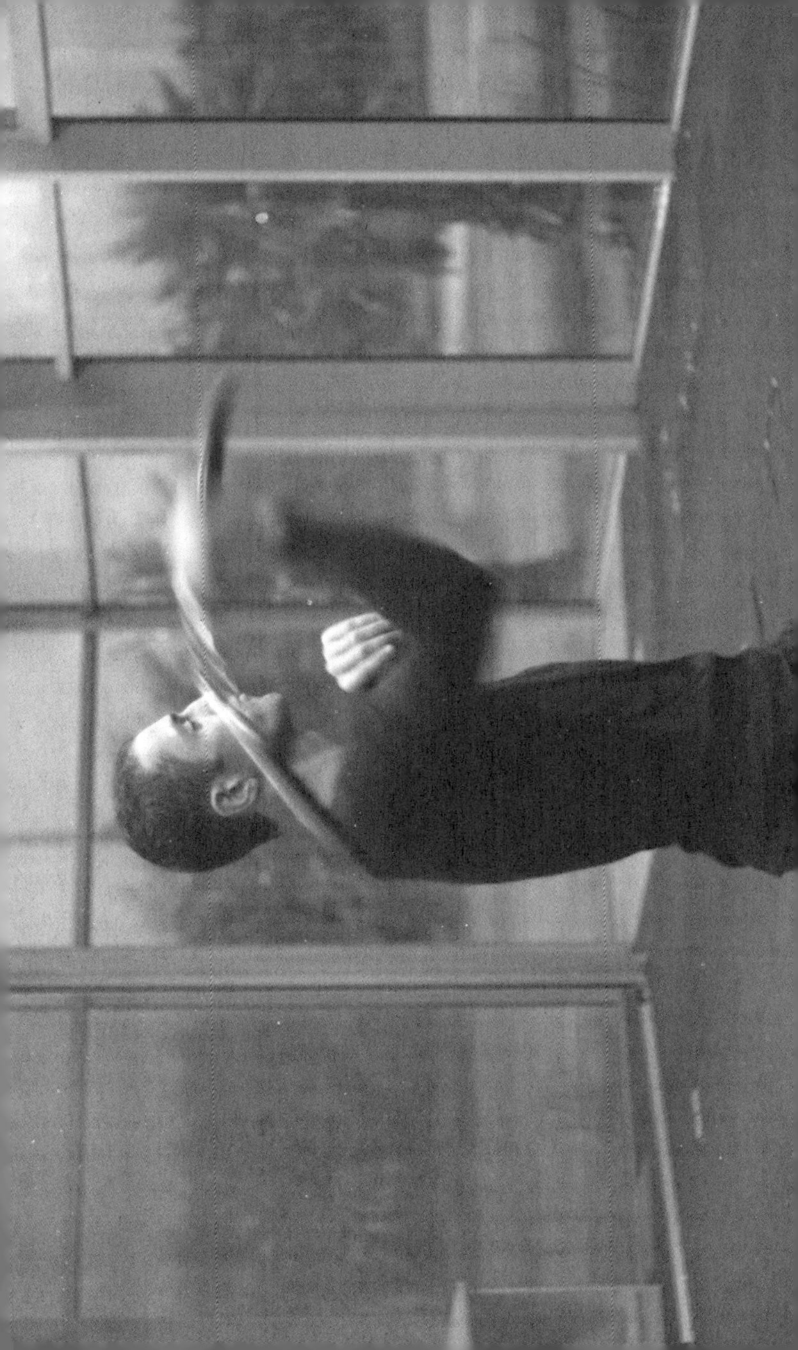

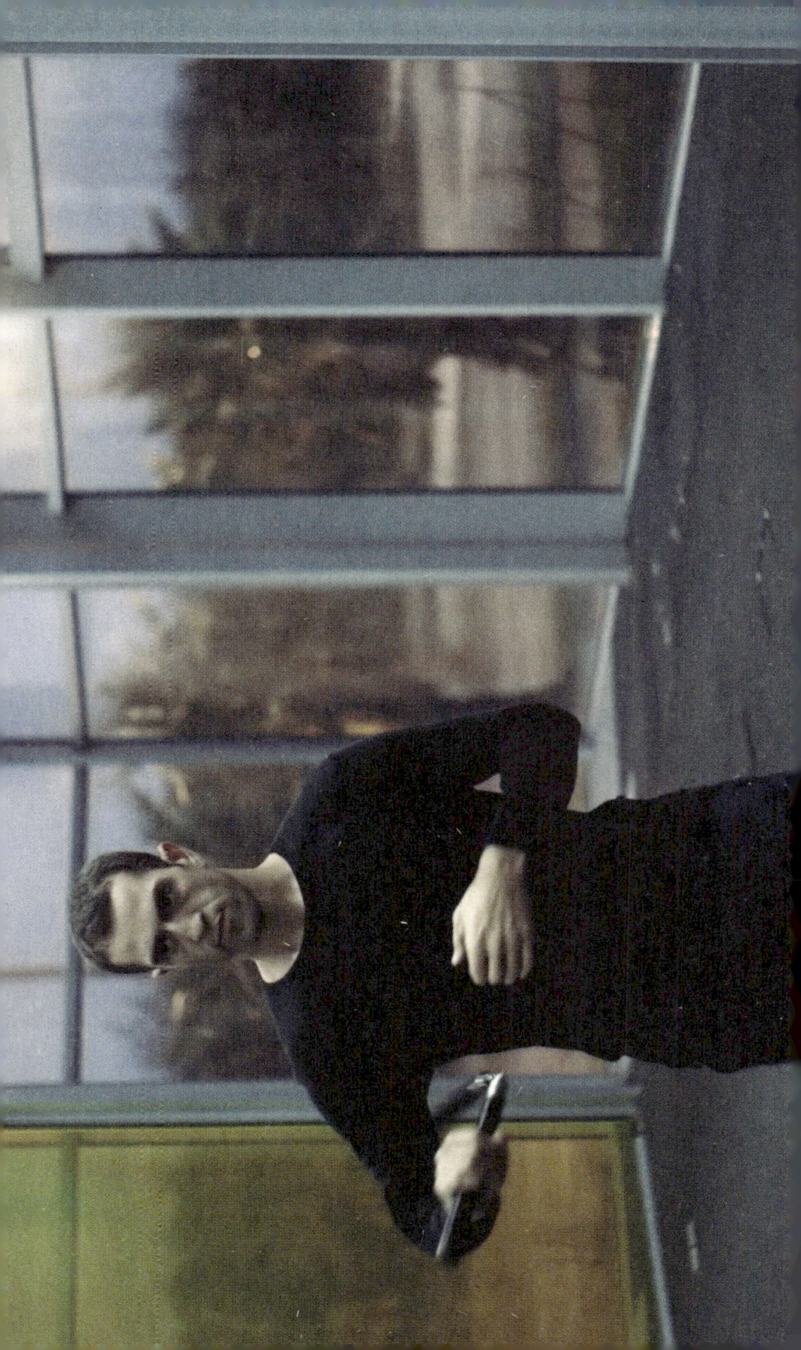

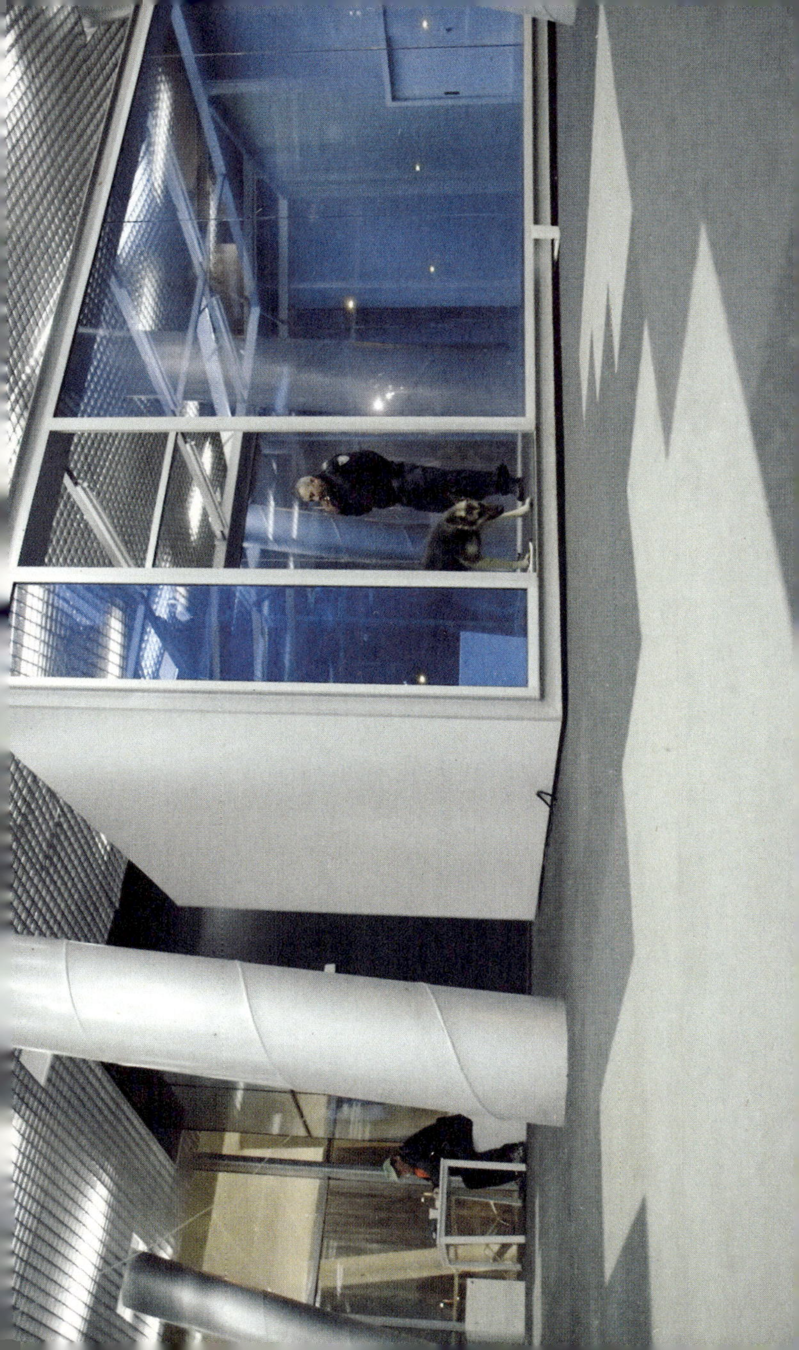

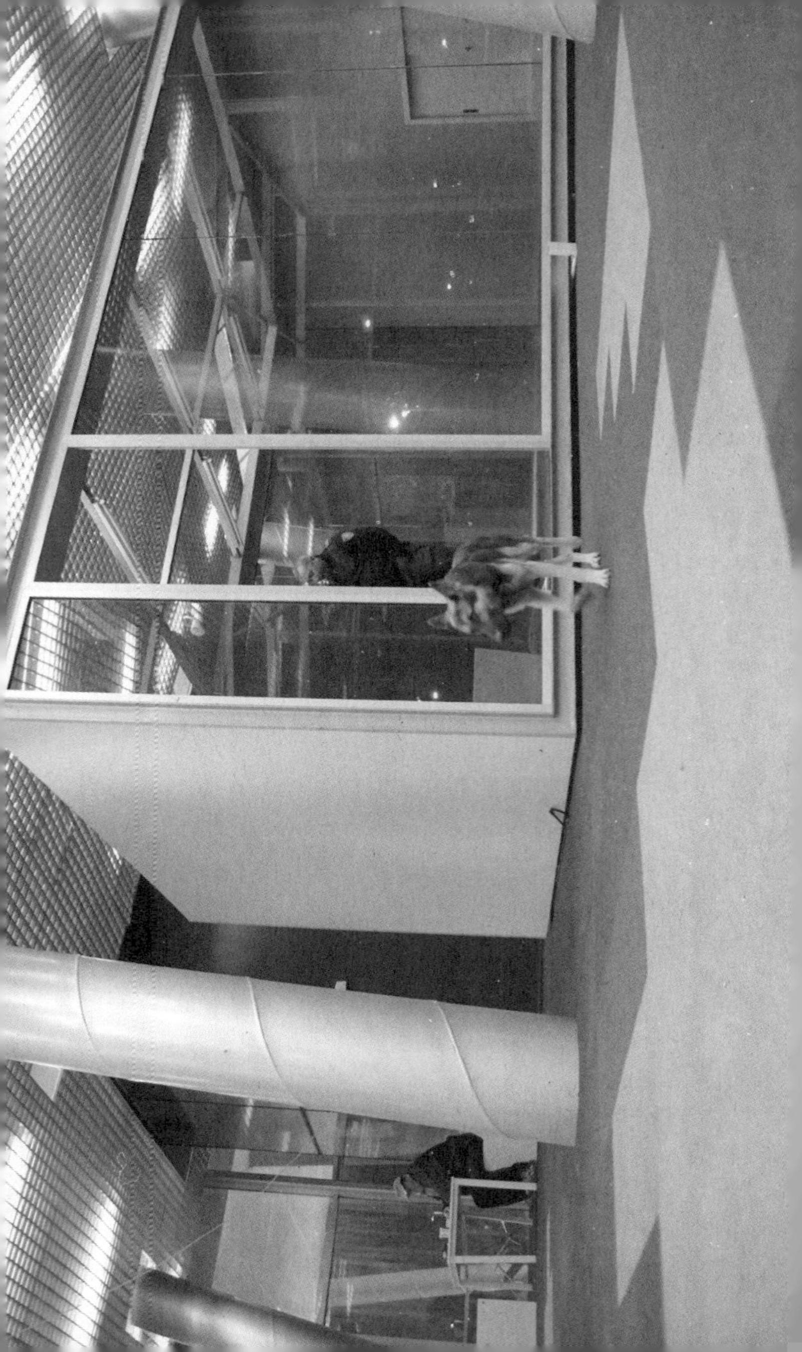

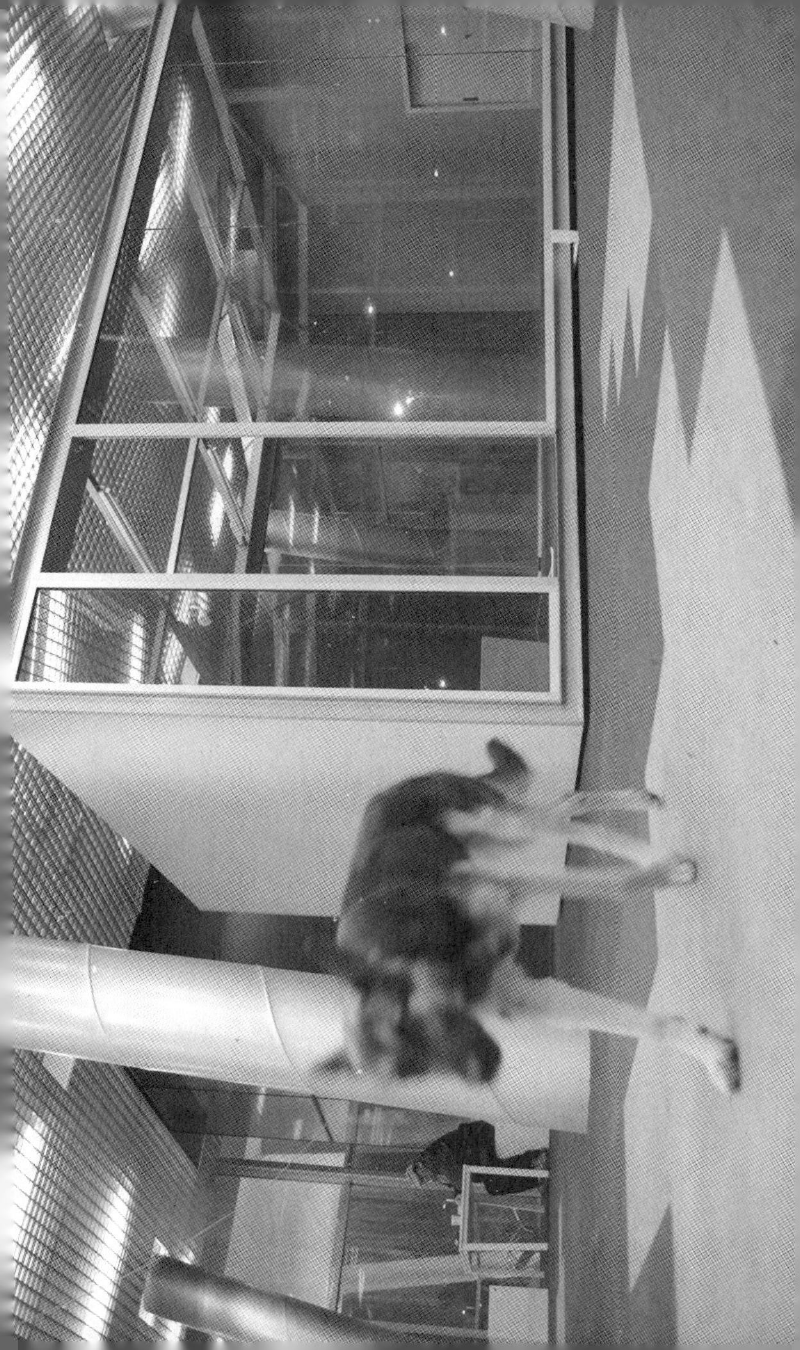

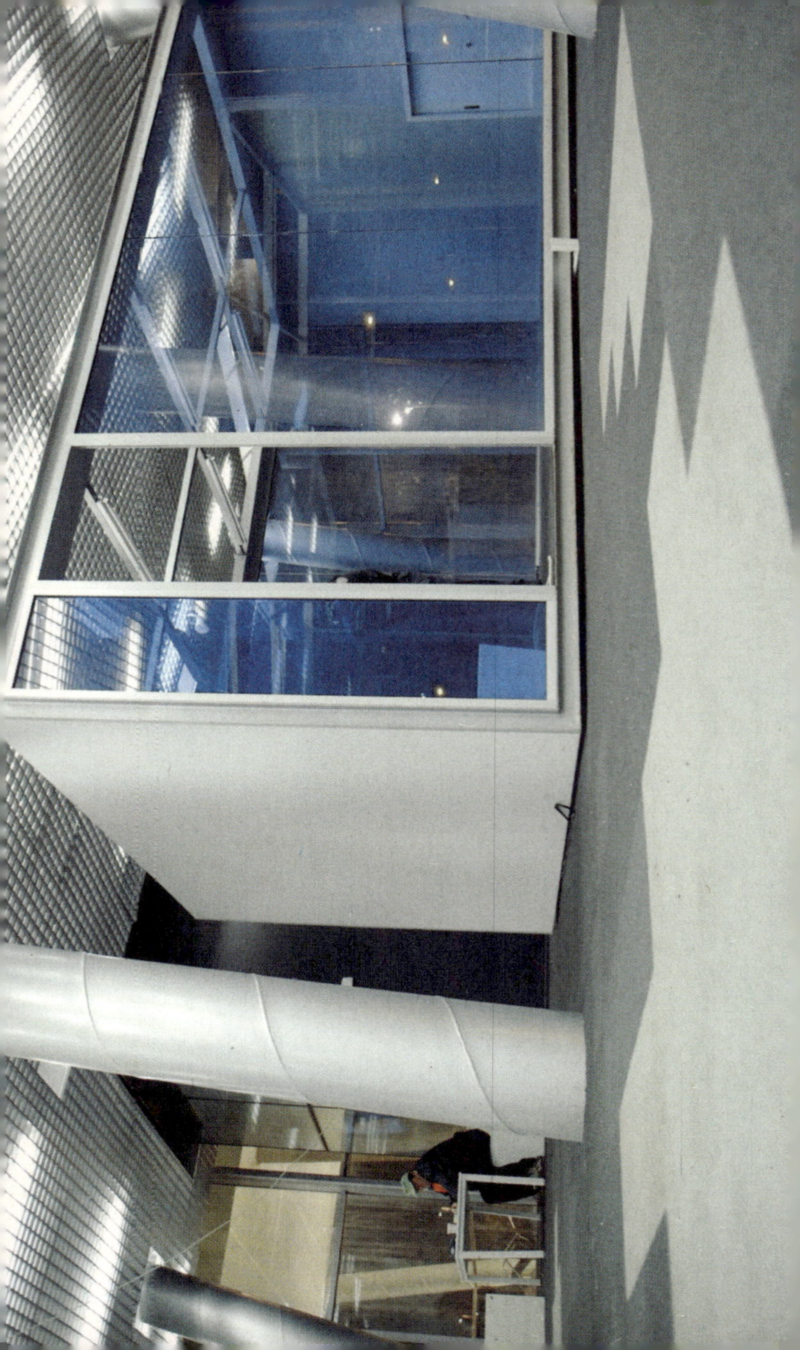

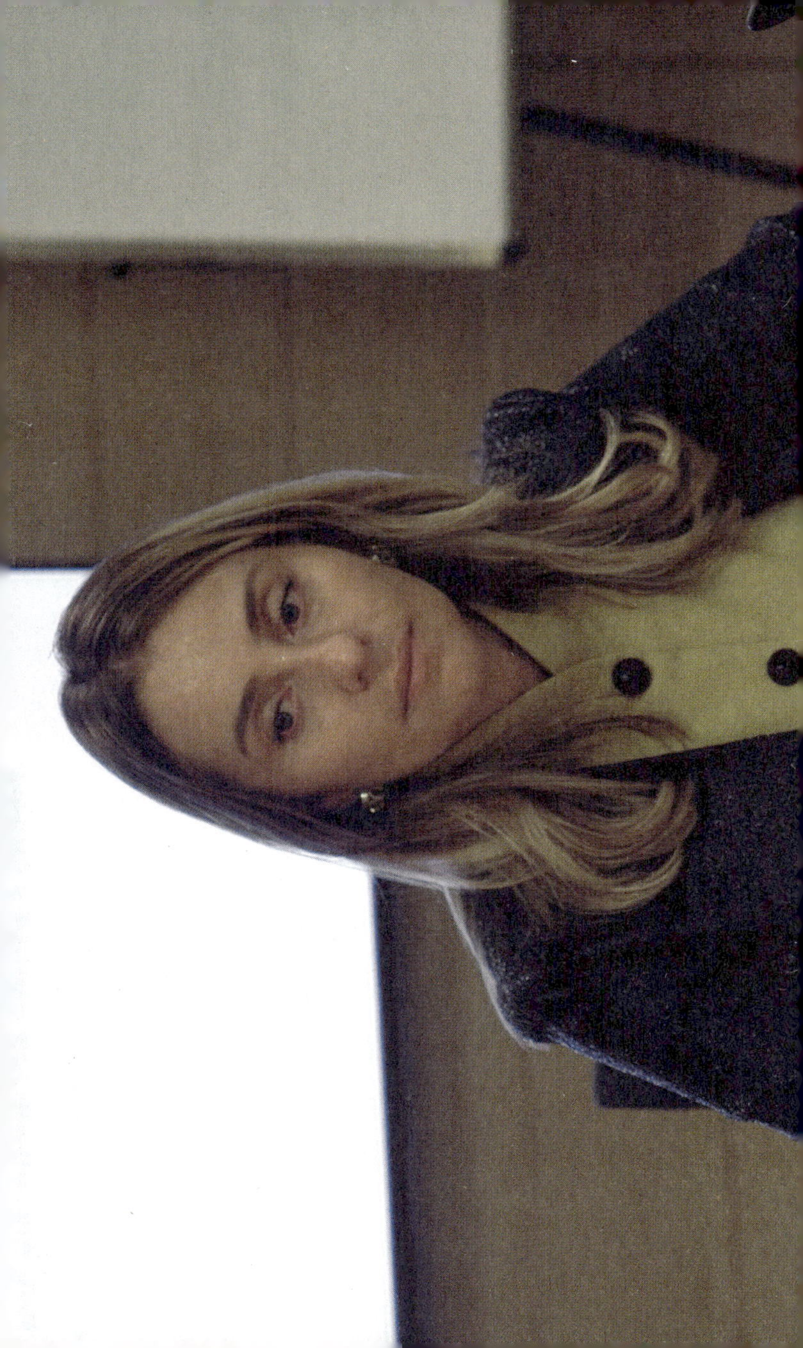

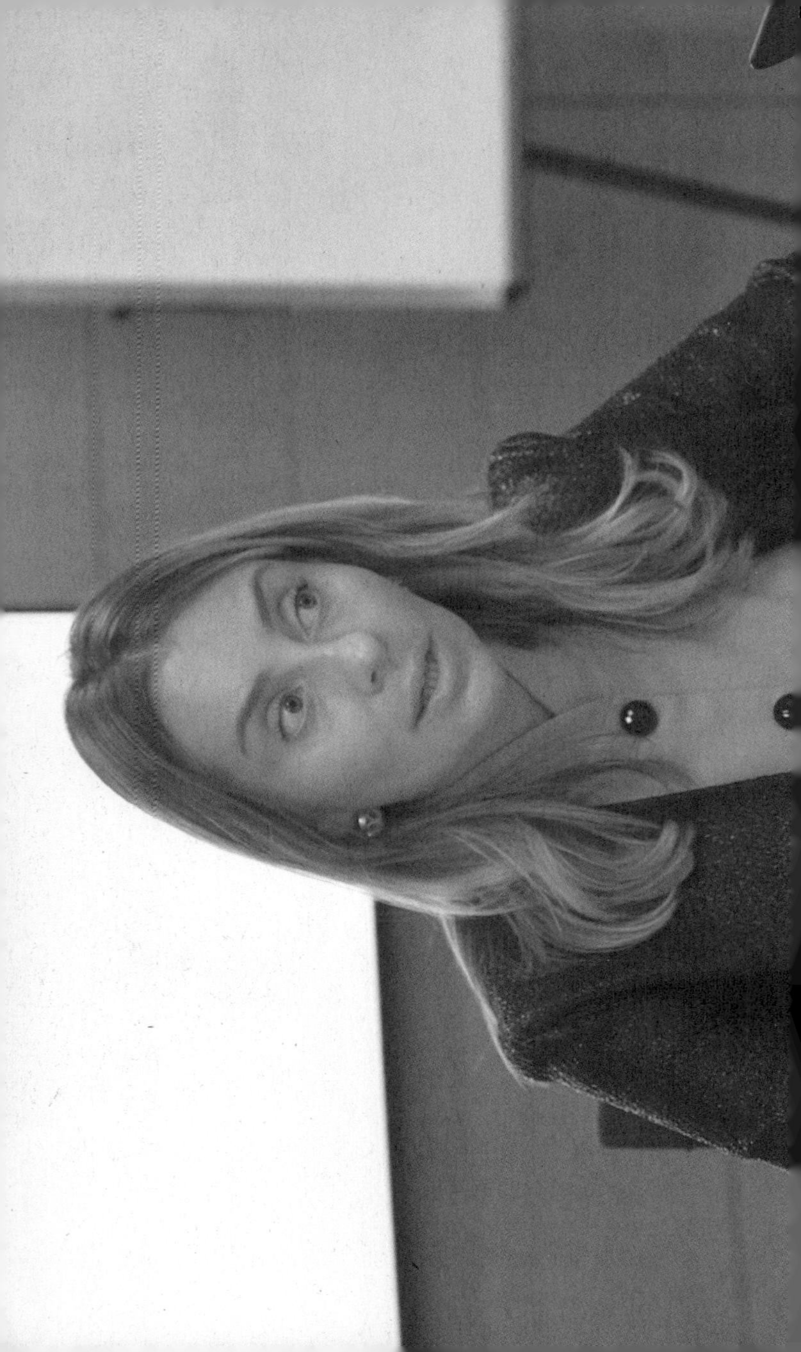

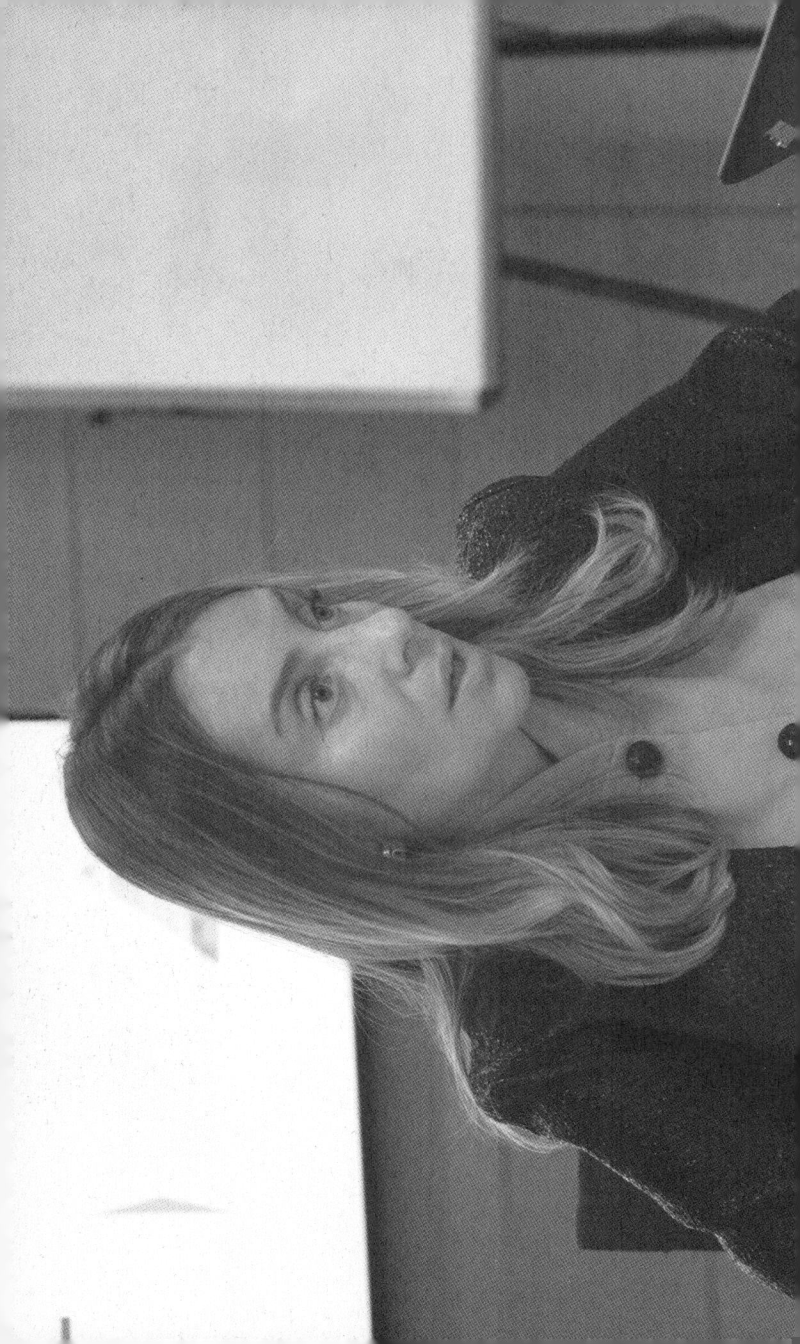

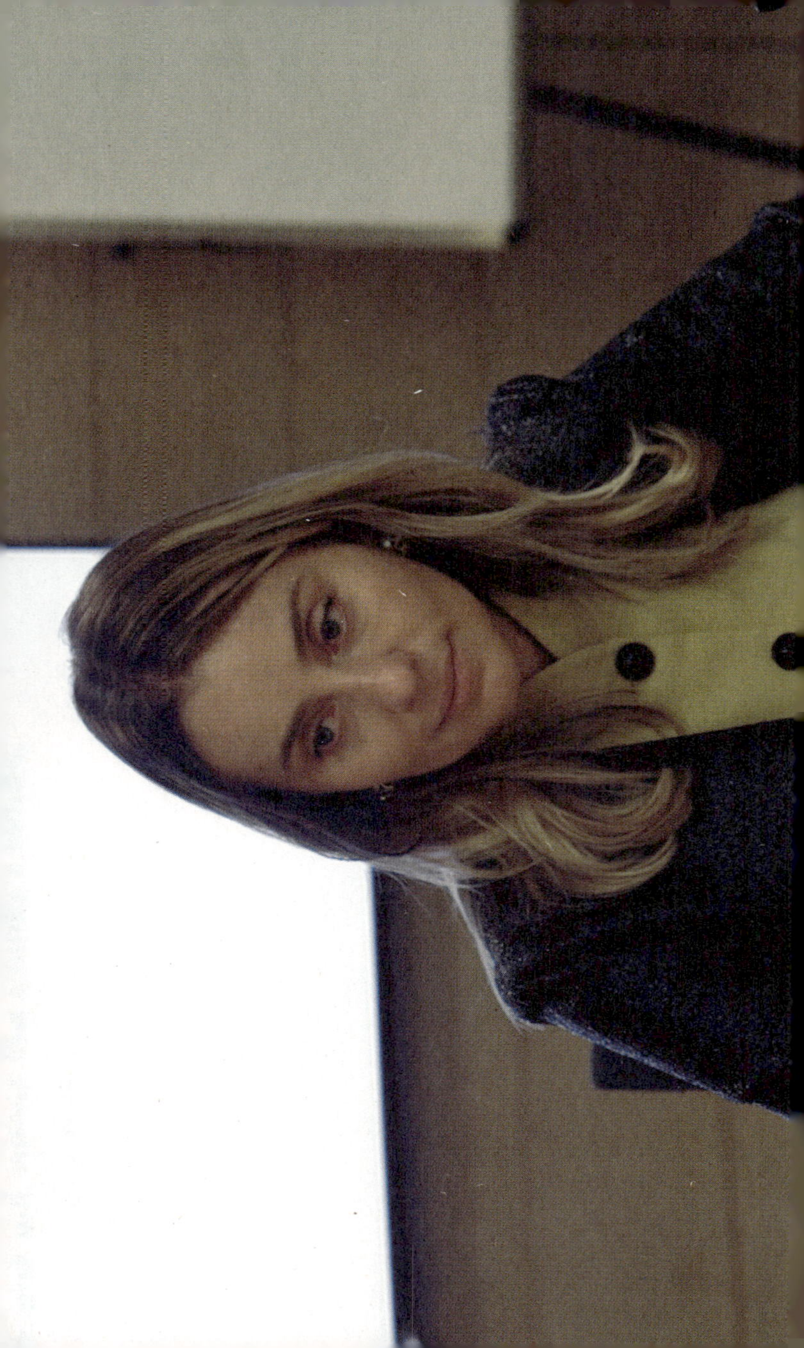

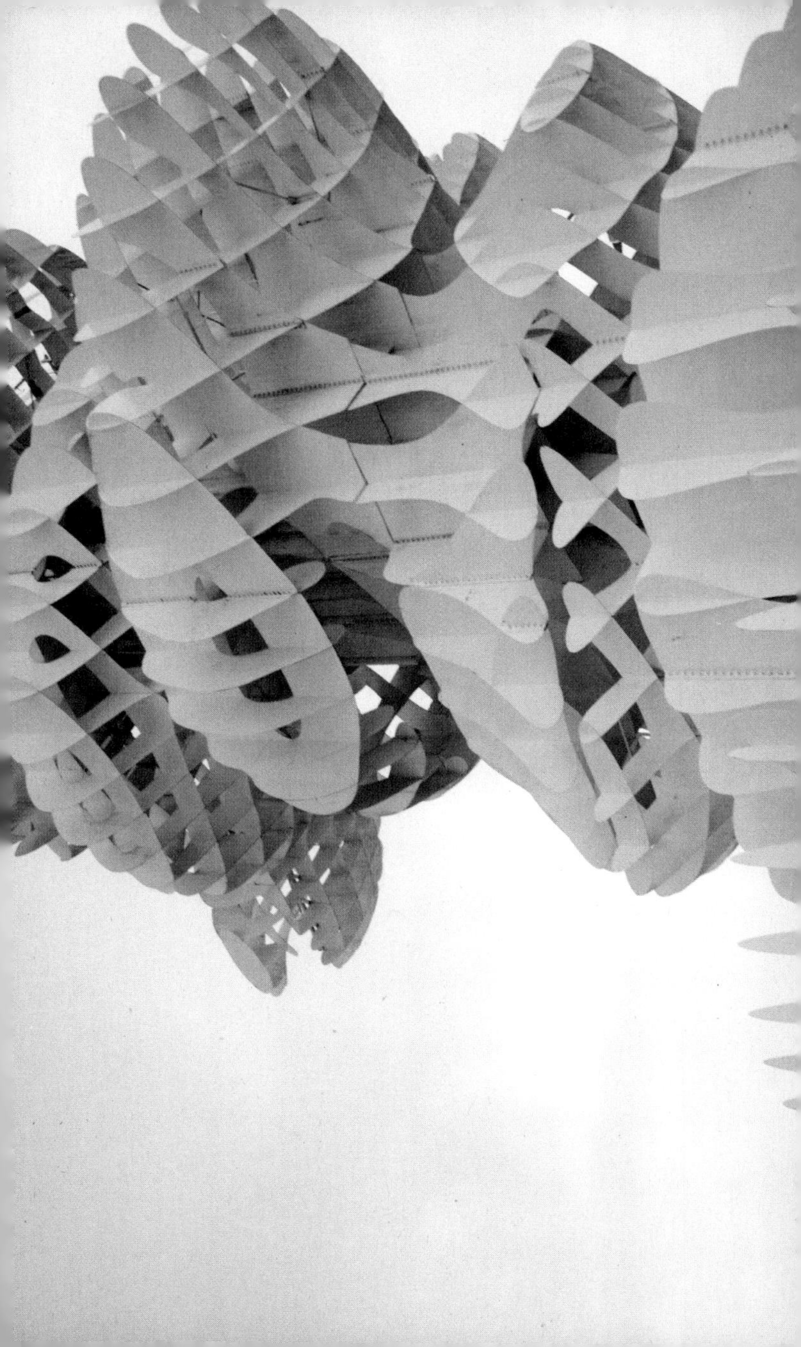

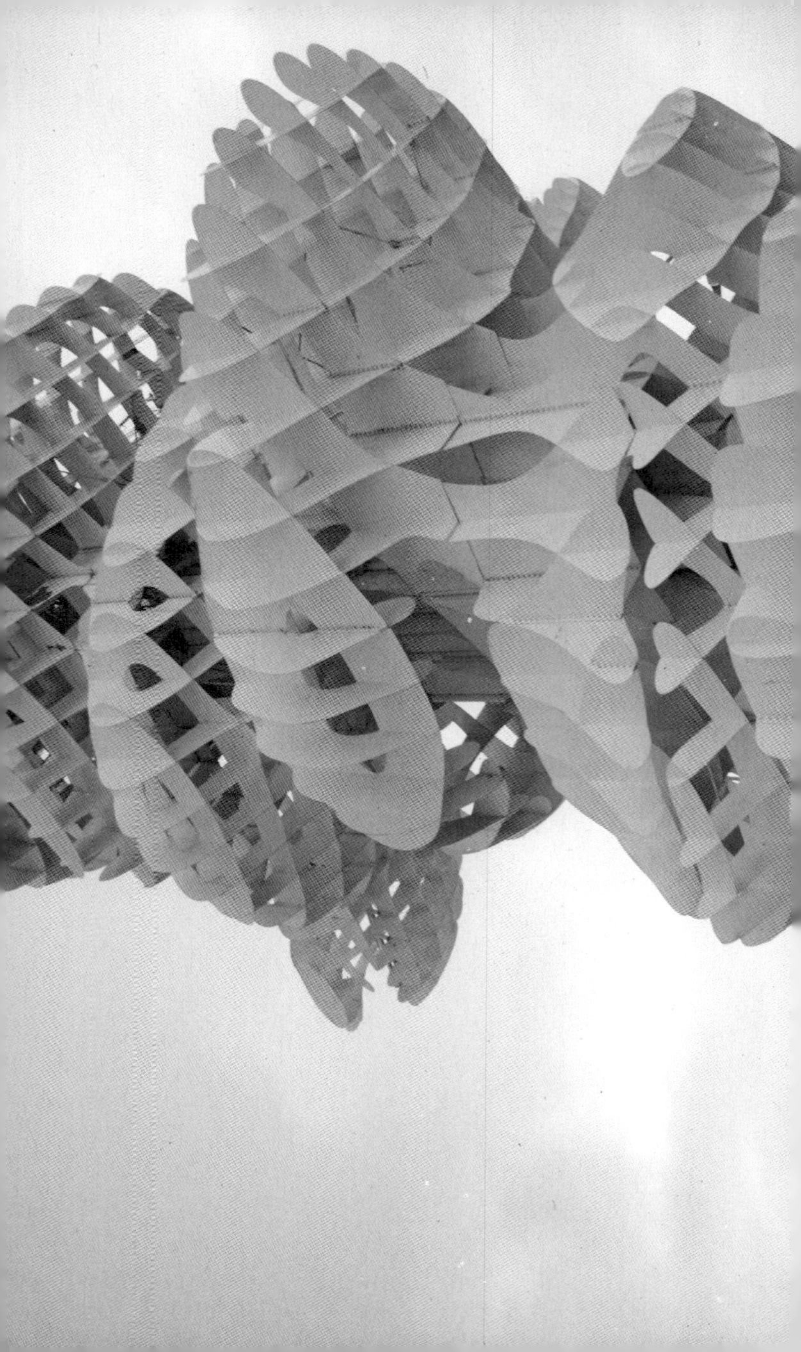

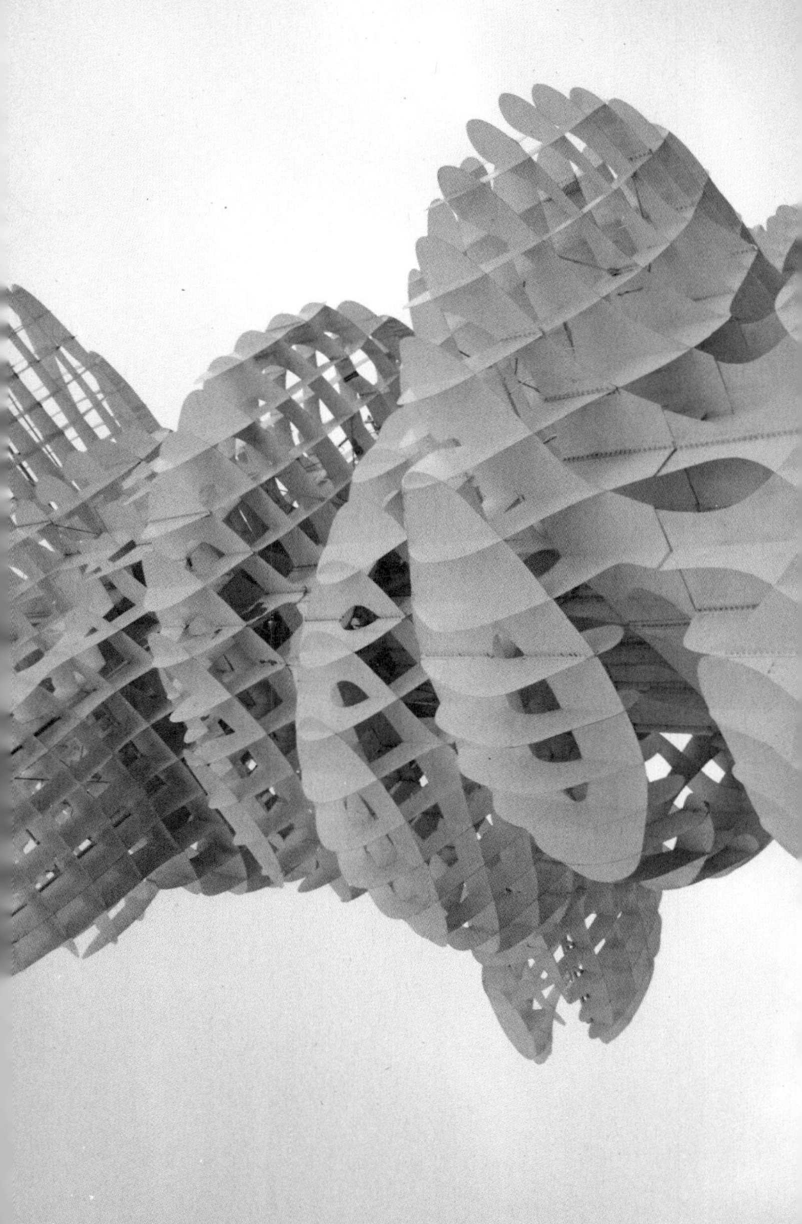

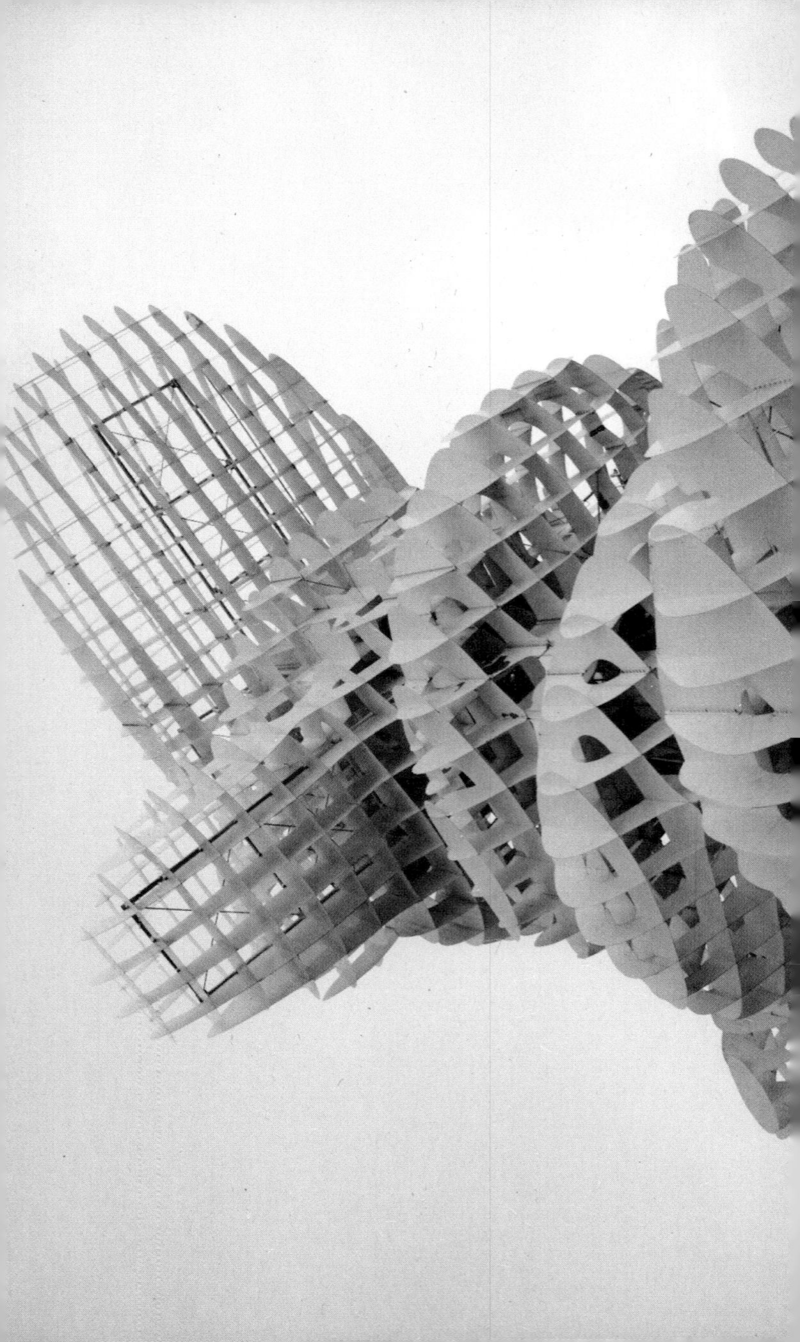

Infrastructures of
Friendship

Evelina Gambino

Writing with a pile of women on my lap
tramontane wind in Cadaques
when the tramontane wind
blew us in Cadaques
I took a picture
a picture of every latent idea
of us in the rented car
I didn't trust your driving
olives driving
with a pile of women on their laps
with holes in their stomachs.[1]

Research can be intimidating. Especially if what one researches is something simultaneously so broad and so intimate as people's everyday lives in times of change. It is not surprising, then, that only a few days after discovering that our respective projects—a film and a doctoral thesis—sought to document the same transformation, Tekla Aslanishvili and I travelled together to the coastal village of Anaklia to embark on our inquiries side by side. A small and unremarkable place, Anaklia was at the centre of the largest infrastructural development in Georgia, aimed at turning it into a logistical hub with global reach. Starting in the spring of 2017, for over two years, we travelled back and forth to Anaklia, taking night trains, coaches, marshutkas and taxis, attending public events, private tours, and spending long days observing the village transform.

When in Anaklia, we lived in a small concrete room with bed frames so bendy they would almost touch the floor under the weight of our bodies. During those days anticipation filled the

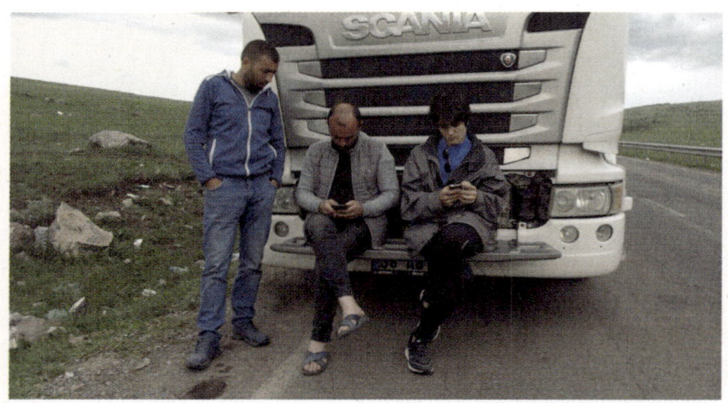

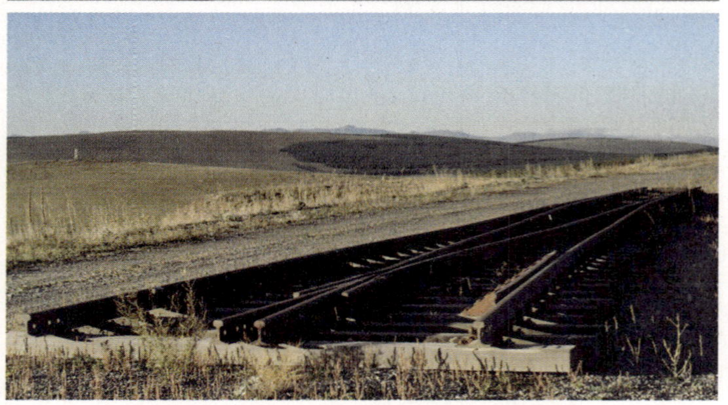

Film stills. Tekla Aslanishvili, *A State in a State*, 2022.

town; villagers readied themselves for a future
as entrepreneurs and workers on large machines
prepared the territory to host the deepest port
in the country. As small vernacular houses were
removed to make space for the port, new buildings
mushroomed across the sea, designed to welcome a new class of people who would settle in
the village once the transformation had been completed. We became part of it, awaiting like others

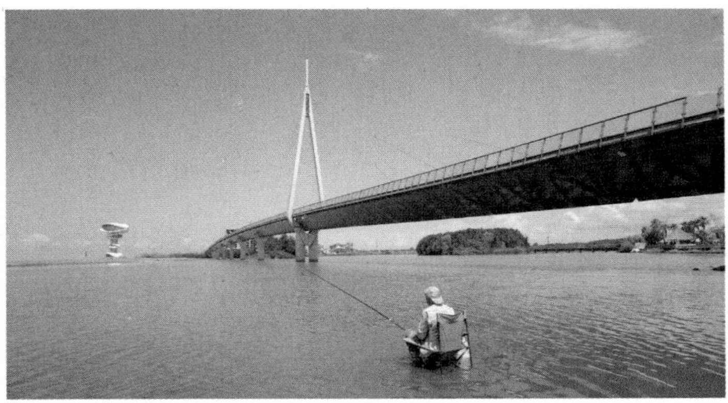

Film still. Tekla Aslanishvili, *The Mountain Speaks to the Sea*, 2024.

to see a new Anaklia being constructed, but also signalling with our presence that something worth immortalising was indeed about to happen.

Logistics, Deborah Cowen[2] writes, entails a recasting of the relation between "making and moving" at the heart of contemporary capitalism. At stake in this recasting are new horizons of profit, not just acquired through producing commodities or extracting materials but from controlling their movements across space. When Tekla and I discussed our projects during our first meeting in Tbilisi we uncovered that our interest in Anaklia's transformation had similar roots: we were concerned with an emerging and increasingly popular script that placed investment in logistical corridors as a gateway for planetary prosperity. Those in charge of rebuilding Anaklia constantly referred to that script as a means of justifying and conferring a worldly allure to their activities. As we mapped the village's makeover,

we observed how that worldly script was translated into a hybrid and elusive promise, incorpo-
rating local dreams that had long preceded
and, in many ways, contradicted it.
Building a port entails a choreography of different
forms of work. While some of these activities
can be understood to be productive—the actual
construction and assembling of its technical
components and material structures—others are
reproductive. These are the acts of work geared at
making uncertain projects like the port of Anaklia
look smooth and coherent in the eyes of potential
investors and publics. The film Tekla was making
traces the contours of this choreography and
maps the frictions that populate it. Alternating
formal interviews with architects, representatives,
CEOs, and critics of the project, with scenes
showing the transformations—sometimes akin
to terraforming—that Anaklia's ecologies and its
inhabitants endured in preparation for the port's
construction, Tekla documented the gap between
the visions of prosperity embodied by the port
and the effective violence and carelessness of
their implementation in Anaklia. The film explores
the theatrical and often farcical nature of many
of the encounters that filled the village in those
days of anticipation: shiny buildings slowly sink-
ing into the wetlands, boastful CEOs attempting
to impress groups of students, and maintenance
routines accentuating the alien-ness of newly
built structures.

Towards the end of 2019, as Tekla moved
into the editing phase of her film and I returned

to London to write my PhD, the building site we had observed for the past two years was abandoned. For months rumours had circulated about a crisis that enveloped the project and speculations abounded over its political and geopolitical motivations. Suddenly the script had been turned upside down and no one could decipher it anymore. The work we had done acquired a different meaning, captured in the title of Tekla's film, *Scenes from Trial and Error*. In the aftermath of the project's collapse, locals were left to reorient their lives away from its promise and Anaklia ceased to be in the spotlight. The trials and errors that the village had sustained and that we partially witnessed have left scars and mark the village up to the present day. In some ways, *Scenes from Trial and Error* functions as an archive of those scars, many of which are depicted in the film as still in the making. Not intending to be a testimony of disaster, the film successfully shows how infrastructural projects are *constantly brokering failure*. A lot of the work that sustains projects like the one that never materialised in Anaklia is not necessarily to prevent failure, rather it is to make sure that investors are shielded by its effects.

Already in 2018 Tekla and I had travelled to the semi-abandoned station of the Baku–Tbilisi–Kars (BTK) train in Akhalkalaki, Georgia. Accompanied by cameraman Nikoloz Tabukashvili, we spent several days exploring and filming the steppe-like landscapes that surround the station and interviewing some of the people who live and work in its proximity. Years later, this short trip became the foundation for the film we developed together titled *A State in a State* (2022). Unlike the port that was set to transform Anaklia, the history of the Baku–Tbilisi–Kars railway reaches as far back as the Russian Empire. Over the years, the same tracks have been repurposed and appropriated for their capacity to materialise profitable forms of connectivity and enforce lasting forms of disconnection. The project we observed is a re-routing of a railway which passed through the Armenian city of Gyumri. Built at the end of the 19th century, this railway remained a key transit infrastructure throughout the Soviet Union. After the Union's collapse and in the aftermath of the first Nagorno-Karabakh War (1988–1994) between Armenia and Azerbaijan, Azerbaijan and Turkey announced their intention to build a new line that passed through Georgia, bypassing Armenia. From its inception the BTK has thus embodied contradictory visions of the future. One pertains to Georgia's developmental goal to become a transit corridor part of the New Silk Road, and the other is a result of Turkey and Azerbaijan's commitment to exclude Armenia from transnational trade routes. These contrasting visions and the territorial and economic conflicts that they have generated are inscribed in the railway. While the traces of these conflicts are all too visible and felt by those who live and work next to the railway, our film sought to construct a visual language communicating that underneath and even inscribed into this infrastructural network, a different kind of connectivity exists. As a socio-technical system of almost unfathomable proportions, the railways that crossed the Soviet Union allowed the emergence and circulation of a set of techno-political relations and subjectivities that have largely been severed in the wake of the Soviet collapse.

Yet, when speaking with veteran railway workers who worked along the Soviet route of the BTK line, we found that a specific infra-structural consciousness remains hinged on what is left of this railway today. At a time when information technologies travelled on the same material tracks as supplies, the railway was the most developed technological system feeding the Soviet Union. In the several interviews we conducted with former workers on the two sides of the line—in Georgia and Armenia—different

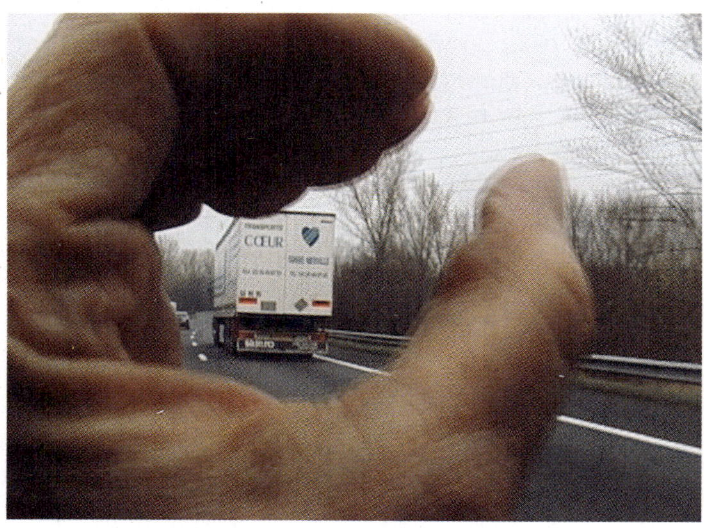

Film still. Agnes Varda, *Les Glaneurs et La Glaneuse*, 1999.

veterans described the railroad as 'a state within a state'. This is because, as they explained, it had its own connectivity, including specific phone codes and lines that facilitated connections between rail workers in all corners of the Union, even in times when connectivity was otherwise not possible. Running parallel to and underneath the governmental apparatus of the Soviet Union, this infrastructural *state* provided its members not just with a series of technological advantages that facilitated connectivity, but was rather a sprawling ecosystem,[3] comprising of specific subjectivities and a relational logic that made acts of identification and solidarity possible.

Infrastructures are made of and make relations. Our documentary excavates the forgotten and lively connectivity that bound railway workers together across borders, taking its name from this "choreography of experimentation"[4] that ties together designs, materials, knowledge, and people as they seek to intervene in the worlds in which they live.

In *The Gleaners and I* (1999), Agnes Varda drives around France looking for people who live off capitalism's leftovers. As she films along a busy highway, she playfully tries to capture the trucks driving past by closing her hand around their moving silhouettes. In his comments on filmmaking's potential as a methodology, Matthew Gandy highlights documentary's ability to stand in for a fragment of the real. Chiming with Varda, Gandy stresses the improvisational and serendipitous quality of filmmaking. I first became attuned to this ability of film to encapsulate fragments of time as I observed Tekla capture scenes from Anaklia's daily life and, subsequently, patch them together into a coherent narrative. However, in watching Tekla at work, improvisation always appeared to be matched by a seemingly incessant amount of technical and conceptual labour necessary to actually bring the film to light. It is in the tension between these two opposing states that—perhaps in contrast with Gandy's experience—I believe film acquires its value as an ethnographic methodology. Film allows the filmmaker to follow serendipitous connections, while simultaneously making visible the labour necessary to capture and link these disparate moments. A labour akin to what Edward Said has called "being of the connection".[5] Filming, much like ethnographic fieldwork, entails negotiations with a range of participants, yet it also implies a different urgency, a heightened attention to atmospheric elements, and coordination with the non-human actors that populate each scene. During the making of *A State in a State* we spent hours waiting for elusive trains to show up. Exposed to all kinds of weather, we embarked in frenzied runs carrying heavy equipment at the faintest sound of carriages on the tracks, letting out elated screams—quickly muffled not to compromise the filming—when we finally caught sight of it. These experiences of working with and within ecosystems are unique to filmmaking, however they are not confined to it. These experiences have directly informed our understanding of infrastructure as patchworked objects and sites of friction, and have allowed us to piece together an account of the BTK railway as a palimpsest of diverse histories.

In my decade-long struggle to become fluent in Georgian, I have learned to pay attention to the etymology of words, as they often tell surprising stories. The English word 'friend', for instance, derives from the Indo-European root meaning 'to love'. Anyone who has ever had a friend would struggle to find this surprising and, indeed, this relation is maintained in other languages such as the Italian 'amica' that derives from the Latin 'amare'. But this is not the end, for there is another word that shares the same root as *friend*, and that is the word 'free'. That loving and caring for others makes you free is perhaps the reason why feminists — and many others engaged in making the world a little less oppressive — have often emphasized collaboration as the basis of their political practice. At its most basic, collaboration can be a means of achieving the kind of reflexivity necessary to recognize the limits of the knowledge that we produce. The stories Tekla and I have assembled are not smooth, instead they confront the seemingly endless cycles of emergence, failure, and aftermath that organize the lives of the infrastructures we have been observing. We have focused our efforts towards *staying with* the troubles we have encountered along our way.[6] But if we have continued working with one another from one infrastructure to the next, it is probably due to something simpler: the sheer pleasure of a friendship spawned through learning and producing knowledge together.

this might be the way I think about it.[7]

1   Fragment from Emilia Weber, "[Writing with a pile of women on my lap]," in Familiars (Bristol: Sad Press, 2017).

2   Deborah Cowen, *The Deadly Life of Logistics: Mapping Violence in Global Trade* (Minneapolis: University of Minnesota Press, 2014), 104.

3   Penelope Harvey, "The Topological Quality of Infrastructural Relation: An Ethnographic Approach," *Theory, Culture & Society* 29, no. 4–5 (2012): 76–92.

4   Soumhya Venkatesan et al., "Attention to infrastructure offers a welcome reconfiguration of anthropological approaches to the political," *Critique Of Anthropology* 38, no. 1 (March 2018): 3–52

5   Edward W. Said, "Representing the Colonized: Anthropology's Interlocutors," *Critical Inquiry* 15, no. 2 (Winter 1989): 205–225.

6   Donna Haraway, *Staying with the Trouble: Making Kin in the Chthulucene* (Durham: Duke University Press, 2016).

7   Fragment from Emilia Weber, "[Writing with a pile of women on my lap]," in Familiars (Bristol: Sad Press, 2017).

Biographies

Alexandra Aroshvili

is an independent researcher and publicist based in Tbilisi, Georgia. She has authored research and publications on social policy, political economy, various forms of inequality, informal and atypical work, women's migration, extractivism, and ecology. She has founded various social movements and public campaigns and collaborated with numerous print and online publications. Over the years, she has worked closely with workers and trade unions, critiqued Georgia's economic policy, and contributed to developing an alternative model of pension reform. She has also worked on Tbilisi's public transport reform. Since 2020, she has been actively engaged in peripheral social and environmental protests involving local populations Currently, she is focused on issues related to hydro energy and infrastructural coloniality as part of the group Fair Energy Politics Collective.

Tekla Aslanishvili

is an artist, filmmaker, and essayist based between Berlin and Tbilisi. Currently, Aslanishvili is a doctoral candidate at the Academy of Fine Arts Vienna and a postgraduate fellow at the Berlin Centre for Advanced Studies in Arts and Sciences (BAS) at Berlin University of the Arts. She completed her bachelors at the Tbilisi State Academy of Arts in 2009 and holds an MA in Experimental Film and New Media from the Berlin University of the Arts. Her work has been screened and exhibited internationally at Berlinische Galerie; SculptureCenter, New York; Taipei Biennial 2023; Wiels, Brussels; Eye Filmmuseum, Amsterdam; Schirn Kunsthalle, Frankfurt; Transmediale 2023, Berlin; LOOP Festival—Fundació Antoni Tàpies, Barcelona; NTU Centre for Contemporary Art Singapore; Neue Berliner Kunstverein; 14th Baltic Triennial; Tbilisi Architecture Biennial; Short Film Festival Oberhausen; and Kunsthalle Münster. She was a Digital Earth Fellow (2019), a nominee for the Ars-Viva Art Prize (2021), and a recipient of the Han Nefkens Foundation—Fundació Antoni Tàpies Video Art Production Award (2020).

Ifor Duncan

is a writer, artist, and interdisciplinary researcher. He is a Postdoctoral Researcher on the ERC project EcoViolence at the Institute of Cultural Inquiry (ICON), University of Utrecht. Duncan's research focuses on political violence against communities in the context of degrading watery spaces, processes, and materialities. He encounters these concerns through visual cultures, cultural memory, and a fieldwork practice that involves submerged audiovisual methods. He completed his PhD and was a lecturer at the Centre for Research Architecture—Department of Visual Cultures, Goldsmiths University of London (2022–24), and a postdoctoral fellow at the New Institute Centre

Biographies

for Environmental Humanities (NICHE), Ca' Foscari University of Venice (2020–22).

Silvia Franceschini

is a curator and editor working across the fields of visual arts, design, and architecture. Currently, she is a Curator at CIVA in Brussels, and the co-founder of Celador, a space for art and writing in Brussels. Between 2018 and 2021 she was a curator at Z33—House for Contemporary Art in Hasselt. Previously, she organized exhibitions in various private and public institutions, including the V-A-C Foundation, Moscow; and Centre Pompidou, Paris. In 2015 she was part of the curatorial team of The School of Kyiv—Kyiv Biennial 2015. Franceschini is an editor of *Curator Without a System. Viktor Misiano: Selected Writings* (Sternberg Press: 2022); *The Politics of Affinity: Experiments in Art, Education and the Social Sphere* (Cittadellarte—Fondazione Pistoletto: 2018); and *Global Tools 1973–1975: When Education Coincides With Life* (Nero Publishing: 2019). She holds a PhD in Design and Visual Cultures from the Polytechnic University of Milan, and was a research fellow at the Liverpool John Moores University and the Strelka Institute for Media, Architecture and Design in Moscow.

Evelina Gambino

is the Margaret Tyler Research Fellow in Geography at Girton College, University of Cambridge. Her research is concerned with a situated analysis of global logistics. Through ethnographic work around connectivity infrastructures in Georgia and the South Caucasus, Gambino's research maps how planetary projects of circulation, such as the Belt and Road Initiative, are translated into local contexts. In dialogue with feminist critiques of capitalism, her analysis highlights the different kinds of work that this translation entails. Gambino's work has been published within and beyond academia. Since 2017 she has collaborated with artist and director Tekla Aslanishvili on several multimedia projects, including the experimental documentary *A State in a State* (2022). She is co-editor of the volume *Gendering Logistics: Feminist Approaches to the Analysis of Supply Chain Capitalism* (Into the Black Box: 2021) and is currently completing a monograph that proposes a feminist, materialist approach to the study of infrastructural failure.

Timothy Mitchell

is a political theorist and historian. He is Professor of Middle Eastern Studies at Columbia University in New York. His areas of research include the place of colonialism in the making of modernity, the material and technical politics of the Middle East, and the role of economics and other forms of expert knowledge in the government of collective life. Trained in the fields of law, history, and political theory, he works across the

Biographies

disciplinary boundaries of history and the social sciences. Like much of his work, this research combines the study of the built world, technical devices, ecological processes, and the history of economic and political concepts. Mitchell is the author of *Colonising Egypt* (University of California Press: 1991), *Rule of Experts: Egypt, Techno-Politics, Modernity* (University of California Press: 2002), and *Carbon Democracy: Political Power in the Age of Oil* (Verso Books: 2011).

Tekla Aslanishvili
The Mountain Speaks to the Sea

Systems & Territories

Onomatopee #261
ISBN 978-94-93382-13-8

2025

Editor — Silvia Franceschini
Publishing editor — Natasha Rijkhoff
Written contributions — Alexandra Aroshvili, Tekla Aslanishvili, Ifor Duncan, Silvia Franceschini, Evelina Gambino, Timothy Mitchell
Graphic design — Kai Udema
Publisher — Onomatopee Projects (Eindhoven, NL) Jesse Muller and Natasha Rijkhoff
Copy editor & proofreader — Annemarie Wadlow
Lithography — Alex Feenstra
Printing — Printon (Tallin, EST)
Typeface — Geigy (Lineto)
Edition — 1000

This book is published on the occasion of the exhibition *Tekla Aslanishvili. The Mountain Speaks to the Sea* which was held at Onomatopee between 11.10.2024 and 15.12.2024. Curator: Silvia Franceschini. Exhibition designer: Natalia Nebieridze. Exhibition coordinator: Robin Roelofs. Communication: Chloë Alyshea. Graphic design: Kai Udema.

The project is supported by the Italian Council program (2024) promoted by the Directorate-General for Contemporary Creativity of the Italian Ministry of Culture, Critical Media Lab HGK Basel FHNW, University of Arts Berlin, Graduate School UdK Berlin, Kommission für künstlerische und wissenschaftliche Vorhaben (KKWV) Berlin, E.A. Shared Space Tbilisi, Cultuur Eindhoven and Mondriaan Fonds.

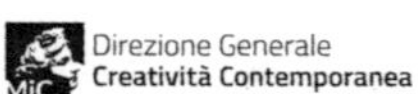

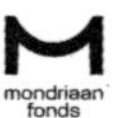

Cover images: Tekla Aslanishvili, *The Mountain Speaks to the Sea*, 2024, film stills. Courtesy: the artist.